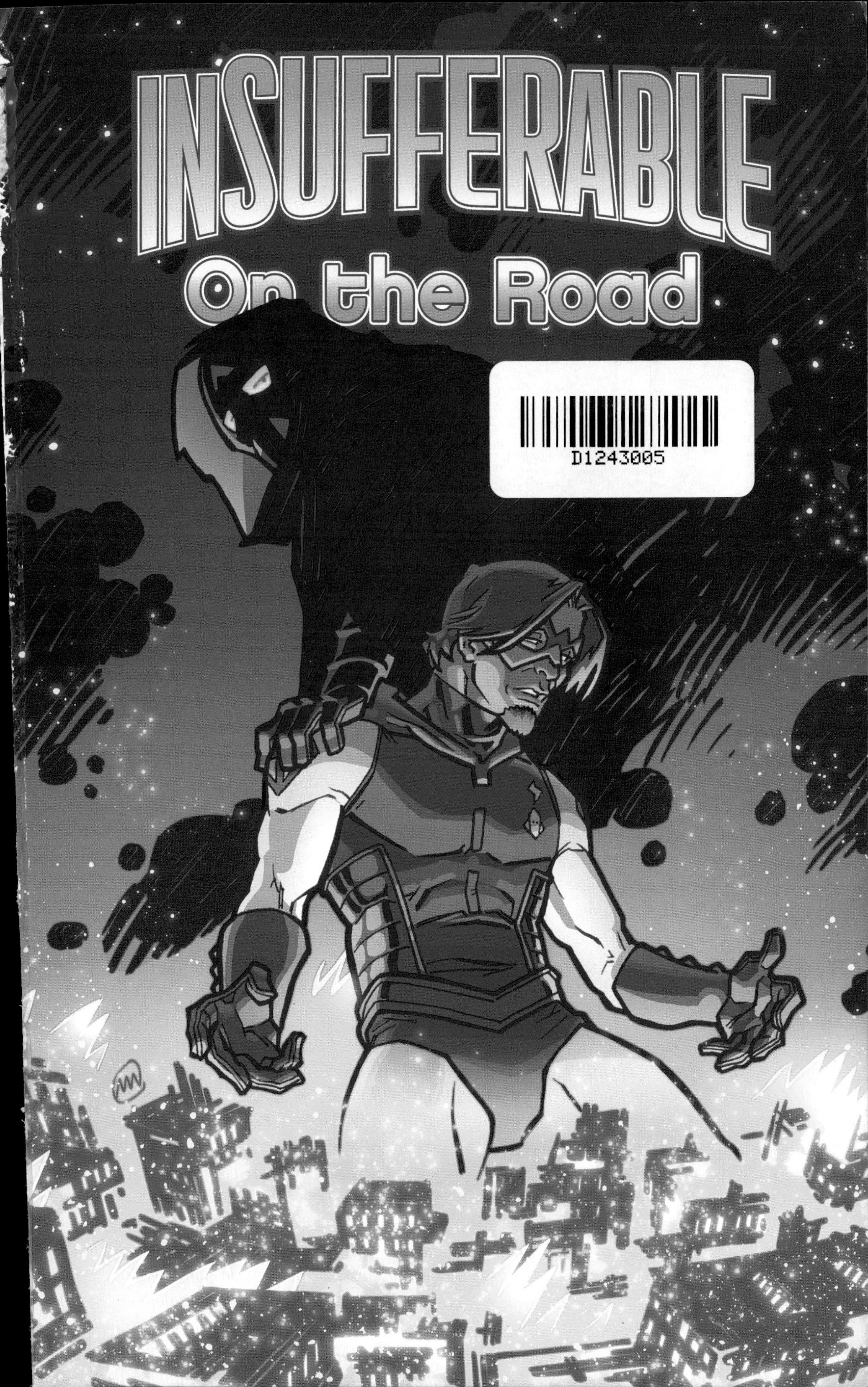
INSUFFERABLE
On the Road

Cover Art by **Peter Krause**

Cover Colors by **Nolan Woodard**

Collection Edits by **Justin Eisinger** and **Alonzo Simon**

Collection Design by **Ron Estevez**

Publisher: **Ted Adams**

ISBN: 978-1-63140-734-5

19 18 17 16   1 2 3 4

www.IDWPUBLISHING.com
IDW founded by Ted Adams, Alex Garner, Kris Oprisko, and Robbie Robbins

Ted Adams, CEO & Publisher
Greg Goldstein, President & COO
Robbie Robbins, EVP/Sr. Graphic Artist
Chris Ryall, Chief Creative Officer/Editor-in-Chief
Laurie Windrow, Senior Vice President of Sales & Marketing
Matthew Ruzicka, CPA, Chief Financial Officer
Dirk Wood, VP of Marketing
Lorelei Bunjes, VP of Digital Services
Jeff Webber, VP of Licensing, Digital and Subsidiary Rights
Jerry Bennington, VP of New Product Development

Facebook: **facebook.com/idwpublishing**
Twitter: **@idwpublishing**
YouTube: **youtube.com/idwpublishing**
Tumblr: **tumblr.idwpublishing.com**
Instagram: **instagram.com/idwpublishing**

Originally published as INSUFFERABLE: ON THE ROAD issues #1–6.

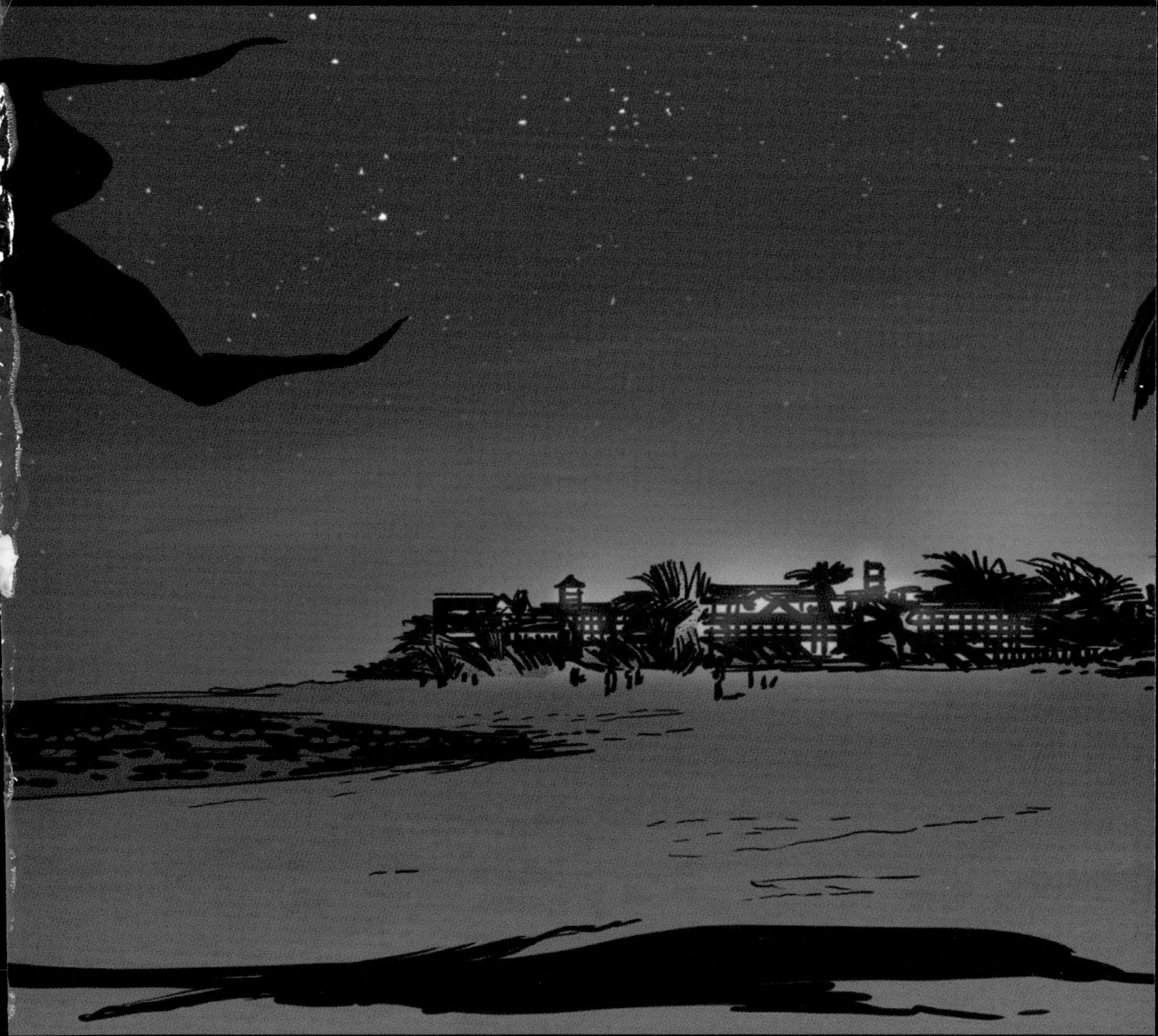

Insufferable created by **Mark Waid** & **Peter Krause**

Writers / Storytellers / Artist
Mark Waid & **Peter Krause**

Colorist
Nolan Woodard

Letterer
Troy Peteri

Series Editor
Michael Benedetto

CHAPTER 1

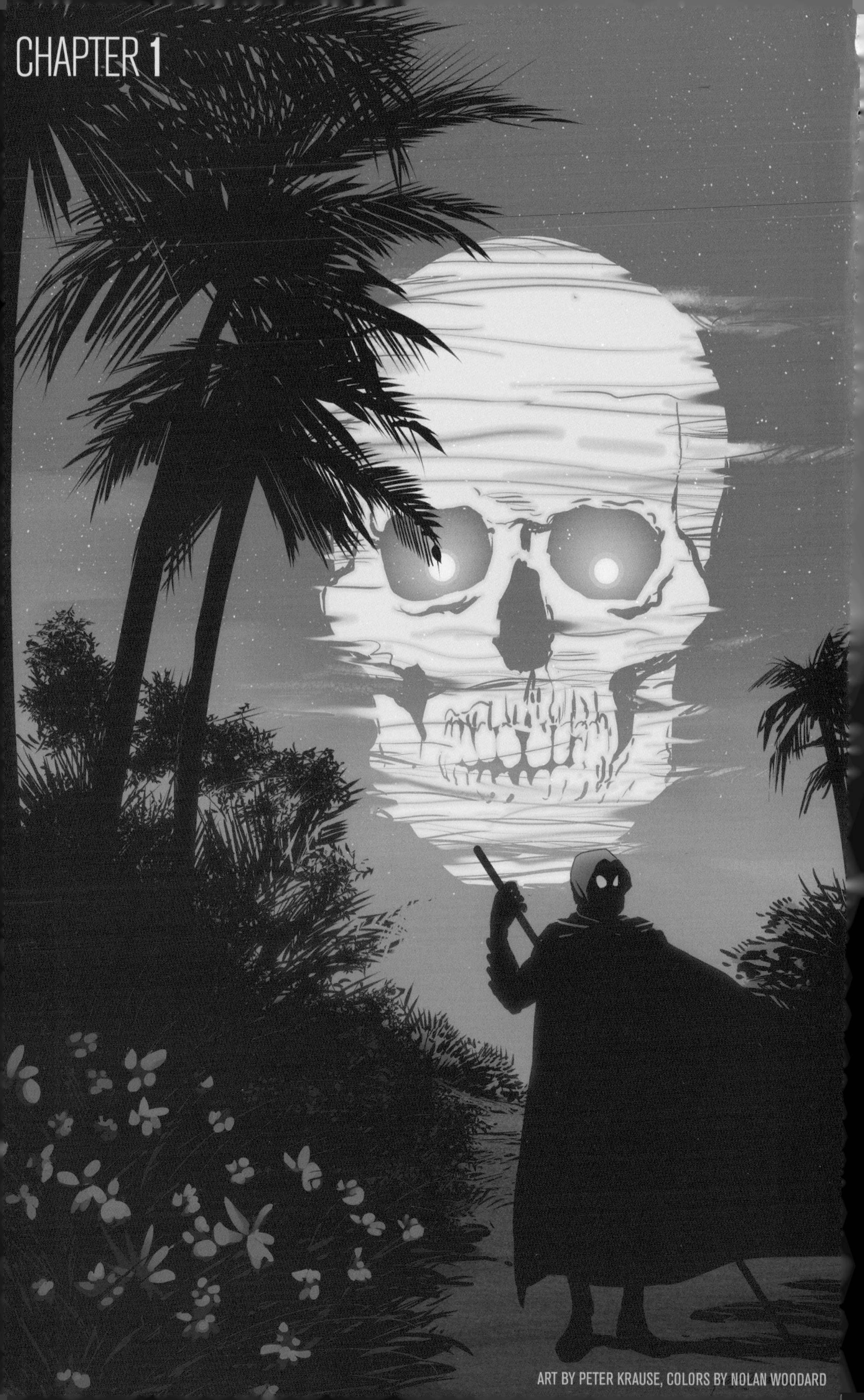

ART BY PETER KRAUSE, COLORS BY NOLAN WOODARD

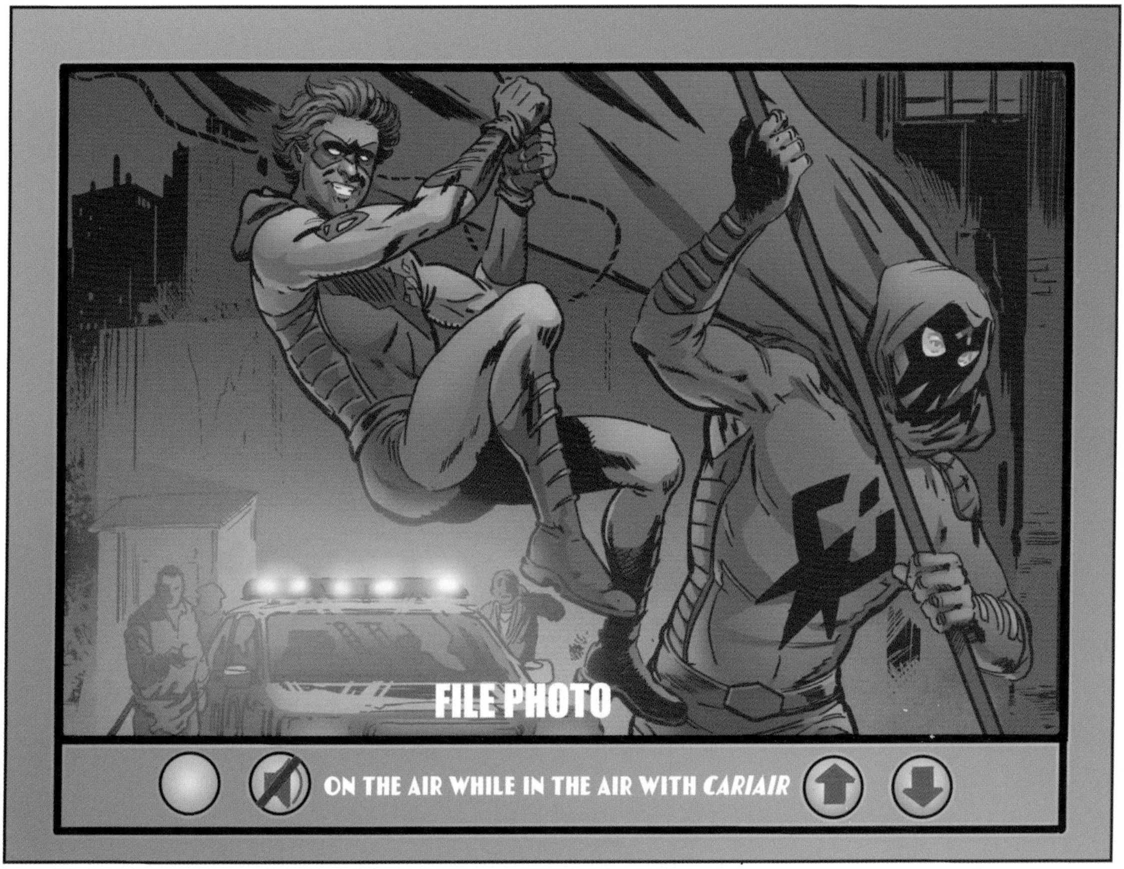
FILE PHOTO
ON THE AIR WHILE IN THE AIR WITH CARIAIR

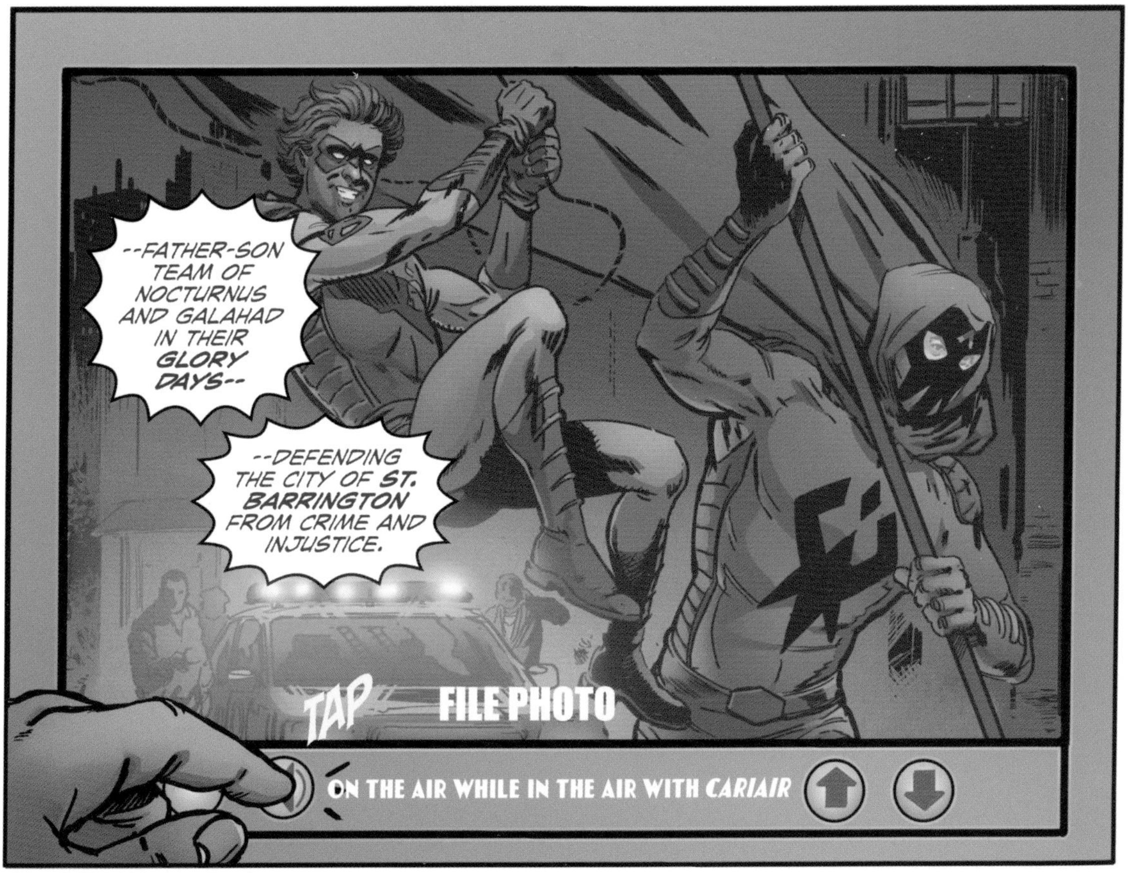
--FATHER-SON TEAM OF NOCTURNUS AND GALAHAD IN THEIR **GLORY DAYS**--
--DEFENDING THE CITY OF **ST. BARRINGTON** FROM CRIME AND INJUSTICE.
TAP
FILE PHOTO
ON THE AIR WHILE IN THE AIR WITH CARIAIR

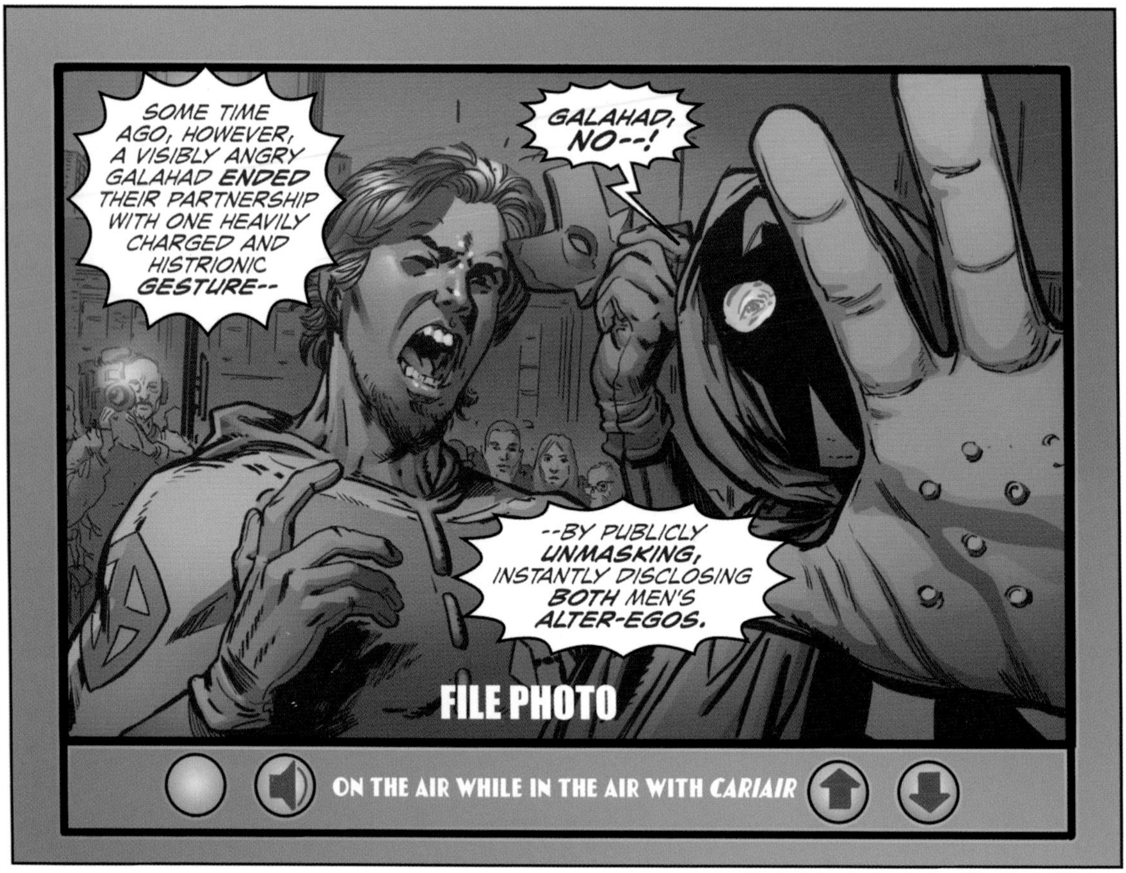
SOME TIME AGO, HOWEVER, A VISIBLY ANGRY GALAHAD ENDED THEIR PARTNERSHIP WITH ONE HEAVILY CHARGED AND HISTRIONIC GESTURE--
GALAHAD, NO--!
--BY PUBLICLY UNMASKING, INSTANTLY DISCLOSING BOTH MEN'S ALTER-EGOS.
FILE PHOTO
ON THE AIR WHILE IN THE AIR WITH CARIAIR

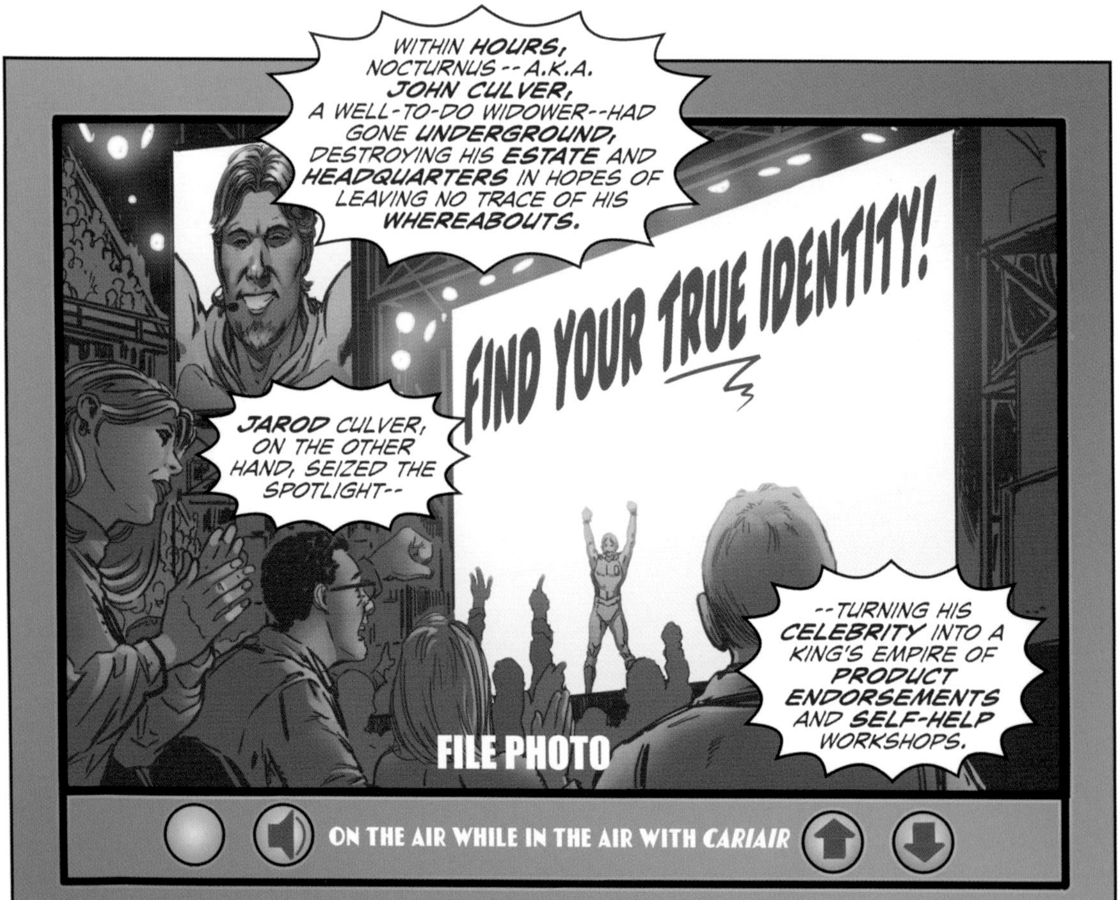
WITHIN HOURS, NOCTURNUS--A.K.A. JOHN CULVER, A WELL-TO-DO WIDOWER--HAD GONE UNDERGROUND, DESTROYING HIS ESTATE AND HEADQUARTERS IN HOPES OF LEAVING NO TRACE OF HIS WHEREABOUTS.
FIND YOUR TRUE IDENTITY!
JAROD CULVER, ON THE OTHER HAND, SEIZED THE SPOTLIGHT--
--TURNING HIS CELEBRITY INTO A KING'S EMPIRE OF PRODUCT ENDORSEMENTS AND SELF-HELP WORKSHOPS.
FILE PHOTO
ON THE AIR WHILE IN THE AIR WITH CARIAIR

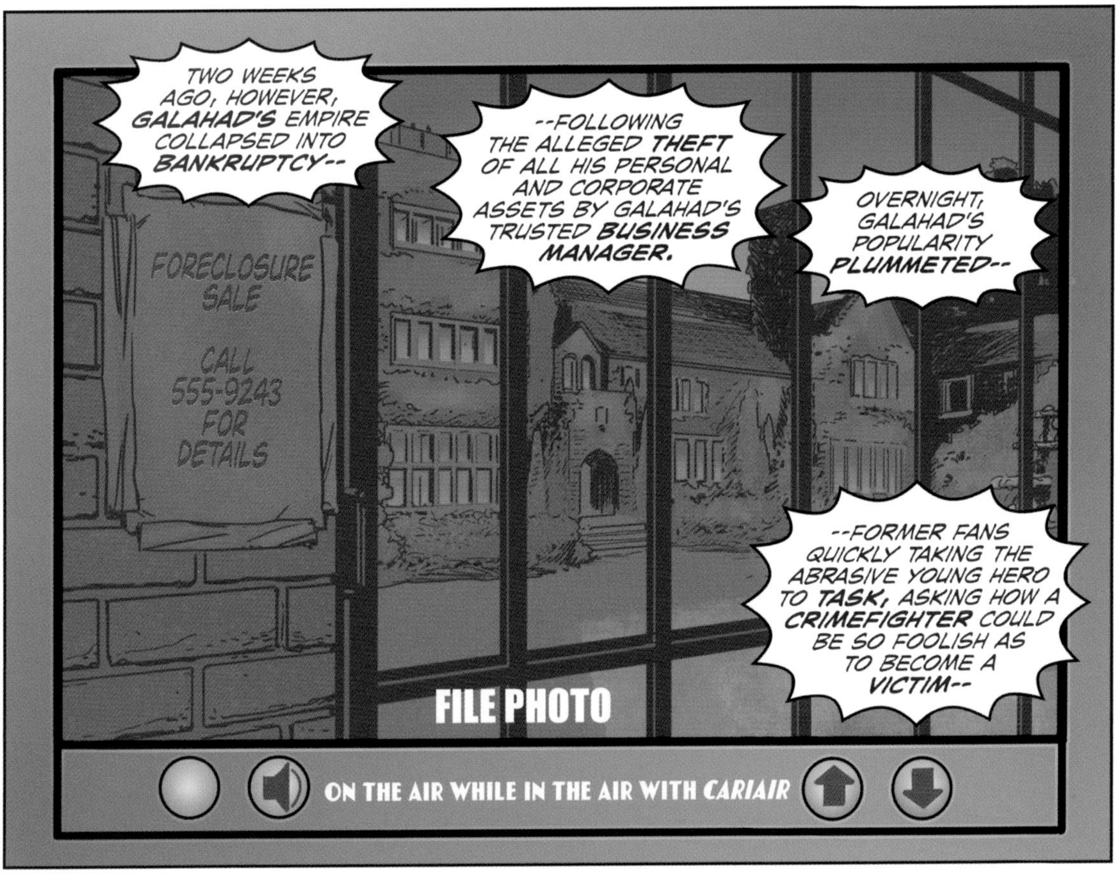
TWO WEEKS AGO, HOWEVER, GALAHAD'S EMPIRE COLLAPSED INTO BANKRUPTCY--
--FOLLOWING THE ALLEGED THEFT OF ALL HIS PERSONAL AND CORPORATE ASSETS BY GALAHAD'S TRUSTED BUSINESS MANAGER.
OVERNIGHT, GALAHAD'S POPULARITY PLUMMETED--
FORECLOSURE SALE CALL 555-9243 FOR DETAILS
--FORMER FANS QUICKLY TAKING THE ABRASIVE YOUNG HERO TO TASK, ASKING HOW A CRIMEFIGHTER COULD BE SO FOOLISH AS TO BECOME A VICTIM--
FILE PHOTO
ON THE AIR WHILE IN THE AIR WITH CARIAIR

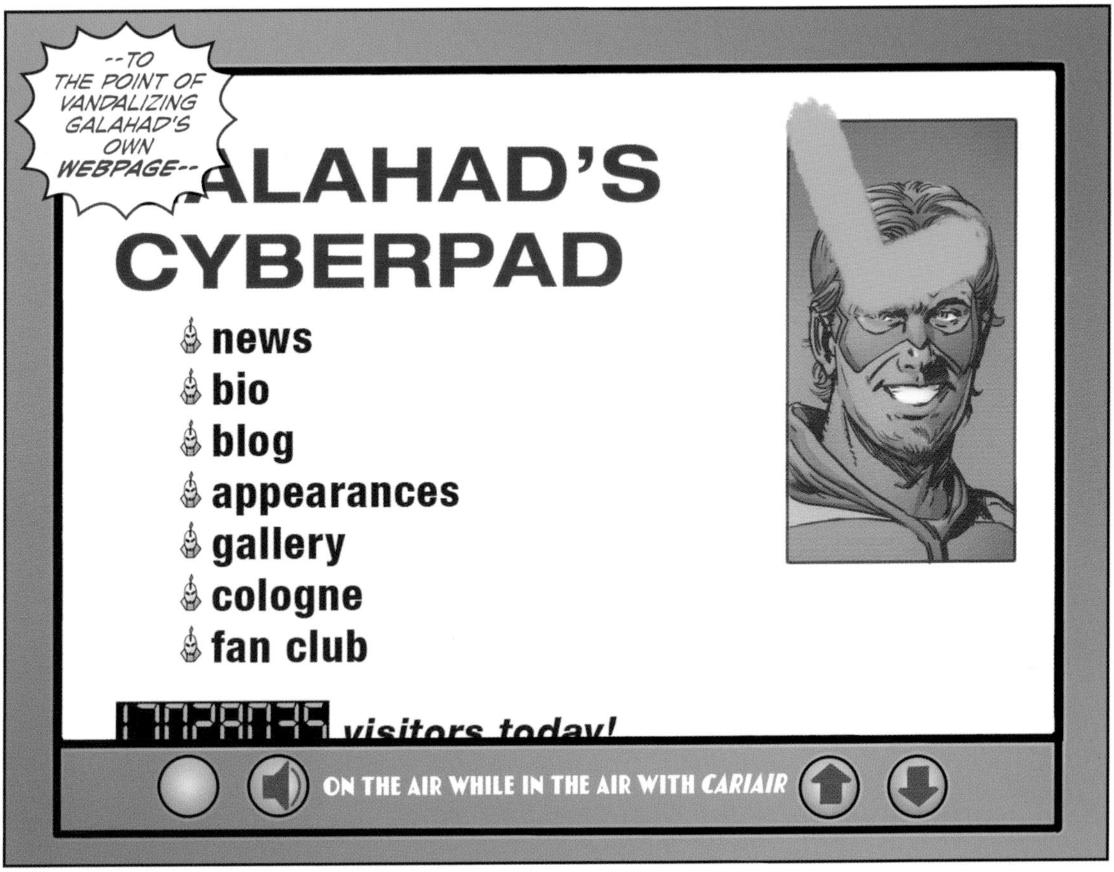
--TO THE POINT OF VANDALIZING GALAHAD'S OWN WEBPAGE--
ALAHAD'S
CYBERPAD
news
bio
blog
appearances
gallery
cologne
fan club
visitors today!
ON THE AIR WHILE IN THE AIR WITH CARIAIR

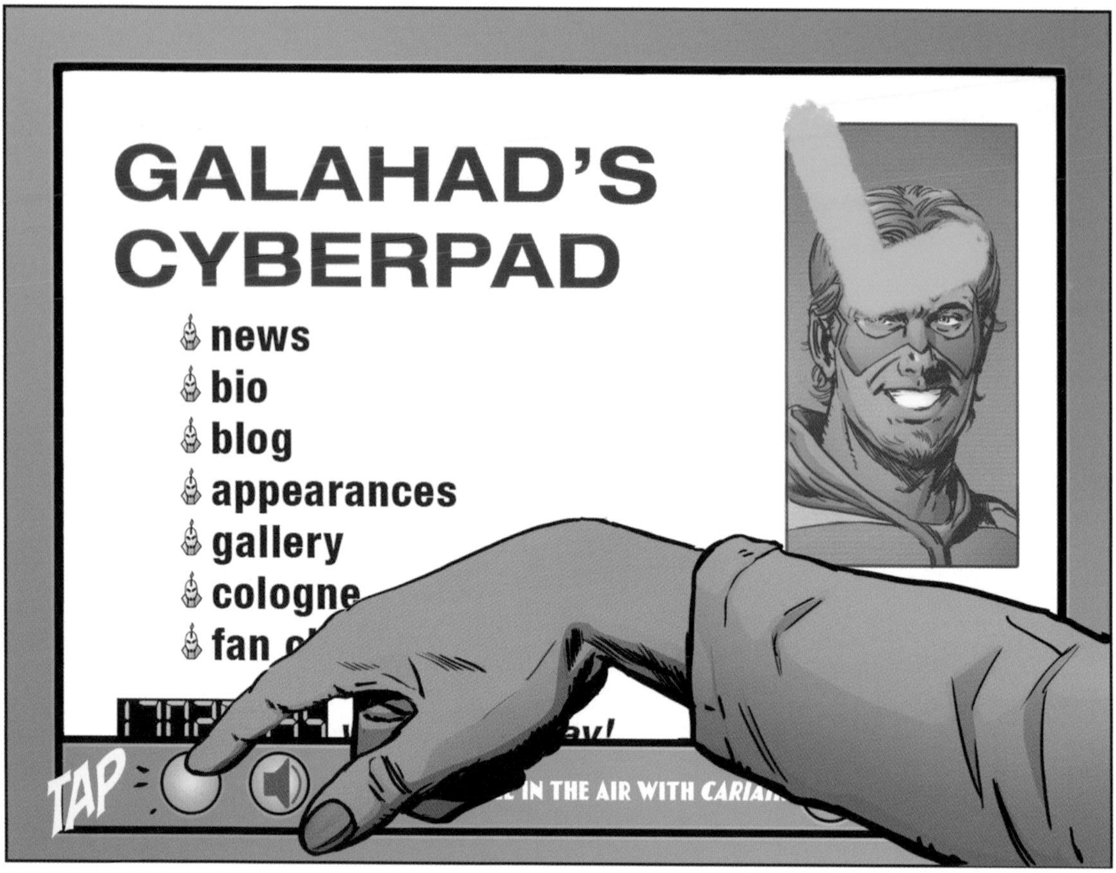
GALAHAD'S CYBERPAD
news
bio
blog
appearances
gallery
cologne
TAP

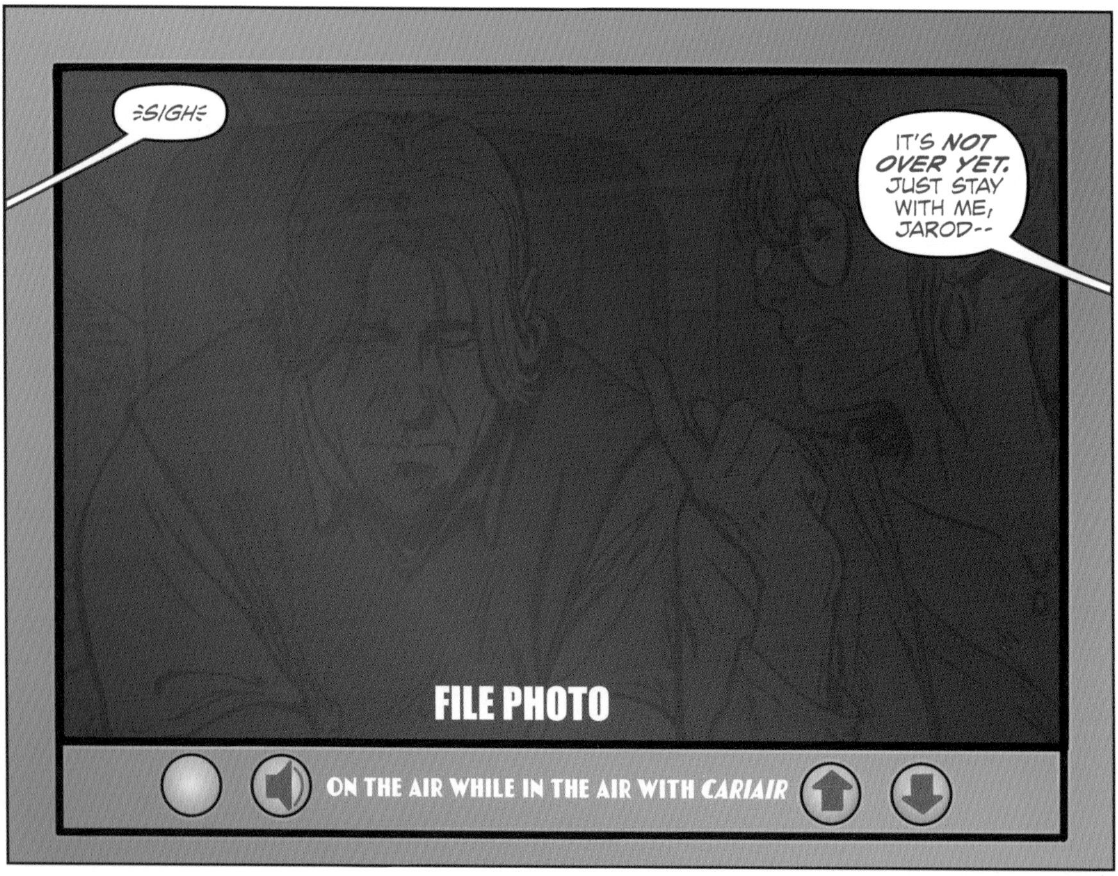
≈SIGH≈
IT'S NOT OVER YET. JUST STAY WITH ME, JAROD--
FILE PHOTO
ON THE AIR WHILE IN THE AIR WITH CARIAIR

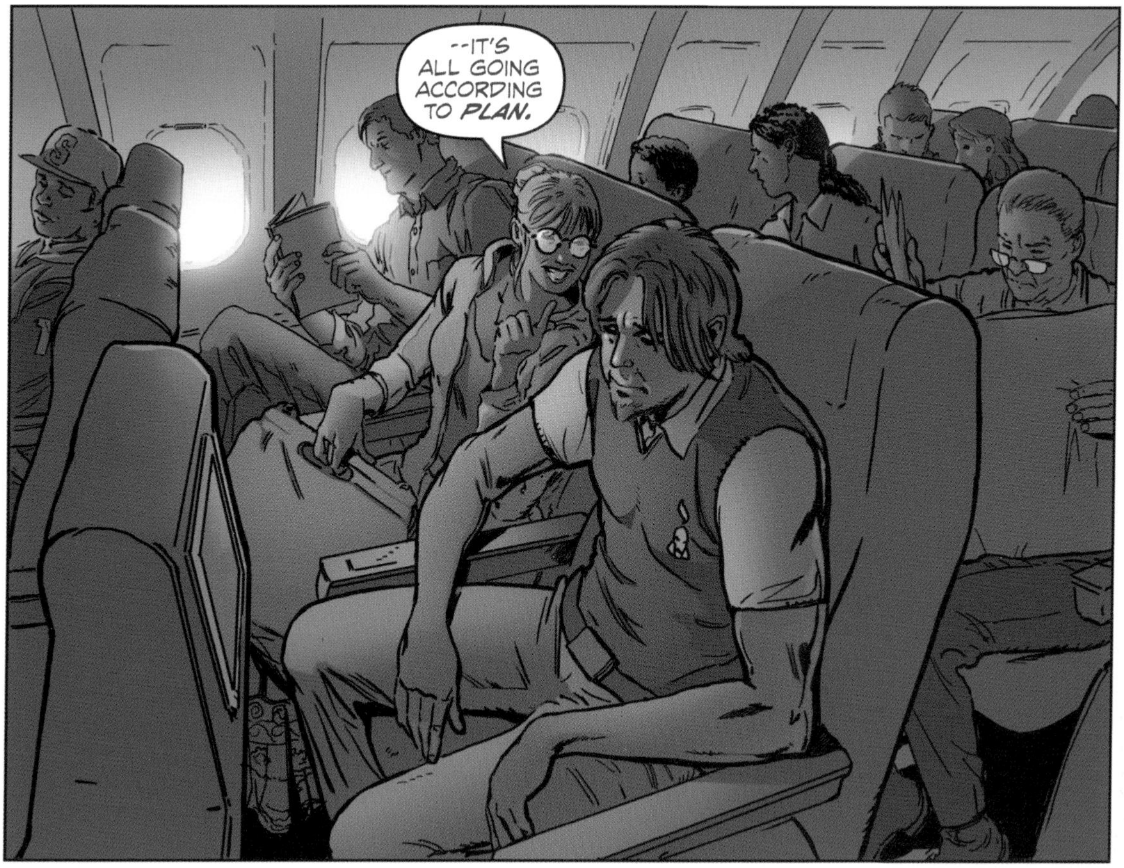
--IT'S ALL GOING ACCORDING TO *PLAN.*

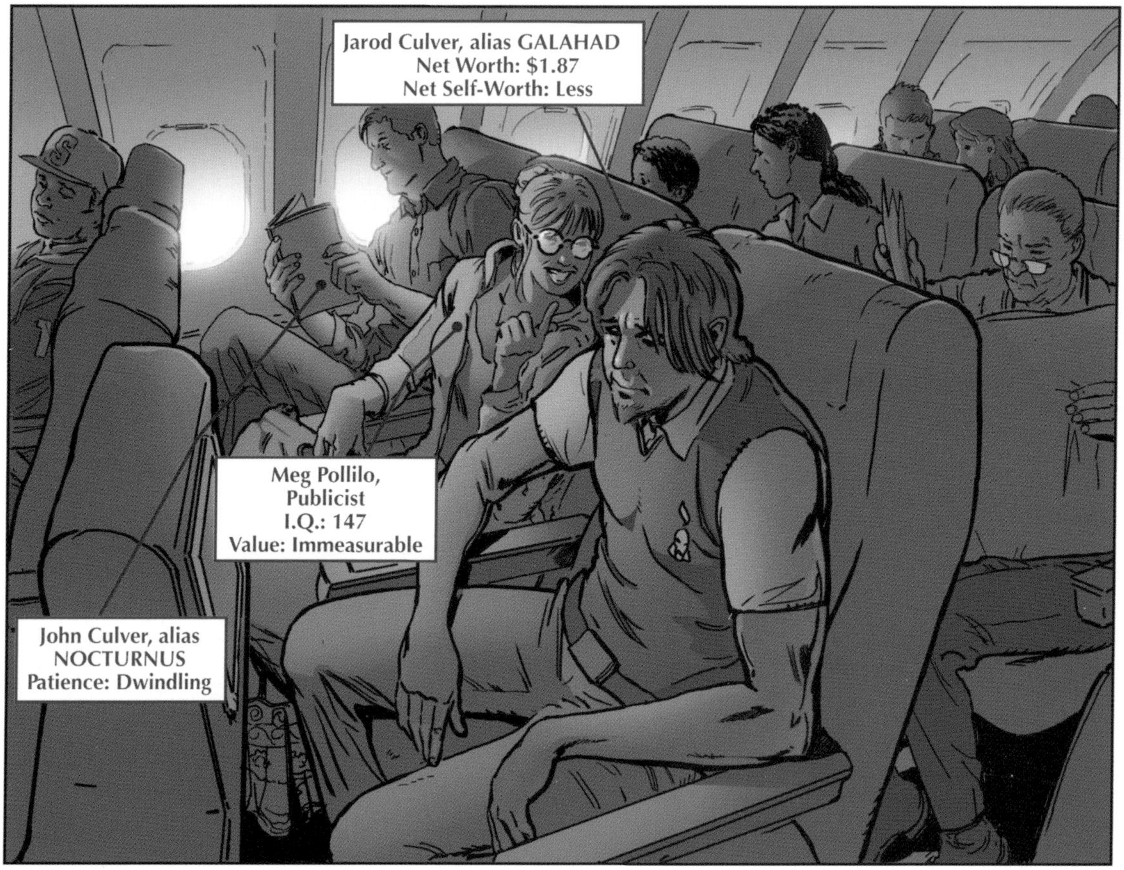
Jarod Culver, alias GALAHAD
Net Worth: $1.87
Net Self-Worth: Less
Meg Pollilo,
Publicist
I.Q.: 147
Value: Immeasurable
John Culver, alias
NOCTURNUS
Patience: Dwindling

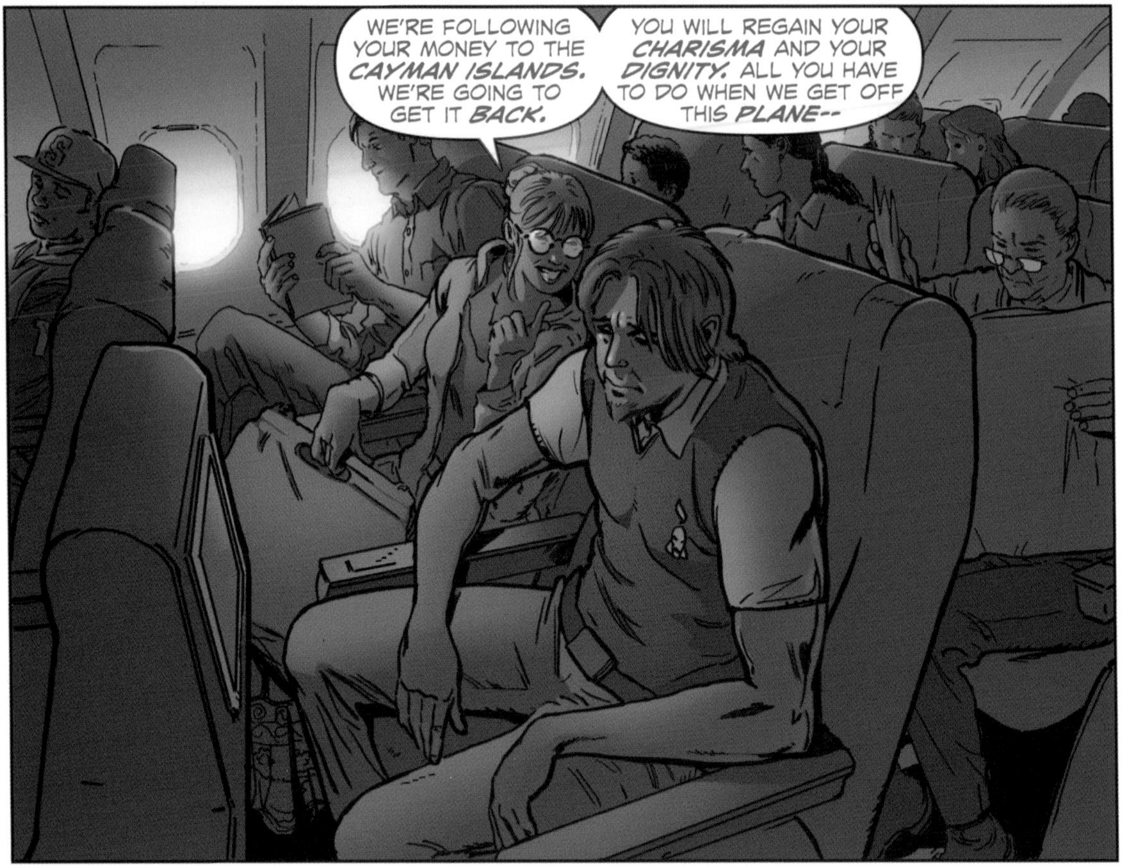
WE'RE FOLLOWING YOUR MONEY TO THE CAYMAN ISLANDS. WE'RE GOING TO GET IT BACK.
YOU WILL REGAIN YOUR CHARISMA AND YOUR DIGNITY. ALL YOU HAVE TO DO WHEN WE GET OFF THIS PLANE--

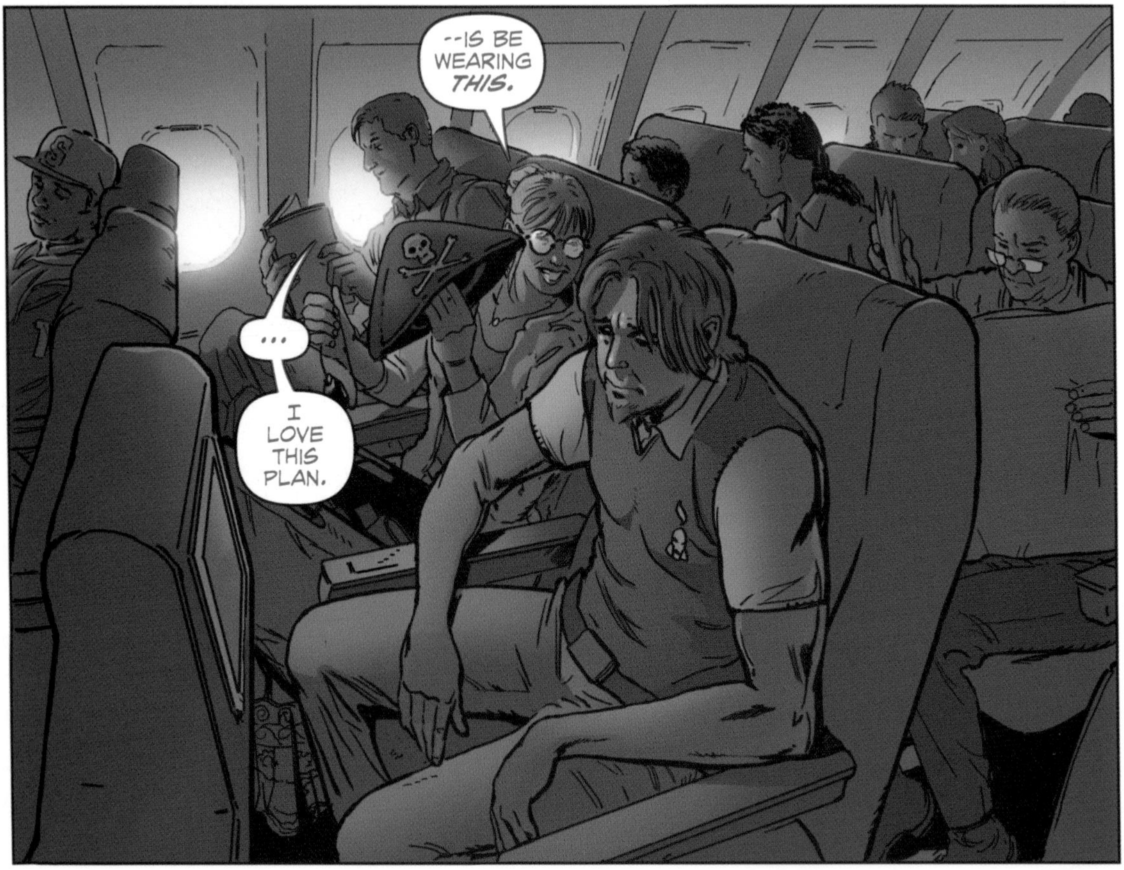
--IS BE WEARING THIS.
...
I LOVE THIS PLAN.

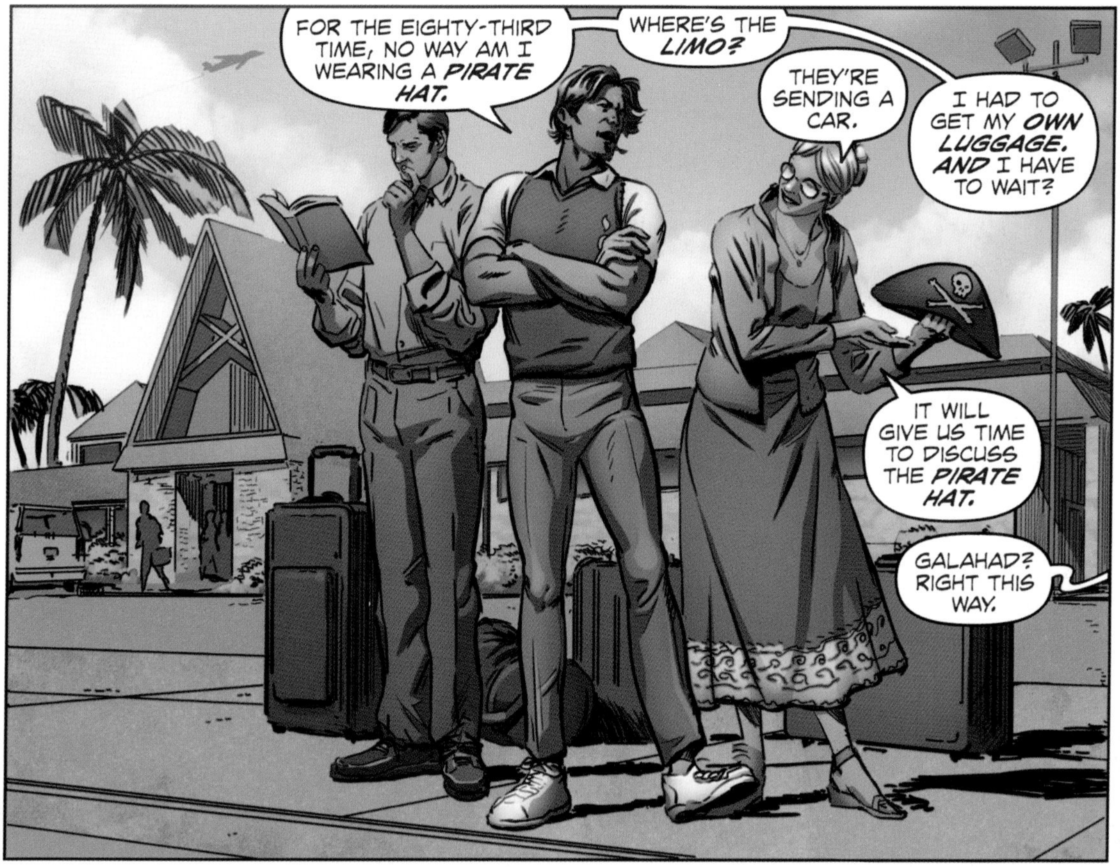
FOR THE EIGHTY-THIRD TIME, NO WAY AM I WEARING A PIRATE HAT.
WHERE'S THE LIMO?
THEY'RE SENDING A CAR.
I HAD TO GET MY OWN LUGGAGE. AND I HAVE TO WAIT?
IT WILL GIVE US TIME TO DISCUSS THE PIRATE HAT.
GALAHAD? RIGHT THIS WAY.

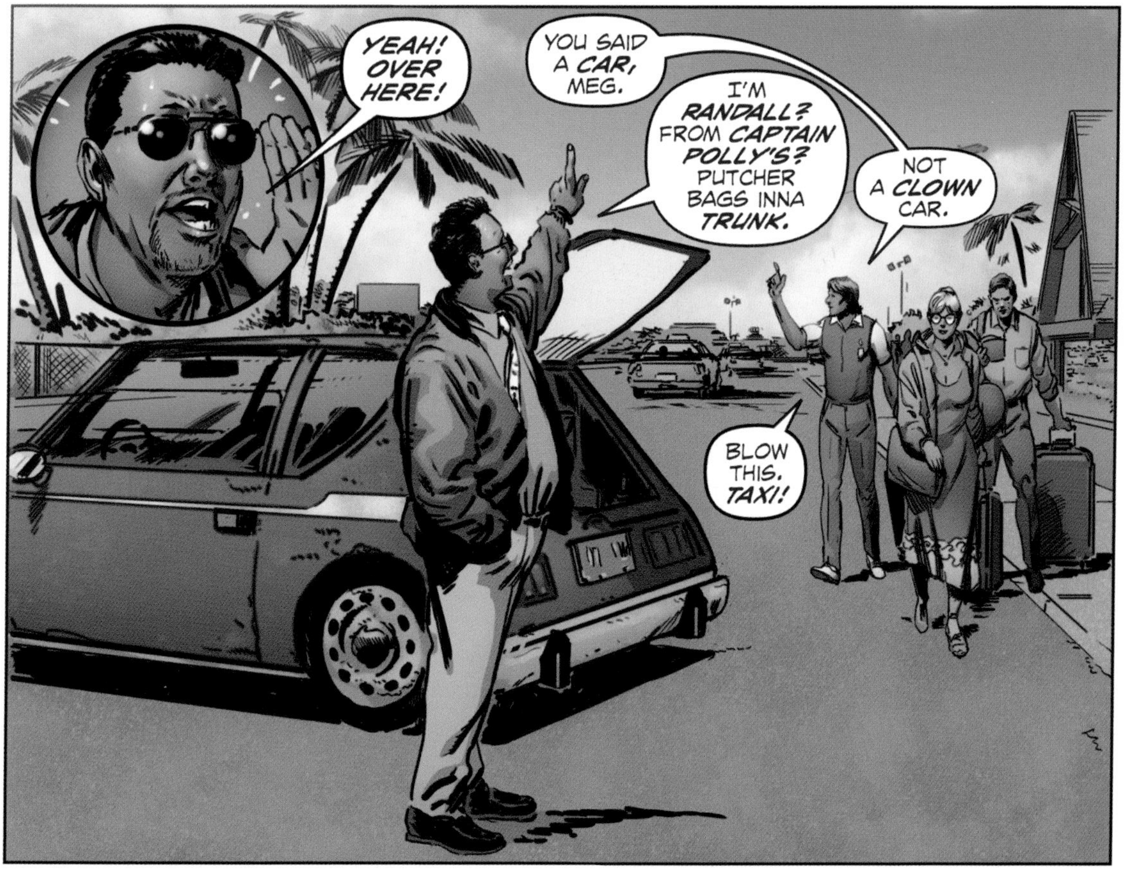
YEAH! OVER HERE!
YOU SAID A CAR, MEG.
I'M RANDALL? FROM CAPTAIN POLLY'S? PUTCHER BAGS INNA TRUNK.
NOT A CLOWN CAR.
BLOW THIS. TAXI!

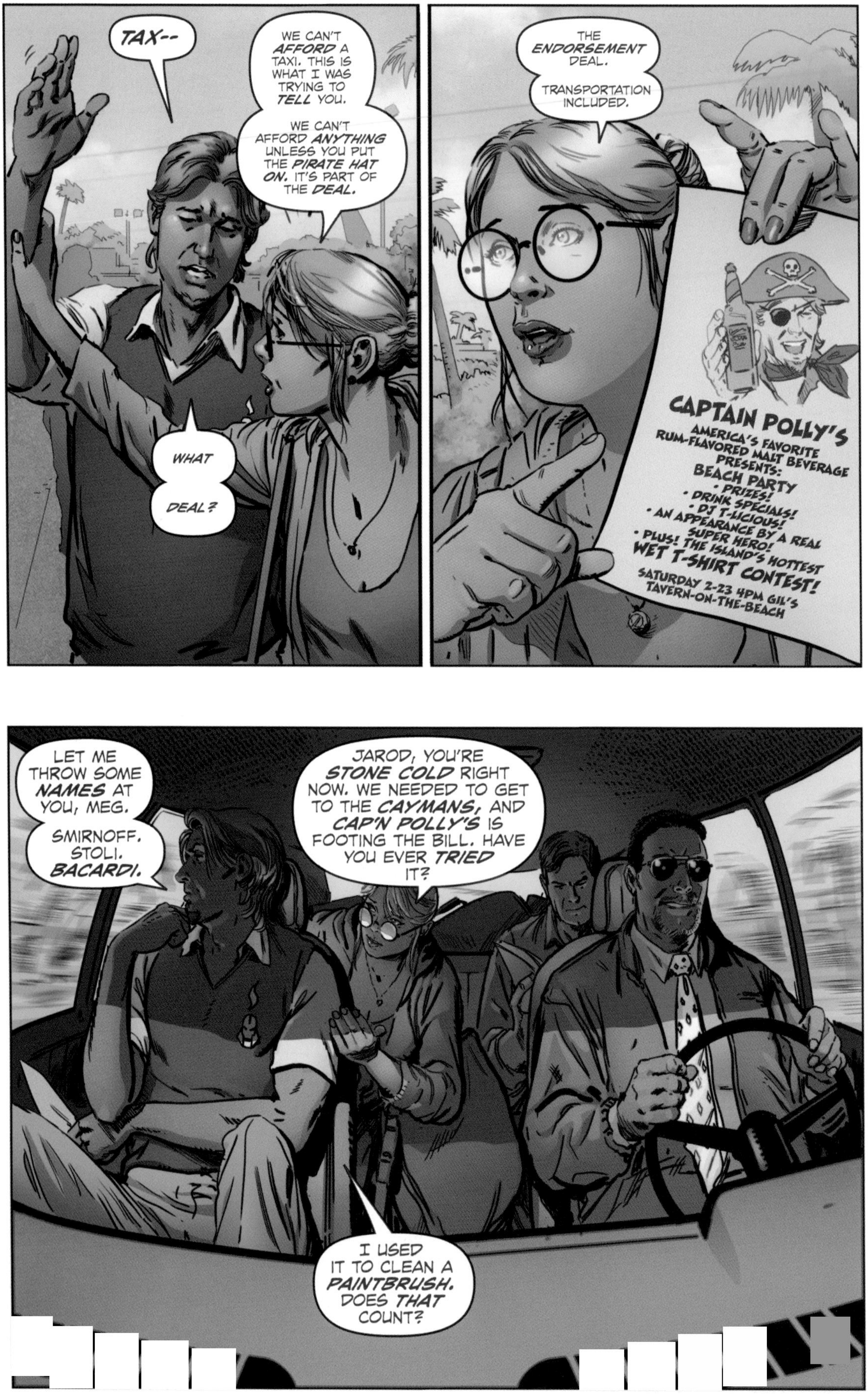
TAX--
WE CAN'T AFFORD A TAXI. THIS IS WHAT I WAS TRYING TO TELL YOU.
WE CAN'T AFFORD ANYTHING UNLESS YOU PUT THE PIRATE HAT ON. IT'S PART OF THE DEAL.
WHAT
DEAL?
THE ENDORSEMENT DEAL.
TRANSPORTATION INCLUDED.
CAPTAIN POLLY'S
AMERICA'S FAVORITE RUM-FLAVORED MALT BEVERAGE PRESENTS:
BEACH PARTY
• PRIZES!
• DRINK SPECIALS!
• DJ T-LICIOUS!
• AN APPEARANCE BY A REAL SUPER HERO!
• PLUS! THE ISLAND'S HOTTEST WET T-SHIRT CONTEST!
SATURDAY 2-23 4PM GIL'S TAVERN-ON-THE-BEACH
LET ME THROW SOME NAMES AT YOU, MEG.
SMIRNOFF. STOLI. BACARDI.
JAROD, YOU'RE STONE COLD RIGHT NOW. WE NEEDED TO GET TO THE CAYMANS, AND CAP'N POLLY'S IS FOOTING THE BILL. HAVE YOU EVER TRIED IT?
I USED IT TO CLEAN A PAINTBRUSH. DOES THAT COUNT?

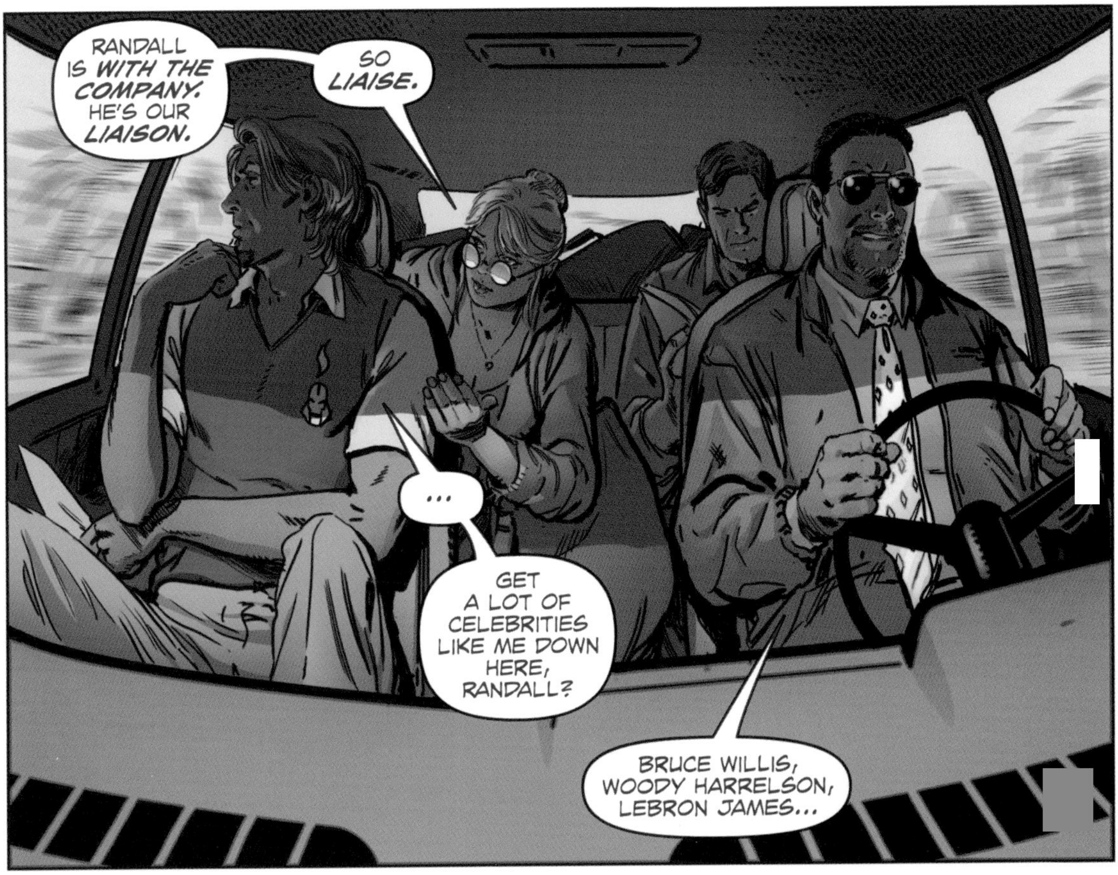
RANDALL IS WITH THE COMPANY. HE'S OUR LIAISON.
SO LIAISE.
...
GET A LOT OF CELEBRITIES LIKE ME DOWN HERE, RANDALL?
BRUCE WILLIS, WOODY HARRELSON, LEBRON JAMES...

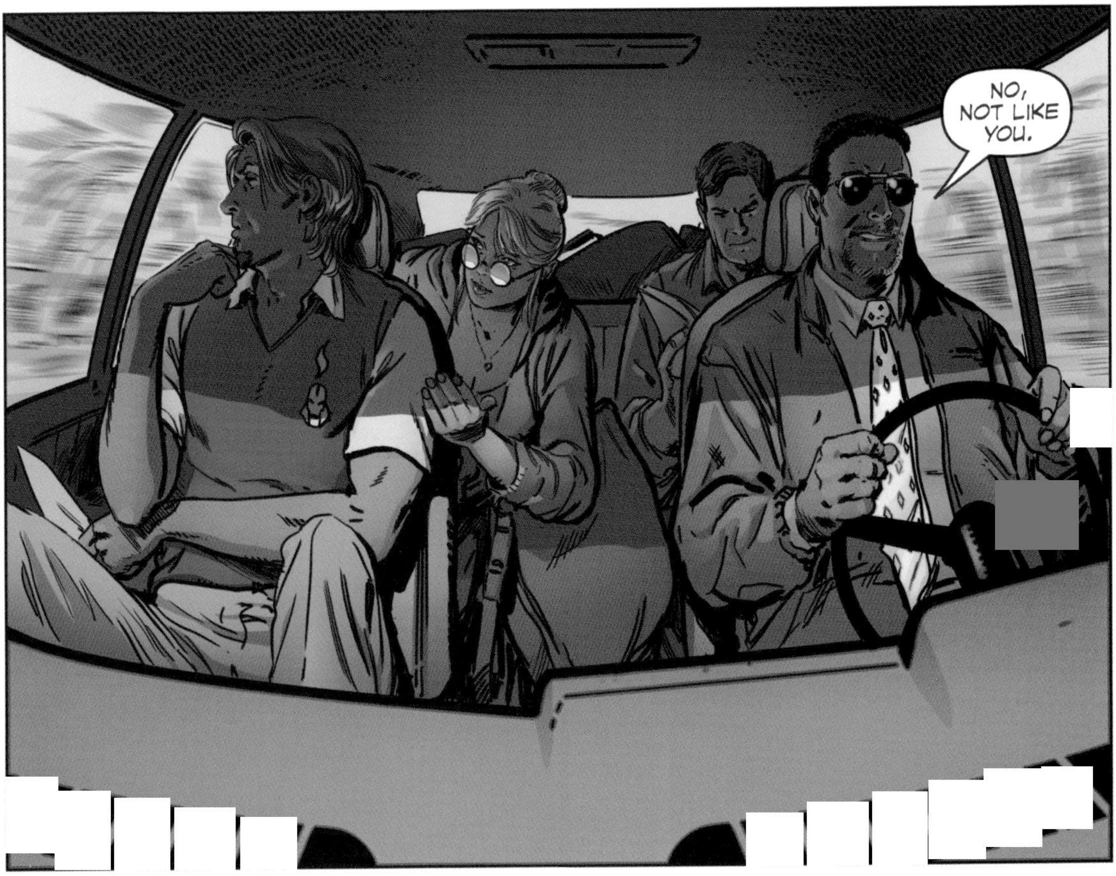
NO, NOT LIKE YOU.

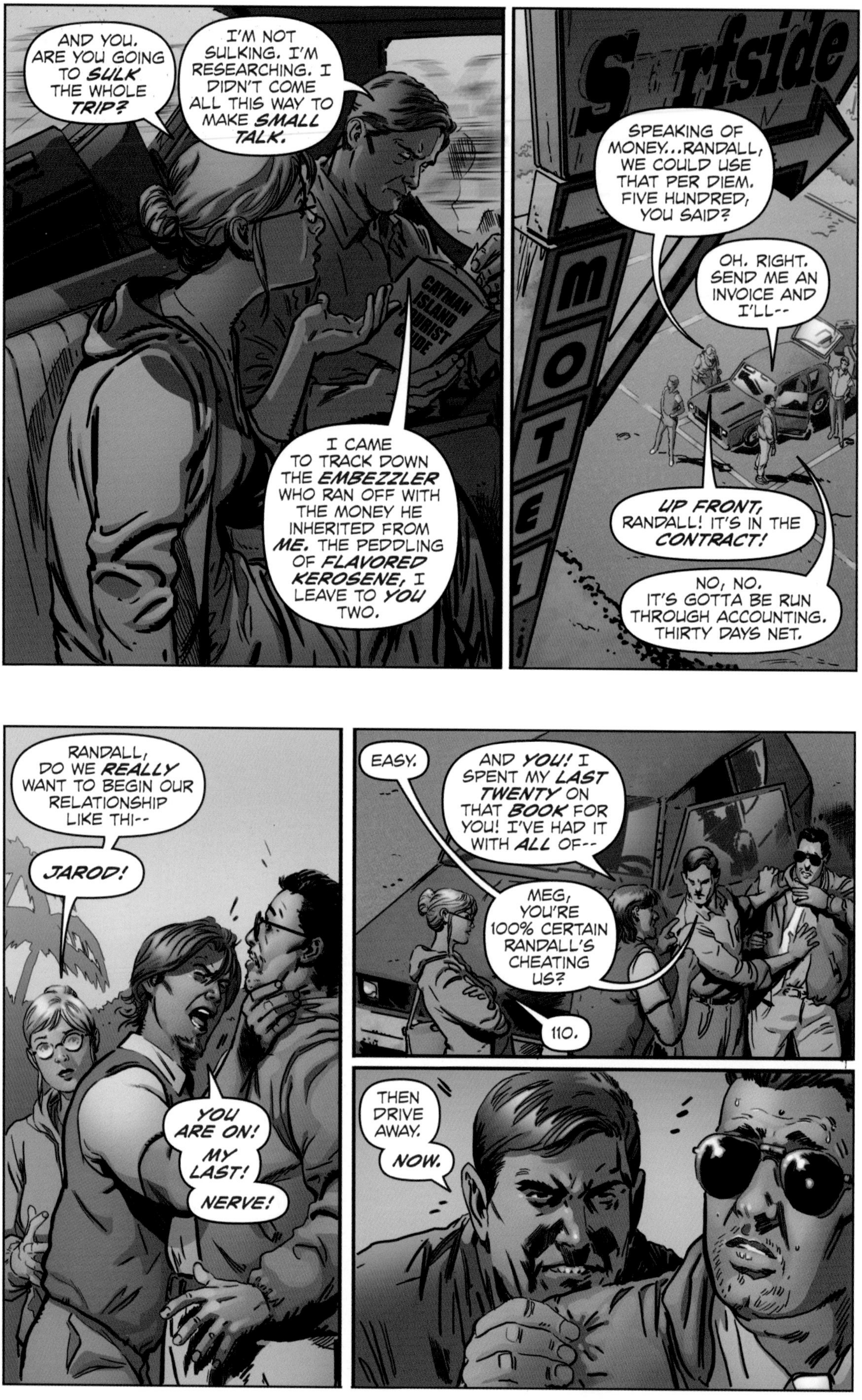
AND YOU. ARE YOU GOING TO SULK THE WHOLE TRIP?
I'M NOT SULKING. I'M RESEARCHING. I DIDN'T COME ALL THIS WAY TO MAKE SMALL TALK.
CAYMAN ISLAND TOURIST GUIDE
I CAME TO TRACK DOWN THE EMBEZZLER WHO RAN OFF WITH THE MONEY HE INHERITED FROM ME. THE PEDDLING OF FLAVORED KEROSENE, I LEAVE TO YOU TWO.
Surfside
MOTEL
SPEAKING OF MONEY...RANDALL, WE COULD USE THAT PER DIEM. FIVE HUNDRED, YOU SAID?
OH. RIGHT. SEND ME AN INVOICE AND I'LL--
UP FRONT, RANDALL! IT'S IN THE CONTRACT!
NO, NO. IT'S GOTTA BE RUN THROUGH ACCOUNTING. THIRTY DAYS NET.
RANDALL, DO WE REALLY WANT TO BEGIN OUR RELATIONSHIP LIKE THI--
JAROD!
YOU ARE ON! MY LAST! NERVE!
EASY.
AND YOU! I SPENT MY LAST TWENTY ON THAT BOOK FOR YOU! I'VE HAD IT WITH ALL OF--
MEG, YOU'RE 100% CERTAIN RANDALL'S CHEATING US?
110.
THEN DRIVE AWAY.
NOW.

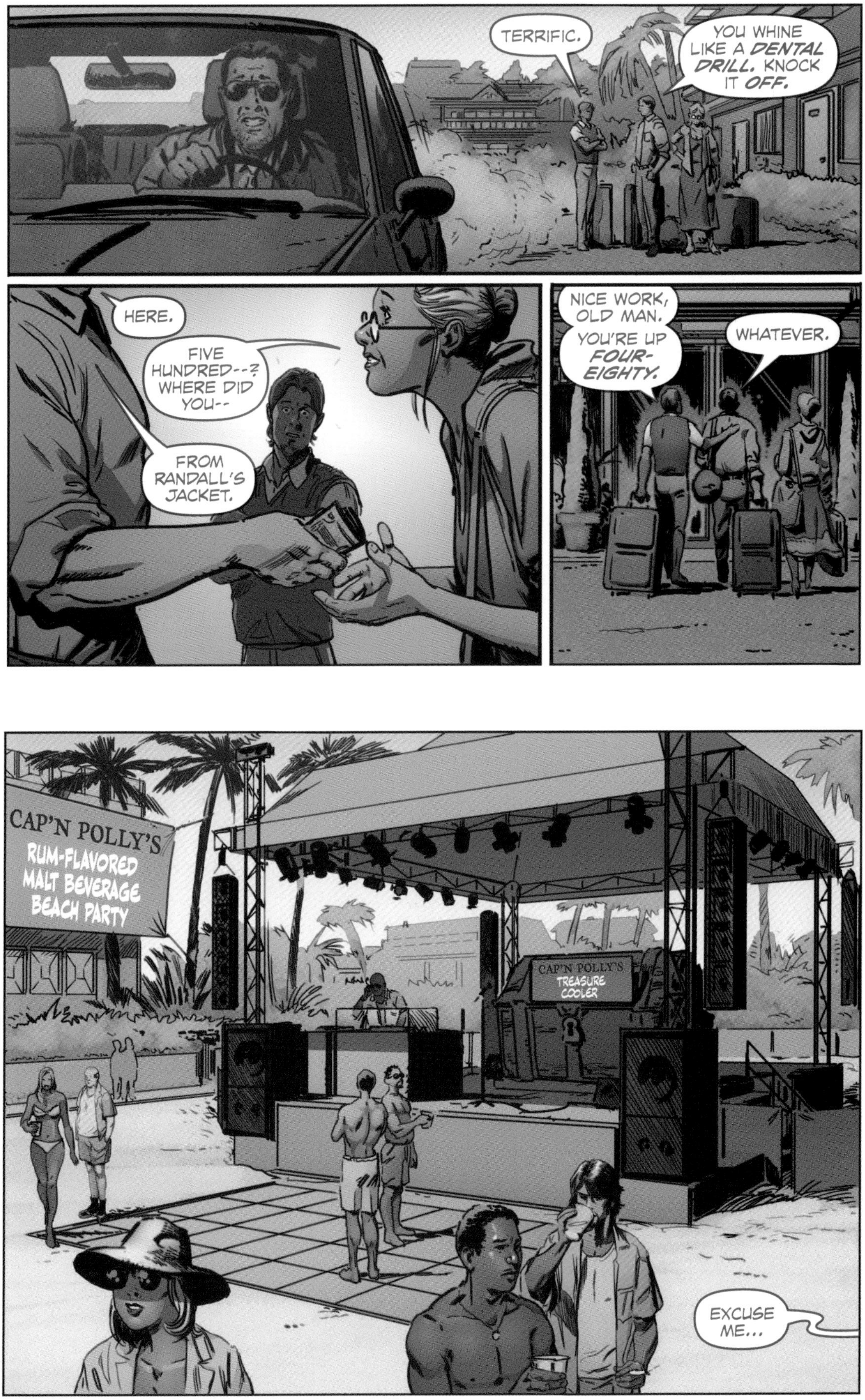
TERRIFIC.
YOU WHINE LIKE A DENTAL DRILL. KNOCK IT OFF.
HERE.
FIVE HUNDRED--? WHERE DID YOU--
FROM RANDALL'S JACKET.
NICE WORK, OLD MAN.
YOU'RE UP FOUR-EIGHTY.
WHATEVER.
CAP'N POLLY'S RUM-FLAVORED MALT BEVERAGE BEACH PARTY
CAP'N POLLY'S TREASURE COOLER
EXCUSE ME...

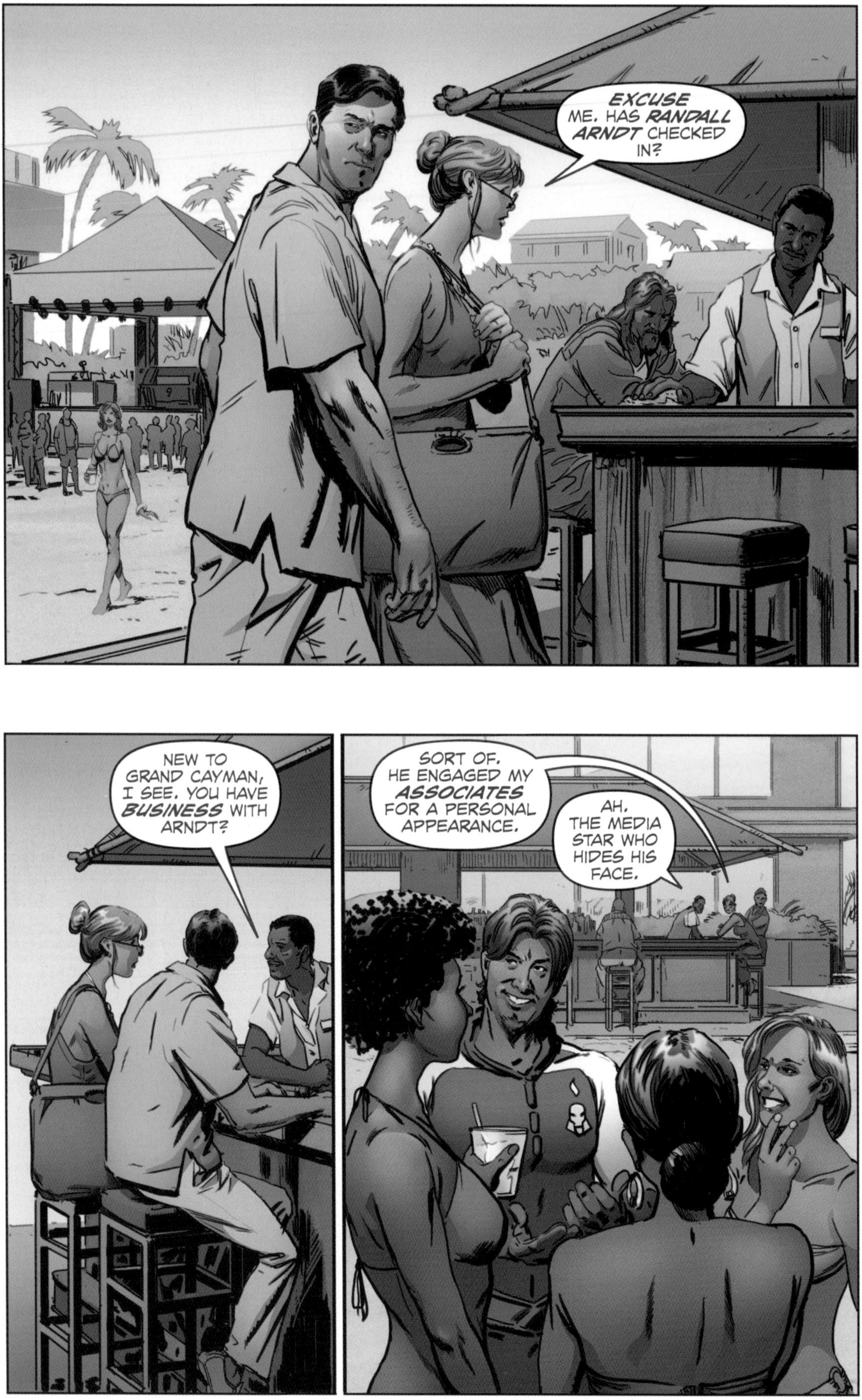
EXCUSE ME. HAS RANDALL ARNDT CHECKED IN?
NEW TO GRAND CAYMAN, I SEE. YOU HAVE BUSINESS WITH ARNDT?
SORT OF. HE ENGAGED MY ASSOCIATES FOR A PERSONAL APPEARANCE.
AH. THE MEDIA STAR WHO HIDES HIS FACE.

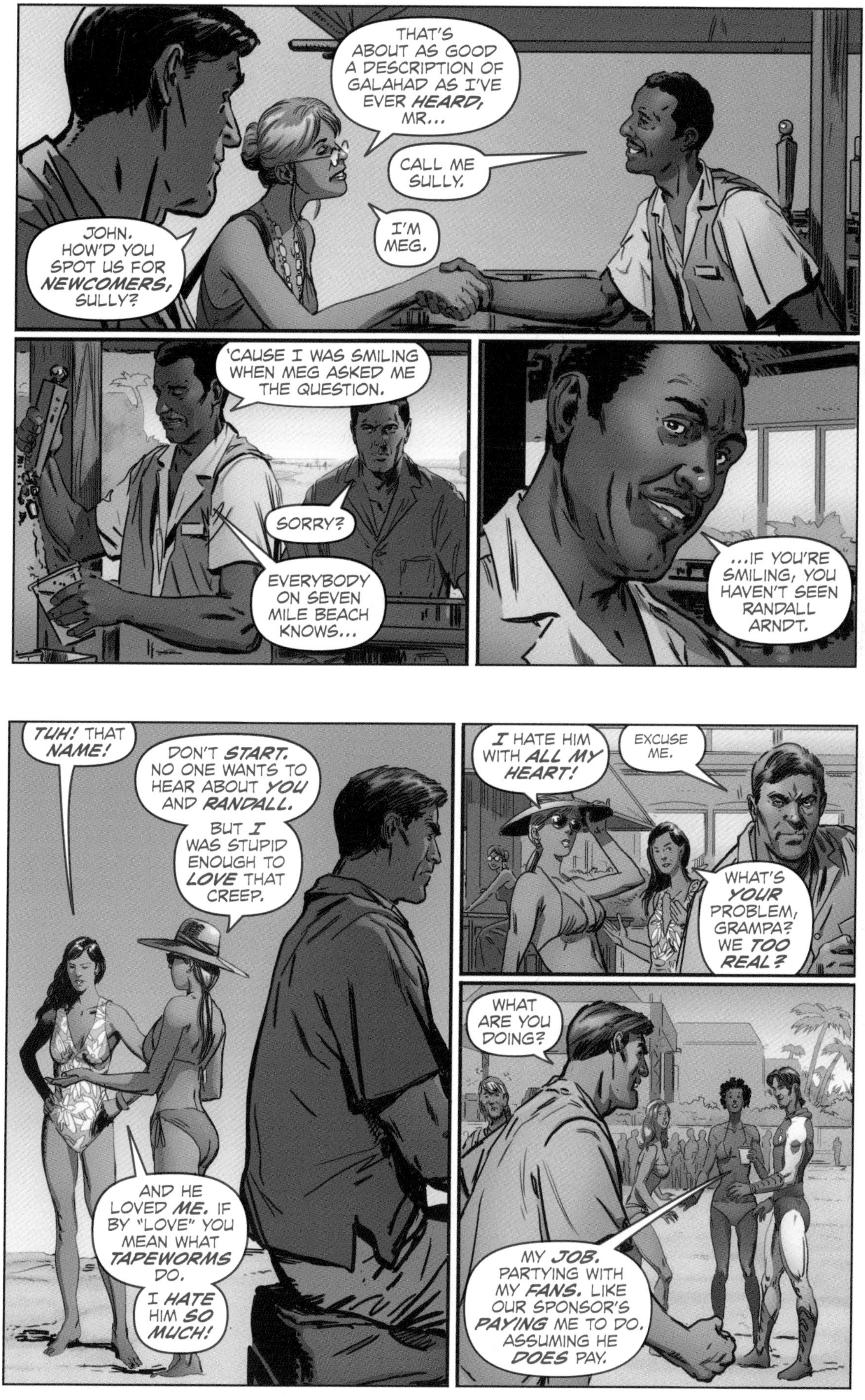

THAT'S ABOUT AS GOOD A DESCRIPTION OF GALAHAD AS I'VE EVER HEARD, MR...
CALL ME SULLY.
I'M MEG.
JOHN. HOW'D YOU SPOT US FOR NEWCOMERS, SULLY?
'CAUSE I WAS SMILING WHEN MEG ASKED ME THE QUESTION.
SORRY?
EVERYBODY ON SEVEN MILE BEACH KNOWS...
...IF YOU'RE SMILING, YOU HAVEN'T SEEN RANDALL ARNDT.
TUH! THAT NAME!
DON'T START. NO ONE WANTS TO HEAR ABOUT YOU AND RANDALL.
BUT I WAS STUPID ENOUGH TO LOVE THAT CREEP.
AND HE LOVED ME. IF BY "LOVE" YOU MEAN WHAT TAPEWORMS DO.
I HATE HIM SO MUCH!
I HATE HIM WITH ALL MY HEART!
EXCUSE ME.
WHAT'S YOUR PROBLEM, GRAMPA? WE TOO REAL?
WHAT ARE YOU DOING?
MY JOB. PARTYING WITH MY FANS. LIKE OUR SPONSOR'S PAYING ME TO DO. ASSUMING HE DOES PAY.

WHOA, WHOA, **WHOA.**

ARNDT? SWINDLER OWES *ME* FOR THE WEBSITE I BUILT HIM! OWED ME SINCE...

...*WHEN*, EXACTLY...WE DIDN'T HAVE ANY LUCK GOOGLING KATE MIDDLETON'S BOOBS, SO IT *HAD* TO BE BEFORE SEPTEMBER...

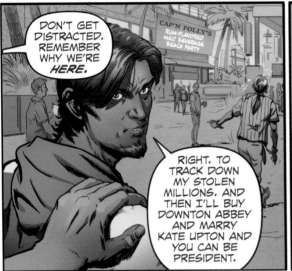

DON'T GET DISTRACTED. REMEMBER WHY WE'RE *HERE.*

CAP'N POLLY'S RUM-FLAVORED MALT BEVERAGE BEACH PARTY

RIGHT. TO TRACK DOWN MY STOLEN MILLIONS. AND THEN I'LL BUY DOWNTON ABBEY AND MARRY KATE UPTON AND YOU CAN BE PRESIDENT.

STOP IT. WE CAN *DO* THIS.

NOW PUT ON THE EMBARRASSING PIRATE HAT, TAKE THE STAGE, AND DO YOUR EIGHT SECONDS.

BECAUSE I'D LIKE TO GET *WORKING* BEFORE YOU DRINK YOURSELF *STUPID.*

YOU'RE NOT MY MOTHER.

I'M YOUR FATHER.

WHEN YOU FEEL LIKE IT.

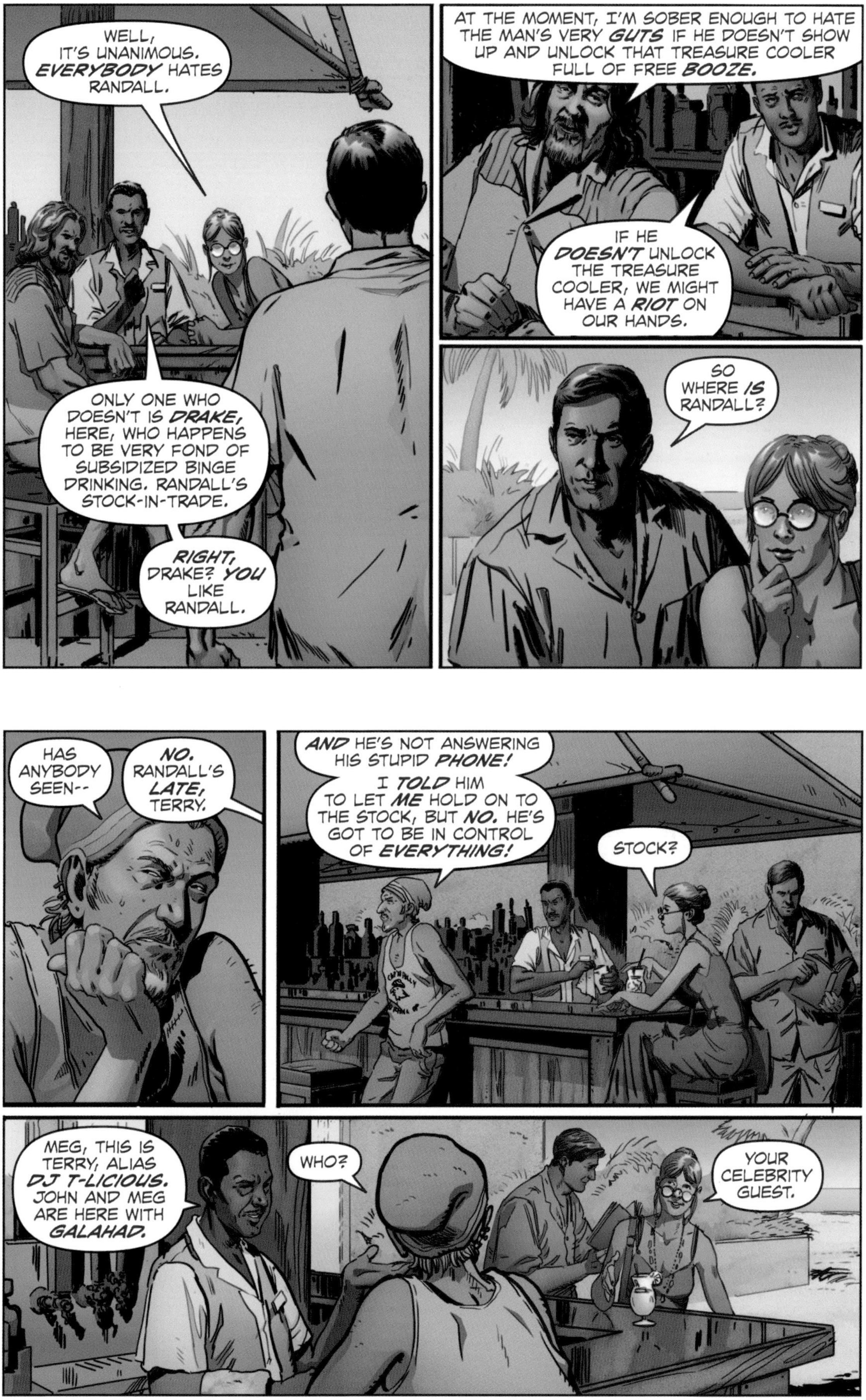

WELL, IT'S UNANIMOUS. EVERYBODY HATES RANDALL.
ONLY ONE WHO DOESN'T IS DRAKE, HERE, WHO HAPPENS TO BE VERY FOND OF SUBSIDIZED BINGE DRINKING. RANDALL'S STOCK-IN-TRADE.
RIGHT, DRAKE? YOU LIKE RANDALL.
AT THE MOMENT, I'M SOBER ENOUGH TO HATE THE MAN'S VERY GUTS IF HE DOESN'T SHOW UP AND UNLOCK THAT TREASURE COOLER FULL OF FREE BOOZE.
IF HE DOESN'T UNLOCK THE TREASURE COOLER, WE MIGHT HAVE A RIOT ON OUR HANDS.
SO WHERE IS RANDALL?
HAS ANYBODY SEEN--
NO. RANDALL'S LATE, TERRY.
AND HE'S NOT ANSWERING HIS STUPID PHONE!
I TOLD HIM TO LET ME HOLD ON TO THE STOCK, BUT NO. HE'S GOT TO BE IN CONTROL OF EVERYTHING!
STOCK?
MEG, THIS IS TERRY, ALIAS DJ T-LICIOUS. JOHN AND MEG ARE HERE WITH GALAHAD.
WHO?
YOUR CELEBRITY GUEST.

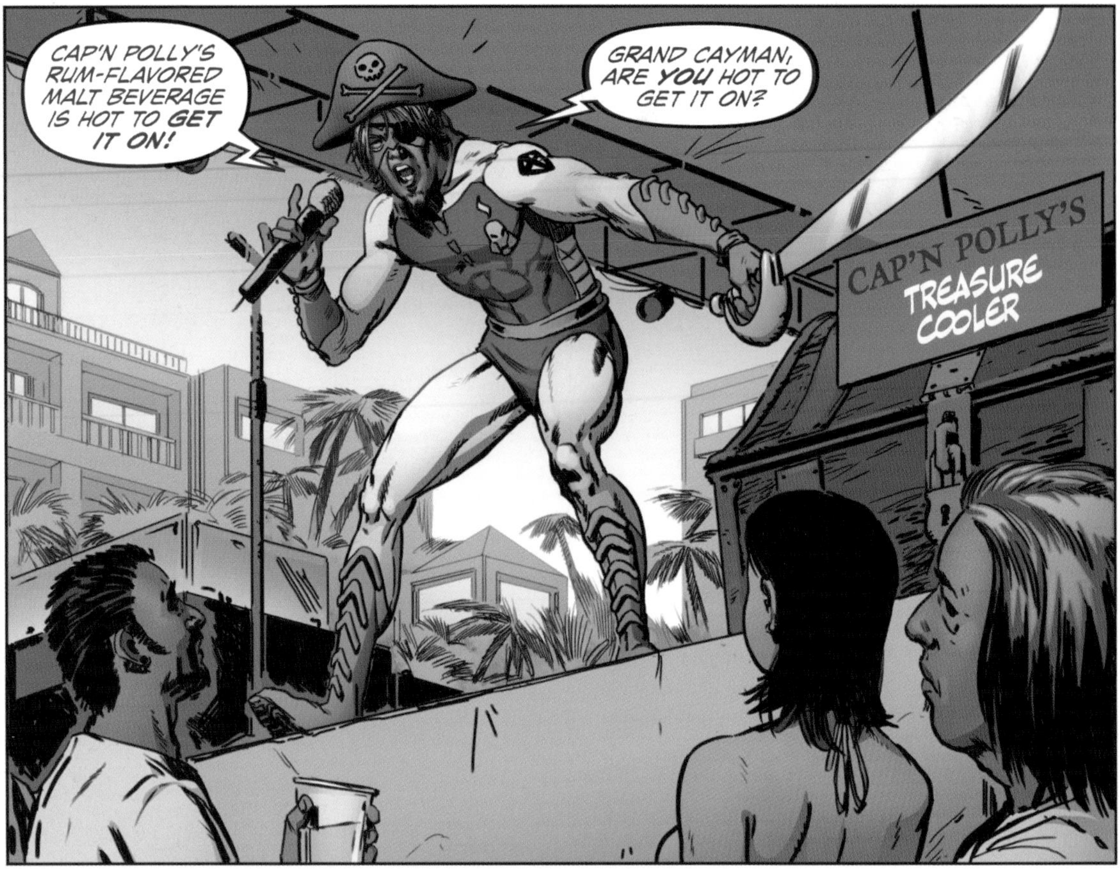
CAP'N POLLY'S RUM-FLAVORED MALT BEVERAGE IS HOT TO GET IT ON!
GRAND CAYMAN, ARE YOU HOT TO GET IT ON?
CAP'N POLLY'S
TREASURE COOLER

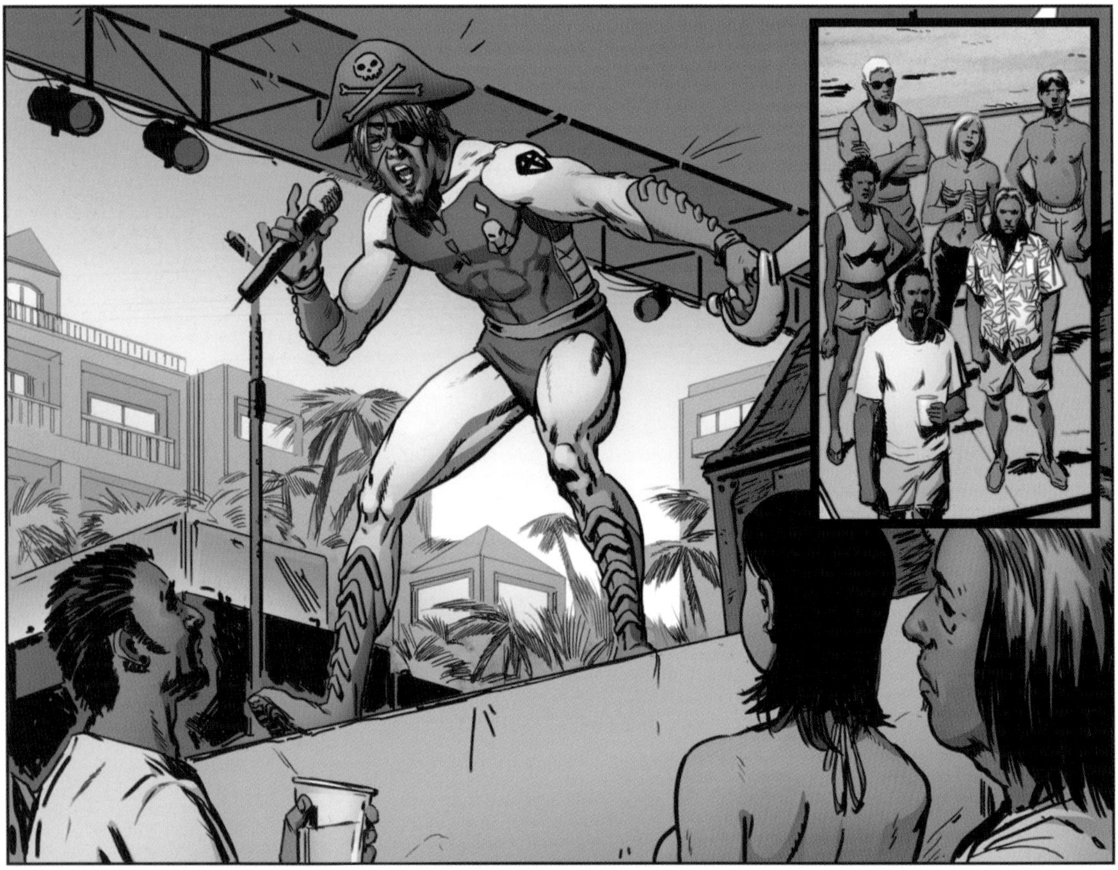

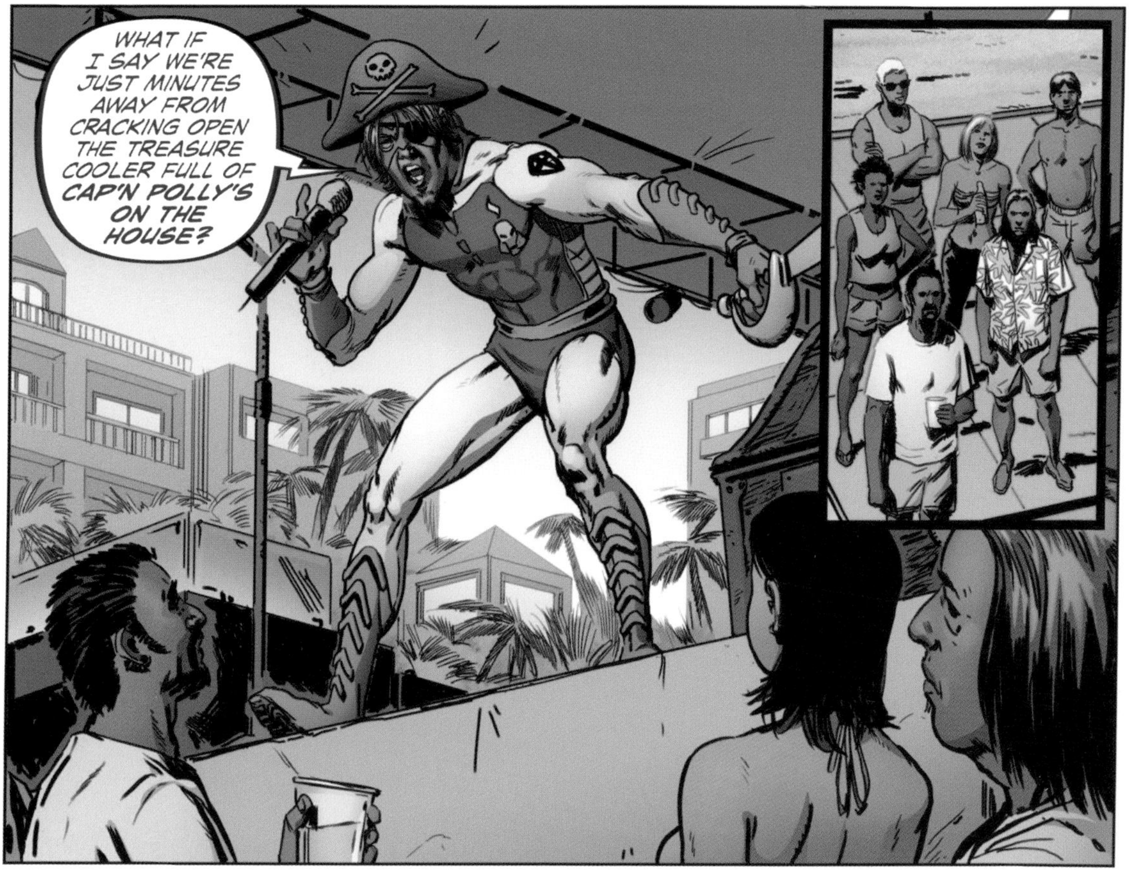
WHAT IF I SAY WE'RE JUST MINUTES AWAY FROM CRACKING OPEN THE TREASURE COOLER FULL OF **CAP'N POLLY'S ON THE HOUSE?**

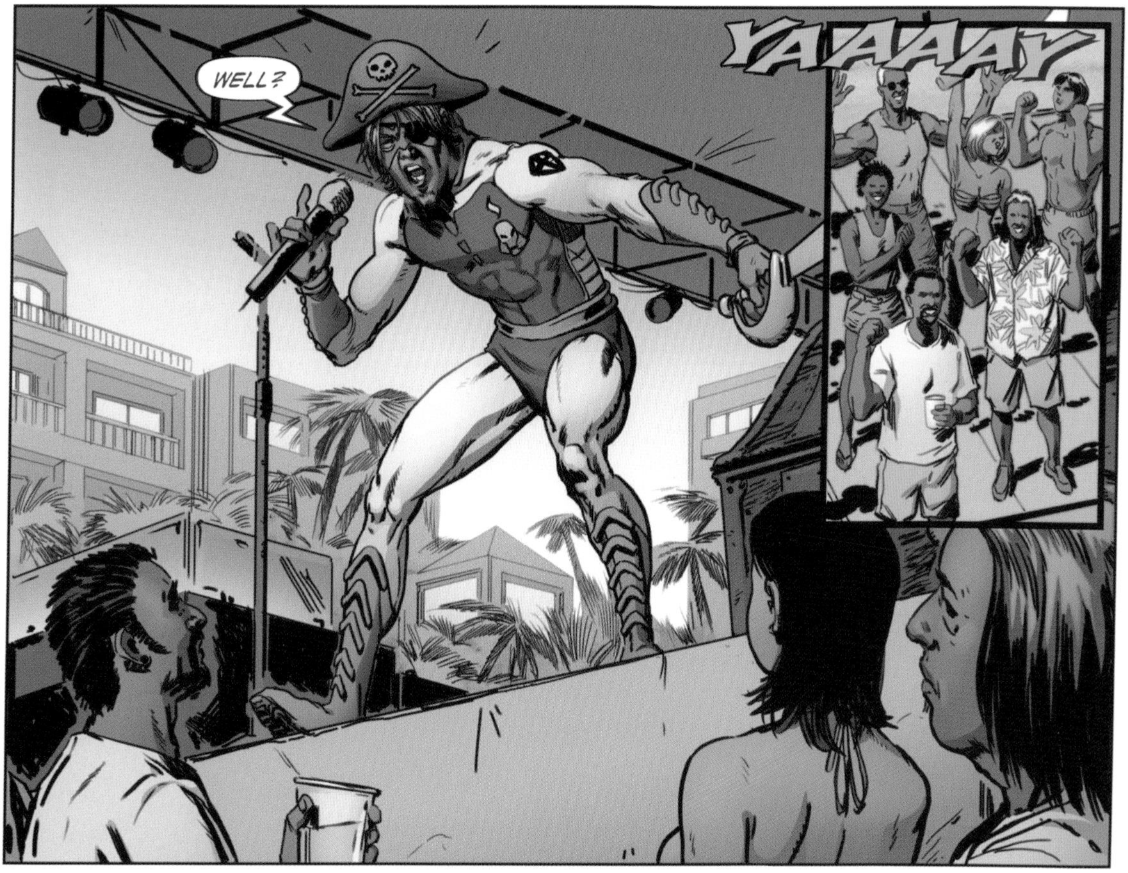
WELL?
YAAAAY

WHATEVER HAPPENED TO CELEBRITIES I *HEARD* OF?

I *KNOW.* THEY KEEP GETTING *YOUNGER,* AND WE *DON'T.* WHAT'S THIS *STOCK* YOU'RE TALKING ABOUT?

CAP'N POLLY T-SHIRTS.

DOESN'T SOUND LIKE MUCH OF AN EMERGENCY.

IT IS IF YOU HAVE TO RUN A *WET T-SHIRT CONTEST!*

I SYMPATHIZE.

HEY!

THIS IS A *RIP-OFF!*

YOU PROMISED *CHEAP* DRINKS AND *FREE* DRINKS! WE PAID OUR WAY *IN* AND *YOU'RE* CHARGIN' A DAMN *LUNG!*

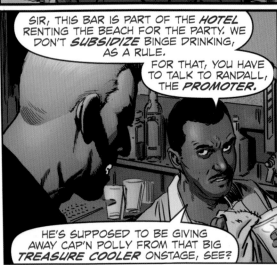

SIR, THIS BAR IS PART OF THE *HOTEL* RENTING THE BEACH FOR THE PARTY. WE DON'T *SUBSIDIZE* BINGE DRINKING, AS A RULE.

FOR THAT, YOU HAVE TO TALK TO RANDALL, THE *PROMOTER.*

HE'S SUPPOSED TO BE GIVING AWAY CAP'N POLLY FROM THAT BIG *TREASURE COOLER* ONSTAGE, SEE?

SO WHERE *IS* THIS RANDALL?

DON'T KNOW.

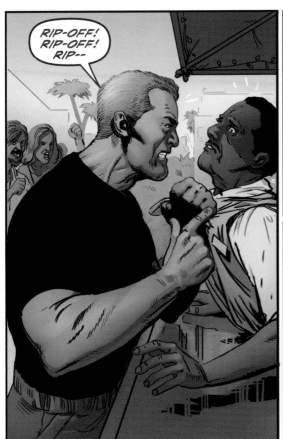

RIP-OFF! RIP-OFF! RIP--

CHUTT

RIP-OFF! RIP-OFF! RIP-OFF!

FUUMP

RIP-OFF! RIP-OFF! RIP-OFF!

OH. NO. LOOK WHAT THIS JERK *STARTED*...

JOHN! WHERE ARE YOU *GOING*?

YOU CAN'T FIGHT THEM *ALL*!

STAY HERE.

RIP-OFF! RIP-OFF!

CUTLASS.

WHAT? WHAT ARE YOU GOING TO *DO*?

RIP-OFF! RIP-OFF!

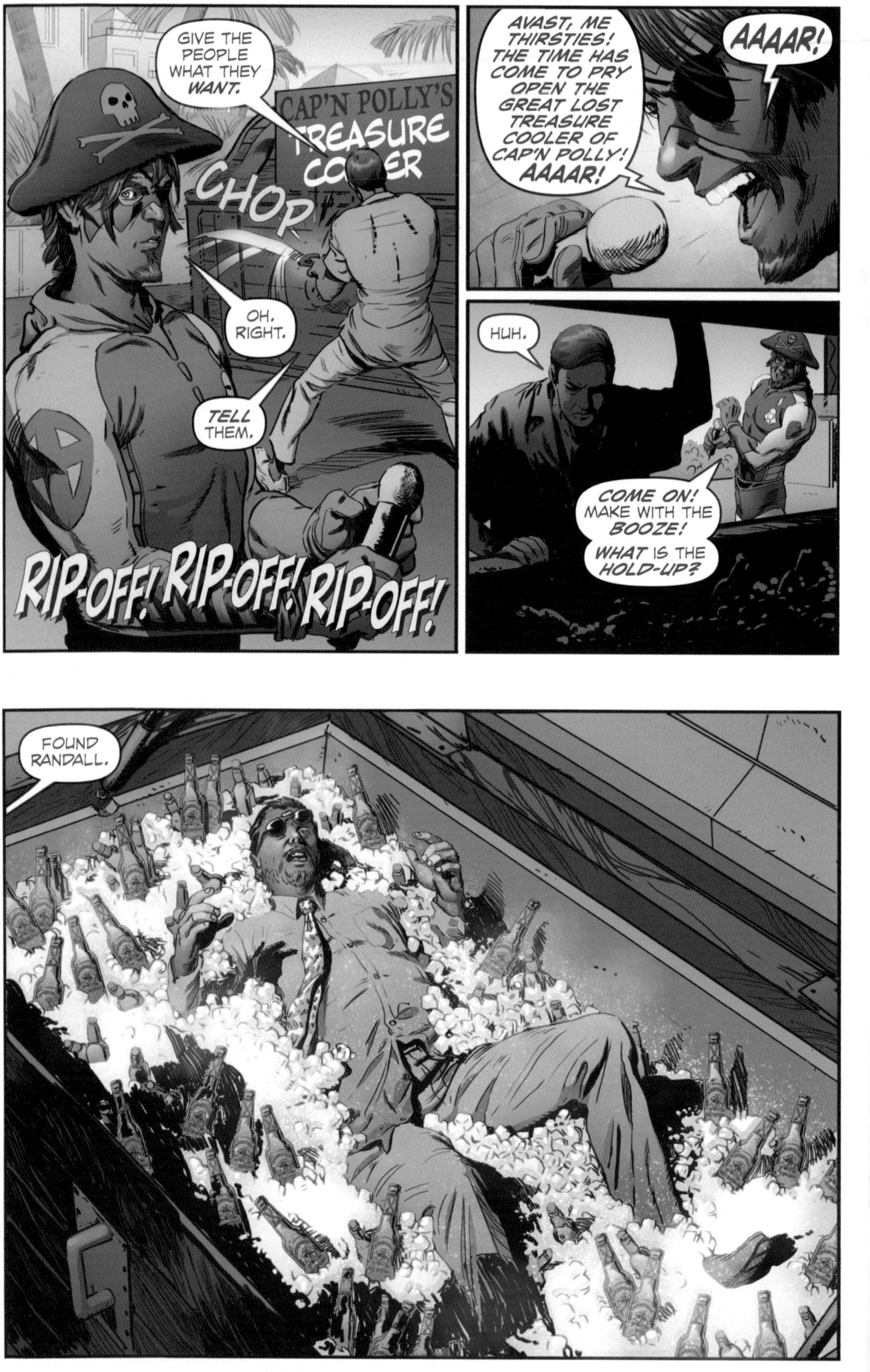
GIVE THE PEOPLE WHAT THEY *WANT.*
CAP'N POLLY'S TREASURE CO ER
CHOP
OH. RIGHT.
TELL THEM.
RIP-OFF! RIP-OFF! RIP-OFF!
AVAST, ME THIRSTIES! THE TIME HAS COME TO PRY OPEN THE GREAT LOST TREASURE COOLER OF CAP'N POLLY! AAAAR!
AAAAR!
HUH.
COME ON! MAKE WITH THE *BOOZE!*
WHAT IS THE *HOLD-UP?*
FOUND RANDALL.

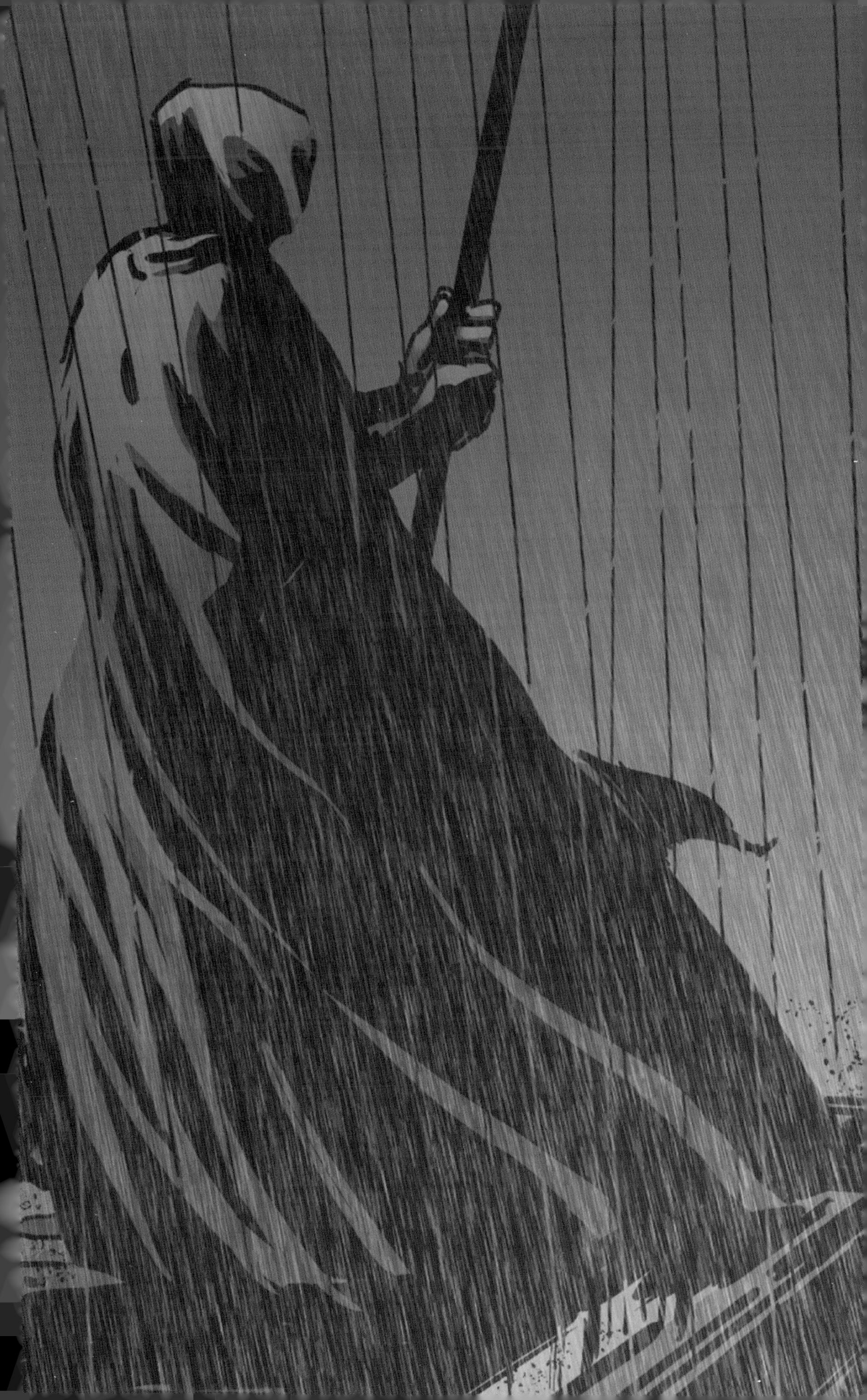

CHAPTER 2

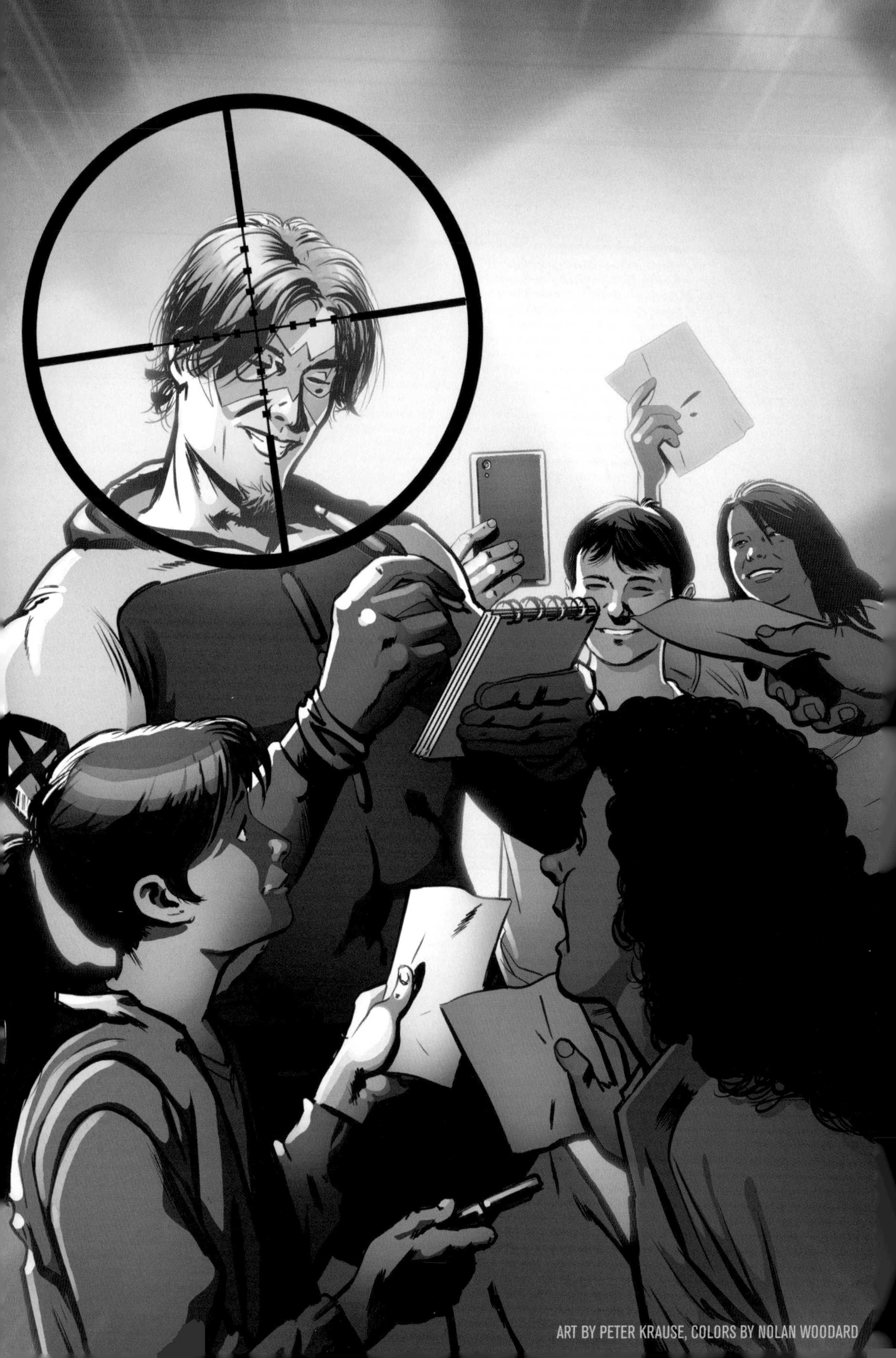

ART BY PETER KRAUSE, COLORS BY NOLAN WOODARD

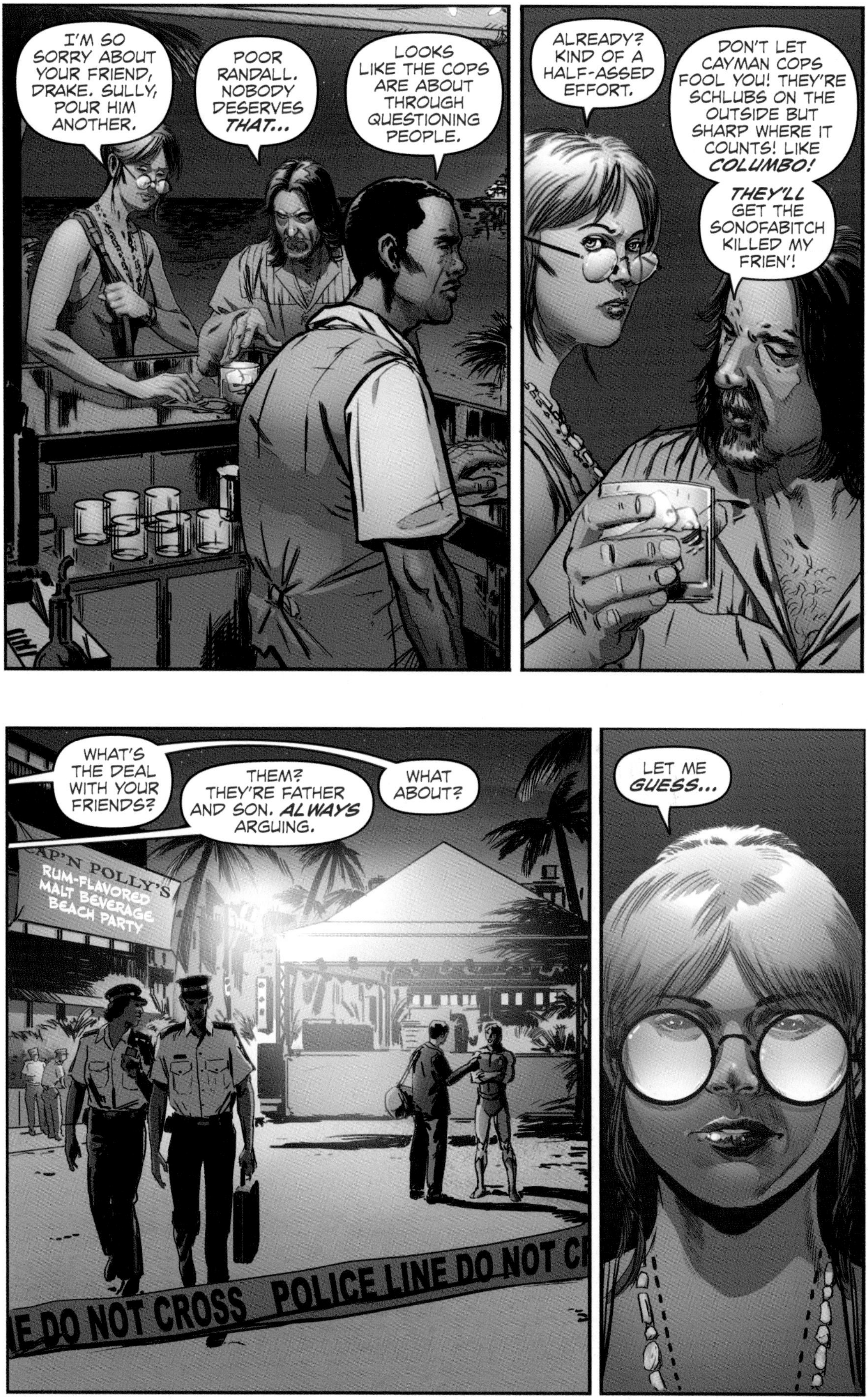
I'M SO SORRY ABOUT YOUR FRIEND, DRAKE. SULLY, POUR HIM ANOTHER.
POOR RANDALL. NOBODY DESERVES *THAT...*
LOOKS LIKE THE COPS ARE ABOUT THROUGH QUESTIONING PEOPLE.
ALREADY? KIND OF A HALF-ASSED EFFORT.
DON'T LET CAYMAN COPS FOOL YOU! THEY'RE SCHLUBS ON THE OUTSIDE BUT SHARP WHERE IT COUNTS! LIKE ***COLUMBO!***
THEY'LL GET THE SONOFABITCH KILLED MY FRIEN'!
WHAT'S THE DEAL WITH YOUR FRIENDS?
THEM? THEY'RE FATHER AND SON. ***ALWAYS*** ARGUING.
WHAT ABOUT?
CAP'N POLLY'S
RUM-FLAVORED MALT BEVERAGE BEACH PARTY
POLICE LINE DO NOT CR
E DO NOT CROSS
LET ME ***GUESS...***

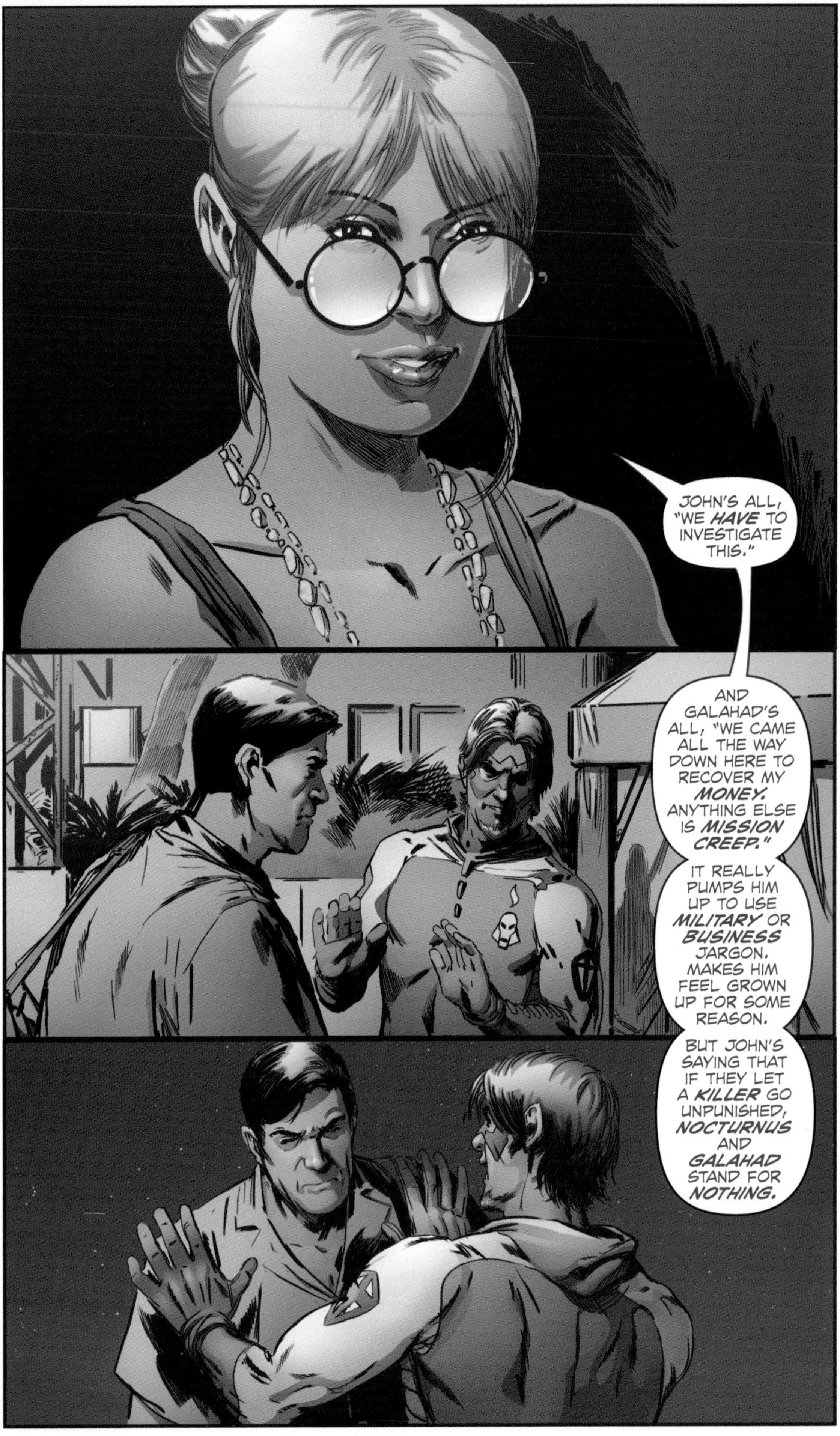
JOHN'S ALL, "WE HAVE TO INVESTIGATE THIS."
AND GALAHAD'S ALL, "WE CAME ALL THE WAY DOWN HERE TO RECOVER MY MONEY. ANYTHING ELSE IS MISSION CREEP."
IT REALLY PUMPS HIM UP TO USE MILITARY OR BUSINESS JARGON. MAKES HIM FEEL GROWN UP FOR SOME REASON.
BUT JOHN'S SAYING THAT IF THEY LET A KILLER GO UNPUNISHED, NOCTURNUS AND GALAHAD STAND FOR NOTHING.

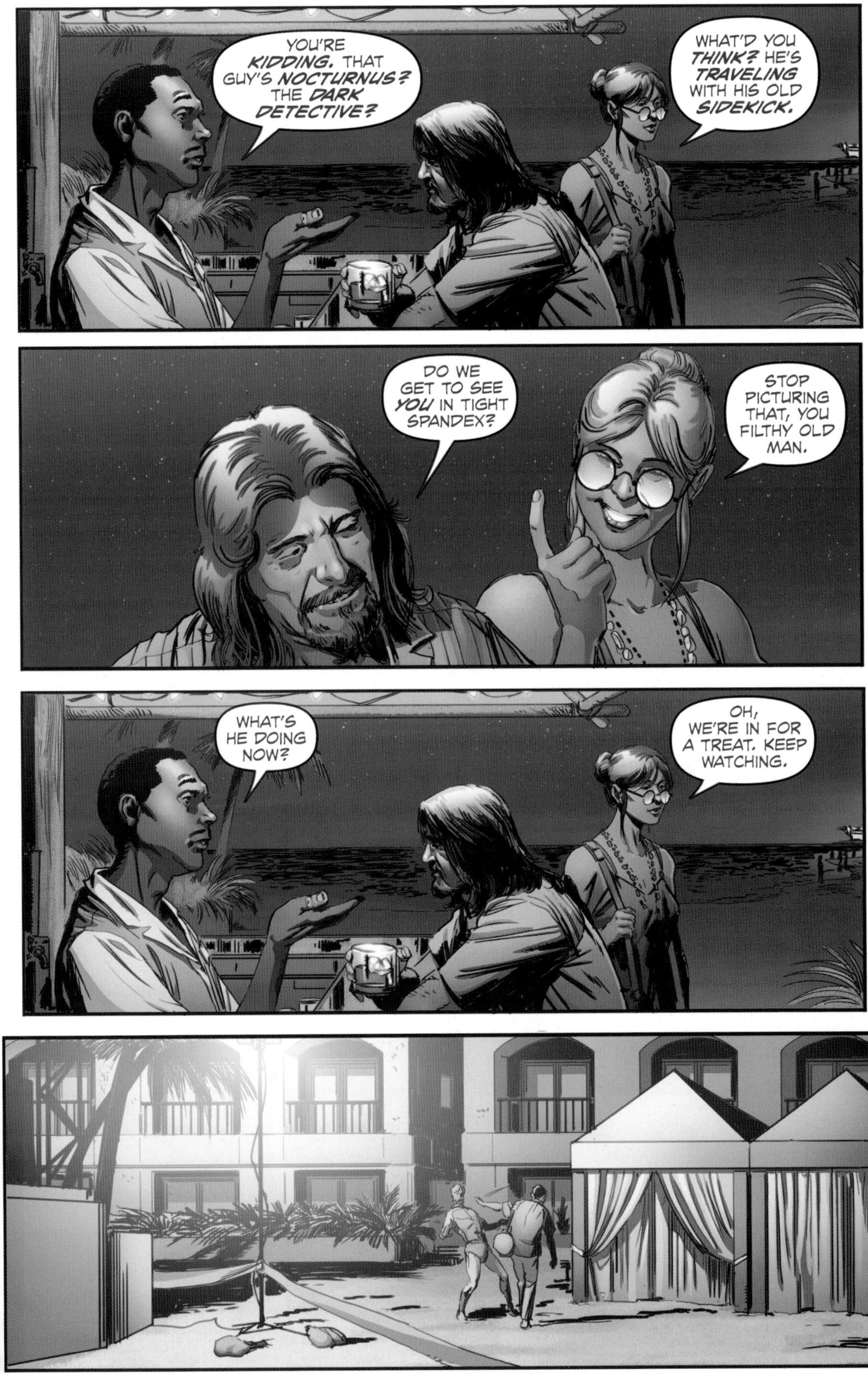
YOU'RE KIDDING. THAT GUY'S NOCTURNUS? THE DARK DETECTIVE?
WHAT'D YOU THINK? HE'S TRAVELING WITH HIS OLD SIDEKICK.
DO WE GET TO SEE YOU IN TIGHT SPANDEX?
STOP PICTURING THAT, YOU FILTHY OLD MAN.
WHAT'S HE DOING NOW?
OH, WE'RE IN FOR A TREAT. KEEP WATCHING.

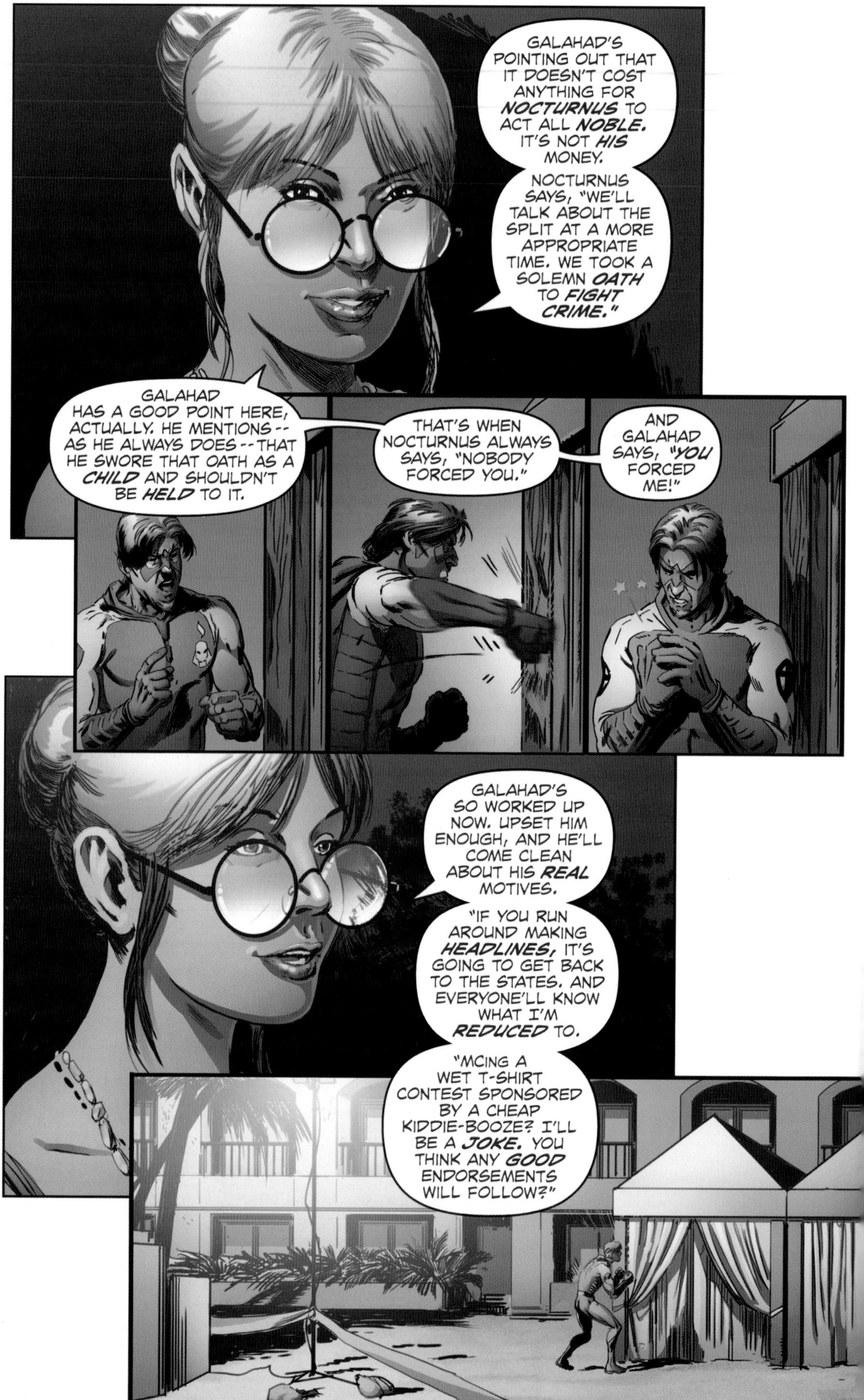
GALAHAD'S POINTING OUT THAT IT DOESN'T COST ANYTHING FOR NOCTURNUS TO ACT ALL NOBLE. IT'S NOT HIS MONEY.
NOCTURNUS SAYS, "WE'LL TALK ABOUT THE SPLIT AT A MORE APPROPRIATE TIME. WE TOOK A SOLEMN OATH TO FIGHT CRIME."
GALAHAD HAS A GOOD POINT HERE, ACTUALLY. HE MENTIONS -- AS HE ALWAYS DOES -- THAT HE SWORE THAT OATH AS A CHILD AND SHOULDN'T BE HELD TO IT.
THAT'S WHEN NOCTURNUS ALWAYS SAYS, "NOBODY FORCED YOU."
AND GALAHAD SAYS, "YOU FORCED ME!"
GALAHAD'S SO WORKED UP NOW. UPSET HIM ENOUGH, AND HE'LL COME CLEAN ABOUT HIS REAL MOTIVES.
"IF YOU RUN AROUND MAKING HEADLINES, IT'S GOING TO GET BACK TO THE STATES. AND EVERYONE'LL KNOW WHAT I'M REDUCED TO.
"MCING A WET T-SHIRT CONTEST SPONSORED BY A CHEAP KIDDIE-BOOZE? I'LL BE A JOKE. YOU THINK ANY GOOD ENDORSEMENTS WILL FOLLOW?"

AND HERE COMES THE TREAT.

SO IT'S SETTLED. NOCTURNUS IS GOING TO BRING RANDALL'S KILLER TO JUSTICE, AND GALAHAD'S GOING TO STAY OUT OF HIS WAY.

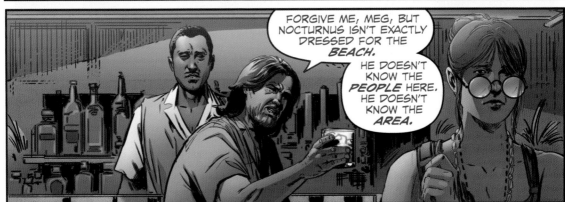

FORGIVE ME, MEG, BUT NOCTURNUS ISN'T EXACTLY DRESSED FOR THE *BEACH*.

HE DOESN'T KNOW THE *PEOPLE* HERE. HE DOESN'T KNOW THE *AREA*.

"HOW'S *HE* EVER GOING TO FIND RANDALL'S KILLER?"

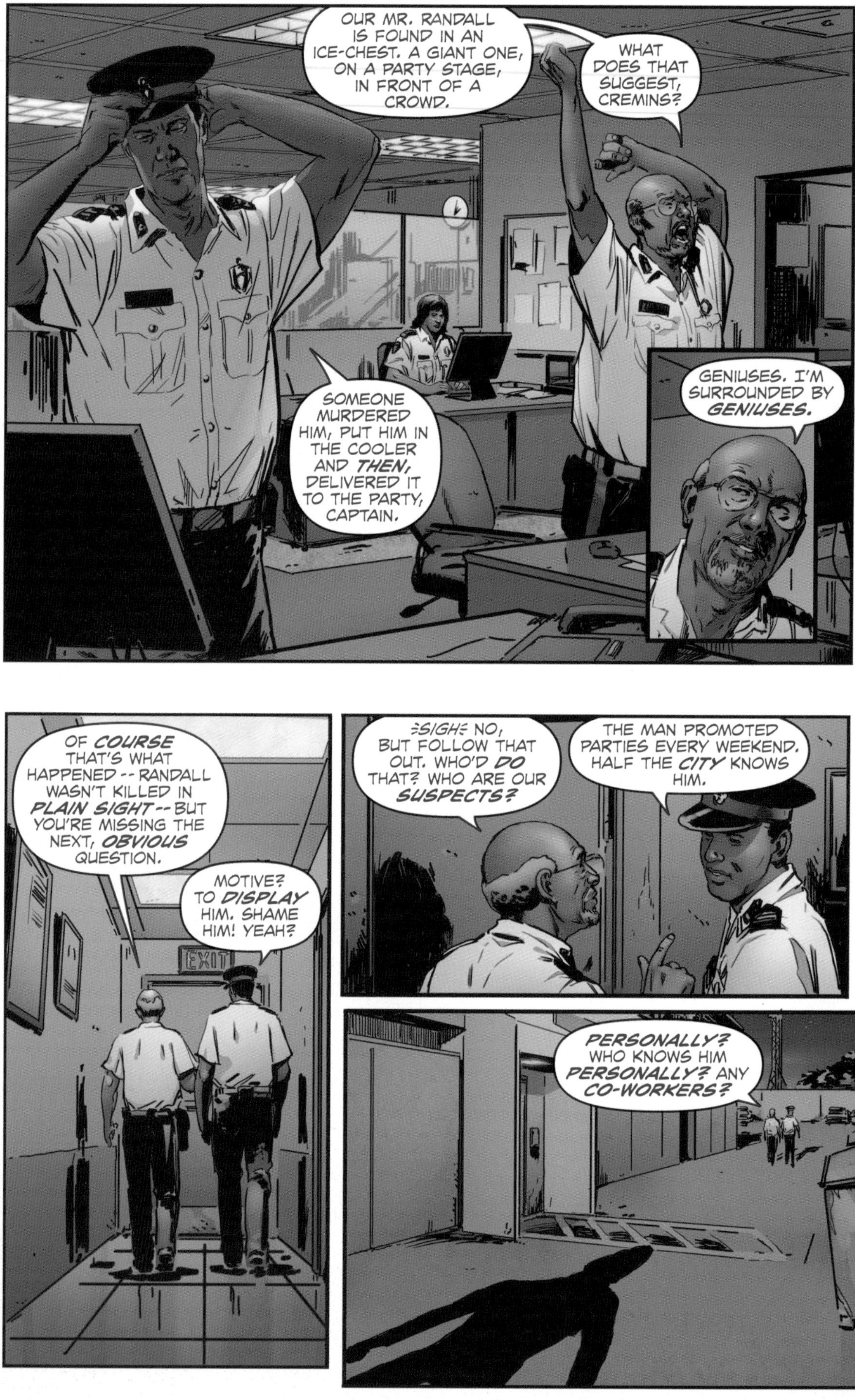
OUR MR. RANDALL IS FOUND IN AN ICE-CHEST. A GIANT ONE, ON A PARTY STAGE, IN FRONT OF A CROWD.
WHAT DOES THAT SUGGEST, CREMINS?
SOMEONE MURDERED HIM, PUT HIM IN THE COOLER AND *THEN,* DELIVERED IT TO THE PARTY, CAPTAIN.
GENIUSES. I'M SURROUNDED BY *GENIUSES.*
OF *COURSE* THAT'S WHAT HAPPENED -- RANDALL WASN'T KILLED IN *PLAIN SIGHT* -- BUT YOU'RE MISSING THE NEXT, *OBVIOUS* QUESTION.
MOTIVE? TO *DISPLAY* HIM. SHAME HIM! YEAH?
EXIT
=SIGH= NO, BUT FOLLOW THAT OUT. WHO'D *DO* THAT? WHO ARE OUR *SUSPECTS?*
THE MAN PROMOTED PARTIES EVERY WEEKEND. HALF THE *CITY* KNOWS HIM.
PERSONALLY? WHO KNOWS HIM *PERSONALLY?* ANY *CO-WORKERS?*

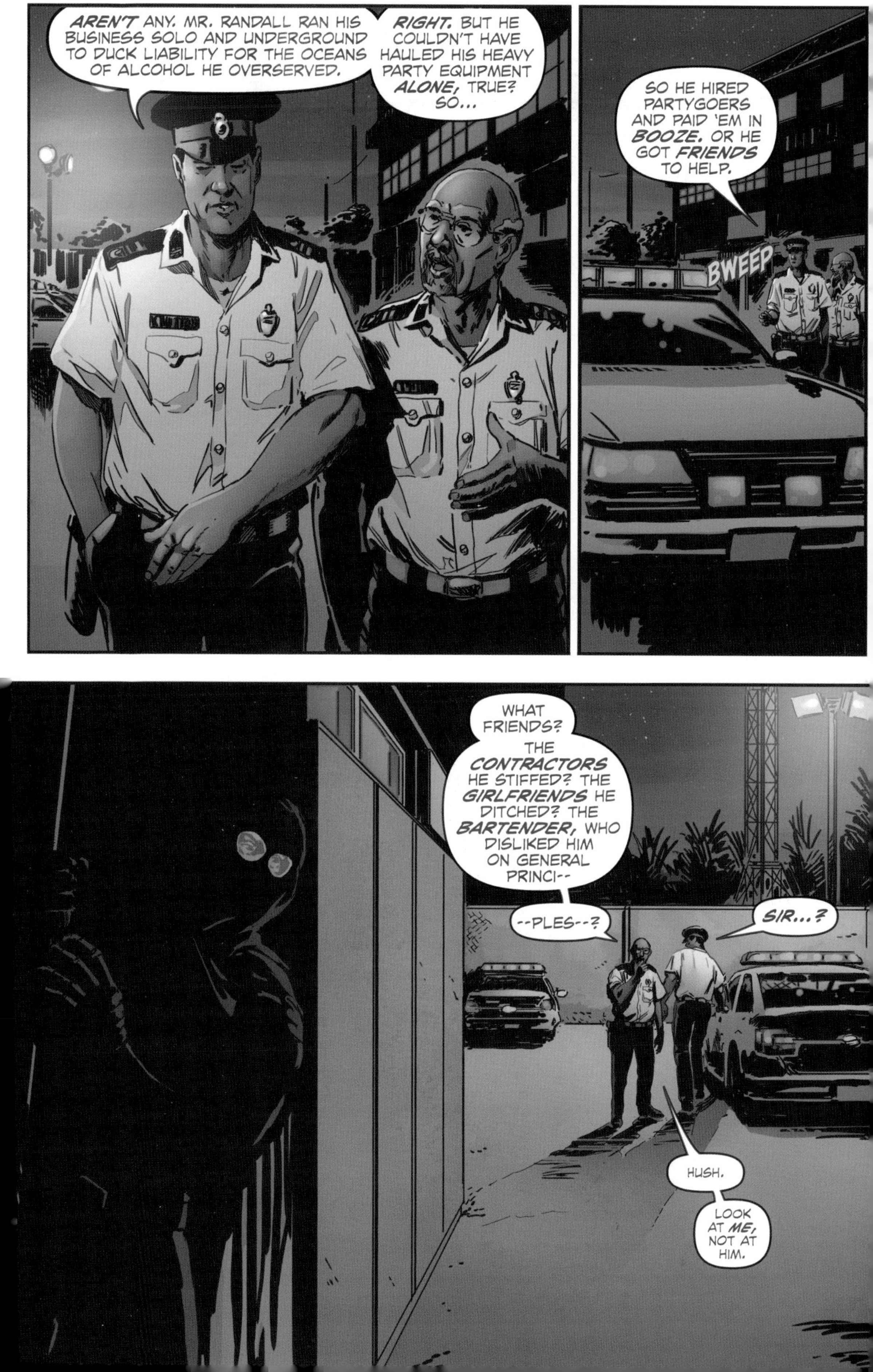

AREN'T ANY. MR. RANDALL RAN HIS BUSINESS SOLO AND UNDERGROUND TO DUCK LIABILITY FOR THE OCEANS OF ALCOHOL HE OVERSERVED.
RIGHT. BUT HE COULDN'T HAVE HAULED HIS HEAVY PARTY EQUIPMENT ALONE, TRUE? SO...
SO HE HIRED PARTYGOERS AND PAID 'EM IN BOOZE. OR HE GOT FRIENDS TO HELP.
BWEEP
WHAT FRIENDS? THE CONTRACTORS HE STIFFED? THE GIRLFRIENDS HE DITCHED? THE BARTENDER, WHO DISLIKED HIM ON GENERAL PRINCI--
--PLES--?
SIR...?
HUSH.
LOOK AT ME, NOT AT HIM.

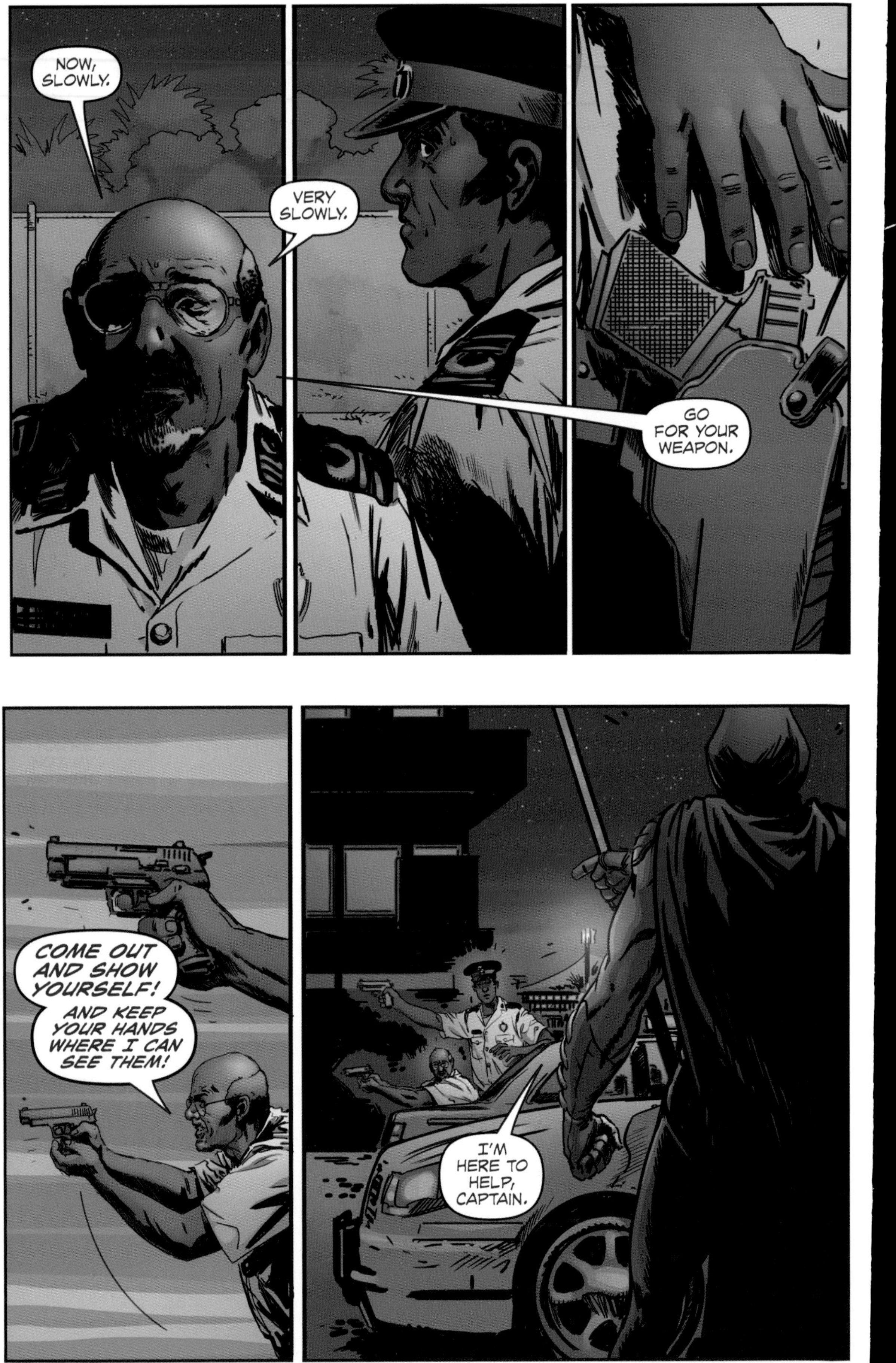
NOW, SLOWLY.
VERY SLOWLY.
GO FOR YOUR WEAPON.
COME OUT AND SHOW YOURSELF!
AND KEEP YOUR HANDS WHERE I CAN SEE THEM!
I'M HERE TO HELP, CAPTAIN.

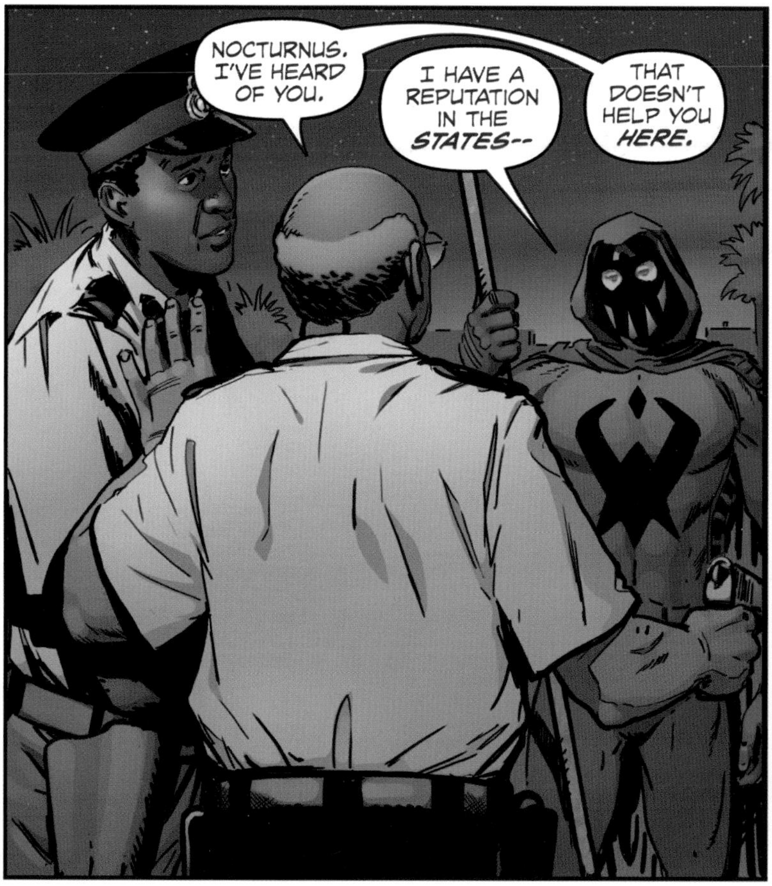
NOCTURNUS. I'VE HEARD OF YOU.
I HAVE A REPUTATION IN THE STATES--
THAT DOESN'T HELP YOU HERE.

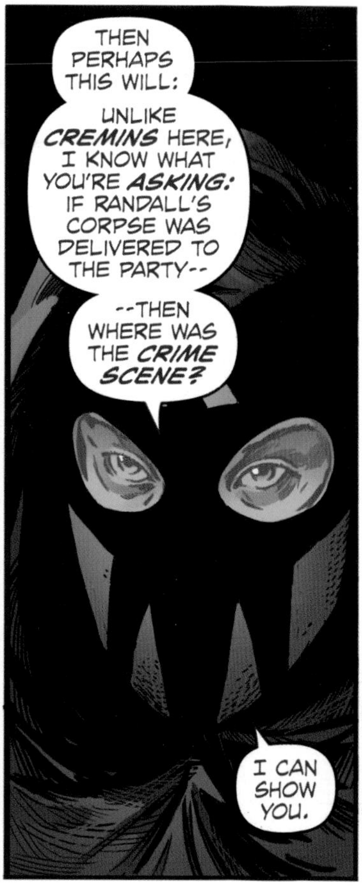
THEN PERHAPS THIS WILL:
UNLIKE CREMINS HERE, I KNOW WHAT YOU'RE ASKING: IF RANDALL'S CORPSE WAS DELIVERED TO THE PARTY--
--THEN WHERE WAS THE CRIME SCENE?
I CAN SHOW YOU.

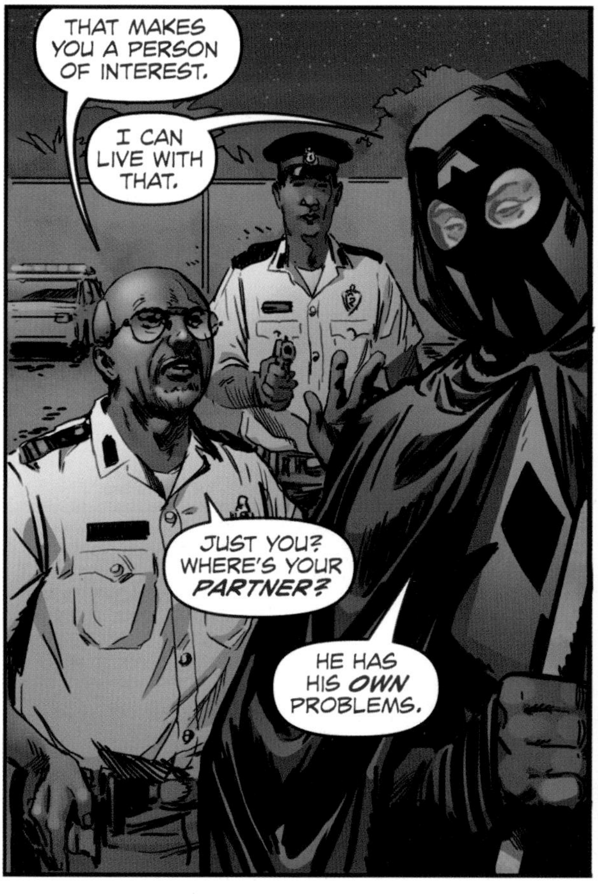
THAT MAKES YOU A PERSON OF INTEREST.
I CAN LIVE WITH THAT.
JUST YOU? WHERE'S YOUR PARTNER?
HE HAS HIS OWN PROBLEMS.

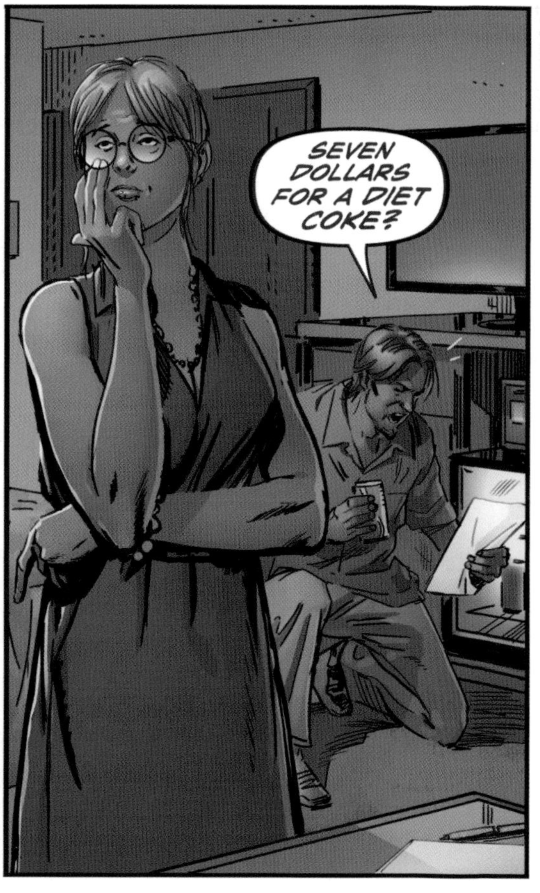
SEVEN DOLLARS FOR A DIET COKE?

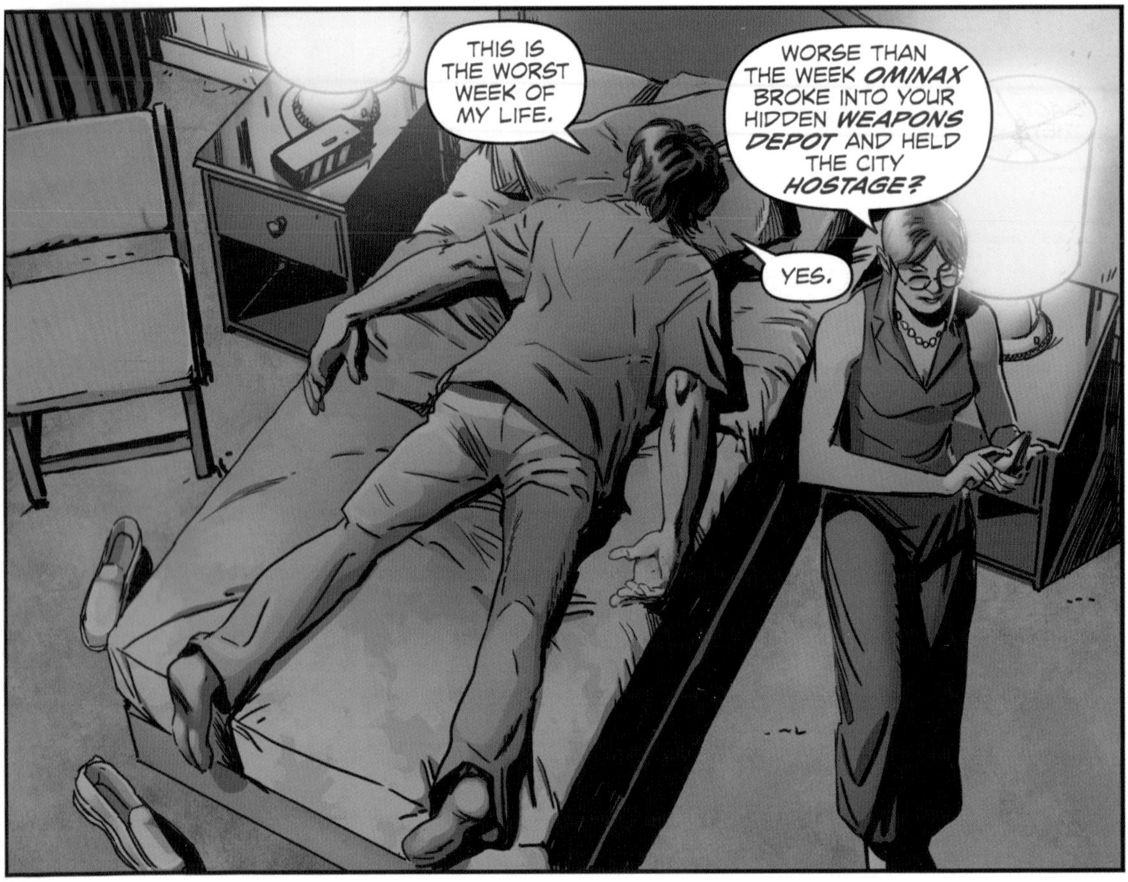
THIS IS THE WORST WEEK OF MY LIFE.
WORSE THAN THE WEEK OMINAX BROKE INTO YOUR HIDDEN WEAPONS DEPOT AND HELD THE CITY HOSTAGE?
YES.

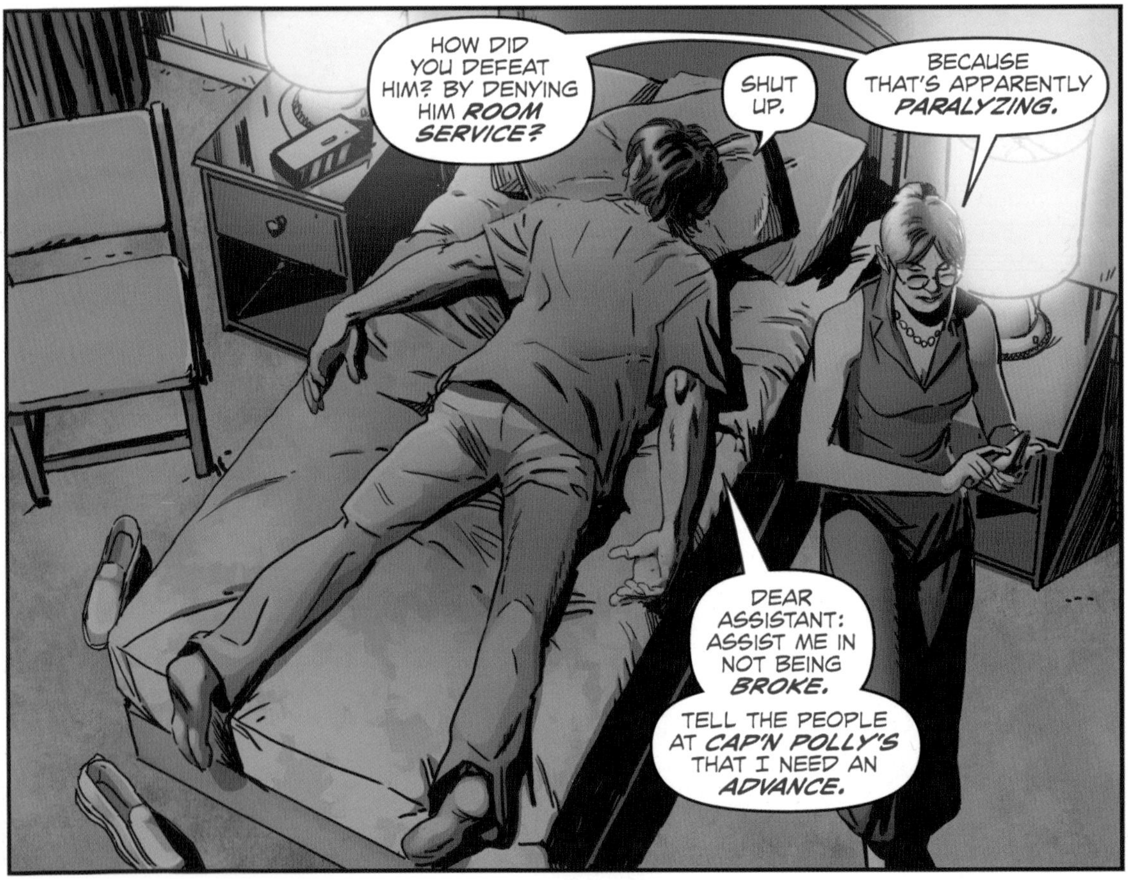
HOW DID YOU DEFEAT HIM? BY DENYING HIM ROOM SERVICE?
SHUT UP.
BECAUSE THAT'S APPARENTLY PARALYZING.
DEAR ASSISTANT: ASSIST ME IN NOT BEING BROKE.
TELL THE PEOPLE AT CAP'N POLLY'S THAT I NEED AN ADVANCE.

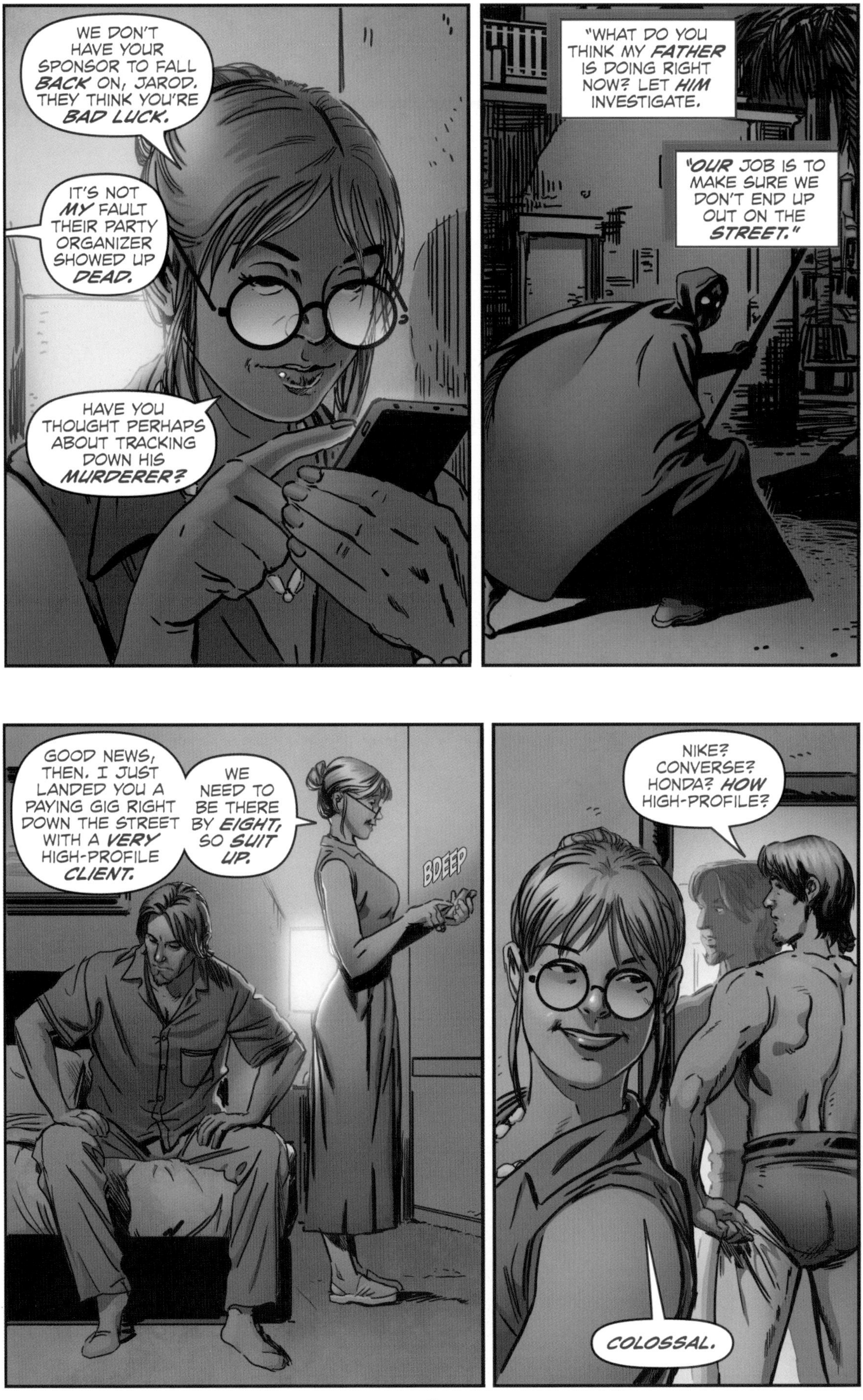
WE DON'T HAVE YOUR SPONSOR TO FALL BACK ON, JAROD. THEY THINK YOU'RE BAD LUCK.
IT'S NOT MY FAULT THEIR PARTY ORGANIZER SHOWED UP DEAD.
HAVE YOU THOUGHT PERHAPS ABOUT TRACKING DOWN HIS MURDERER?
"WHAT DO YOU THINK MY FATHER IS DOING RIGHT NOW? LET HIM INVESTIGATE.
"OUR JOB IS TO MAKE SURE WE DON'T END UP OUT ON THE STREET."
GOOD NEWS, THEN. I JUST LANDED YOU A PAYING GIG RIGHT DOWN THE STREET WITH A VERY HIGH-PROFILE CLIENT.
WE NEED TO BE THERE BY EIGHT, SO SUIT UP.
BDEEP
NIKE? CONVERSE? HONDA? HOW HIGH-PROFILE?
COLOSSAL.

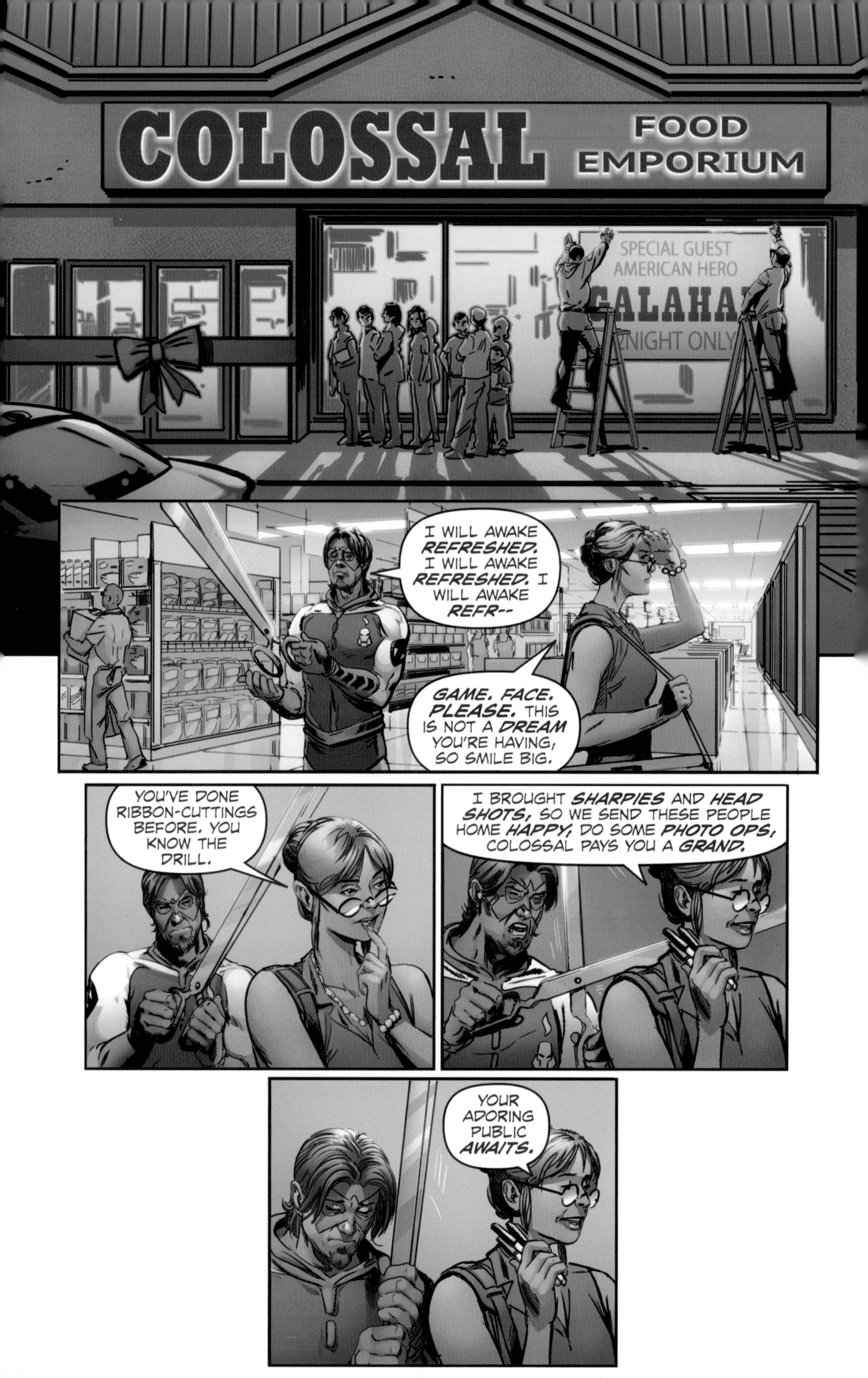
COLOSSAL FOOD EMPORIUM
SPECIAL GUEST AMERICAN HERO GALAHA 2NIGHT ONLY
I WILL AWAKE REFRESHED. I WILL AWAKE REFRESHED. I WILL AWAKE REFR--
GAME. FACE. PLEASE. THIS IS NOT A DREAM YOU'RE HAVING, SO SMILE BIG.
YOU'VE DONE RIBBON-CUTTINGS BEFORE. YOU KNOW THE DRILL.
I BROUGHT SHARPIES AND HEAD SHOTS, SO WE SEND THESE PEOPLE HOME HAPPY, DO SOME PHOTO OPS, COLOSSAL PAYS YOU A GRAND.
YOUR ADORING PUBLIC AWAITS.

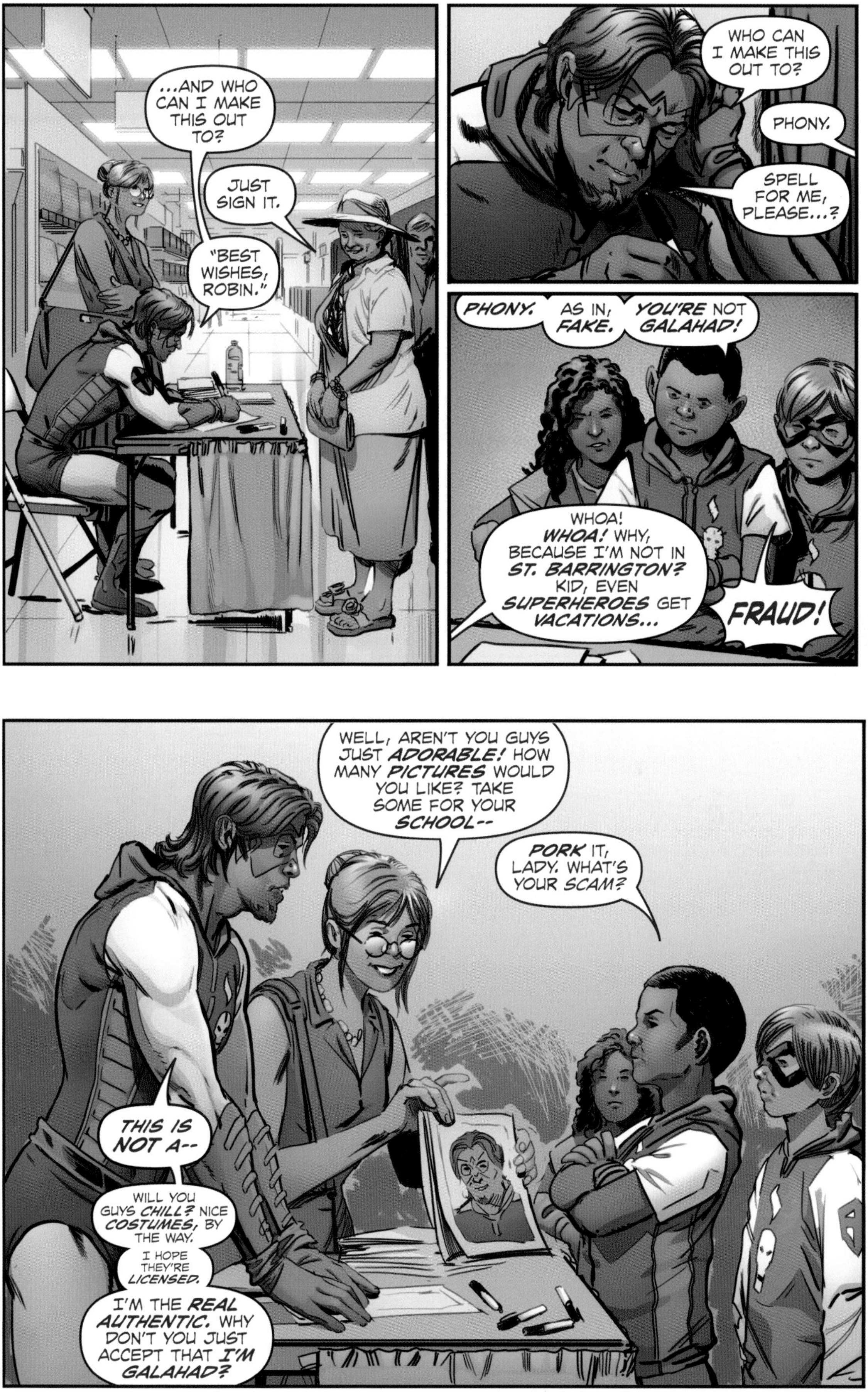
...AND WHO CAN I MAKE THIS OUT TO?
JUST SIGN IT.
"BEST WISHES, ROBIN."
WHO CAN I MAKE THIS OUT TO?
PHONY.
SPELL FOR ME, PLEASE...?
PHONY.
AS IN, FAKE.
YOU'RE NOT GALAHAD!
WHOA! WHOA! WHY, BECAUSE I'M NOT IN ST. BARRINGTON? KID, EVEN SUPERHEROES GET VACATIONS...
FRAUD!
WELL, AREN'T YOU GUYS JUST ADORABLE! HOW MANY PICTURES WOULD YOU LIKE? TAKE SOME FOR YOUR SCHOOL--
PORK IT, LADY. WHAT'S YOUR SCAM?
THIS IS NOT A--
WILL YOU GUYS CHILL? NICE COSTUMES, BY THE WAY.
I HOPE THEY'RE LICENSED.
I'M THE REAL AUTHENTIC. WHY DON'T YOU JUST ACCEPT THAT I'M GALAHAD?

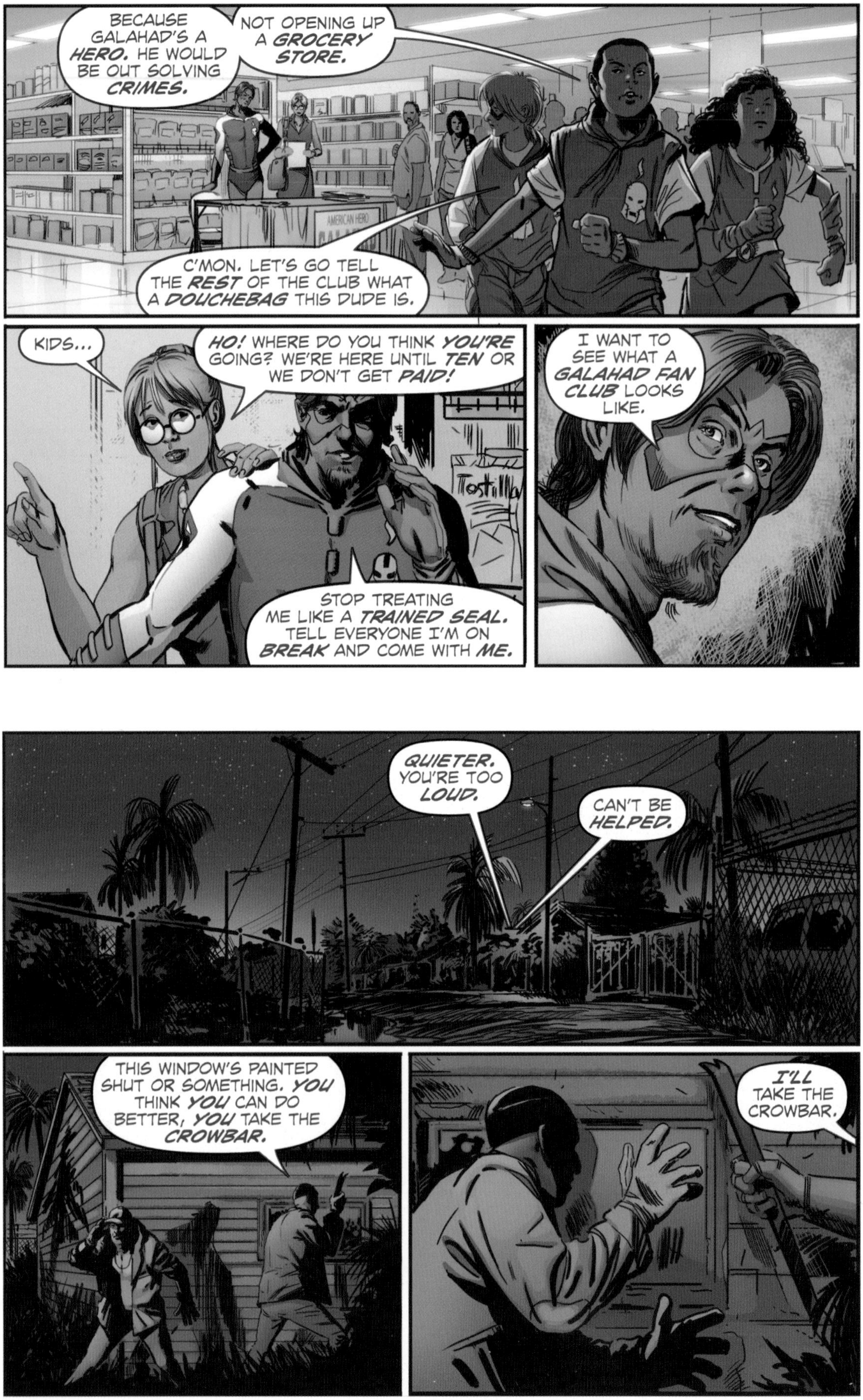
BECAUSE GALAHAD'S A HERO. HE WOULD BE OUT SOLVING CRIMES.
NOT OPENING UP A GROCERY STORE.
C'MON. LET'S GO TELL THE REST OF THE CLUB WHAT A DOUCHEBAG THIS DUDE IS.
KIDS...
HO! WHERE DO YOU THINK YOU'RE GOING? WE'RE HERE UNTIL TEN OR WE DON'T GET PAID!
STOP TREATING ME LIKE A TRAINED SEAL. TELL EVERYONE I'M ON BREAK AND COME WITH ME.
I WANT TO SEE WHAT A GALAHAD FAN CLUB LOOKS LIKE.
QUIETER. YOU'RE TOO LOUD.
CAN'T BE HELPED.
THIS WINDOW'S PAINTED SHUT OR SOMETHING. YOU THINK YOU CAN DO BETTER, YOU TAKE THE CROWBAR.
I'LL TAKE THE CROWBAR.

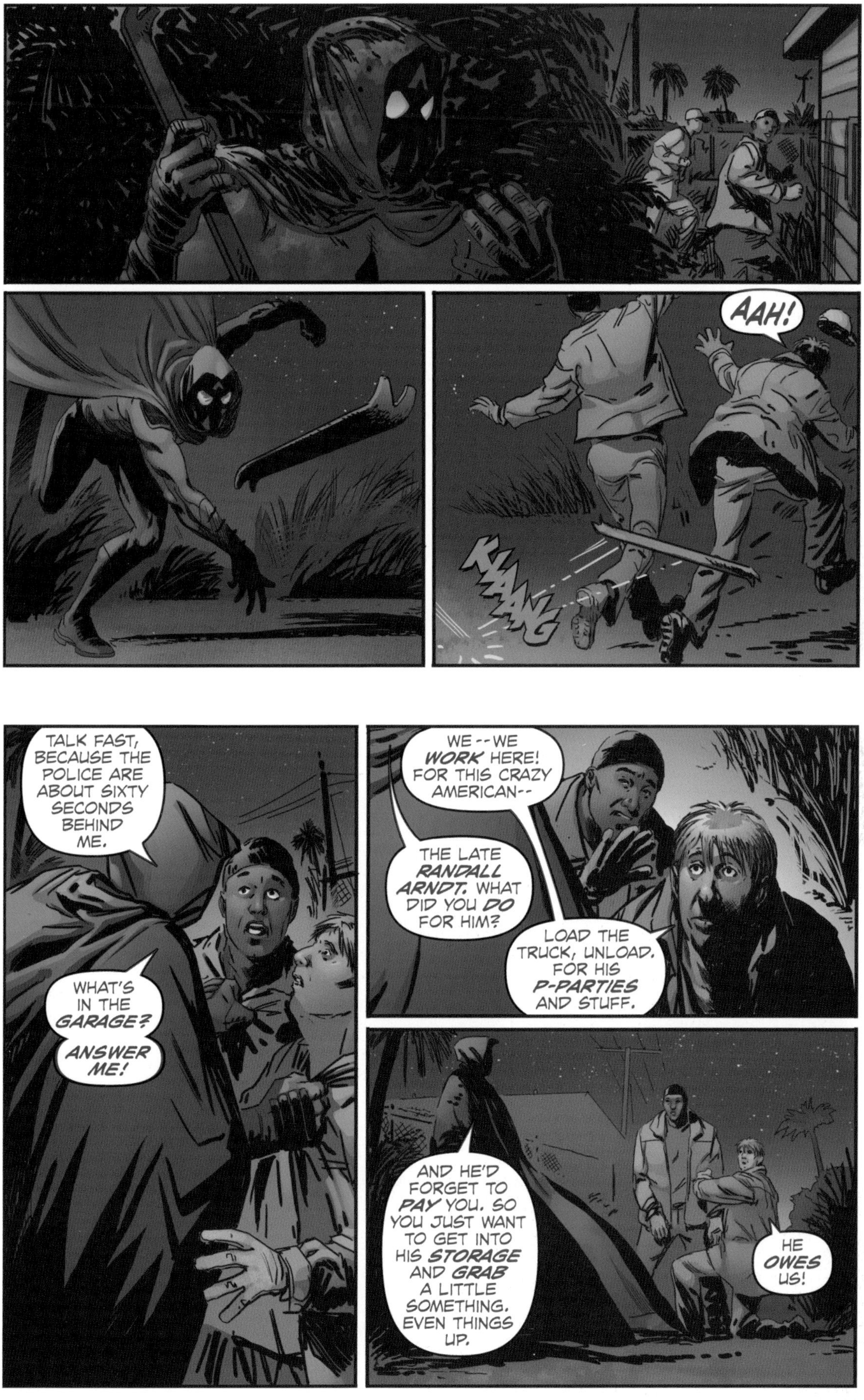
AAH!
KWAANG
TALK FAST, BECAUSE THE POLICE ARE ABOUT SIXTY SECONDS BEHIND ME.
WHAT'S IN THE GARAGE?
ANSWER ME!
WE--WE WORK HERE! FOR THIS CRAZY AMERICAN--
THE LATE RANDALL ARNDT. WHAT DID YOU DO FOR HIM?
LOAD THE TRUCK, UNLOAD. FOR HIS P-PARTIES AND STUFF.
AND HE'D FORGET TO PAY YOU. SO YOU JUST WANT TO GET INTO HIS STORAGE AND GRAB A LITTLE SOMETHING. EVEN THINGS UP.
HE OWES US!

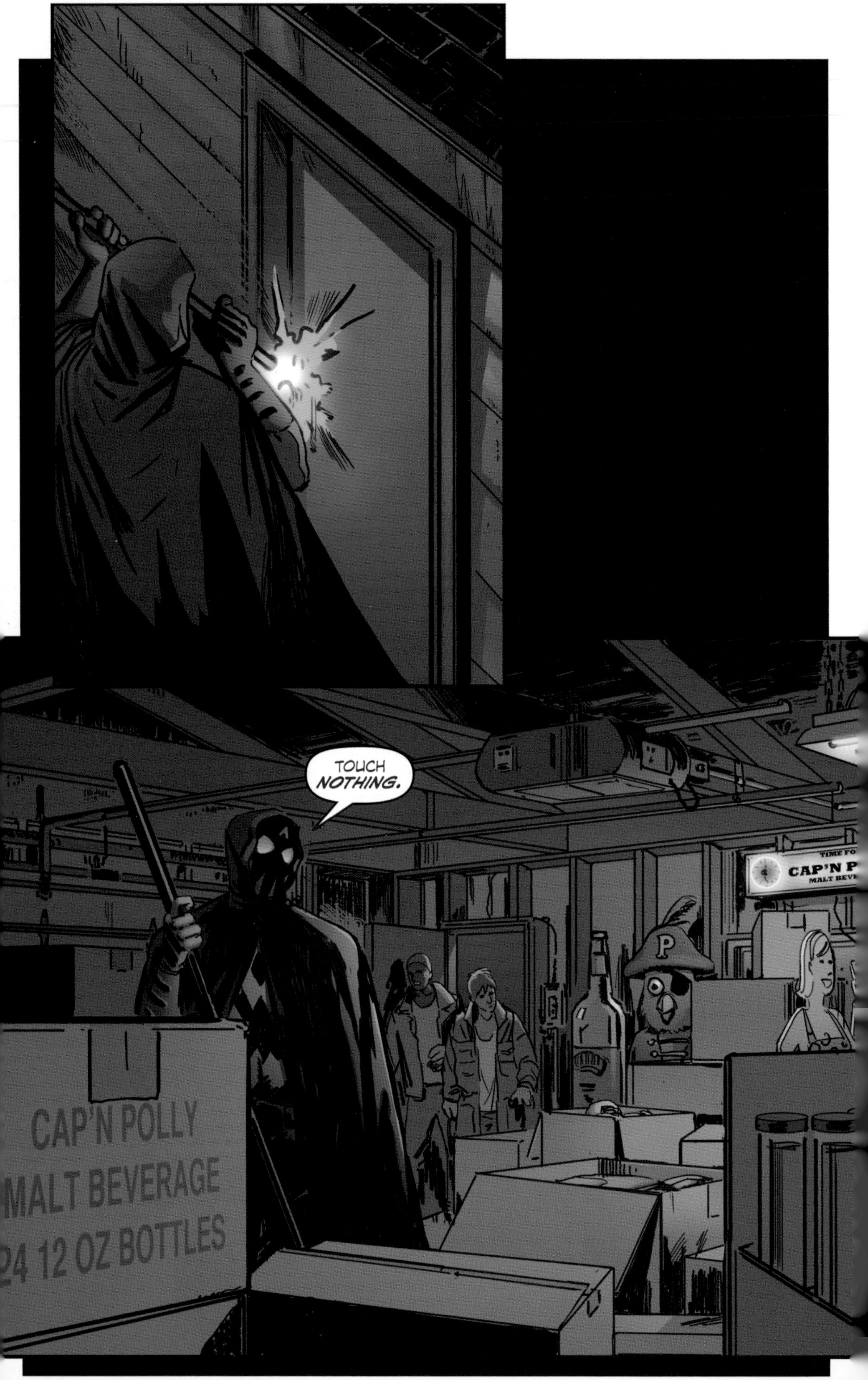
TOUCH NOTHING.
CAP'N POLLY
MALT BEVERAGE
24 12 OZ BOTTLES

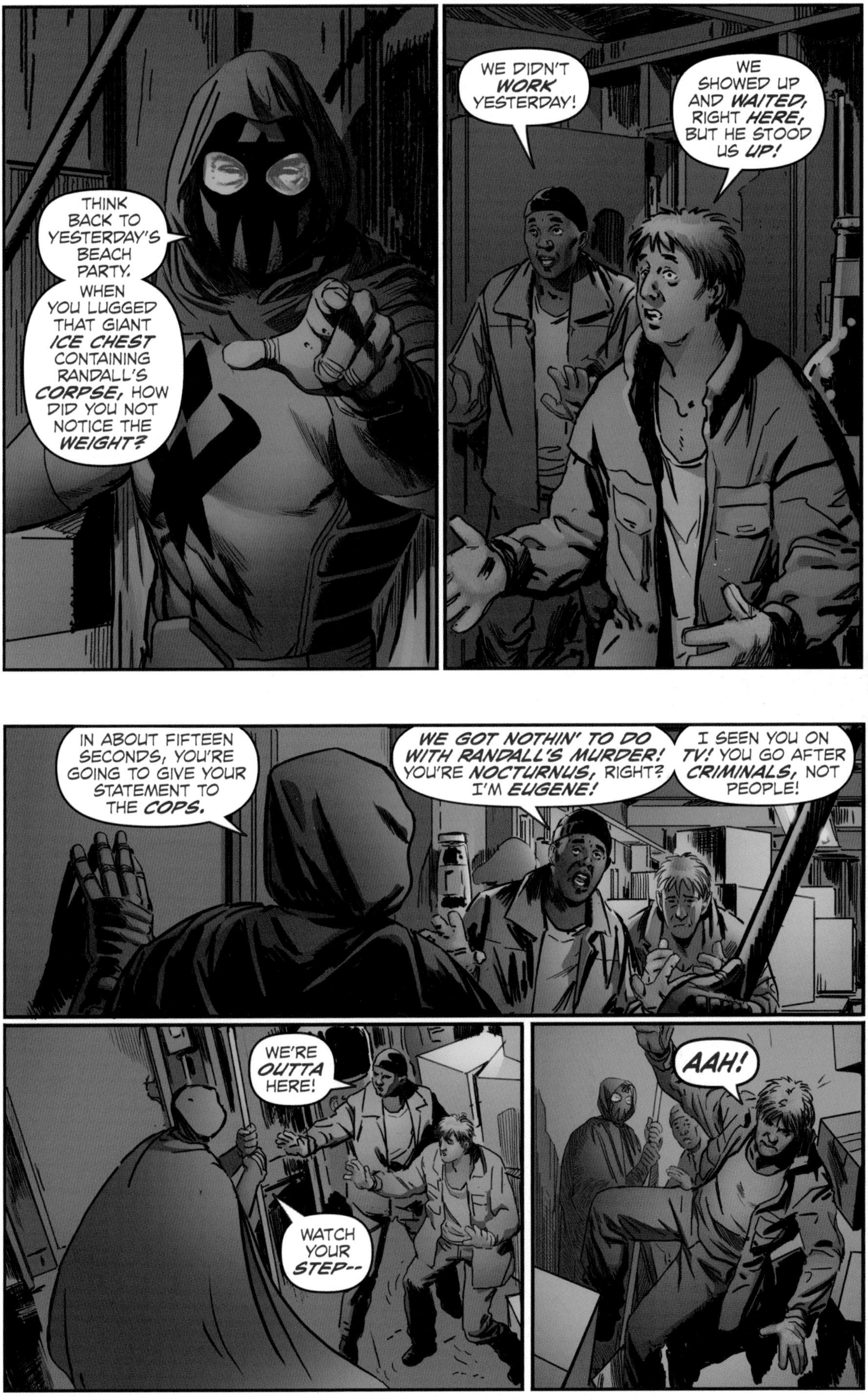
THINK BACK TO YESTERDAY'S BEACH PARTY.
WHEN YOU LUGGED THAT GIANT ICE CHEST CONTAINING RANDALL'S CORPSE, HOW DID YOU NOT NOTICE THE WEIGHT?
WE DIDN'T WORK YESTERDAY!
WE SHOWED UP AND WAITED, RIGHT HERE, BUT HE STOOD US UP!
IN ABOUT FIFTEEN SECONDS, YOU'RE GOING TO GIVE YOUR STATEMENT TO THE COPS.
WE GOT NOTHIN' TO DO WITH RANDALL'S MURDER! YOU'RE NOCTURNUS, RIGHT? I'M EUGENE!
I SEEN YOU ON TV! YOU GO AFTER CRIMINALS, NOT PEOPLE!
WE'RE OUTTA HERE!
WATCH YOUR STEP--
AAH!

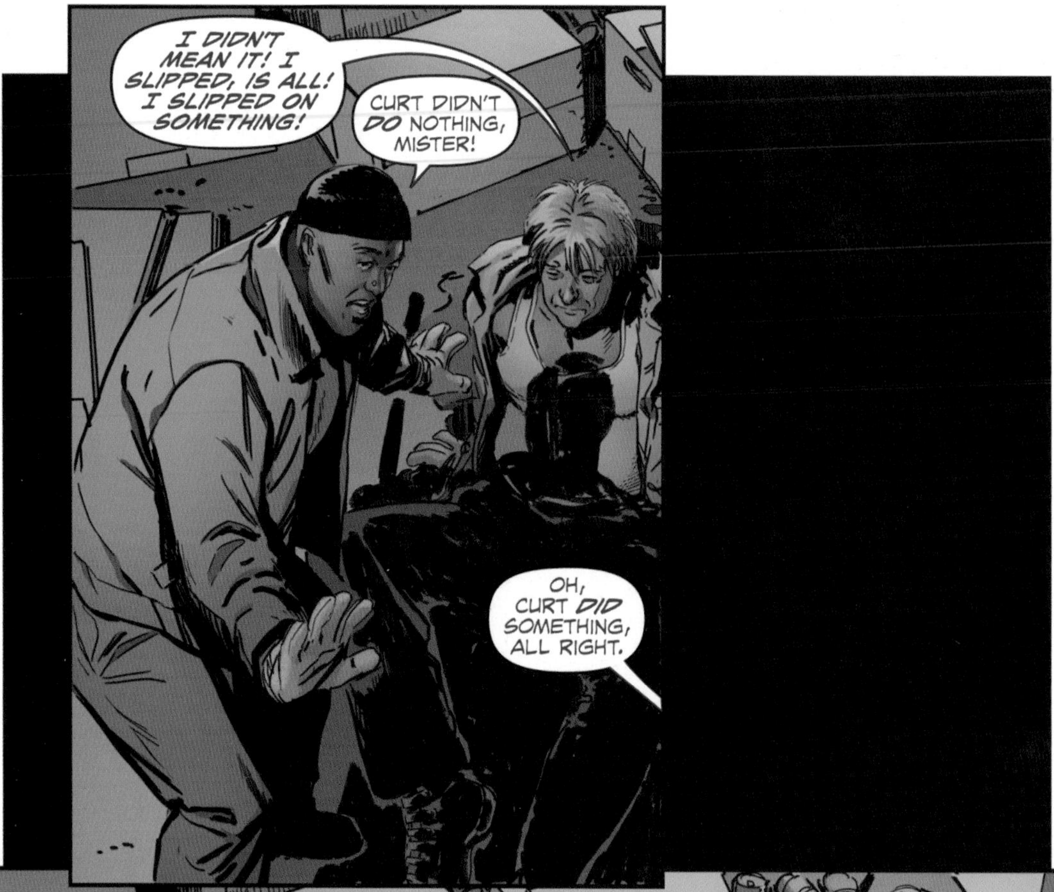
I DIDN'T MEAN IT! I SLIPPED, IS ALL! I SLIPPED ON SOMETHING!
CURT DIDN'T DO NOTHING, MISTER!
OH, CURT DID SOMETHING, ALL RIGHT.

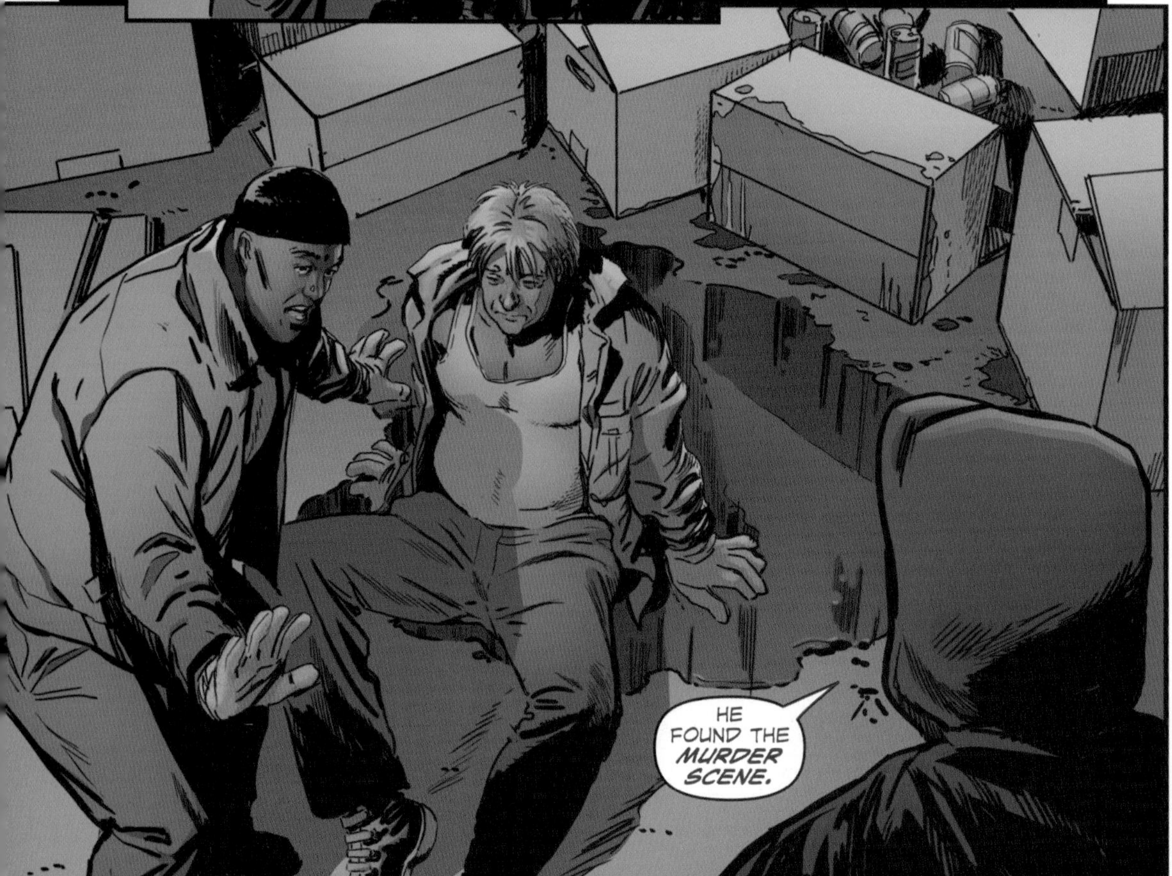
HE FOUND THE MURDER SCENE.

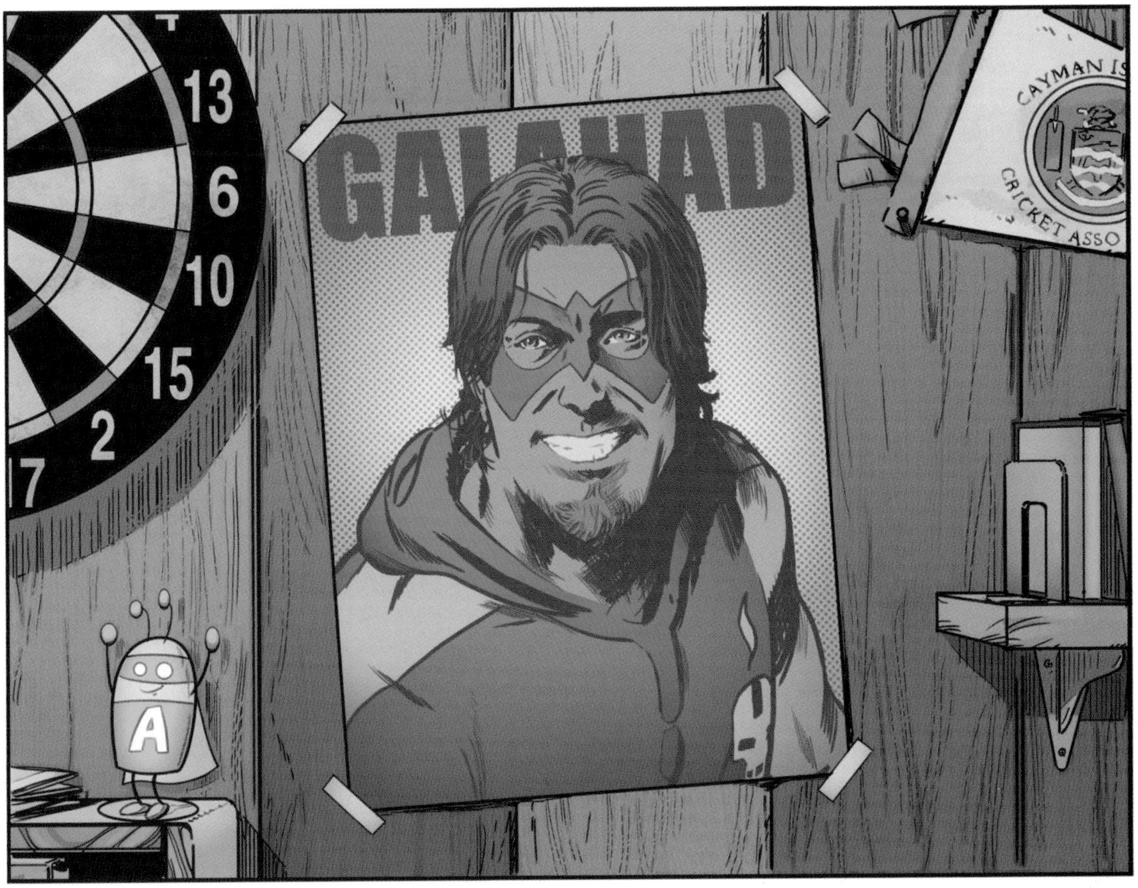
13
6
10
15
2
17
GALAHAD
CAYMAN IS
CRICKET ASSO

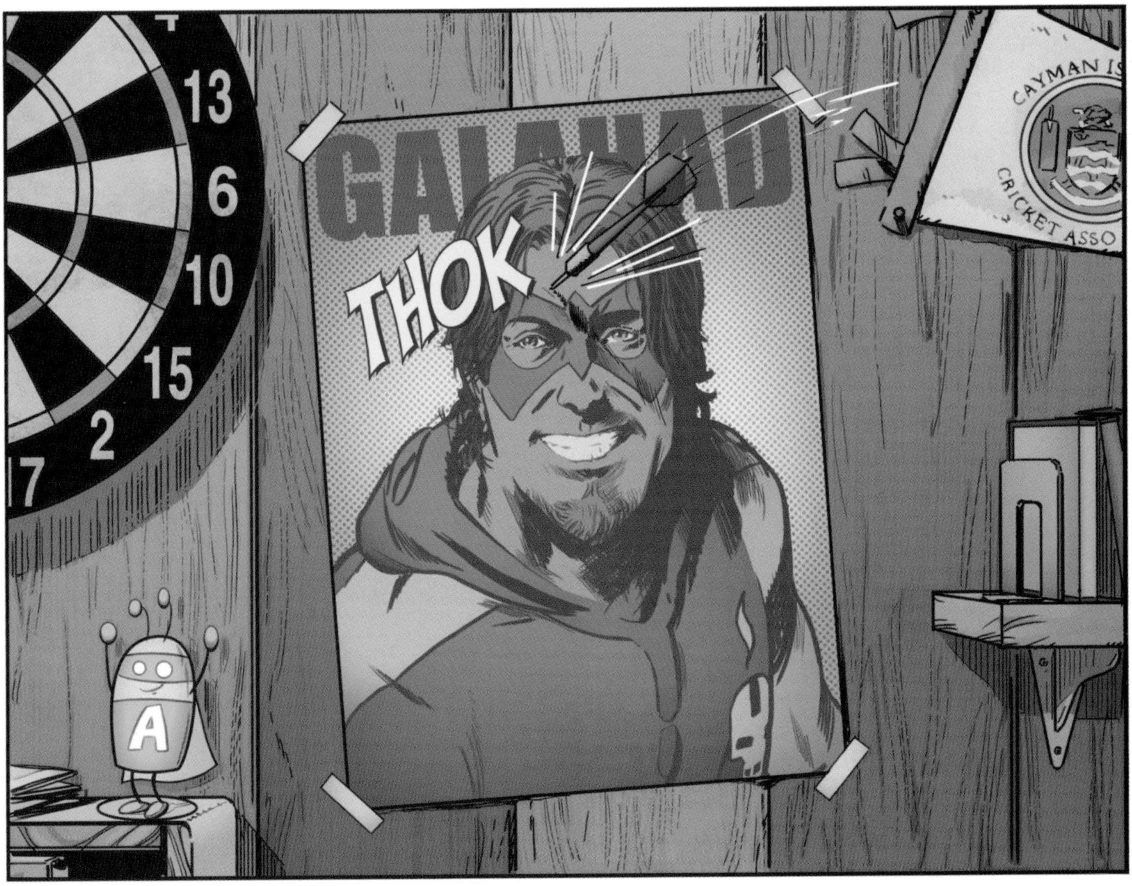
13
6
10
15
2
17
GALAHAD
THOK
CAYMAN IS
CRICKET ASSO

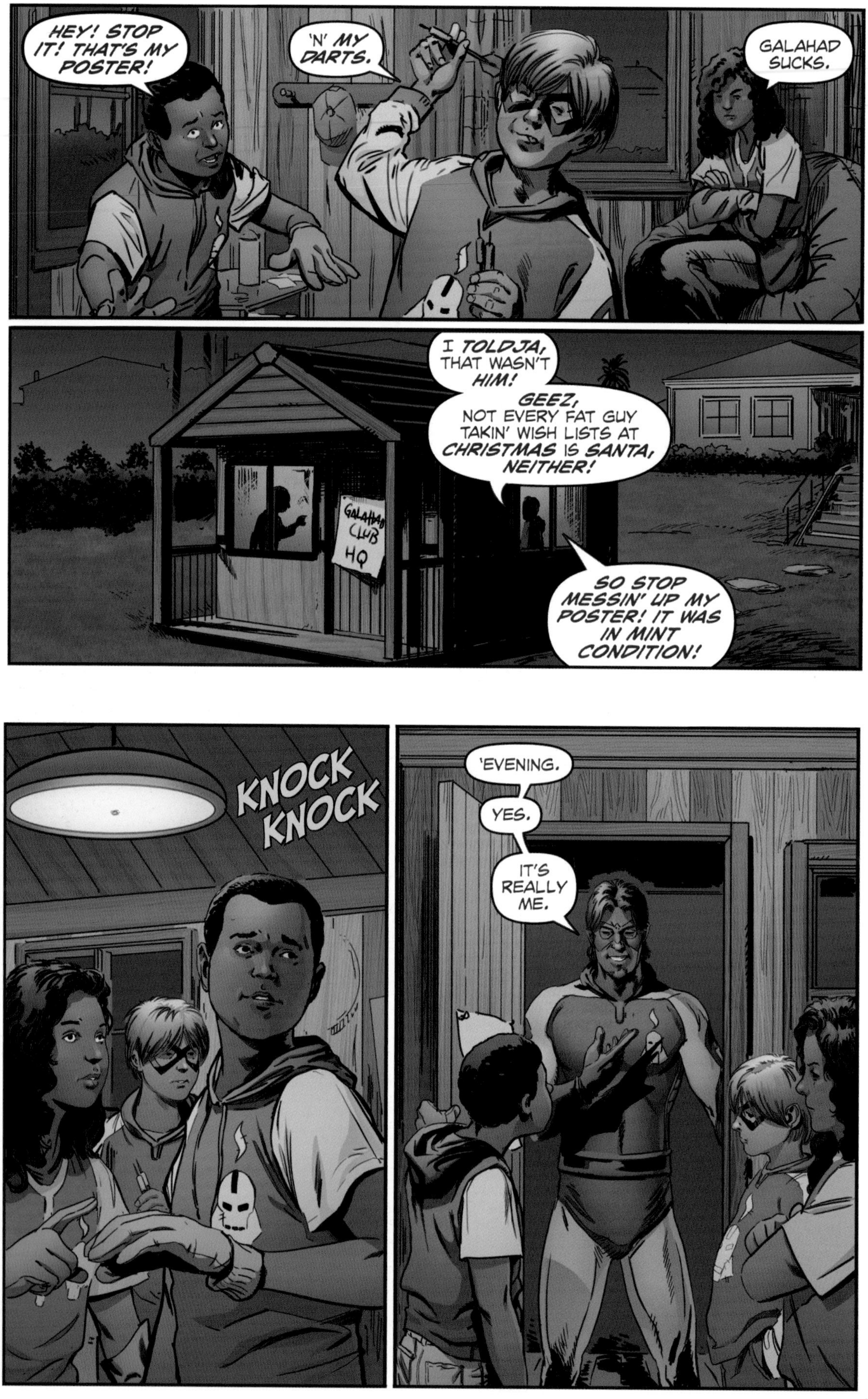

HEY! STOP IT! THAT'S MY POSTER!
'N' MY DARTS.
GALAHAD SUCKS.
I TOLDJA, THAT WASN'T HIM!
GEEZ, NOT EVERY FAT GUY TAKIN' WISH LISTS AT CHRISTMAS IS SANTA, NEITHER!
GALAHAD CLUB HQ
SO STOP MESSIN' UP MY POSTER! IT WAS IN MINT CONDITION!
KNOCK KNOCK
'EVENING.
YES.
IT'S REALLY ME.

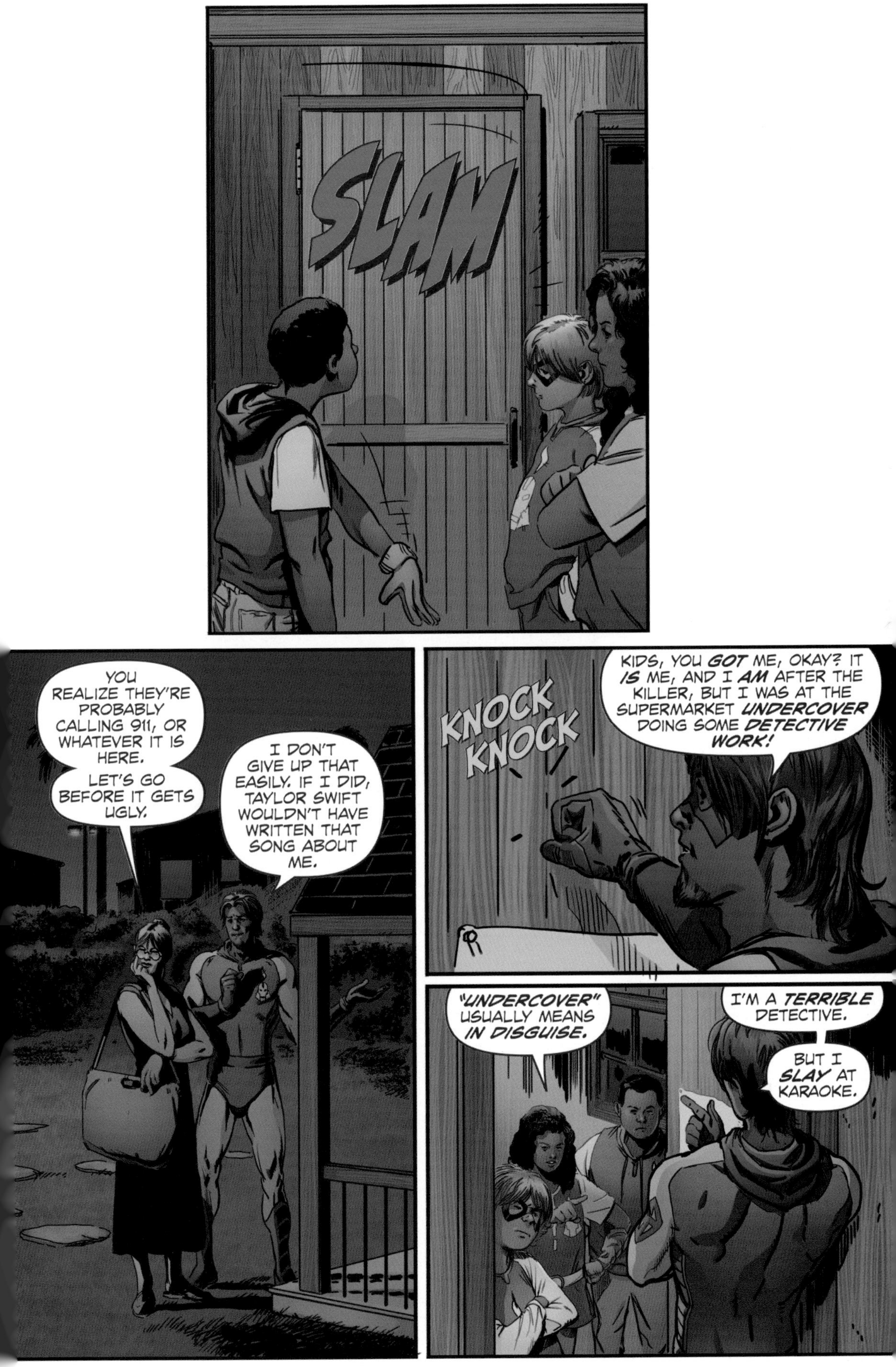

SLAM
YOU REALIZE THEY'RE PROBABLY CALLING 911, OR WHATEVER IT IS HERE.
LET'S GO BEFORE IT GETS UGLY.
I DON'T GIVE UP THAT EASILY. IF I DID, TAYLOR SWIFT WOULDN'T HAVE WRITTEN THAT SONG ABOUT ME.
KNOCK KNOCK
KIDS, YOU GOT ME, OKAY? IT IS ME, AND I AM AFTER THE KILLER, BUT I WAS AT THE SUPERMARKET UNDERCOVER DOING SOME DETECTIVE WORK!
"UNDERCOVER" USUALLY MEANS IN DISGUISE.
I'M A TERRIBLE DETECTIVE.
BUT I SLAY AT KARAOKE.

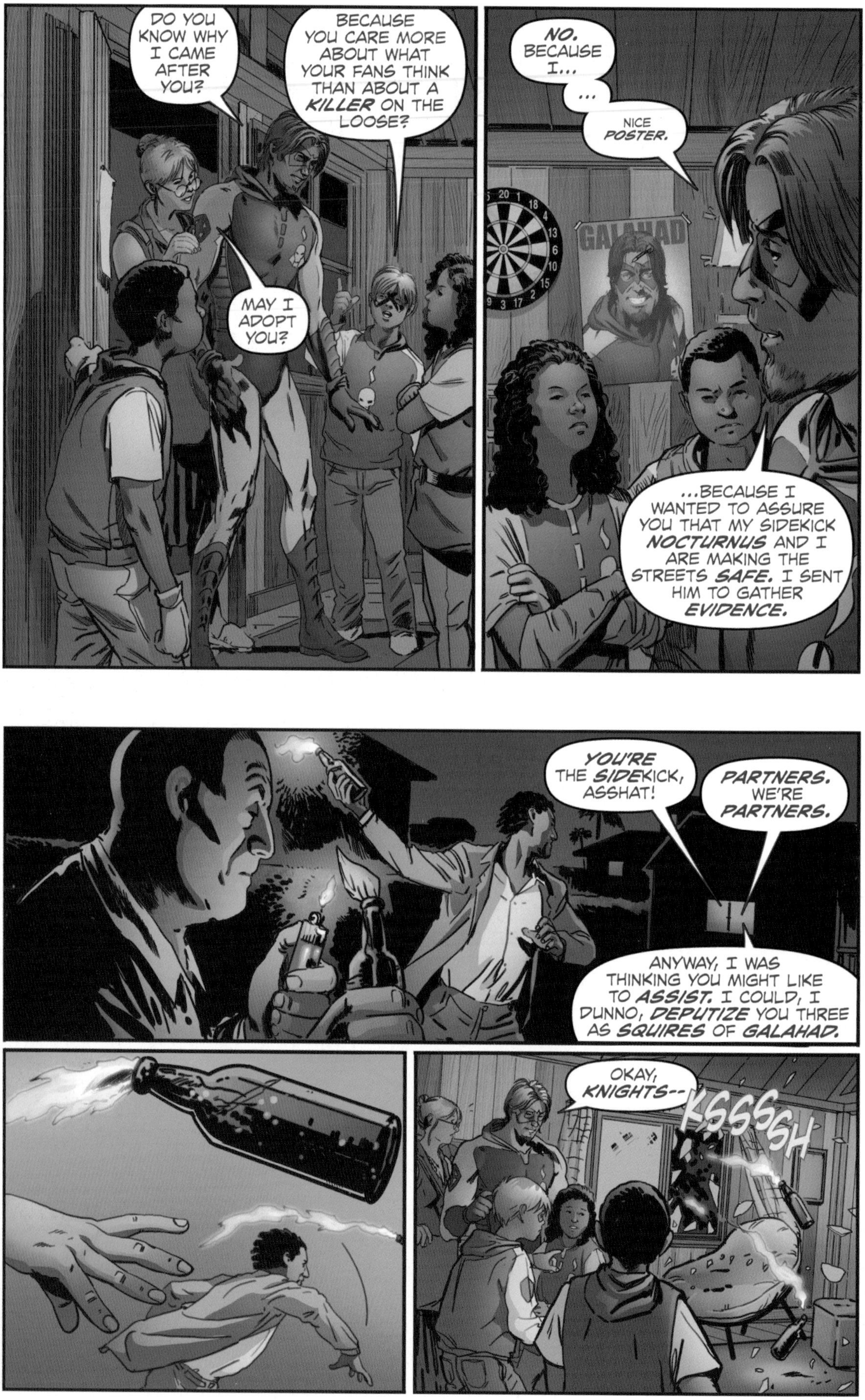
DO YOU KNOW WHY I CAME AFTER YOU?
BECAUSE YOU CARE MORE ABOUT WHAT YOUR FANS THINK THAN ABOUT A KILLER ON THE LOOSE?
MAY I ADOPT YOU?
NO. BECAUSE I...
...
NICE POSTER.
GALAHAD
...BECAUSE I WANTED TO ASSURE YOU THAT MY SIDEKICK NOCTURNUS AND I ARE MAKING THE STREETS SAFE. I SENT HIM TO GATHER EVIDENCE.
YOU'RE THE SIDEKICK, ASSHAT!
PARTNERS. WE'RE PARTNERS.
ANYWAY, I WAS THINKING YOU MIGHT LIKE TO ASSIST. I COULD, I DUNNO, DEPUTIZE YOU THREE AS SQUIRES OF GALAHAD.
OKAY, KNIGHTS--
KSSSSH

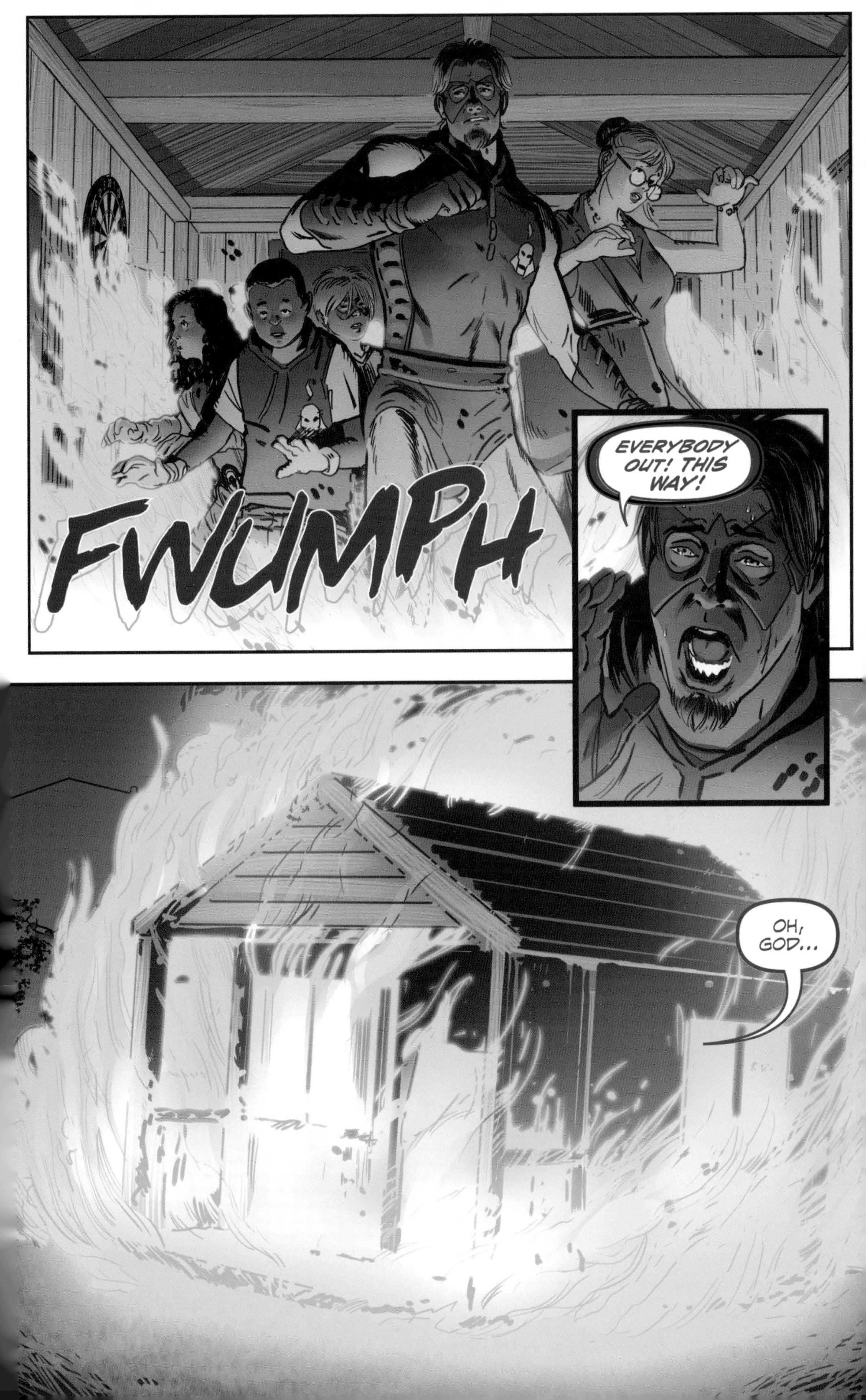
FWUMPH
EVERYBODY OUT! THIS WAY!
OH, GOD...

CHAPTER 3

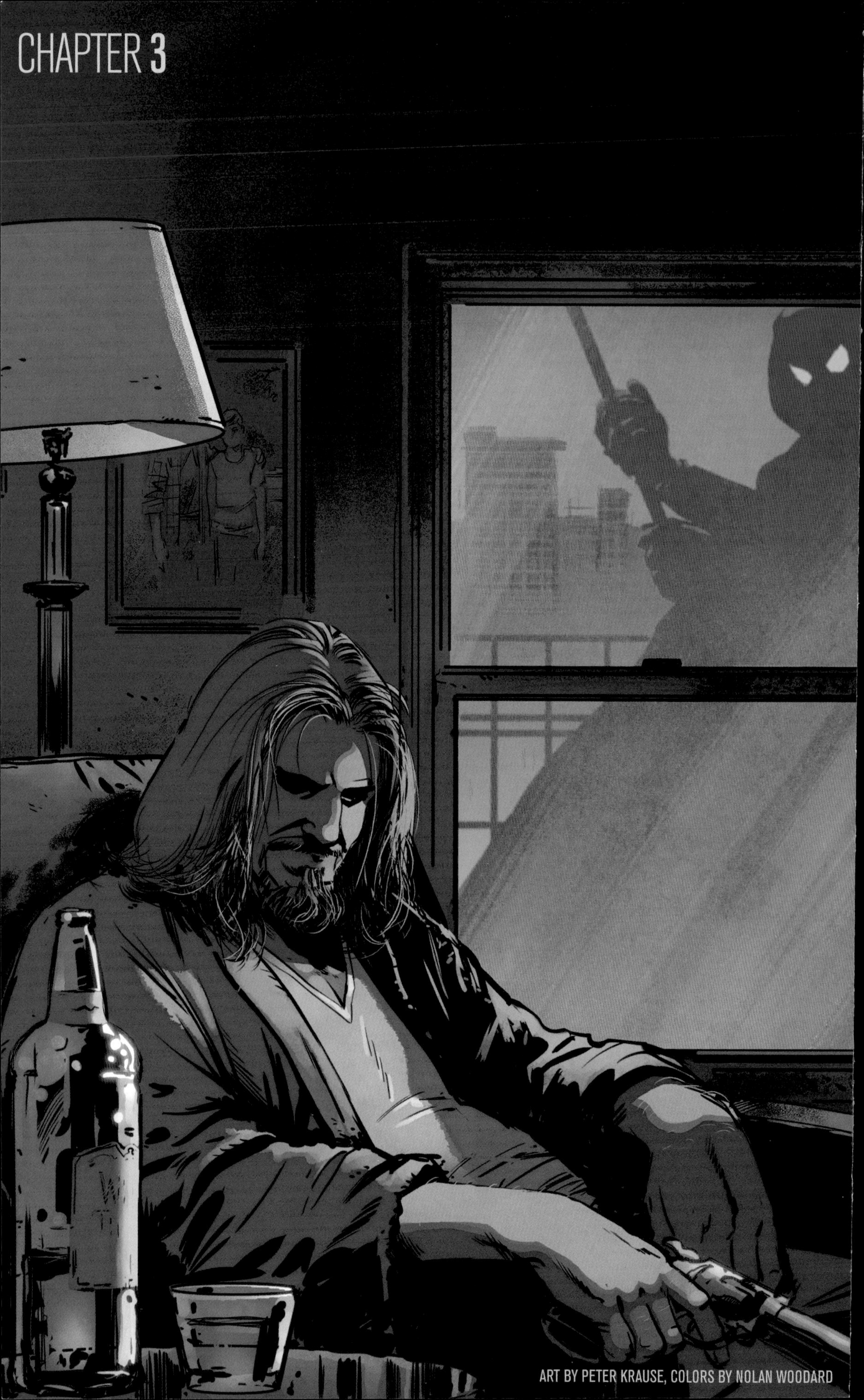

ART BY PETER KRAUSE, COLORS BY NOLAN WOODARD

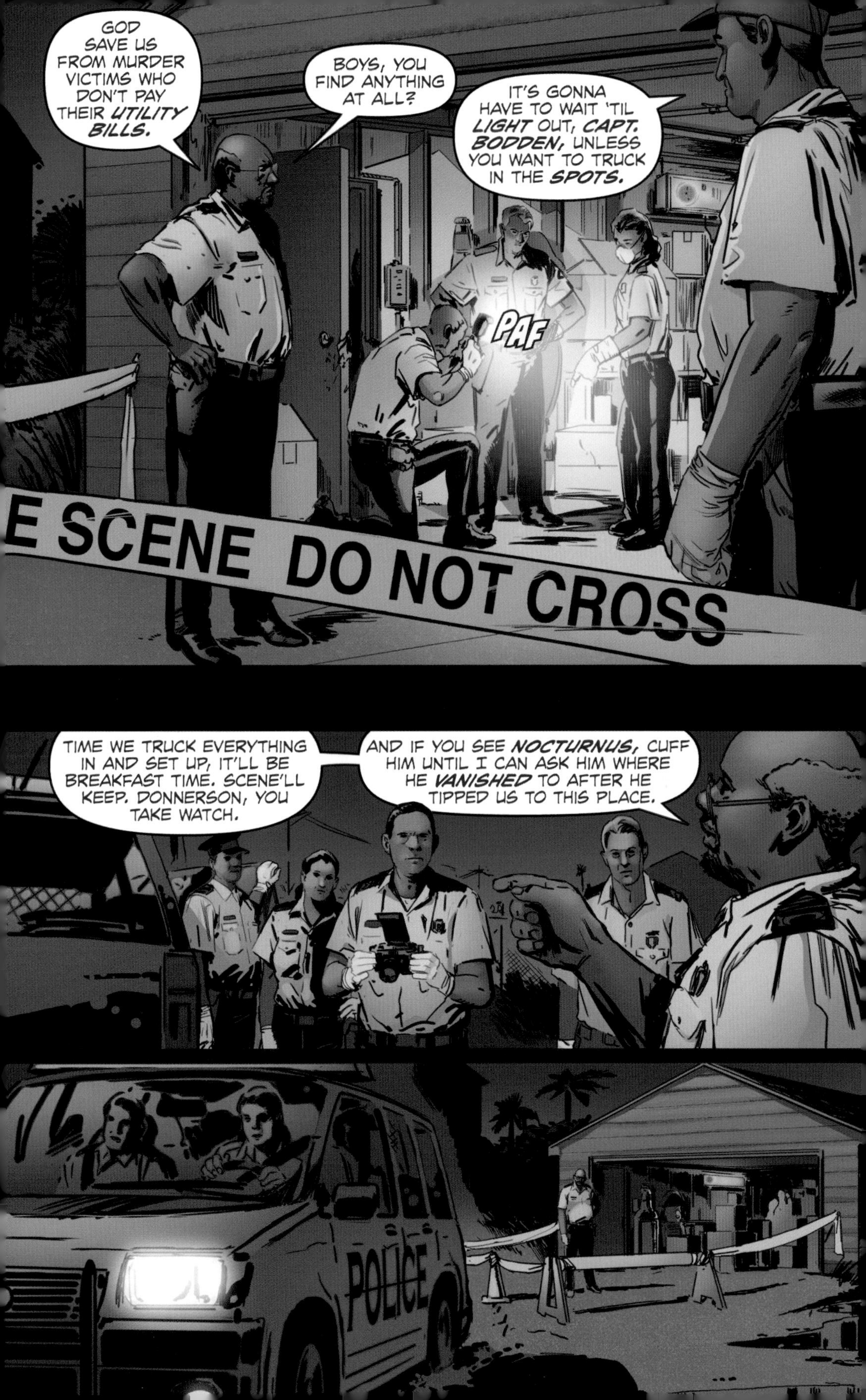
GOD SAVE US FROM MURDER VICTIMS WHO DON'T PAY THEIR UTILITY BILLS.
BOYS, YOU FIND ANYTHING AT ALL?
PAF
IT'S GONNA HAVE TO WAIT 'TIL LIGHT OUT, CAPT. BODDEN, UNLESS YOU WANT TO TRUCK IN THE SPOTS.
E SCENE DO NOT CROSS
TIME WE TRUCK EVERYTHING IN AND SET UP, IT'LL BE BREAKFAST TIME. SCENE'LL KEEP. DONNERSON, YOU TAKE WATCH.
AND IF YOU SEE NOCTURNUS, CUFF HIM UNTIL I CAN ASK HIM WHERE HE VANISHED TO AFTER HE TIPPED US TO THIS PLACE.
POLICE

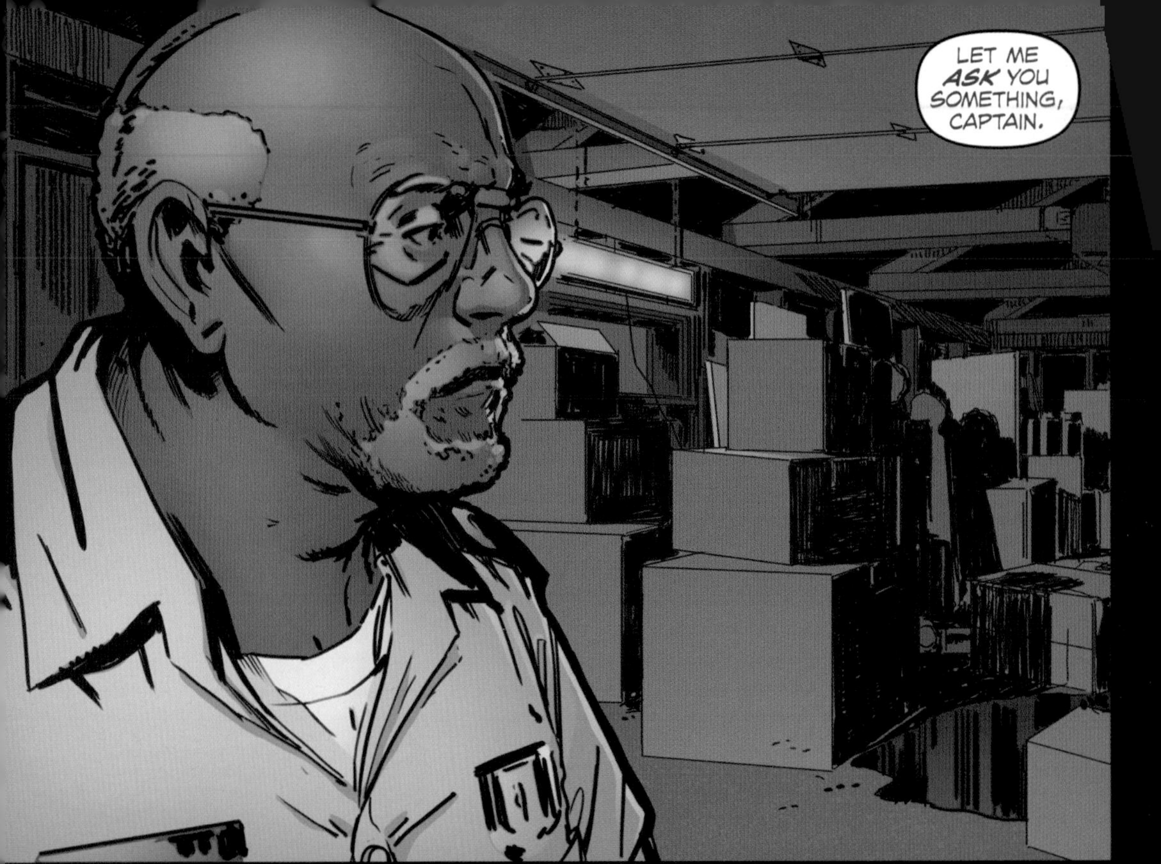
LET ME ASK YOU SOMETHING, CAPTAIN.

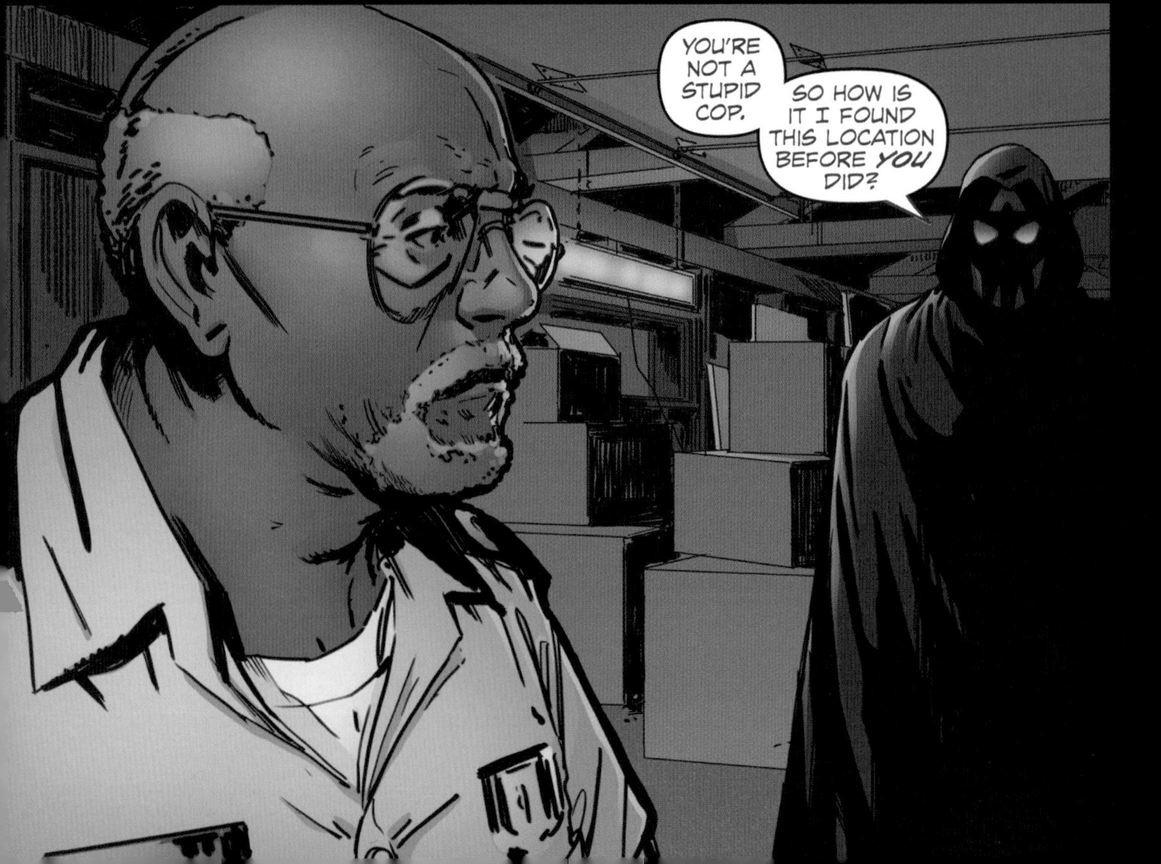
YOU'RE NOT A STUPID COP.
SO HOW IS IT I FOUND THIS LOCATION BEFORE YOU DID?

I SUSPECT YOU WERE MOTIVATED TO *LOOK* HARDER.

HERE'S THE THING ABOUT MR. RANDALL ARNDT.

HE HAD A REPUTATION AS A CREATIVE PROMOTER, BUT THAT WAS CRAP. REALLY, HE KNEW ONLY ONE TRICK:

ROUND UP YOUNG PEOPLE AND GET 'EM DRUNK.

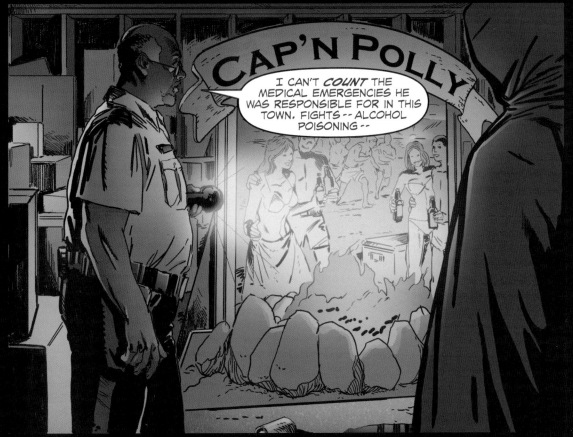

CAP'N POLLY

I CAN'T *COUNT* THE MEDICAL EMERGENCIES HE WAS RESPONSIBLE FOR IN THIS TOWN. FIGHTS -- ALCOHOL POISONING --

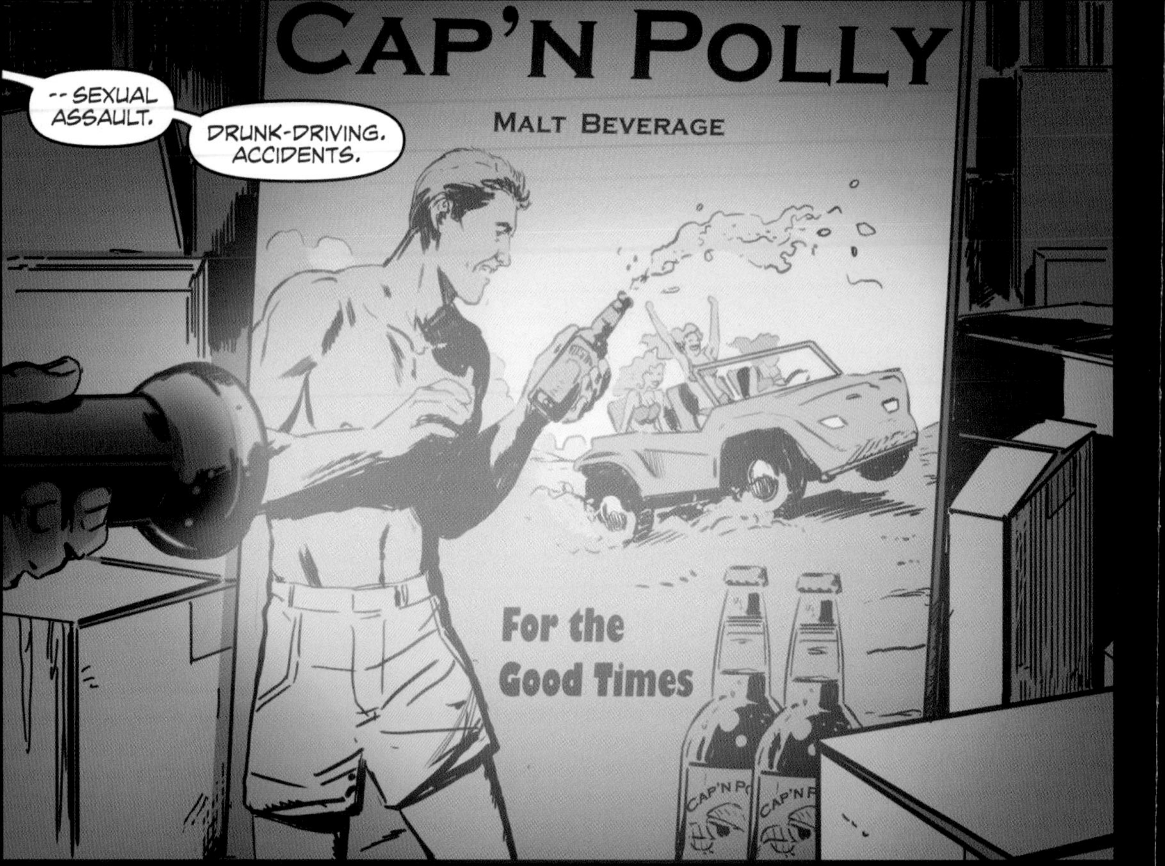
CAP'N POLLY
-- SEXUAL ASSAULT.
DRUNK-DRIVING. ACCIDENTS.
MALT BEVERAGE
For the Good Times

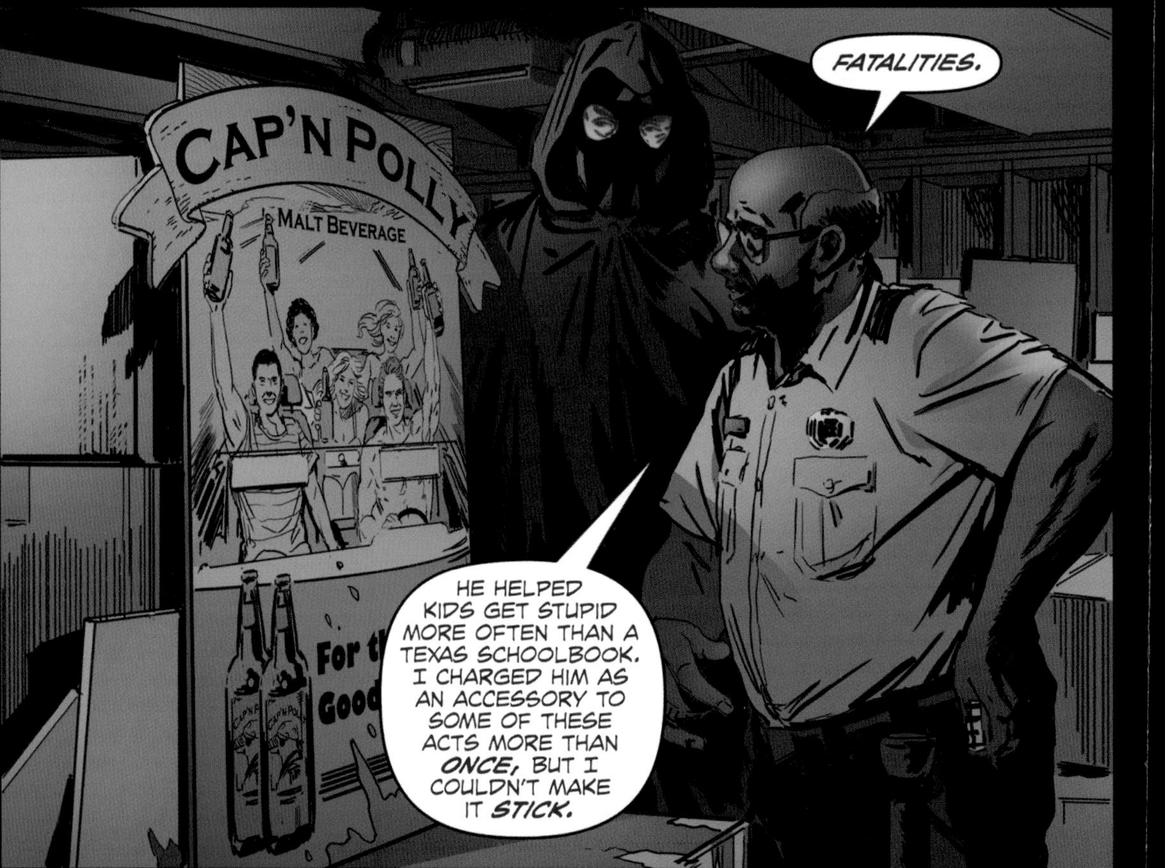
FATALITIES.
CAP'N POLLY
MALT BEVERAGE
HE HELPED KIDS GET STUPID MORE OFTEN THAN A TEXAS SCHOOLBOOK. I CHARGED HIM AS AN ACCESSORY TO SOME OF THESE ACTS MORE THAN *ONCE*, BUT I COULDN'T MAKE IT *STICK*.

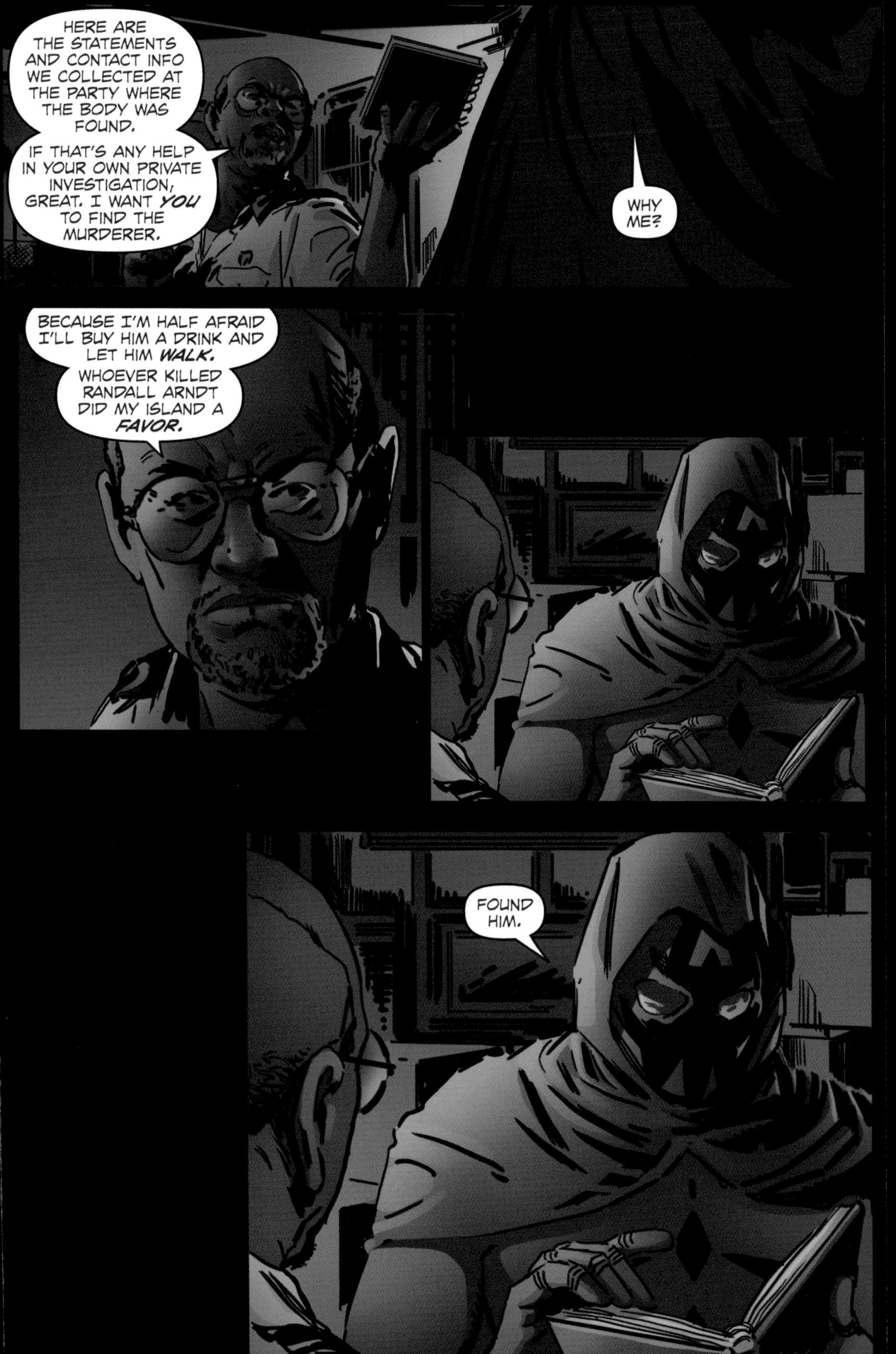
HERE ARE THE STATEMENTS AND CONTACT INFO WE COLLECTED AT THE PARTY WHERE THE BODY WAS FOUND.
IF THAT'S ANY HELP IN YOUR OWN PRIVATE INVESTIGATION, GREAT. I WANT *YOU* TO FIND THE MURDERER.
WHY ME?
BECAUSE I'M HALF AFRAID I'LL BUY HIM A DRINK AND LET HIM *WALK.*
WHOEVER KILLED RANDALL ARNDT DID MY ISLAND A *FAVOR.*
FOUND HIM.

NOCTURNUS CASE FILE: RANDALL ARNDT

This is what I get for trying to prove something to my idiot son.

Because Jarod had allowed "his" fortune to be embezzled away to an offshore account in the Caymans, I thought it would be good to reinforce upon my idiot son the value of detective work, so I suggested we follow the money.

His assistant, Meg, funded our trip to the Caymans by arranging, of all things, a sponsor. Transportation and expenses would be comped so long as my idiot son used what's left of his celebrity to promote a bottled furniture polish called "Cap'n Polly's, America's Favorite Rum-Flavored Malt Beverage."

Upon our arrival, we were met by Cap'n Polly's regional promotions manager, a low-rent huckster named Randall Arndt...

...who was found murdered on the first leg of my idiot son's promotional tour, his corpse hidden inside a giant beer cooler.

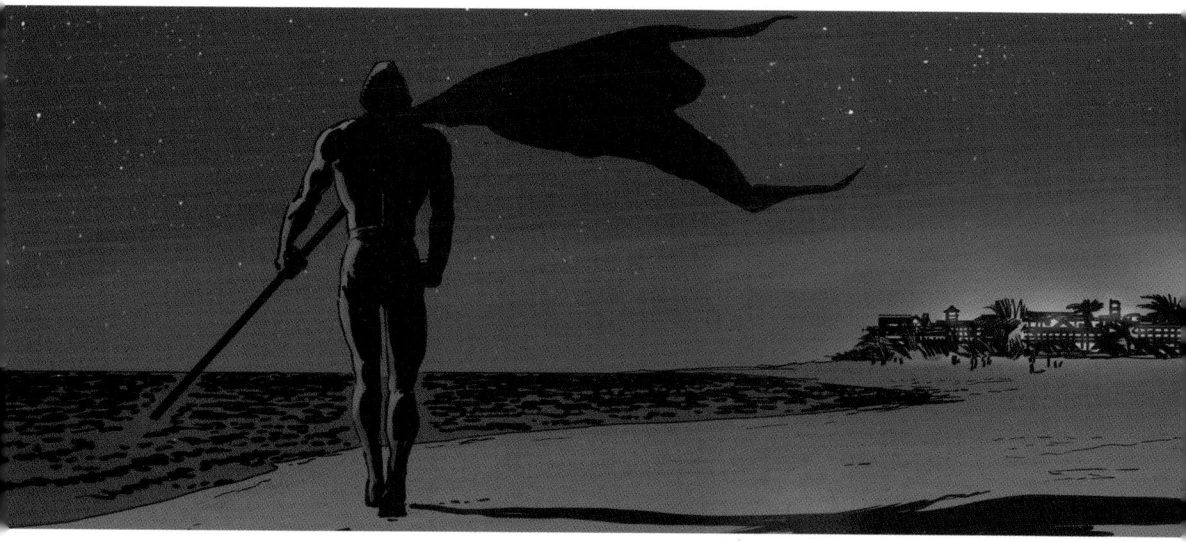

So I set out in search of the murderer.

I would love to say that I did this purely out of a thirst for justice, but that would be dishonest.

Or even that I was investigating because apprehending Arndt's killer seems the best way to relaunch this now-scuttled promotional tour and not be left stranded and penniless away from home.

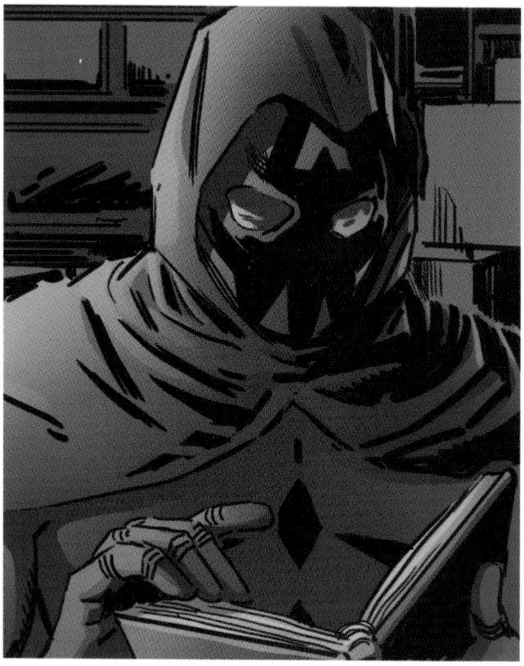

But that's not it, either. That's not why I've let the Arndt mystery divert my attention, and I know it.

Still, dwelling on it won't do anything other than drag this case out.

I've already done my homework.
I have a suspect in mind. Let's see who Police Captain Bodden has already interviewed.

Sully, the hotel bartender at the scene of the body's dramatic unveiling. Nice dragnet, Bodden, good coverage.
But Sully has no real motive.

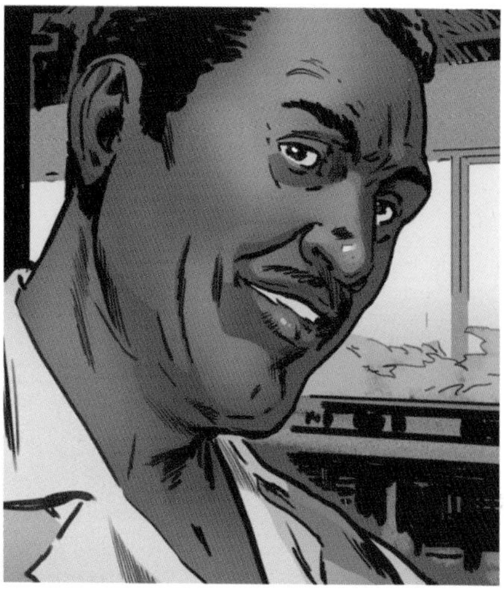

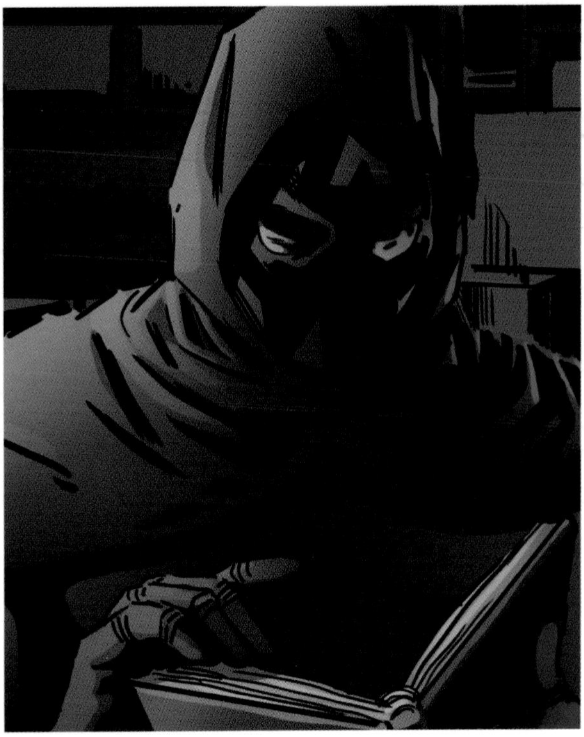

Flowers, on the other hand, is a faded beach hippie who'd built Arndt's website and then couldn't collect payment. Spacey, but that could be an act.

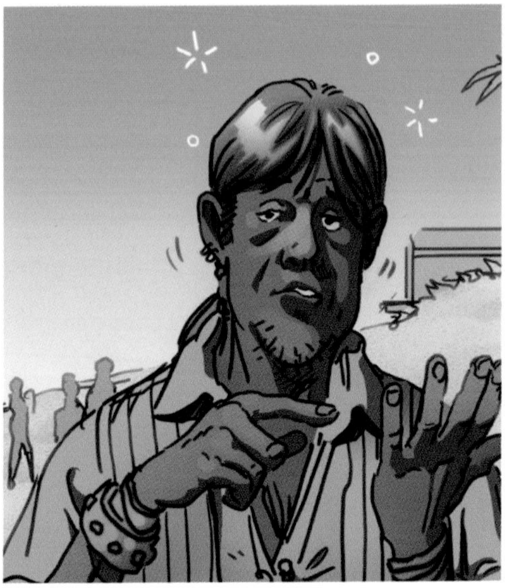

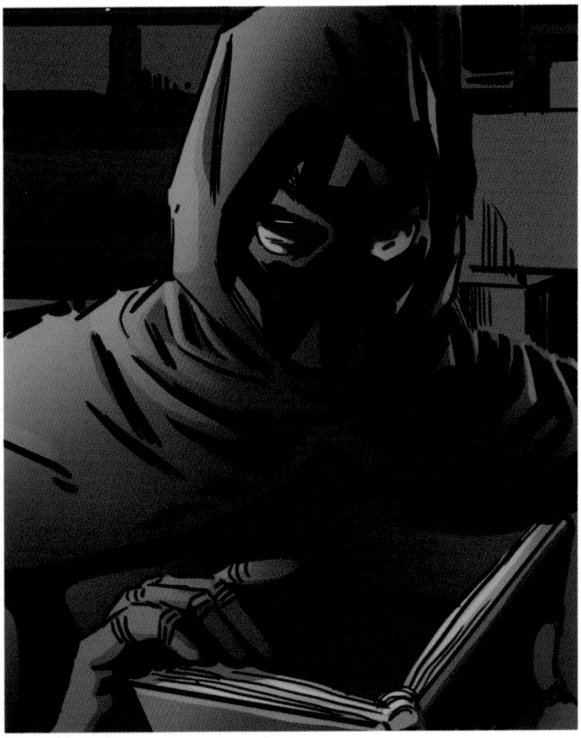

Terry, a.k.a. "DJ T-Licious," Arndt's sometimes-business partner and fellow panderer to the inebriated.

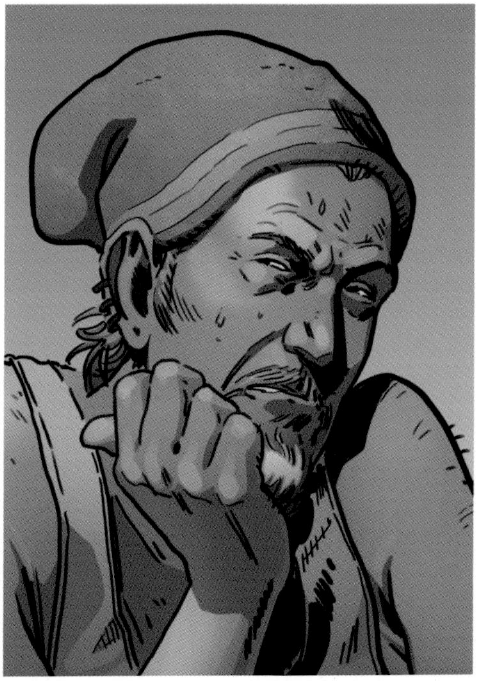

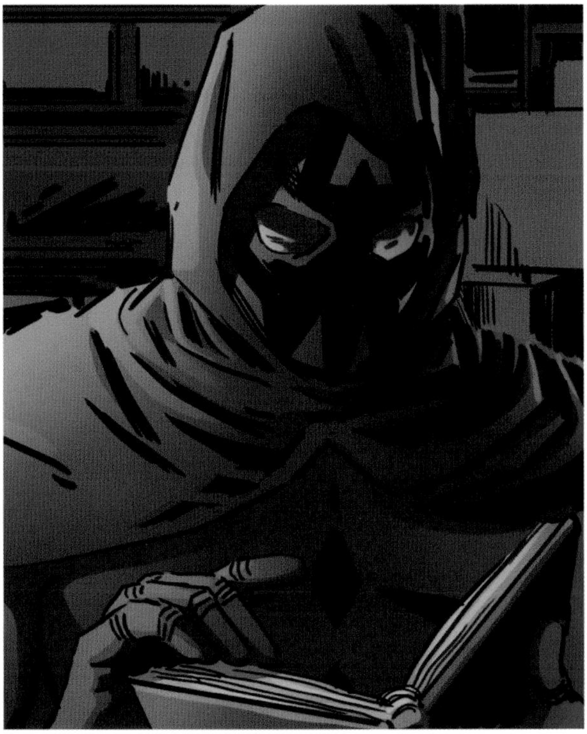

Drake, a barfly who, thus far, is the only carbon-based lifeform in the Milky Way to express any regret that Arndt is dead. Given the grief he's shown, he seems the most unlikely killer.

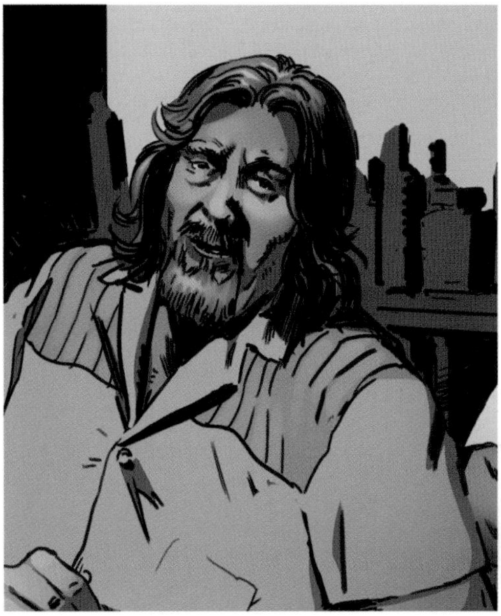

But here's the thing about Drake that Bodden's overlooked.

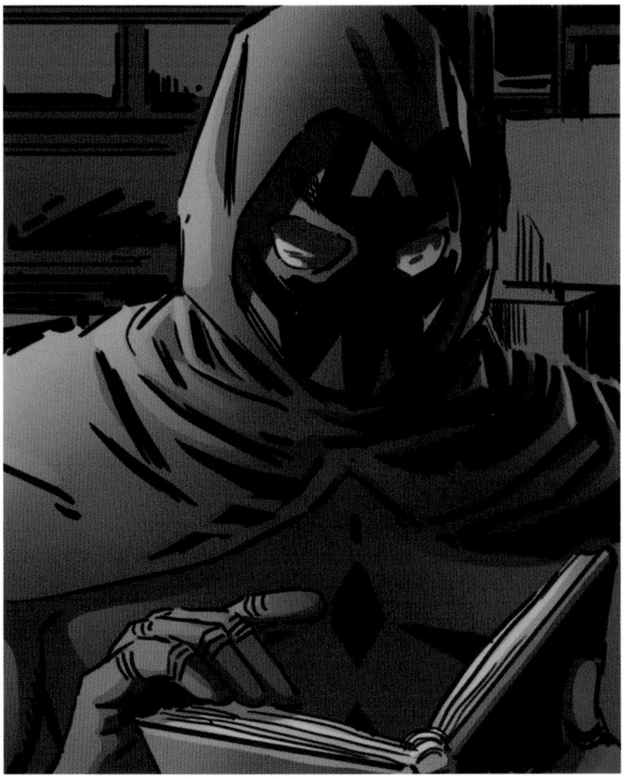

I know why he drinks.

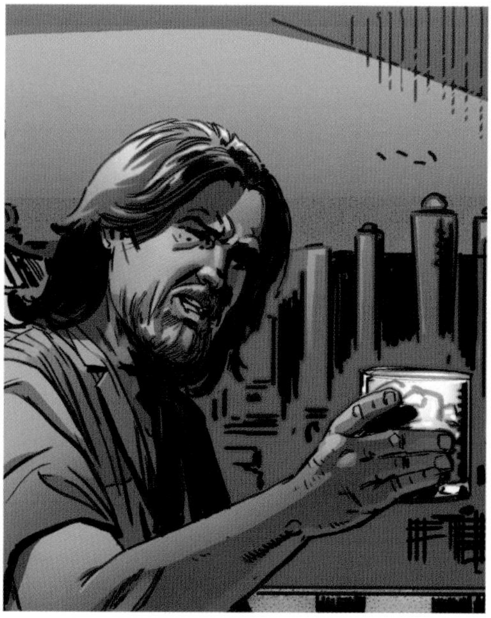

And why he took a knife to Randall Arndt.

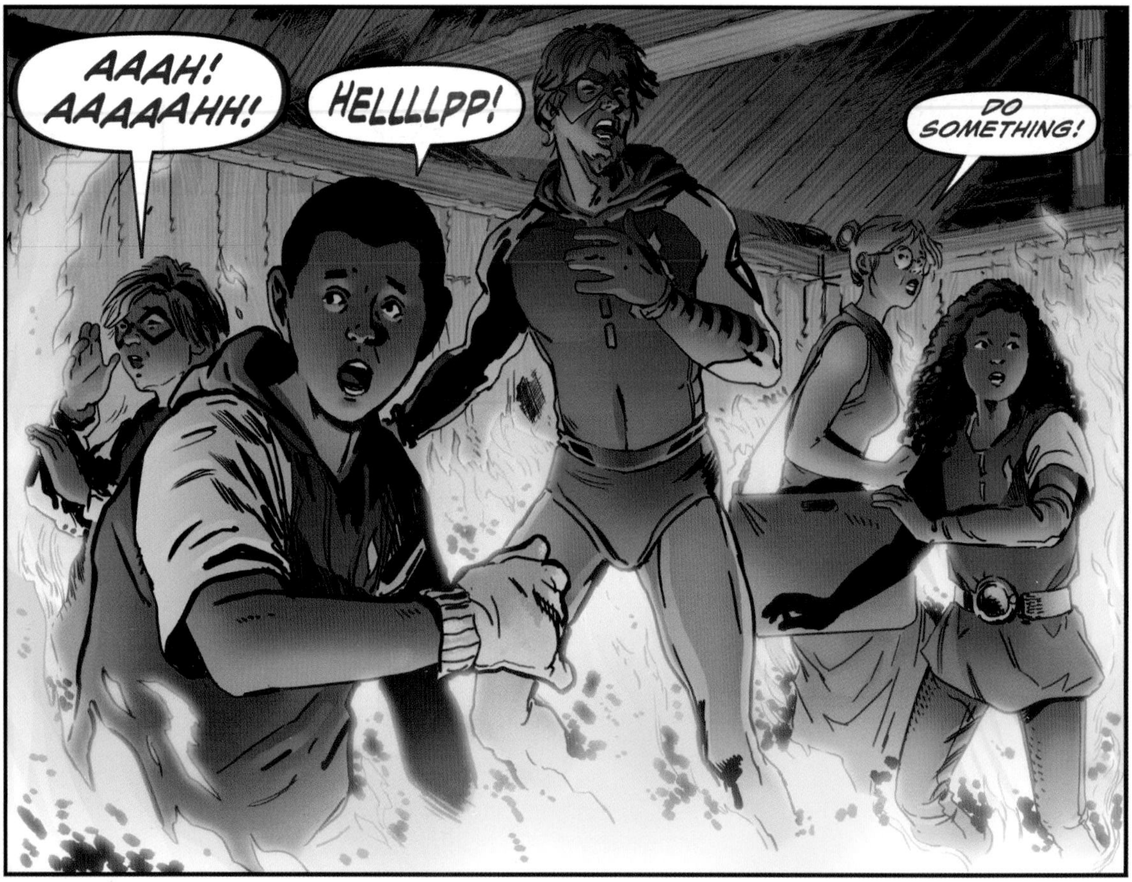
AAAH! AAAAAHH!
HELLLLPP!
DO SOMETHING!

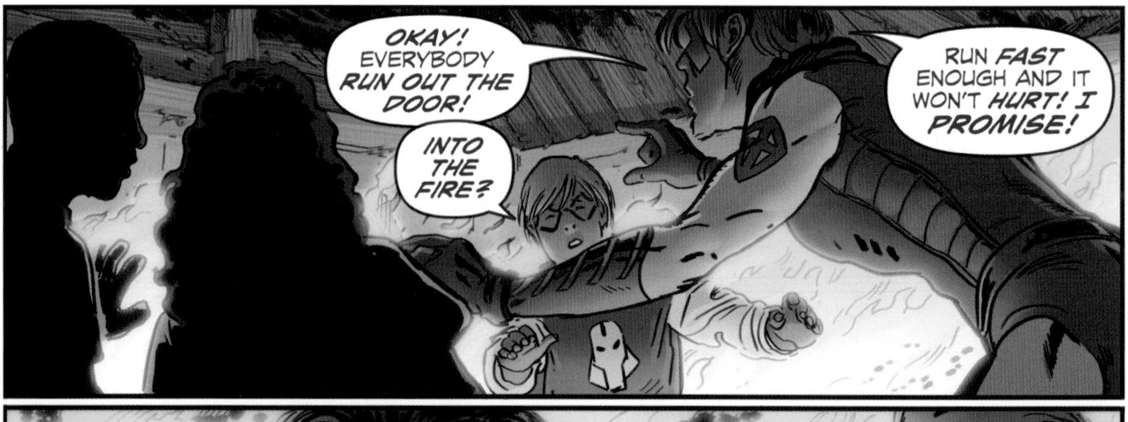
OKAY! EVERYBODY RUN OUT THE DOOR!
INTO THE FIRE?
RUN FAST ENOUGH AND IT WON'T HURT! I PROMISE!

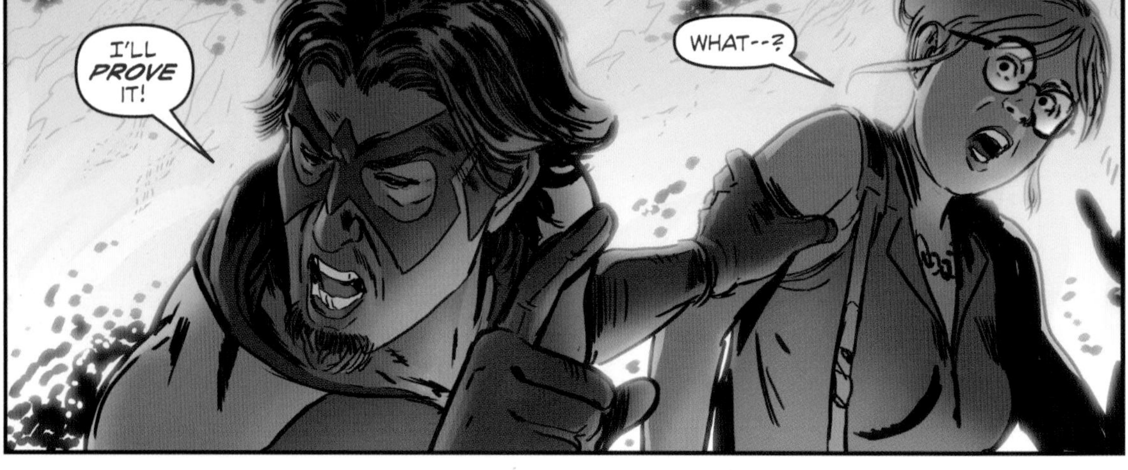
I'LL PROVE IT!
WHAT--?

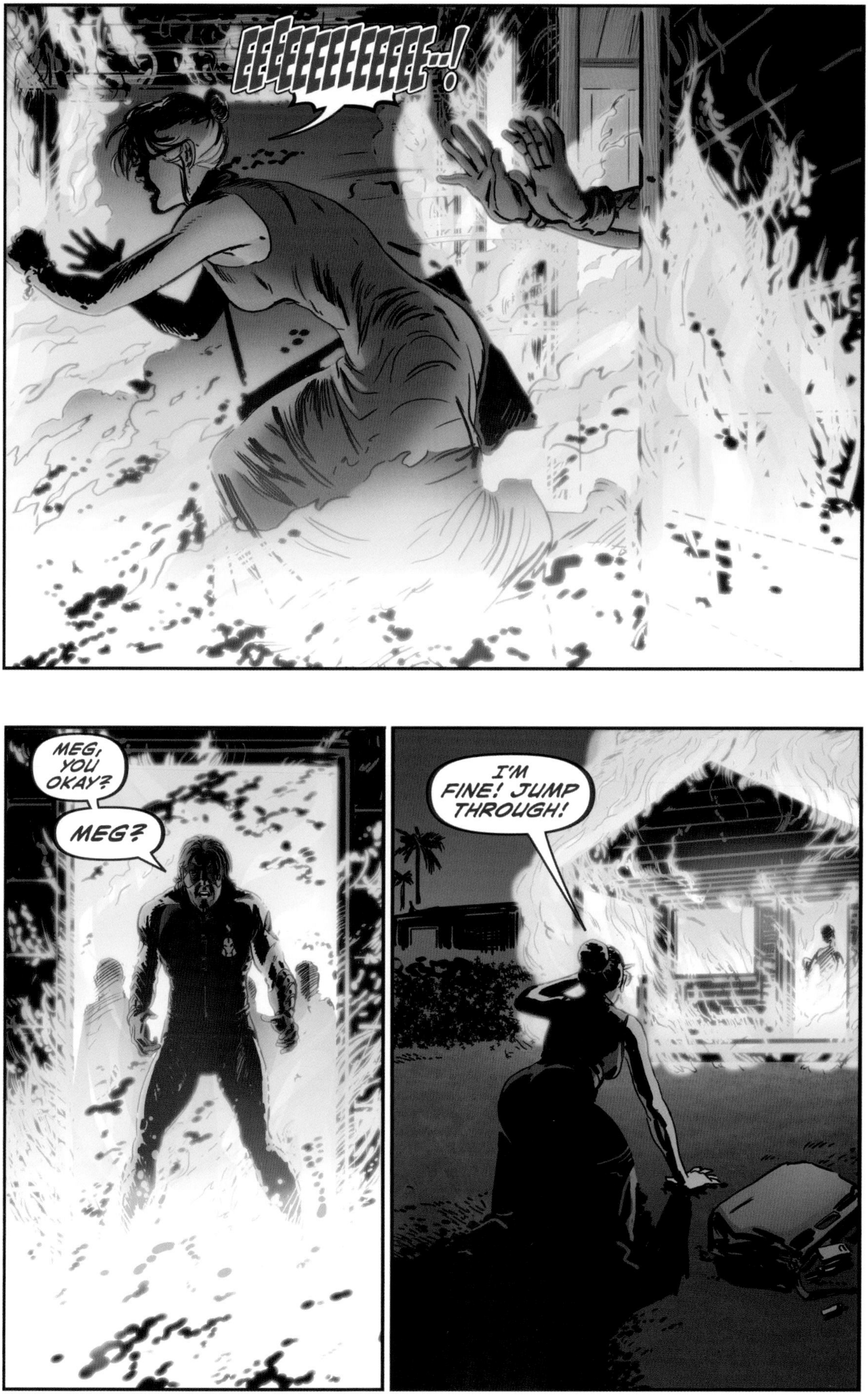
EEEEEEEEEEEE..!
MEG, YOU OKAY?
MEG?
I'M FINE! JUMP THROUGH!

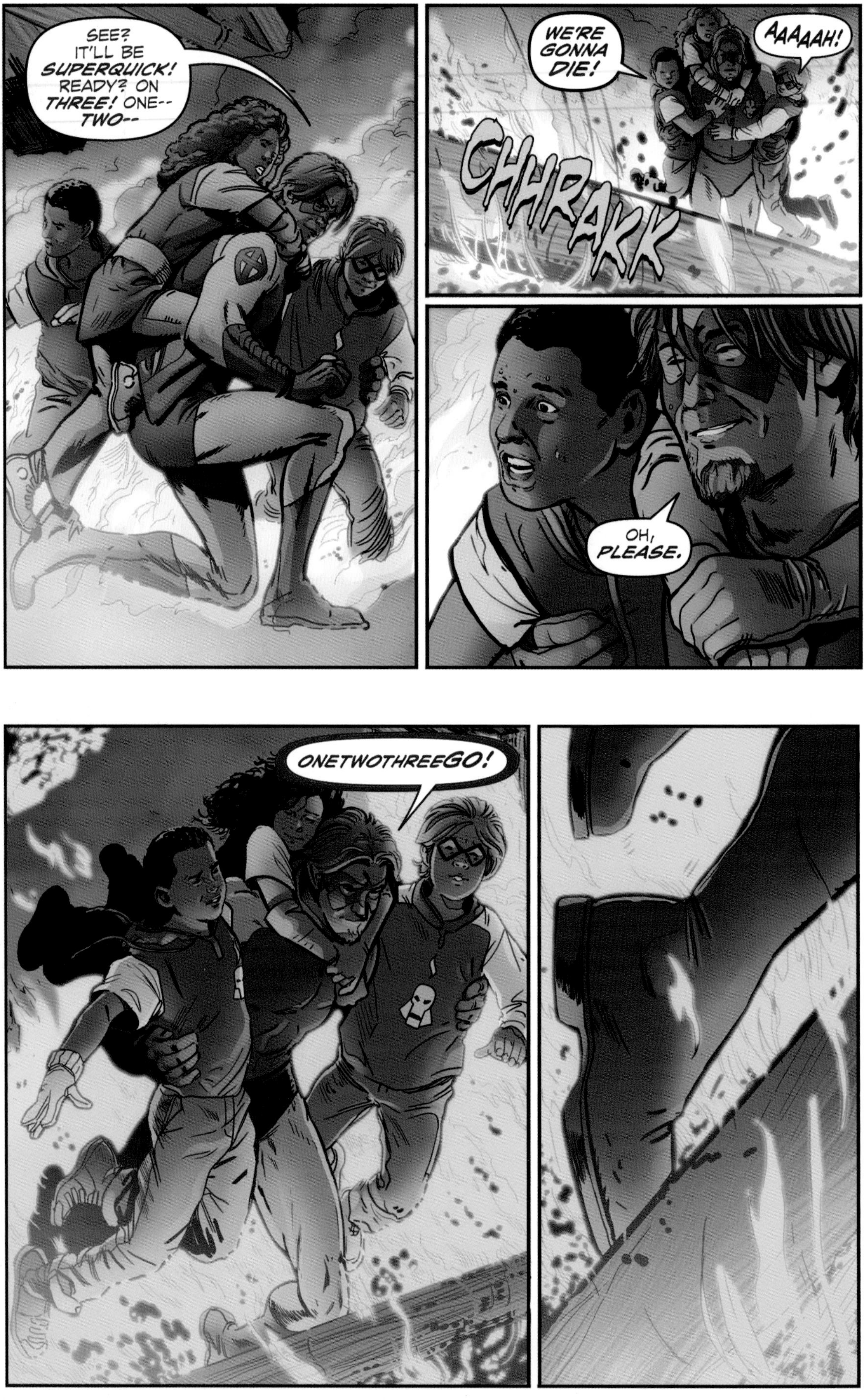
SEE? IT'LL BE SUPERQUICK! READY? ON THREE! ONE-- TWO--
WE'RE GONNA DIE!
AAAAAH!
CHHRAKK
OH, PLEASE.
ONETWOTHREEGO!

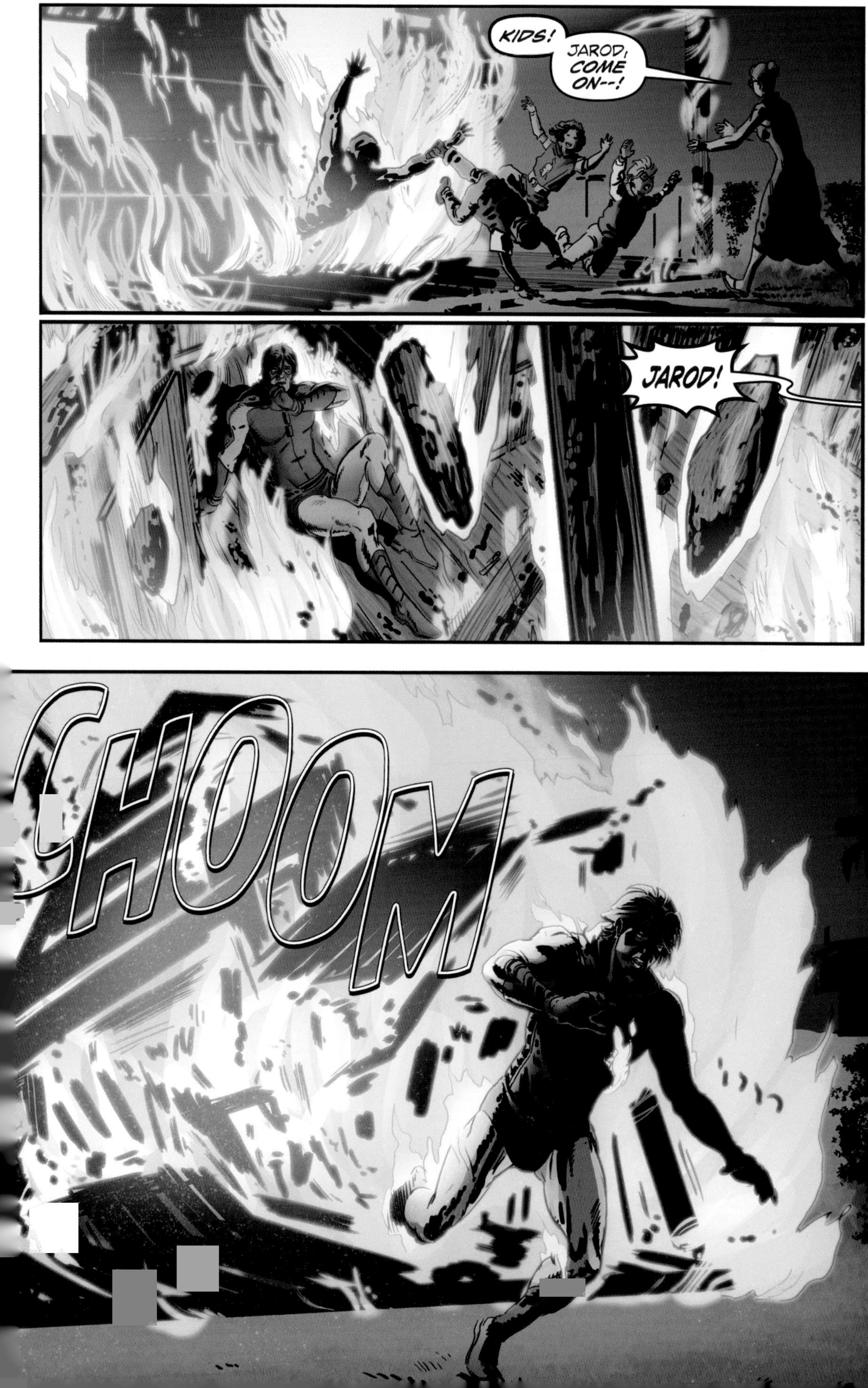
KIDS!
JAROD, COME ON--!
JAROD!
CHOOOM

DROP AND ROLL!

IT'S ALL GOOD! IS ANYONE HURT?

NO? SEE? NOT ON MY WATCH!

EVERYTHING'S JUST FINE.

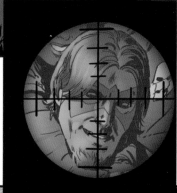

KRAK

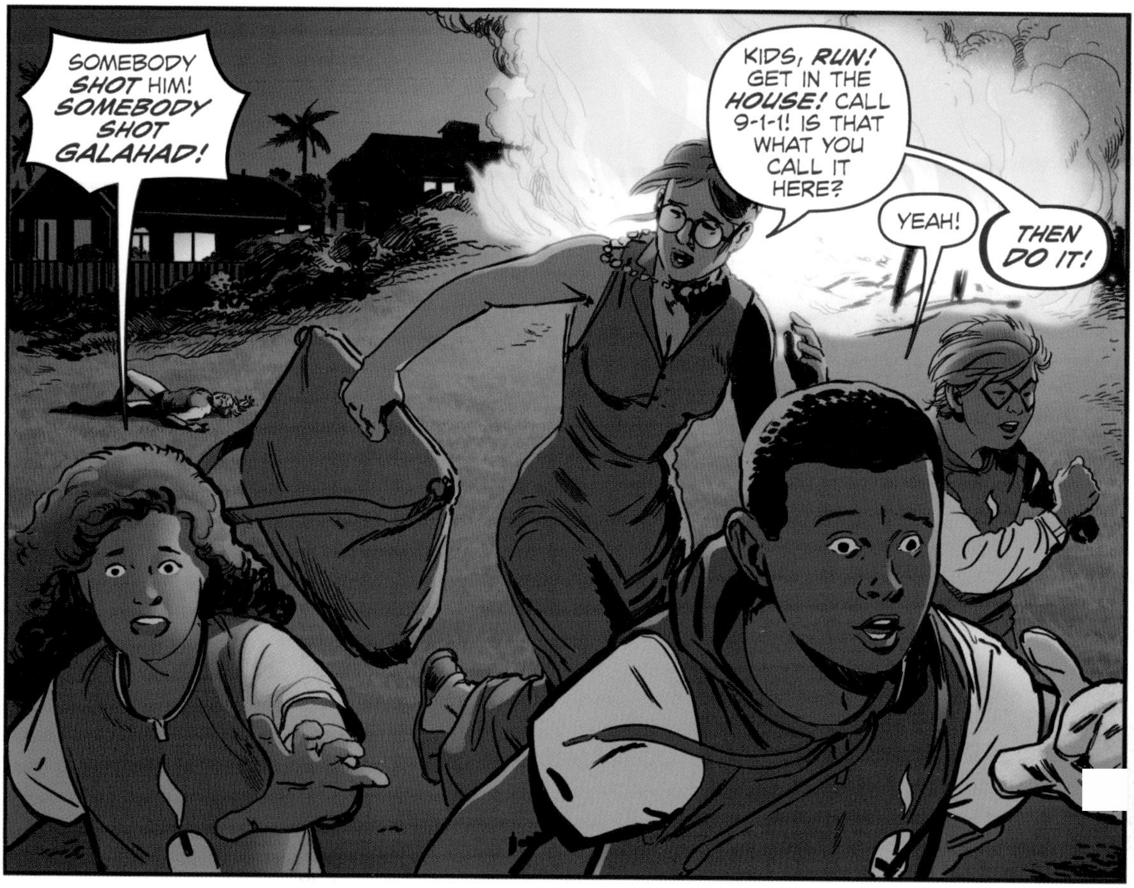
SOMEBODY SHOT HIM! SOMEBODY SHOT GALAHAD!
KIDS, RUN! GET IN THE HOUSE! CALL 9-1-1! IS THAT WHAT YOU CALL IT HERE?
YEAH!
THEN DO IT!

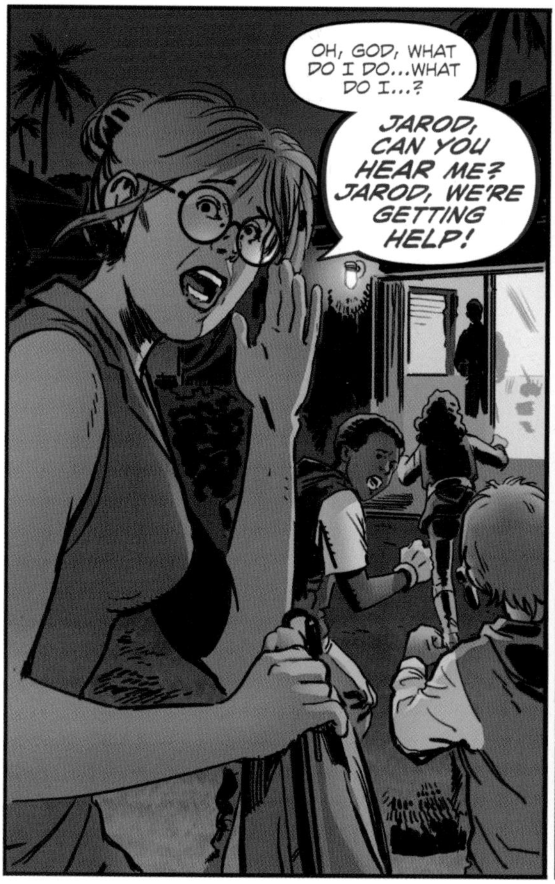
OH, GOD, WHAT DO I DO...WHAT DO I...?
JAROD, CAN YOU HEAR ME? JAROD, WE'RE GETTING HELP!

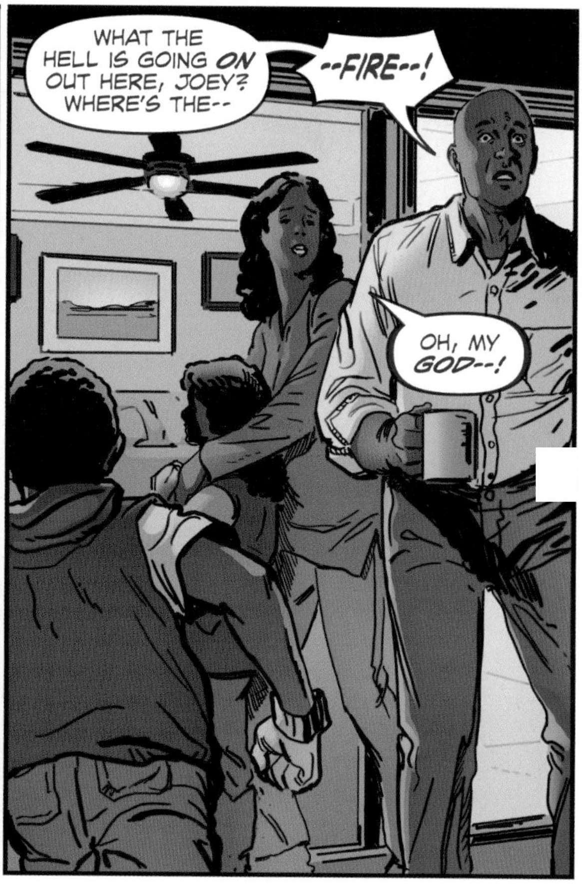
WHAT THE HELL IS GOING ON OUT HERE, JOEY? WHERE'S THE--
--FIRE--!
OH, MY GOD--!

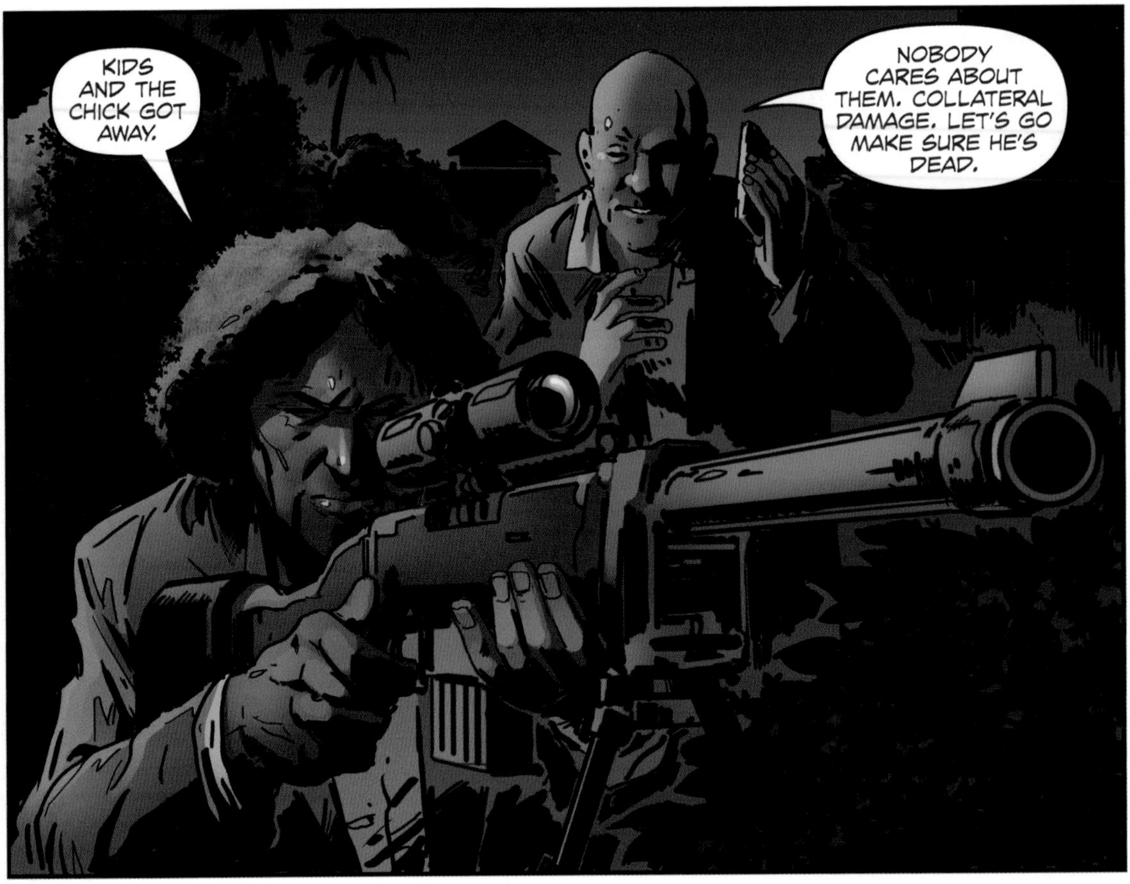
KIDS AND THE CHICK GOT AWAY.
NOBODY CARES ABOUT THEM. COLLATERAL DAMAGE. LET'S GO MAKE SURE HE'S DEAD.

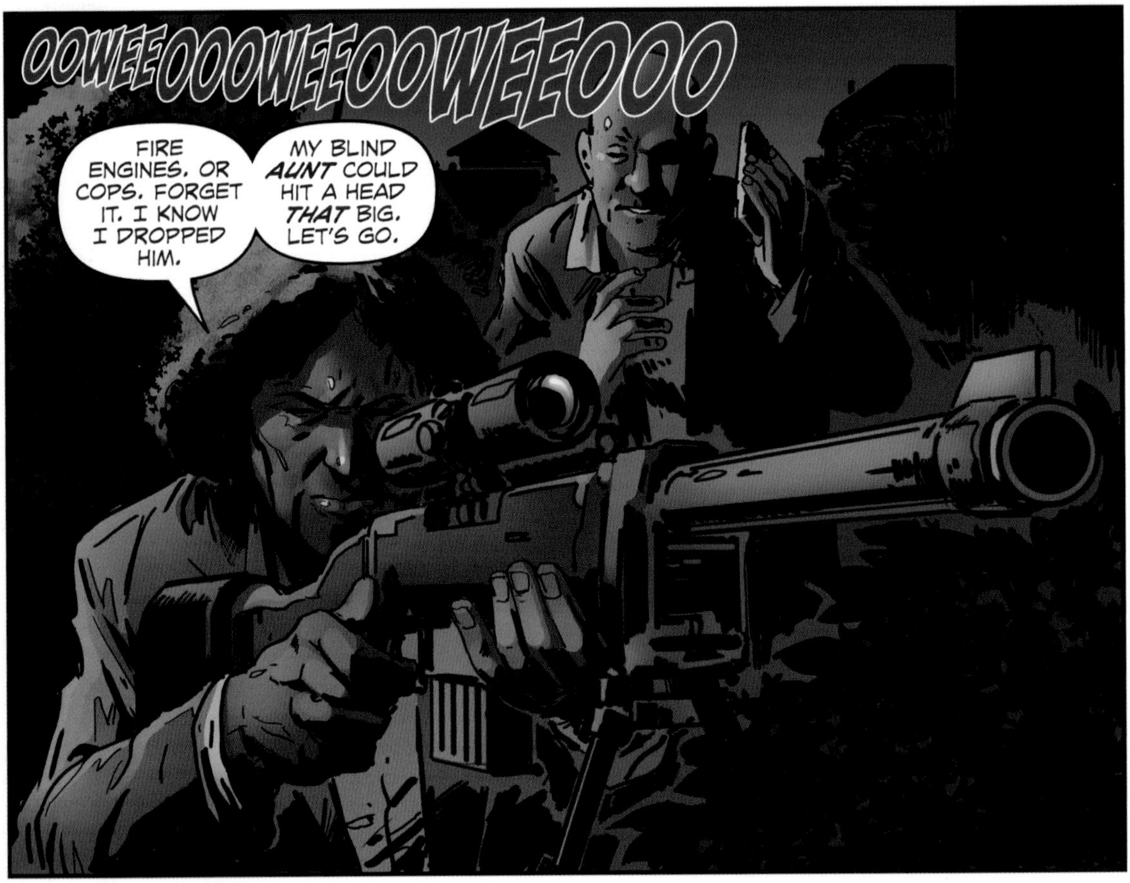
OOWEEOOOWEEOOWEEOOO
FIRE ENGINES. OR COPS. FORGET IT. I KNOW I DROPPED HIM.
MY BLIND *AUNT* COULD HIT A HEAD *THAT* BIG. LET'S GO.

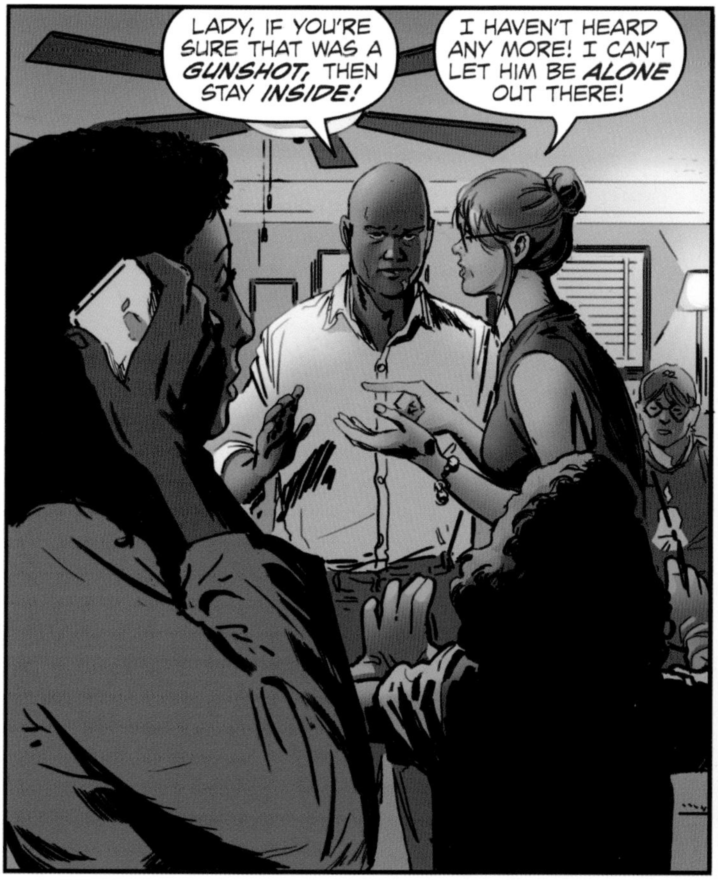
LADY, IF YOU'RE SURE THAT WAS A *GUNSHOT,* THEN STAY *INSIDE!*
I HAVEN'T HEARD ANY MORE! I CAN'T LET HIM BE *ALONE* OUT THERE!

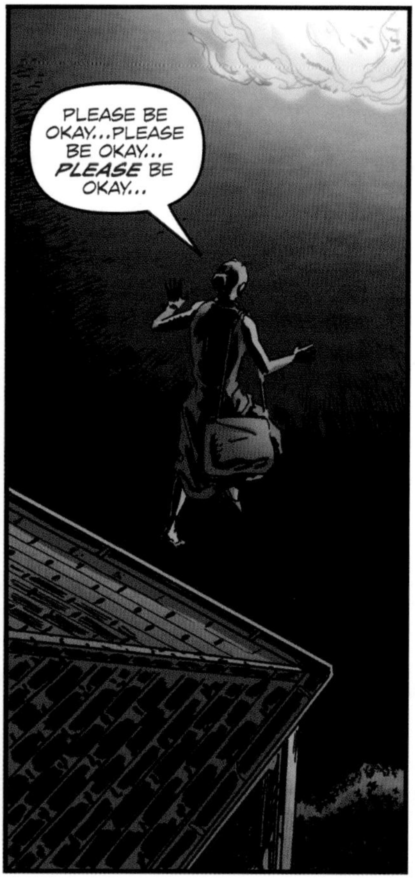
PLEASE BE OKAY...PLEASE BE OKAY... *PLEASE* BE OKAY...

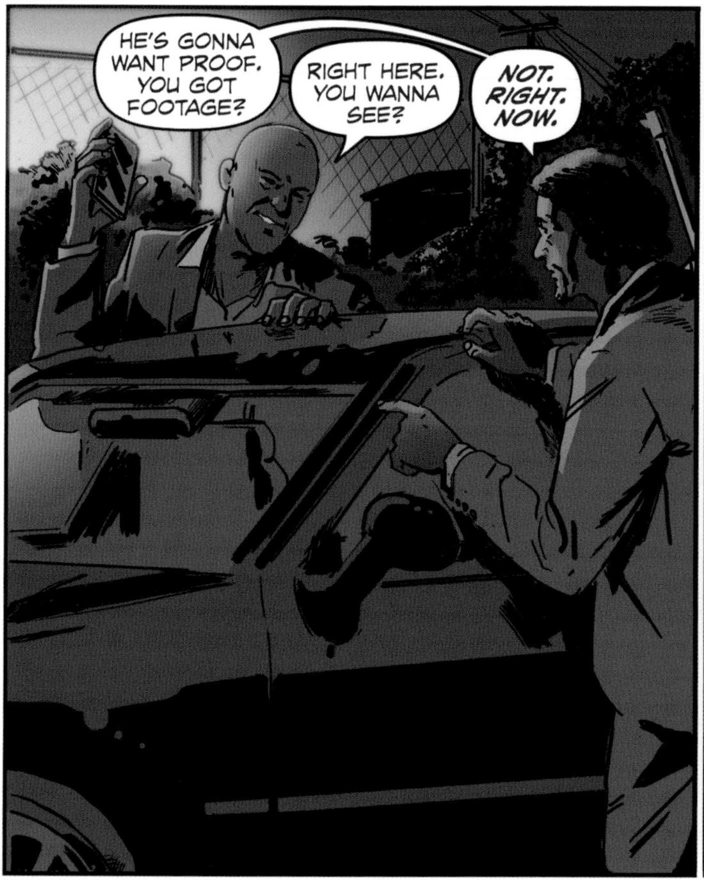
HE'S GONNA WANT PROOF. YOU GOT FOOTAGE?
RIGHT HERE. YOU WANNA SEE?
NOT. RIGHT. NOW.

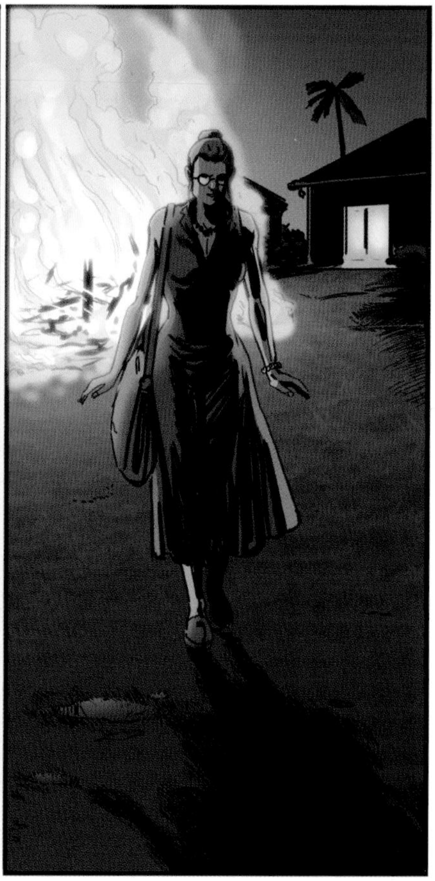

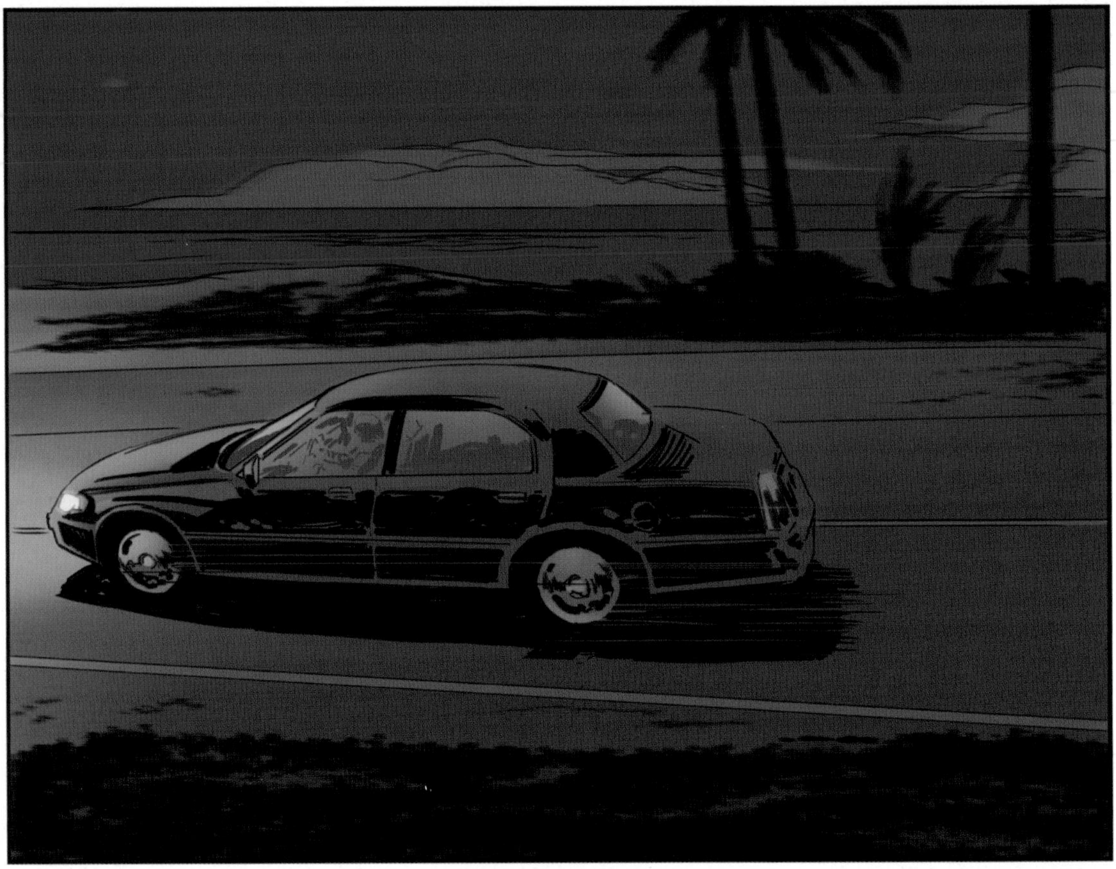

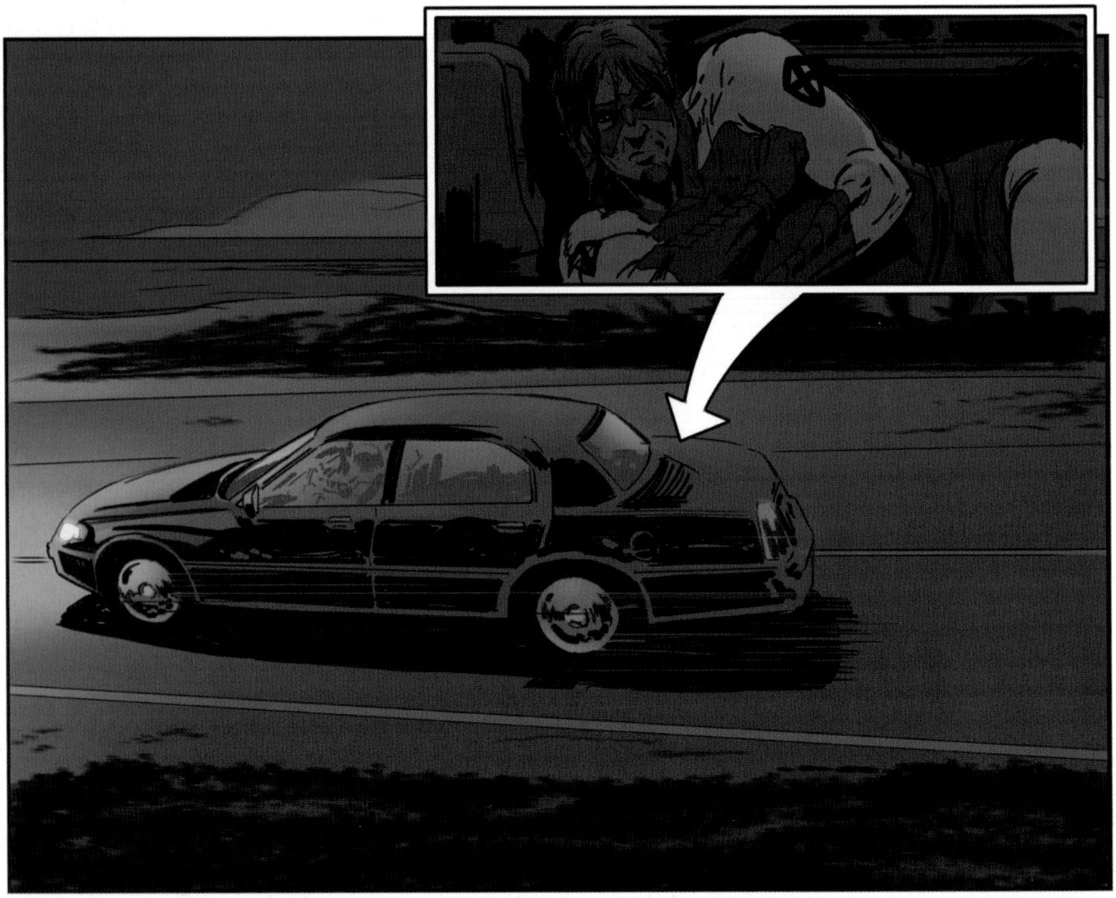

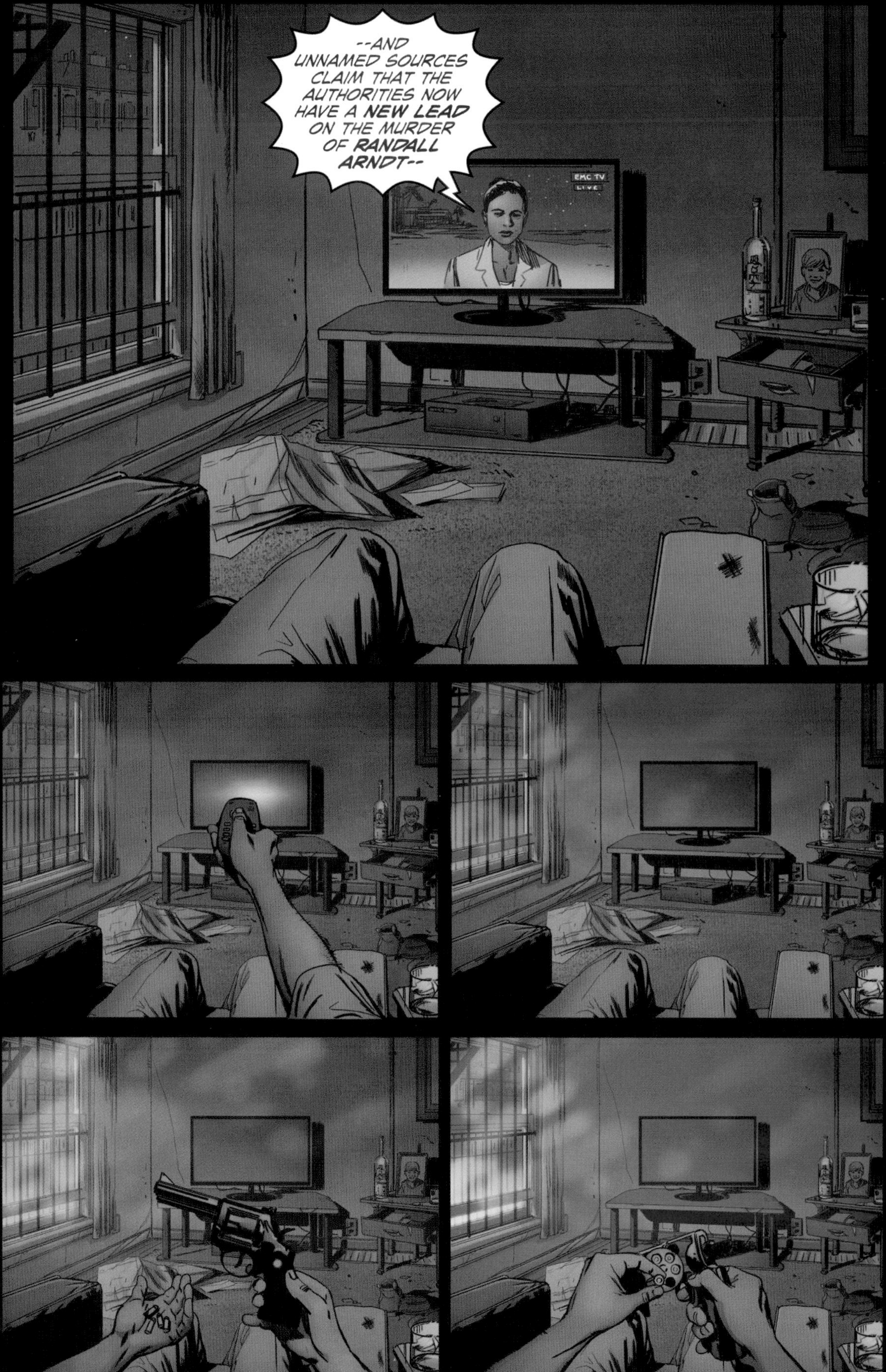
--AND UNNAMED SOURCES CLAIM THAT THE AUTHORITIES NOW HAVE A NEW LEAD ON THE MURDER OF RANDALL ARNDT--
EMC TV
LIVE

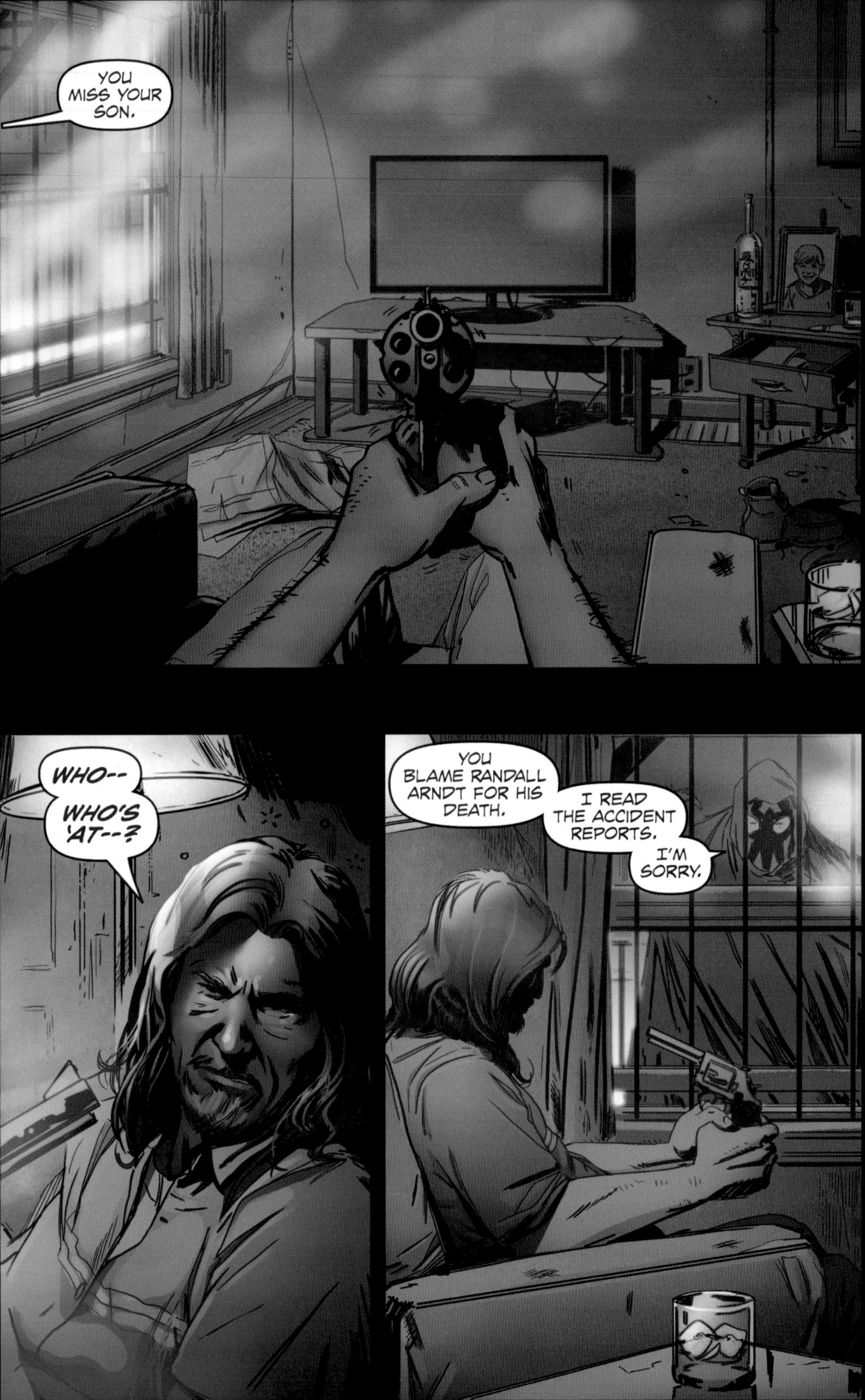
YOU MISS YOUR SON.
WHO--
WHO'S 'AT--?
YOU BLAME RANDALL ARNDT FOR HIS DEATH.
I READ THE ACCIDENT REPORTS.
I'M SORRY.

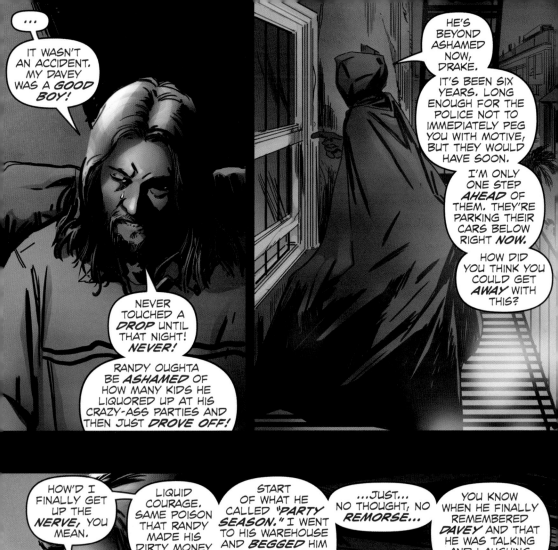

...

IT WASN'T AN ACCIDENT. MY DAVEY WAS A *GOOD BOY!*

NEVER TOUCHED A *DROP* UNTIL THAT NIGHT! *NEVER!*

RANDY OUGHTA BE *ASHAMED* OF HOW MANY KIDS HE LIQUORED UP AT HIS CRAZY-ASS PARTIES AND THEN JUST *DROVE OFF!*

HE'S BEYOND ASHAMED NOW, DRAKE.

IT'S BEEN SIX YEARS. LONG ENOUGH FOR THE POLICE NOT TO IMMEDIATELY PEG YOU WITH MOTIVE, BUT THEY WOULD HAVE SOON.

I'M ONLY ONE STEP *AHEAD* OF THEM. THEY'RE PARKING THEIR CARS BELOW RIGHT *NOW.*

HOW DID YOU THINK YOU COULD GET *AWAY* WITH THIS?

HOW'D I FINALLY GET UP THE *NERVE,* YOU MEAN.

LIQUID COURAGE. SAME POISON THAT RANDY MADE HIS DIRTY MONEY FROM.

START OF WHAT HE CALLED *"PARTY SEASON."* I WENT TO HIS WAREHOUSE AND *BEGGED* HIM TO THINK ABOUT THE *KIDS,* BUT THE WAY HE *TALKED* ABOUT 'EM...

...JUST... NO THOUGHT, NO *REMORSE...*

YOU KNOW WHEN HE FINALLY REMEMBERED *DAVEY* AND THAT HE WAS TALKING AND LAUGHING ABOUT *MY BOY?* ABOUT THE TIME THE *KNIFE* WENT IN.

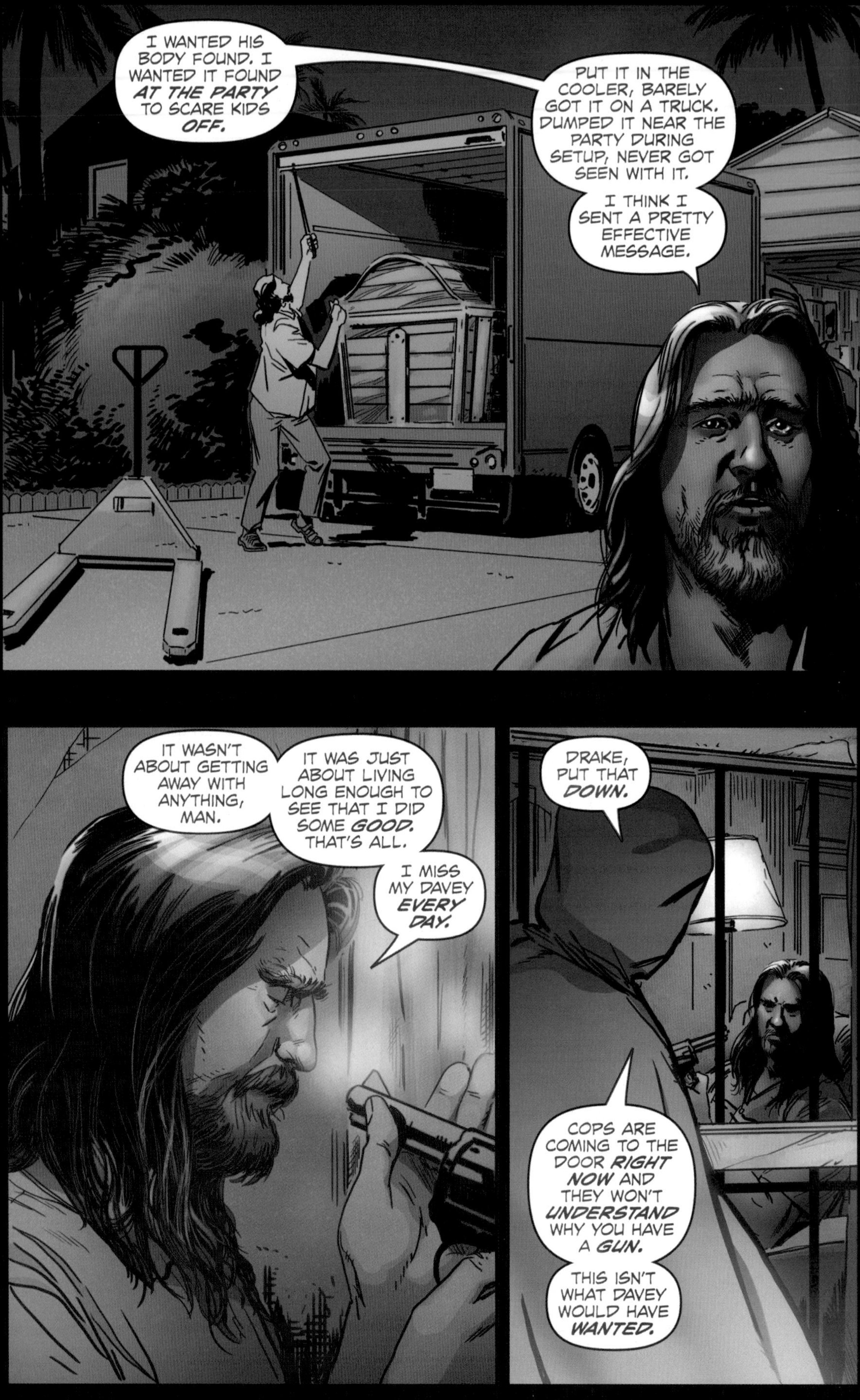
I WANTED HIS BODY FOUND. I WANTED IT FOUND *AT THE PARTY* TO SCARE KIDS *OFF.*
PUT IT IN THE COOLER, BARELY GOT IT ON A TRUCK. DUMPED IT NEAR THE PARTY DURING SETUP, NEVER GOT SEEN WITH IT.
I THINK I SENT A PRETTY EFFECTIVE MESSAGE.
IT WASN'T ABOUT GETTING AWAY WITH ANYTHING, MAN.
IT WAS JUST ABOUT LIVING LONG ENOUGH TO SEE THAT I DID SOME *GOOD.* THAT'S ALL.
I MISS MY DAVEY *EVERY DAY.*
DRAKE, PUT THAT *DOWN.*
COPS ARE COMING TO THE DOOR *RIGHT NOW* AND THEY WON'T *UNDERSTAND* WHY YOU HAVE A *GUN.*
THIS ISN'T WHAT DAVEY WOULD HAVE *WANTED.*

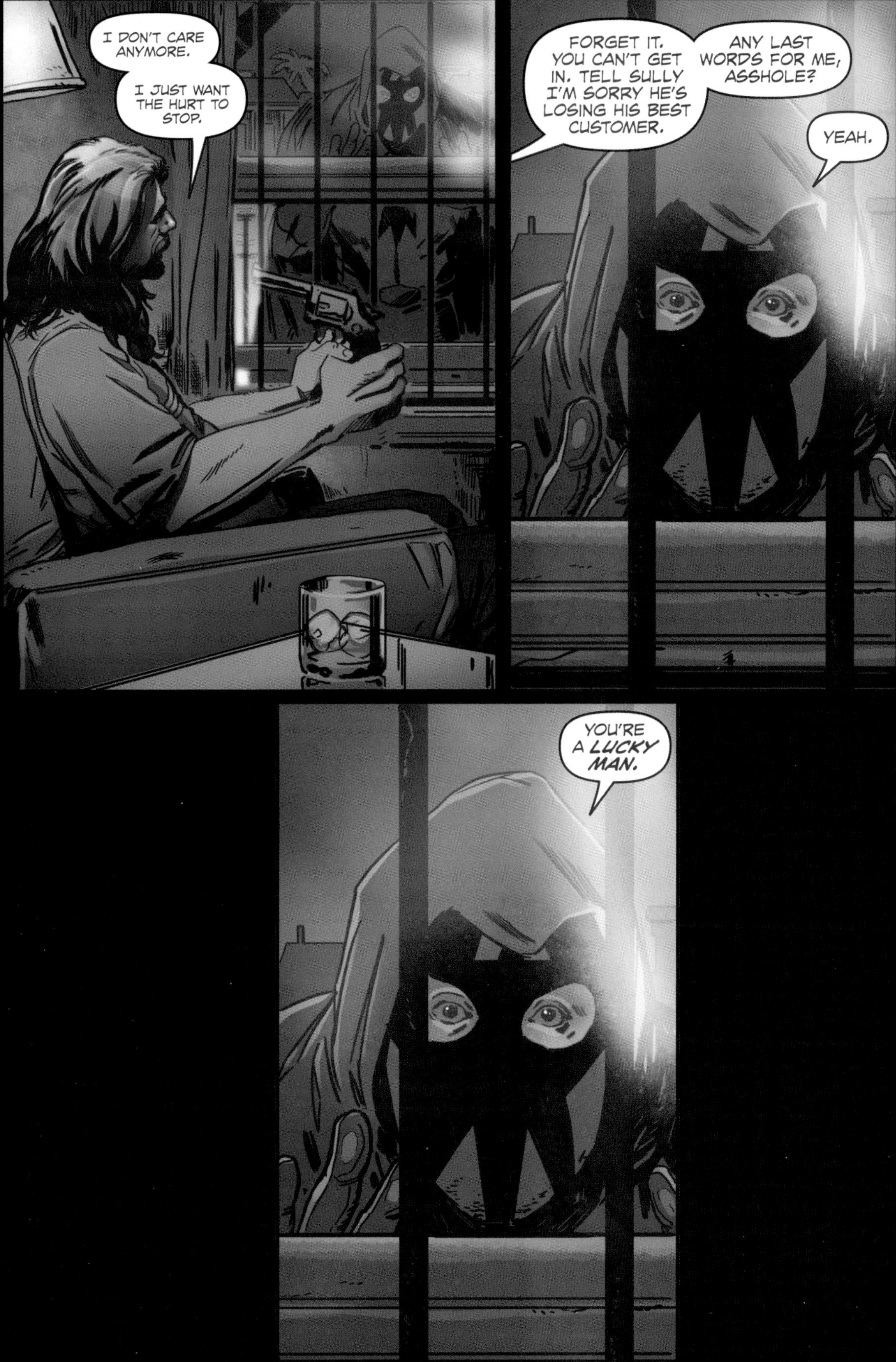
I DON'T CARE ANYMORE.
I JUST WANT THE HURT TO STOP.
FORGET IT. YOU CAN'T GET IN. TELL SULLY I'M SORRY HE'S LOSING HIS BEST CUSTOMER.
ANY LAST WORDS FOR ME, ASSHOLE?
YEAH.
YOU'RE A *LUCKY MAN.*

CHAPTER 4

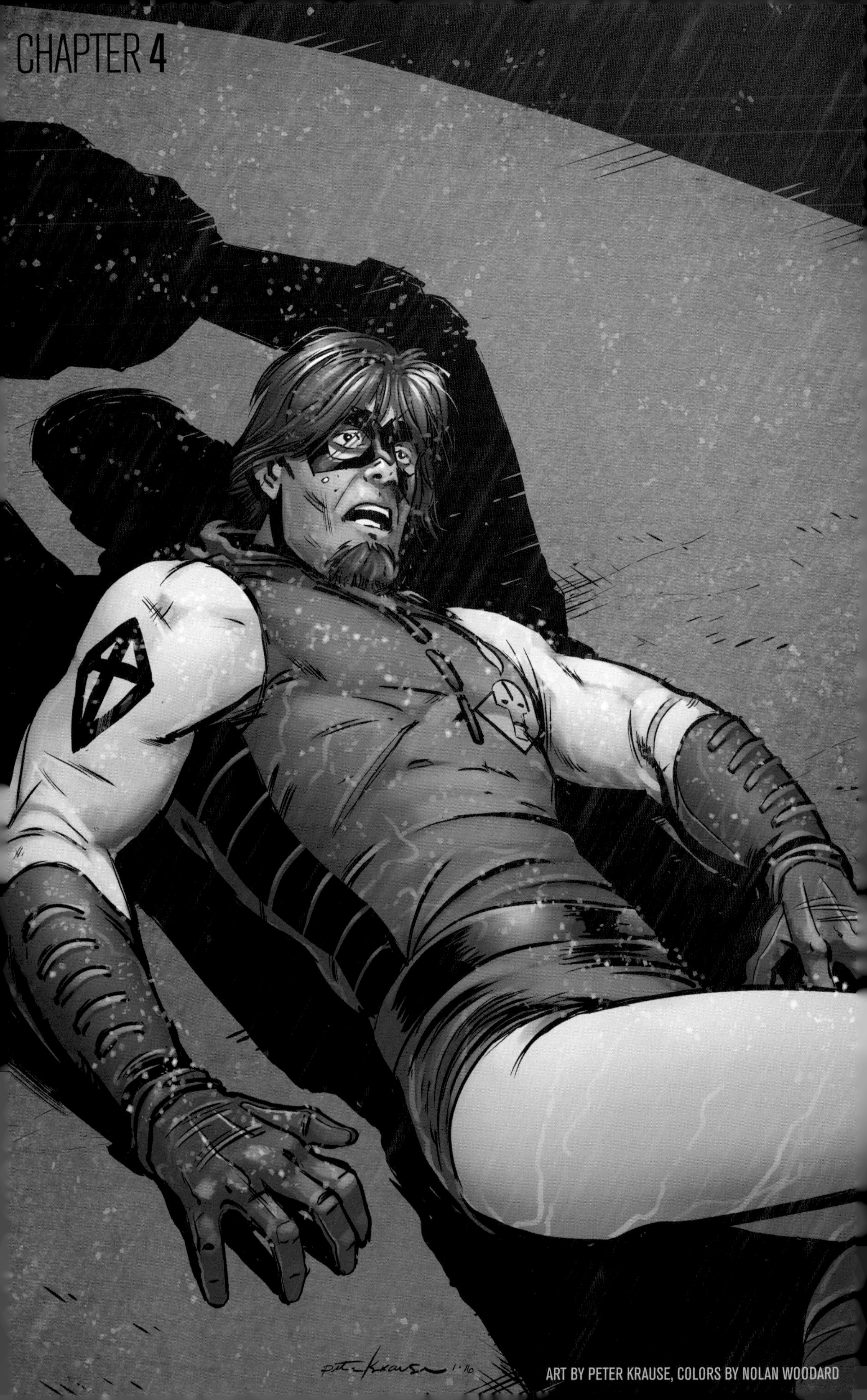

ART BY PETER KRAUSE, COLORS BY NOLAN WOODARD

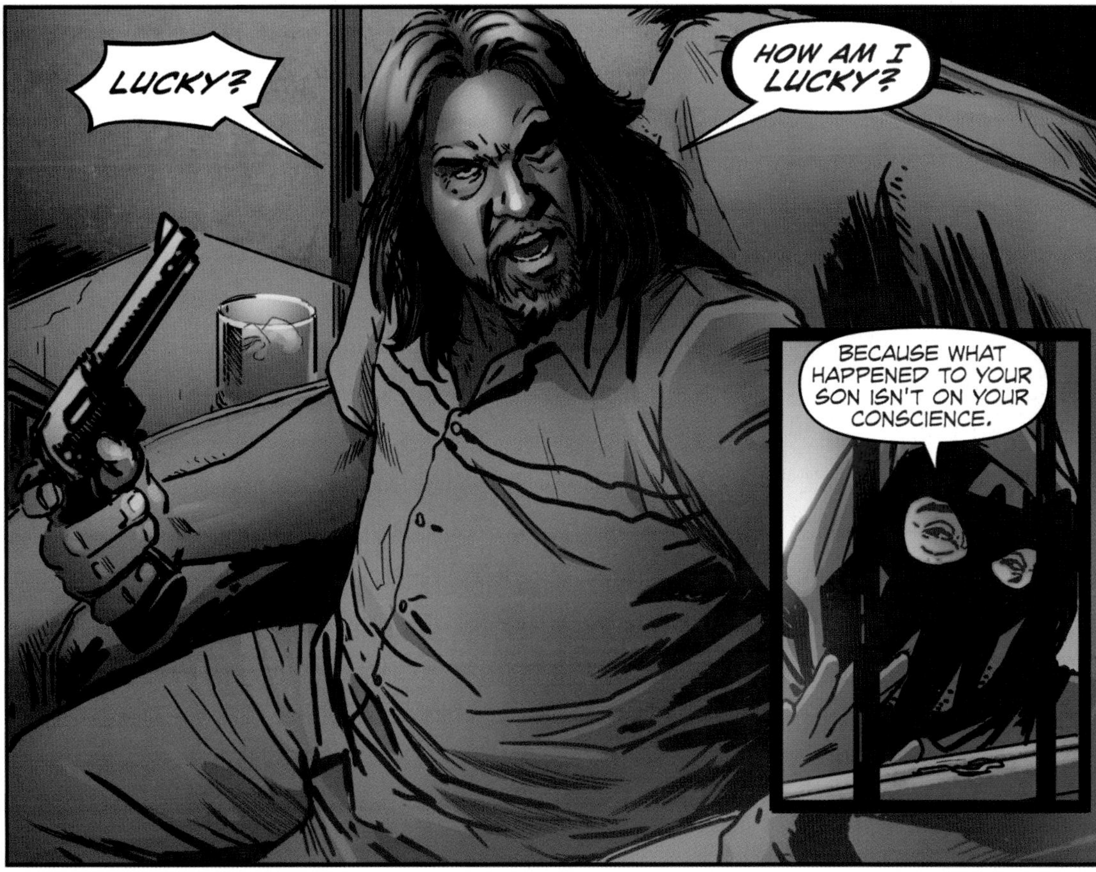
LUCKY?
HOW AM I LUCKY?
BECAUSE WHAT HAPPENED TO YOUR SON ISN'T ON YOUR CONSCIENCE.

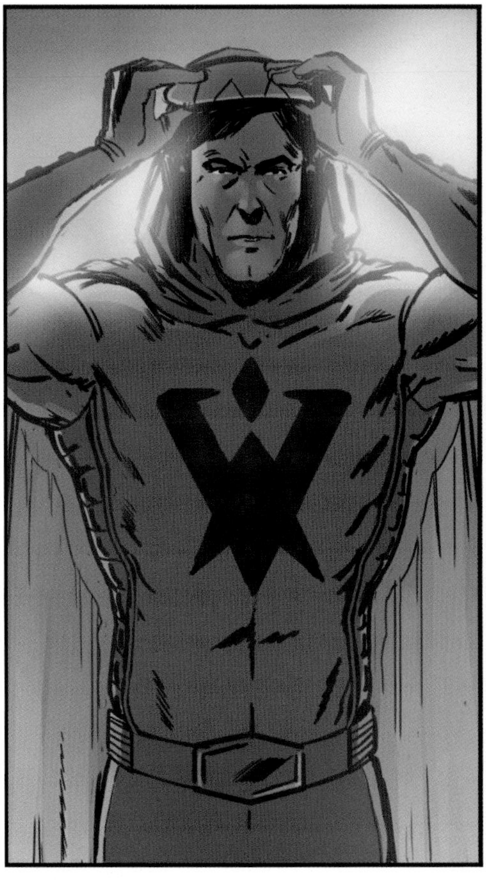

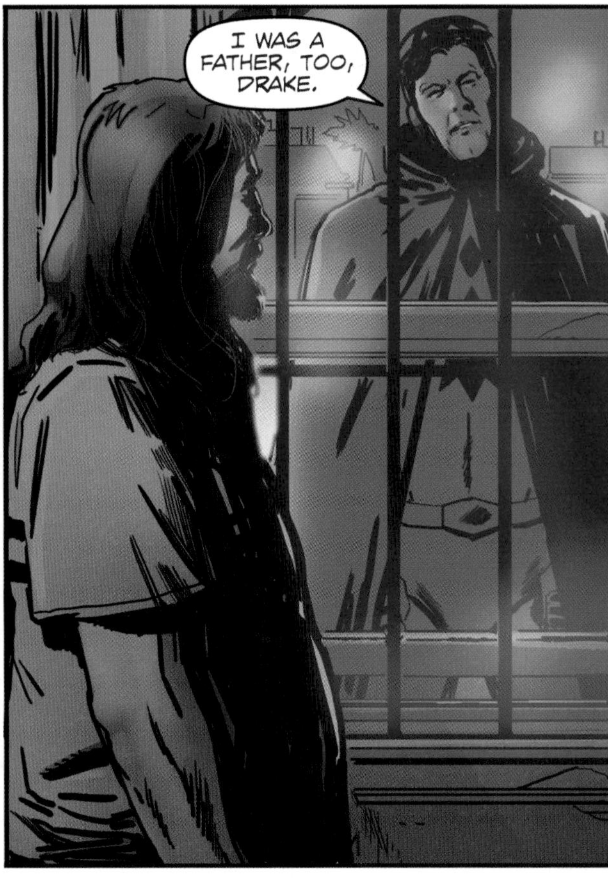
I WAS A FATHER, TOO, DRAKE.

AND I KNOW WHAT YOU'RE GOING THROUGH.

I LOST MY *WIFE* IN A CAR ACCIDENT YEARS AGO. NEARLY KILLED ME. LIKE YOU, I HAD A LOVED ONE WHOSE ABSENCE JUST DESTROYED ME.

AND AS AWFUL AS THAT WAS, I CAN VOUCH THAT THERE'S NOTHING WORSE THAN LOSING YOUR ONLY CHILD.

THAN NOT HAVING HIM IN YOUR LIFE ANYMORE.

I'M SORRY THAT YOUR BOY IS GONE.

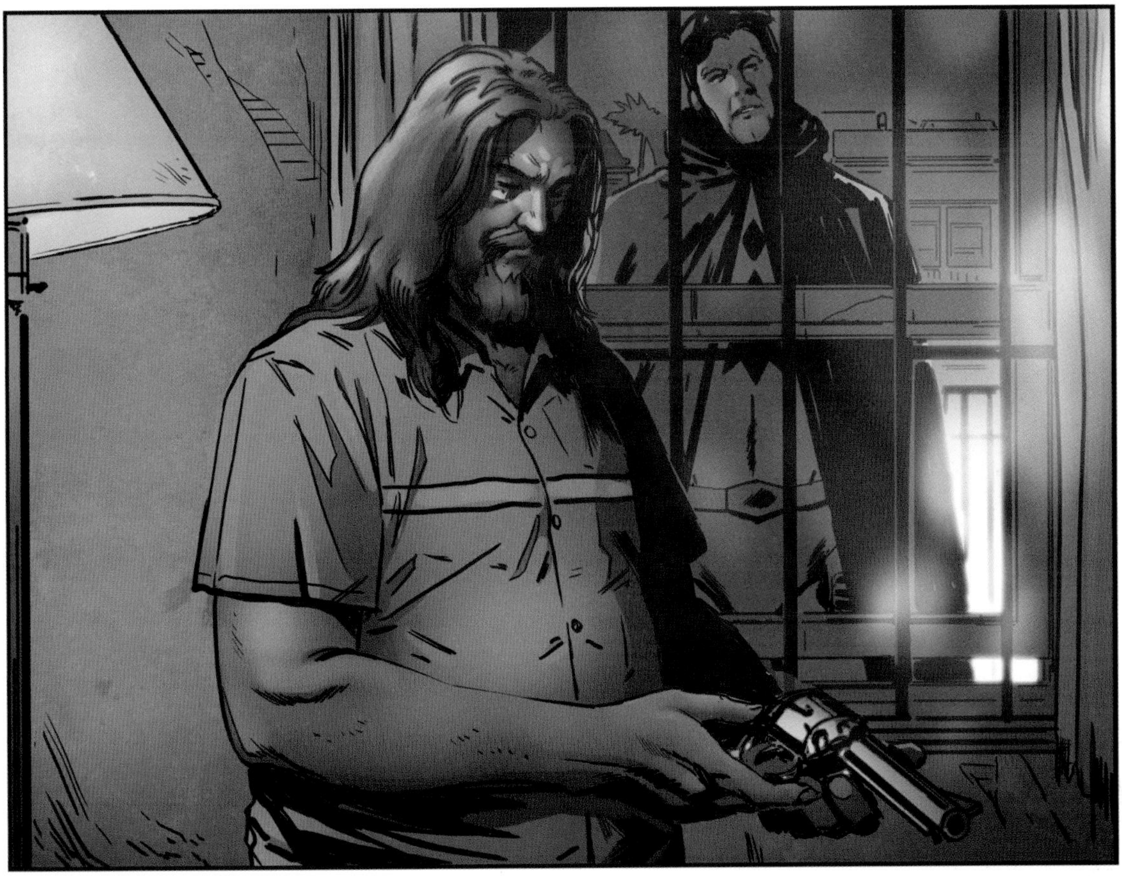

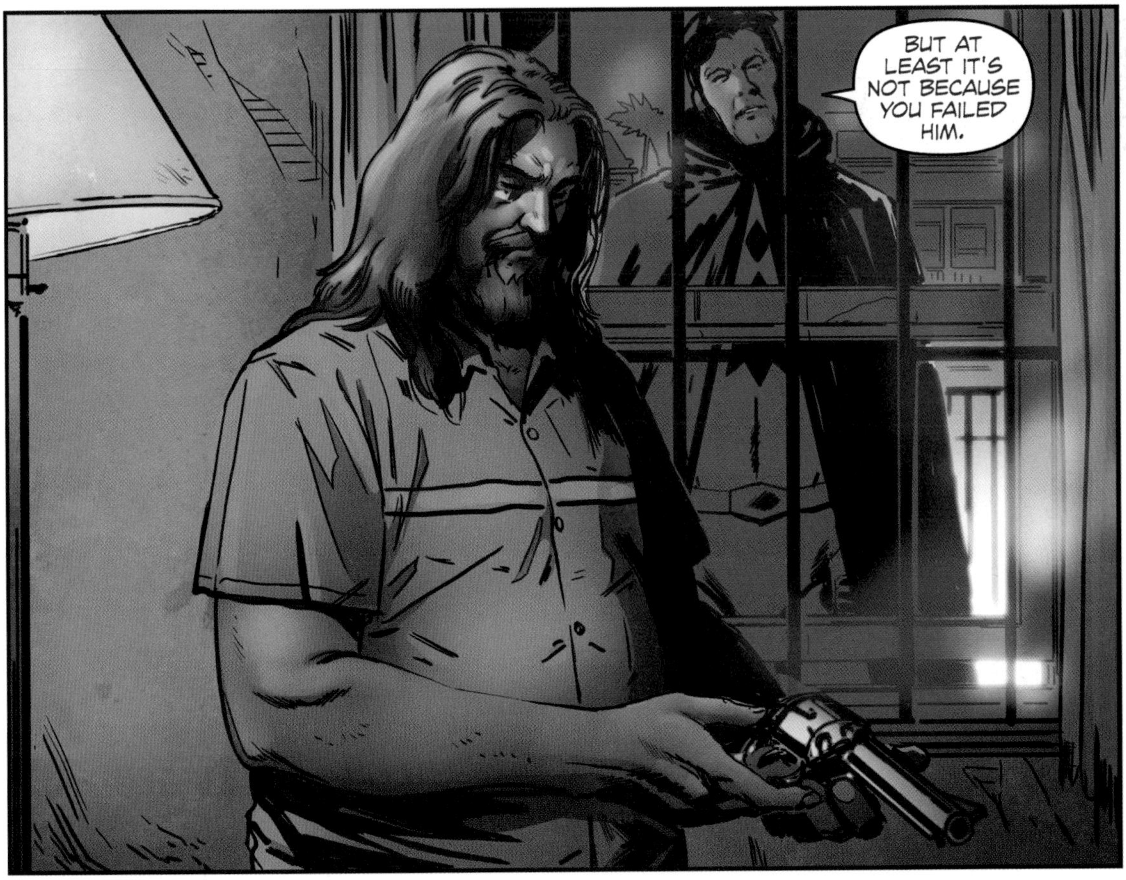
BUT AT LEAST IT'S NOT BECAUSE YOU FAILED HIM.

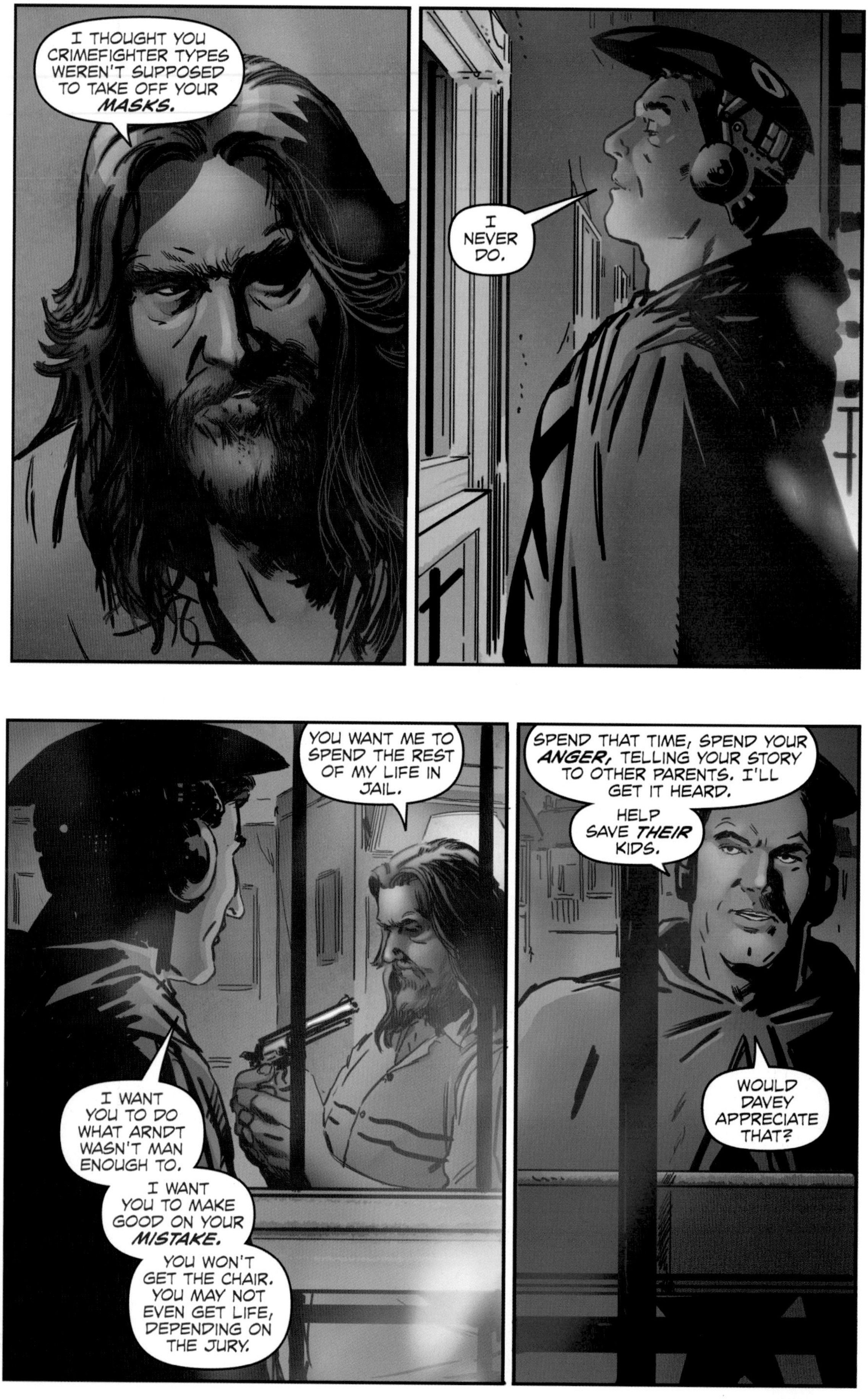

I THOUGHT YOU CRIMEFIGHTER TYPES WEREN'T SUPPOSED TO TAKE OFF YOUR MASKS.
I NEVER DO.
YOU WANT ME TO SPEND THE REST OF MY LIFE IN JAIL.
I WANT YOU TO DO WHAT ARNDT WASN'T MAN ENOUGH TO.
I WANT YOU TO MAKE GOOD ON YOUR MISTAKE.
YOU WON'T GET THE CHAIR. YOU MAY NOT EVEN GET LIFE, DEPENDING ON THE JURY.
SPEND THAT TIME, SPEND YOUR ANGER, TELLING YOUR STORY TO OTHER PARENTS. I'LL GET IT HEARD.
HELP SAVE THEIR KIDS.
WOULD DAVEY APPRECIATE THAT?

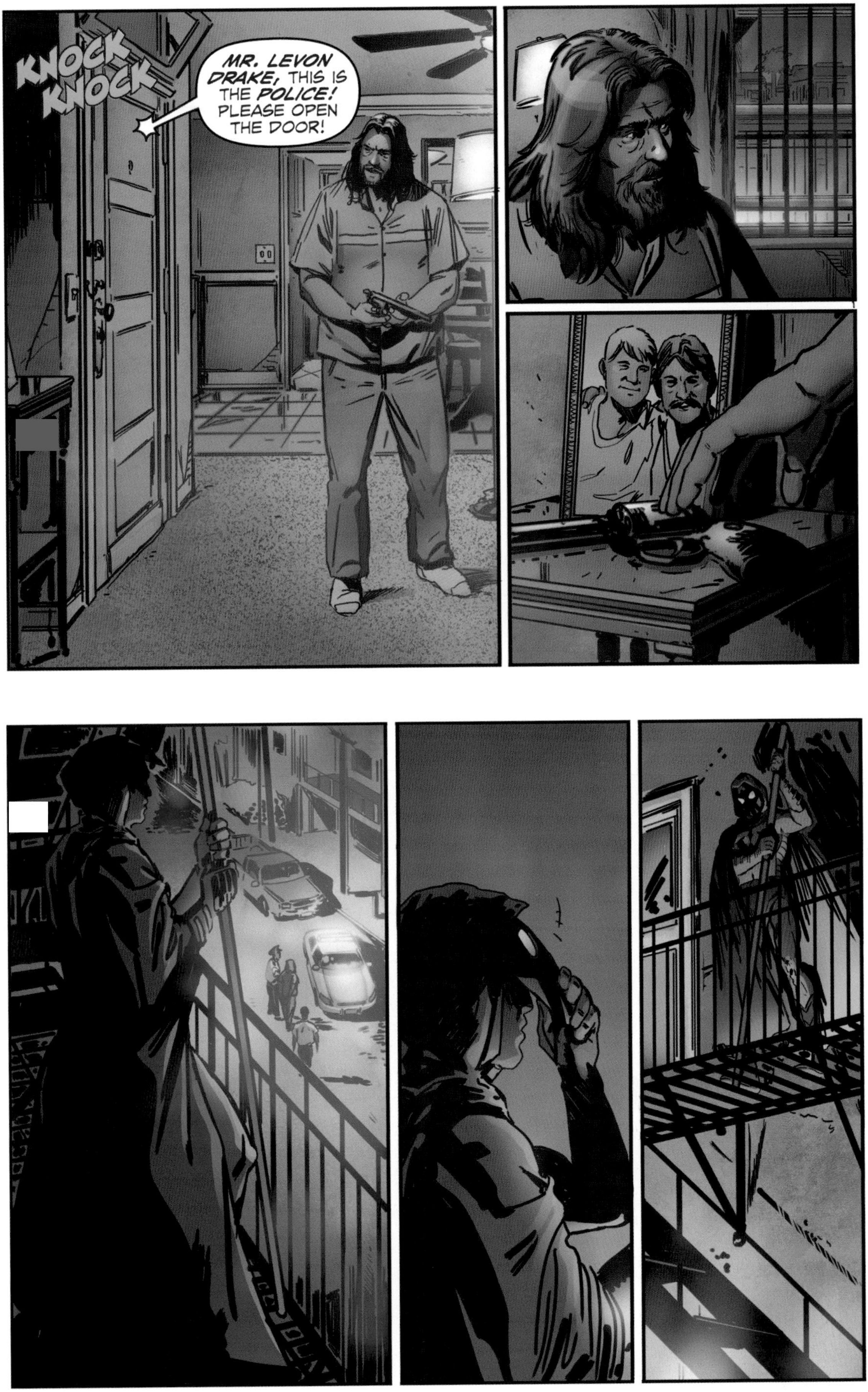
KNOCK KNOCK
MR. LEVON DRAKE, THIS IS THE POLICE! PLEASE OPEN THE DOOR!

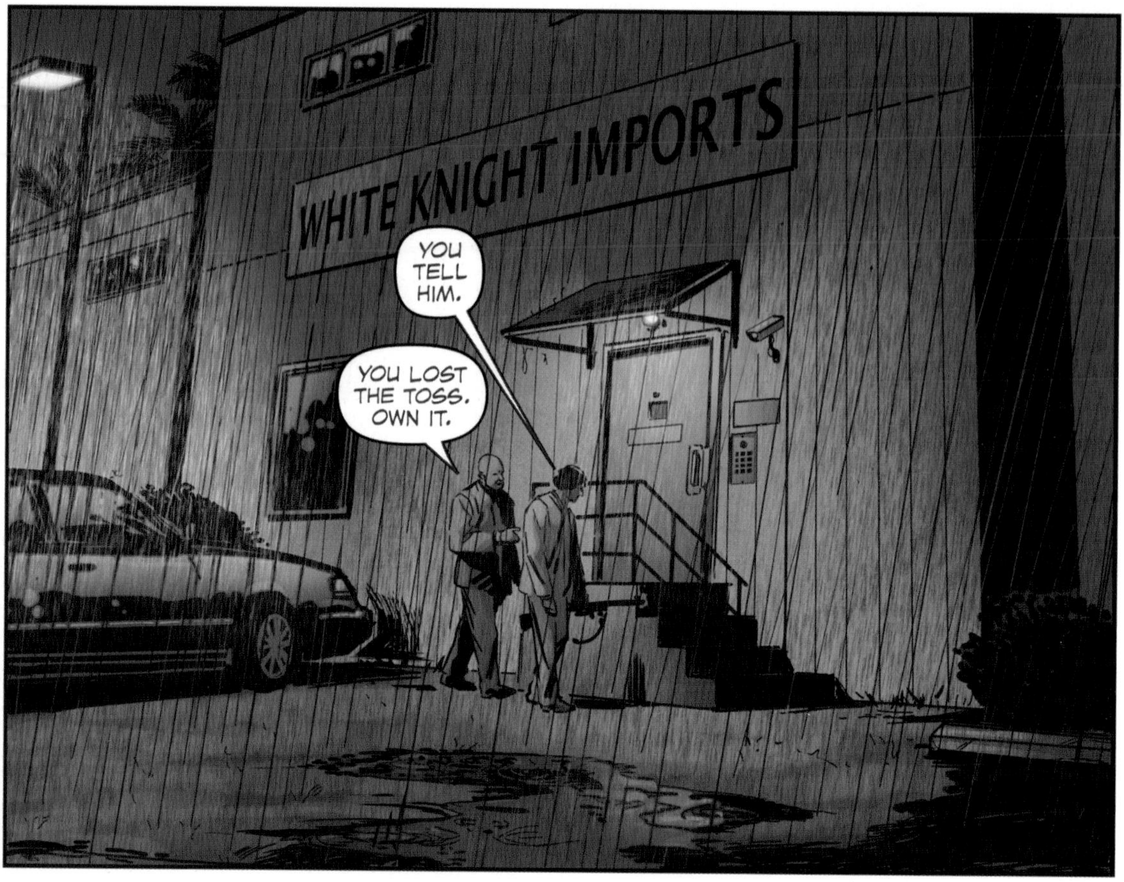
WHITE KNIGHT IMPORTS
YOU TELL HIM.
YOU LOST THE TOSS. OWN IT.

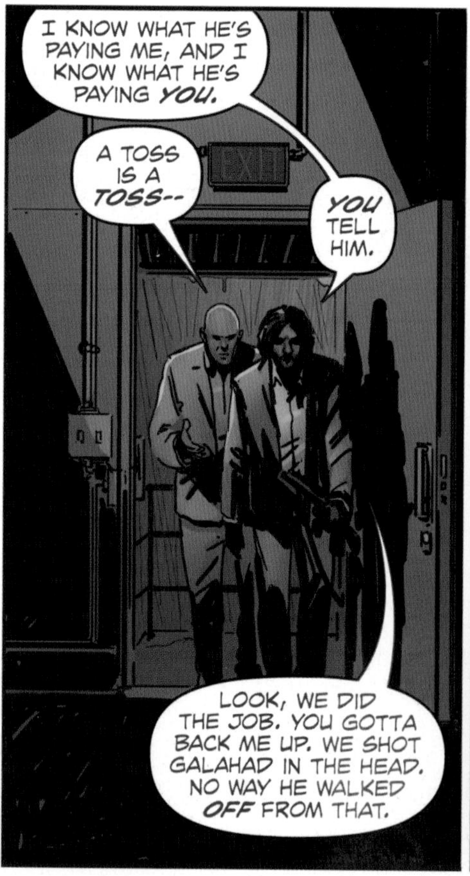
I KNOW WHAT HE'S PAYING ME, AND I KNOW WHAT HE'S PAYING *YOU.*
A TOSS IS A *TOSS--*
YOU TELL HIM.
LOOK, WE DID THE JOB. YOU GOTTA BACK ME UP. WE SHOT GALAHAD IN THE HEAD. NO WAY HE WALKED *OFF* FROM THAT.

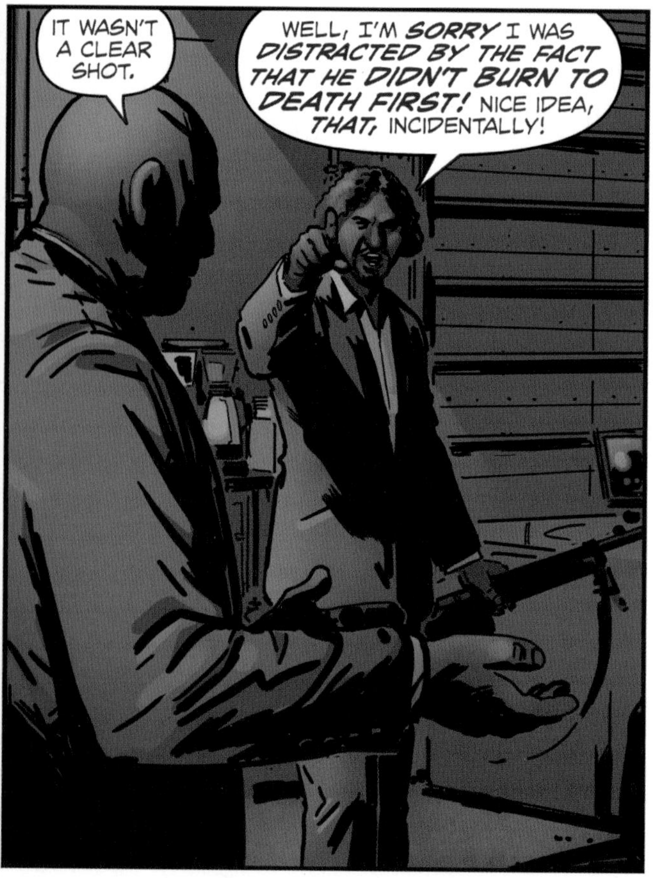
IT WASN'T A CLEAR SHOT.
WELL, I'M *SORRY* I WAS *DISTRACTED BY THE FACT THAT HE DIDN'T BURN TO DEATH FIRST!* NICE IDEA, *THAT,* INCIDENTALLY!

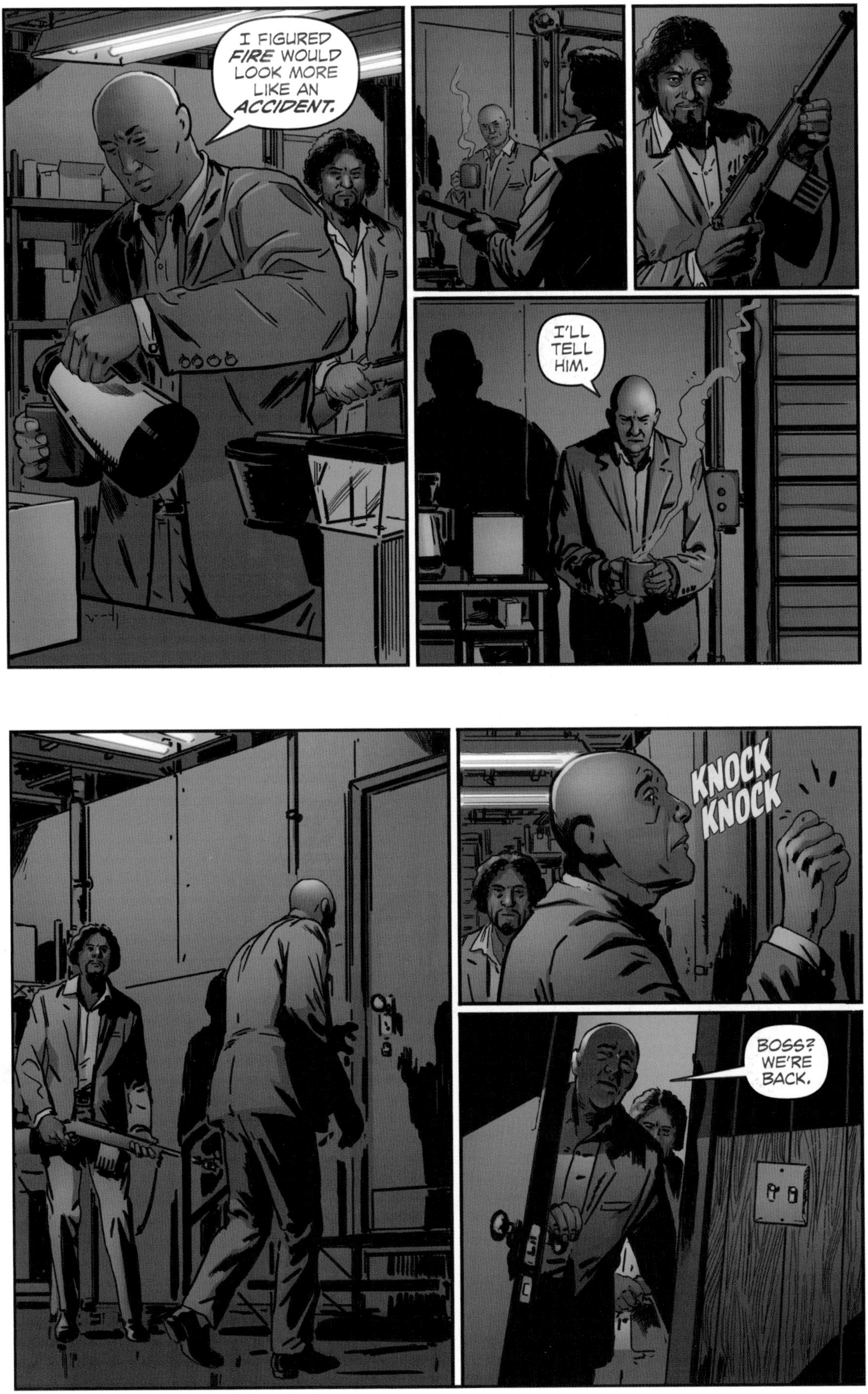

I FIGURED FIRE WOULD LOOK MORE LIKE AN ACCIDENT.
I'LL TELL HIM.
KNOCK KNOCK
BOSS? WE'RE BACK.

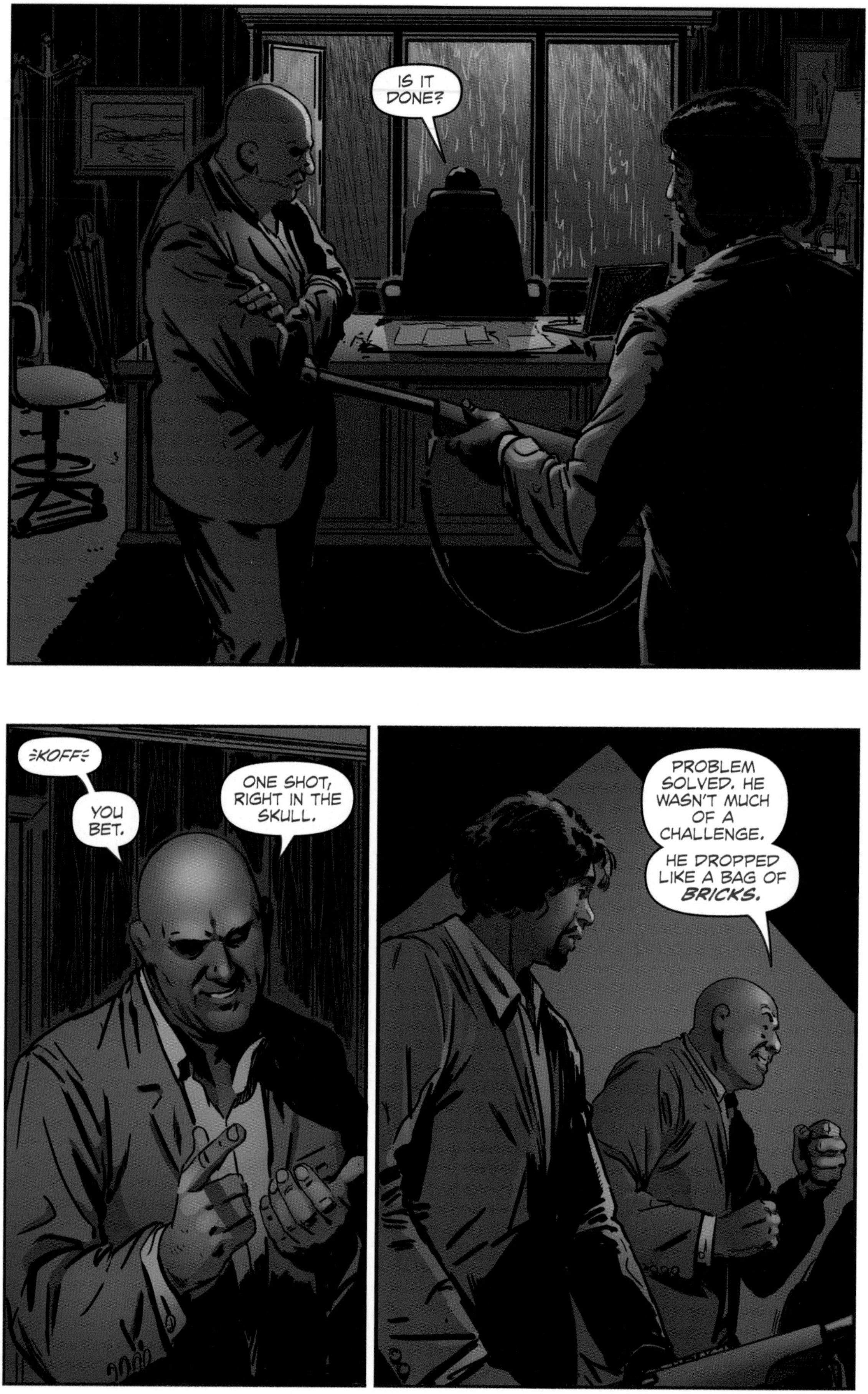
IS IT DONE?
≈KOFF≈
YOU BET.
ONE SHOT, RIGHT IN THE SKULL.
PROBLEM SOLVED. HE WASN'T MUCH OF A CHALLENGE.
HE DROPPED LIKE A BAG OF ***BRICKS.***

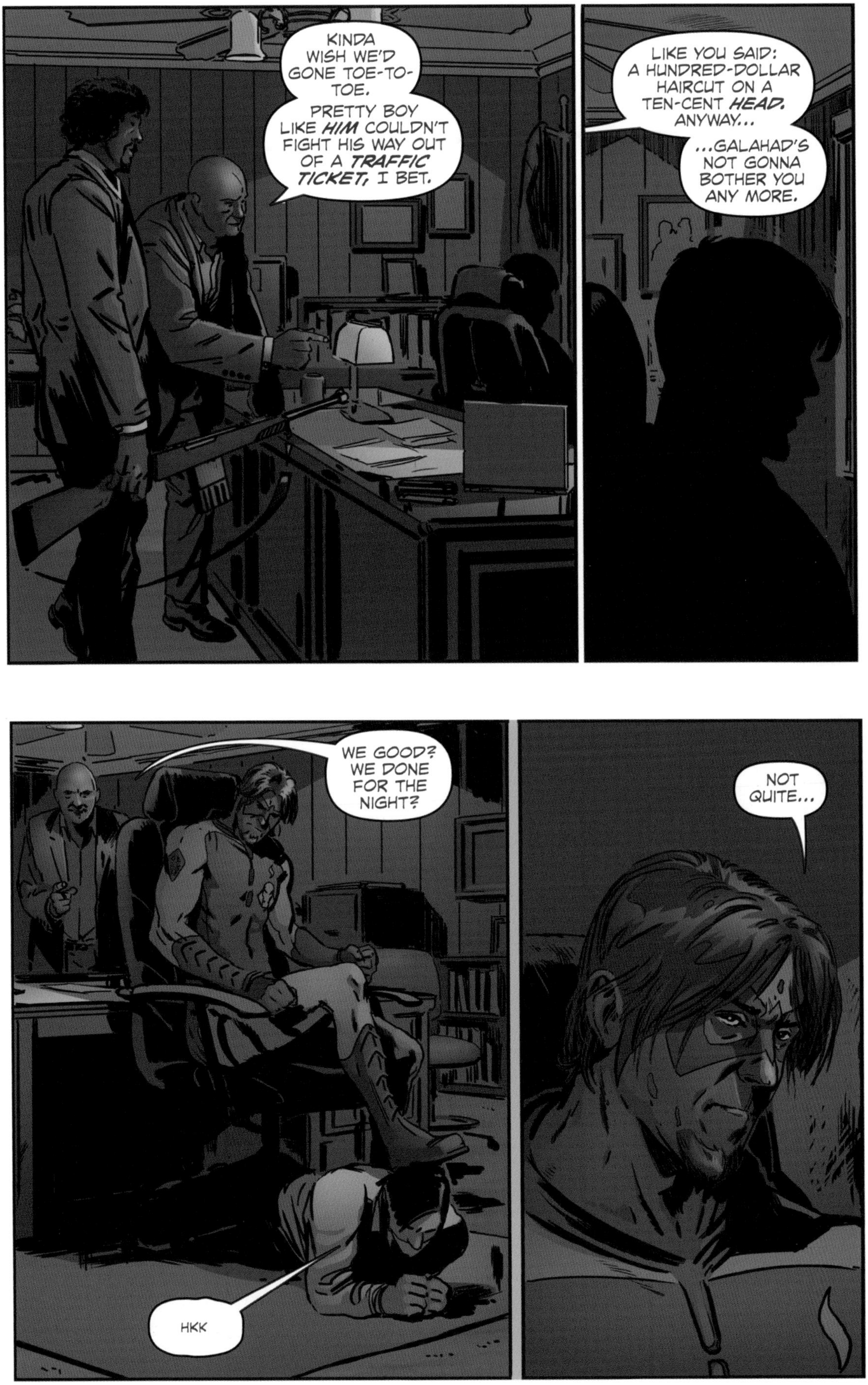
KINDA WISH WE'D GONE TOE-TO-TOE.
PRETTY BOY LIKE *HIM* COULDN'T FIGHT HIS WAY OUT OF A *TRAFFIC TICKET,* I BET.
LIKE YOU SAID: A HUNDRED-DOLLAR HAIRCUT ON A TEN-CENT *HEAD.* ANYWAY...
...GALAHAD'S NOT GONNA BOTHER YOU ANY MORE.
WE GOOD? WE DONE FOR THE NIGHT?
HKK
NOT QUITE...

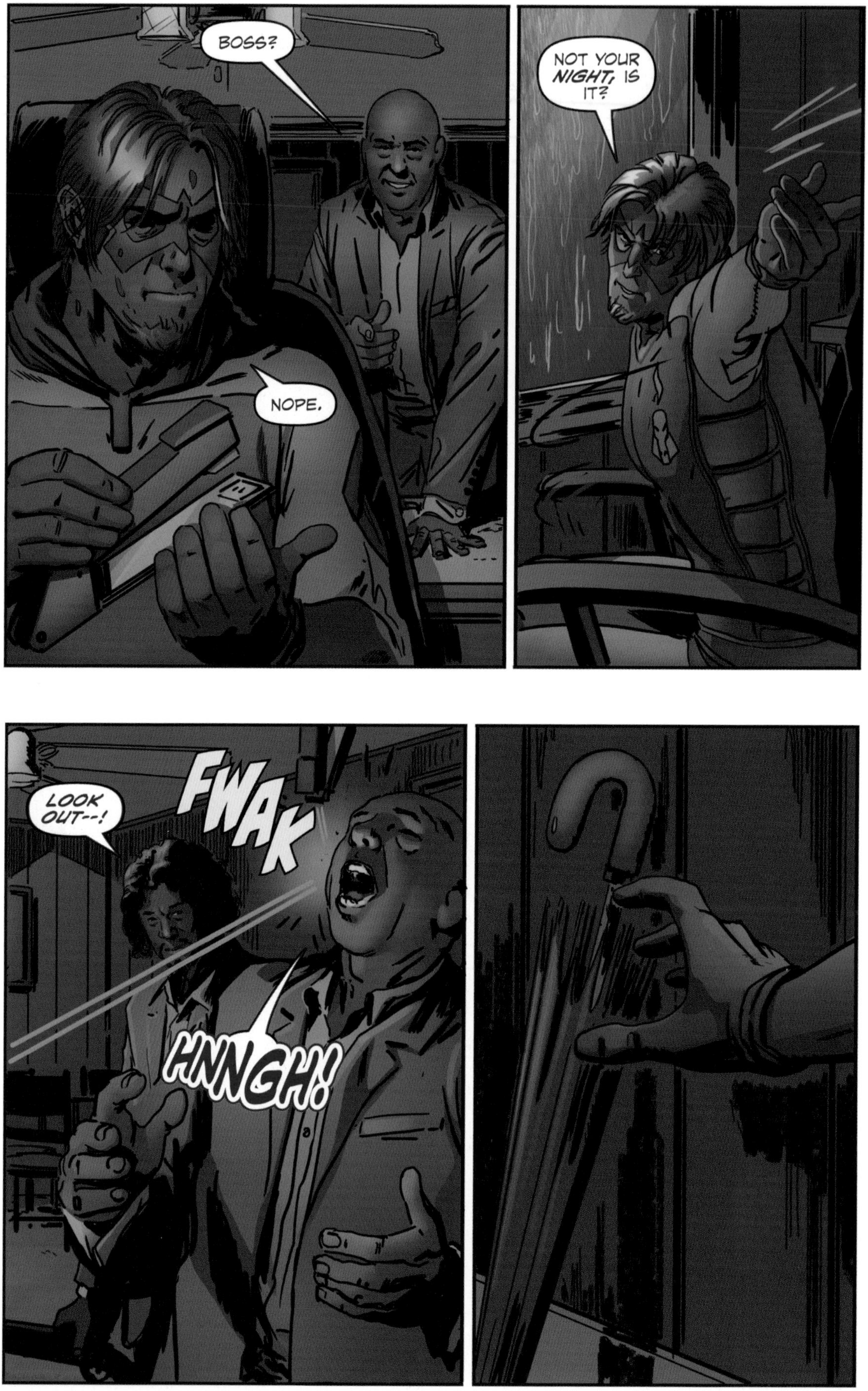
BOSS?
NOPE.
NOT YOUR NIGHT, IS IT?
LOOK OUT--!
FWAK
HNNGH!

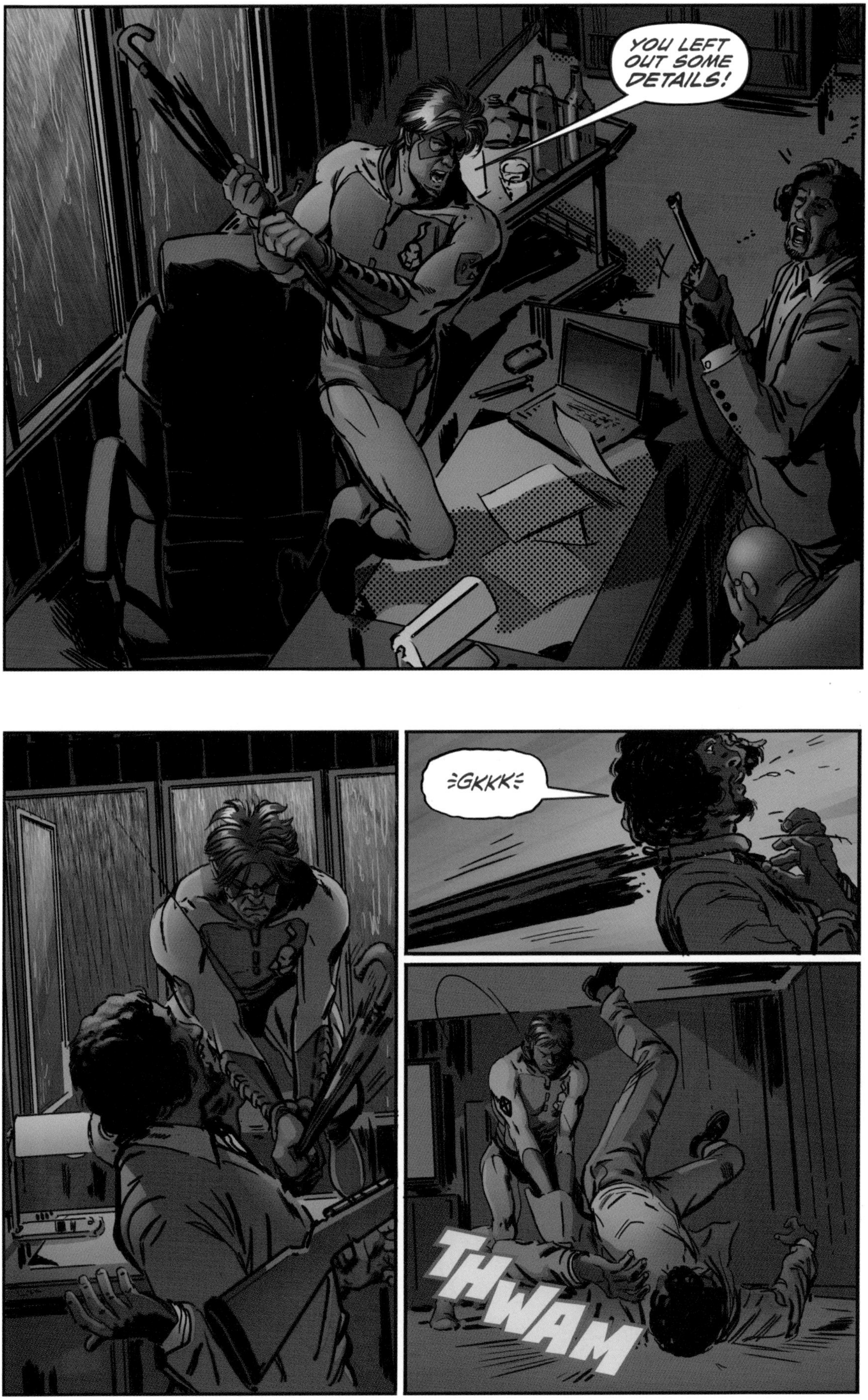
YOU LEFT OUT SOME DETAILS!
GKKK
THWAM

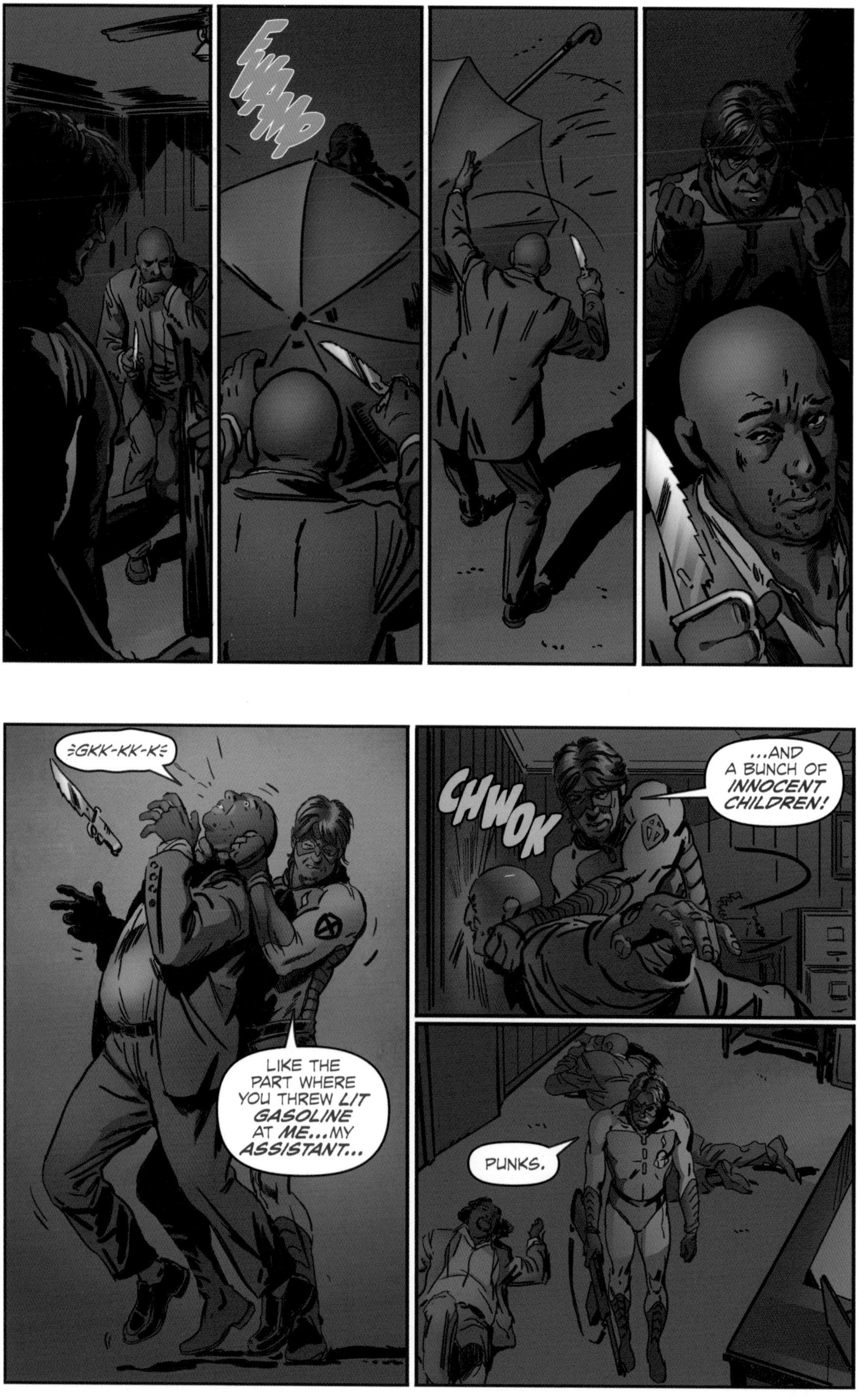

=GKK-KK-K=
LIKE THE PART WHERE YOU THREW *LIT GASOLINE* AT *ME*... MY *ASSISTANT*...
CHWOK
...AND A BUNCH OF *INNOCENT CHILDREN!*
PUNKS.

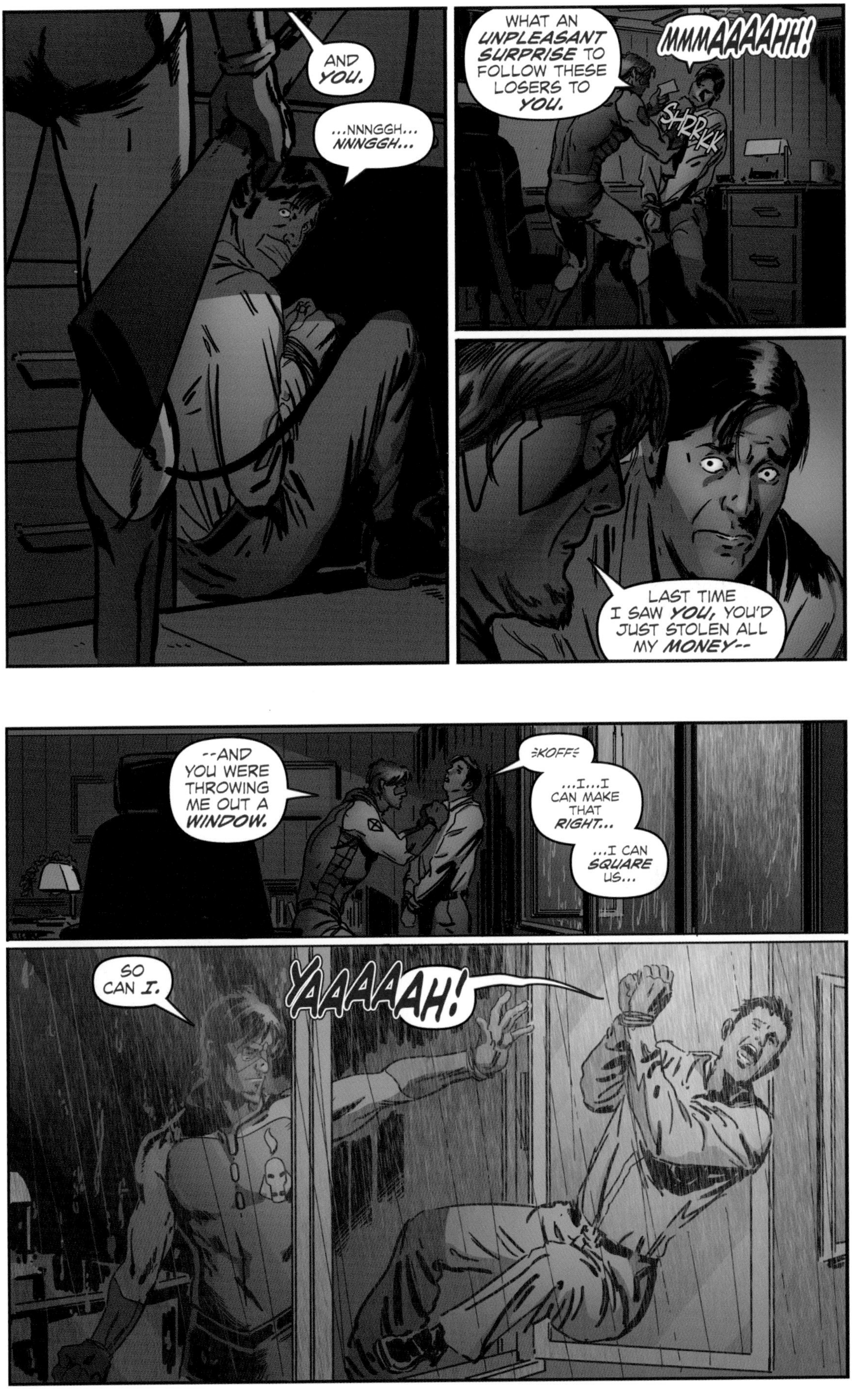
AND YOU.
...NNNGGH... NNNGGH...
WHAT AN UNPLEASANT SURPRISE TO FOLLOW THESE LOSERS TO YOU.
MMMAAAAHH!
SHRRKK
LAST TIME I SAW YOU, YOU'D JUST STOLEN ALL MY MONEY--
--AND YOU WERE THROWING ME OUT A WINDOW.
KOFF
...I...I CAN MAKE THAT RIGHT...
...I CAN SQUARE US...
SO CAN I.
YAAAAAH!

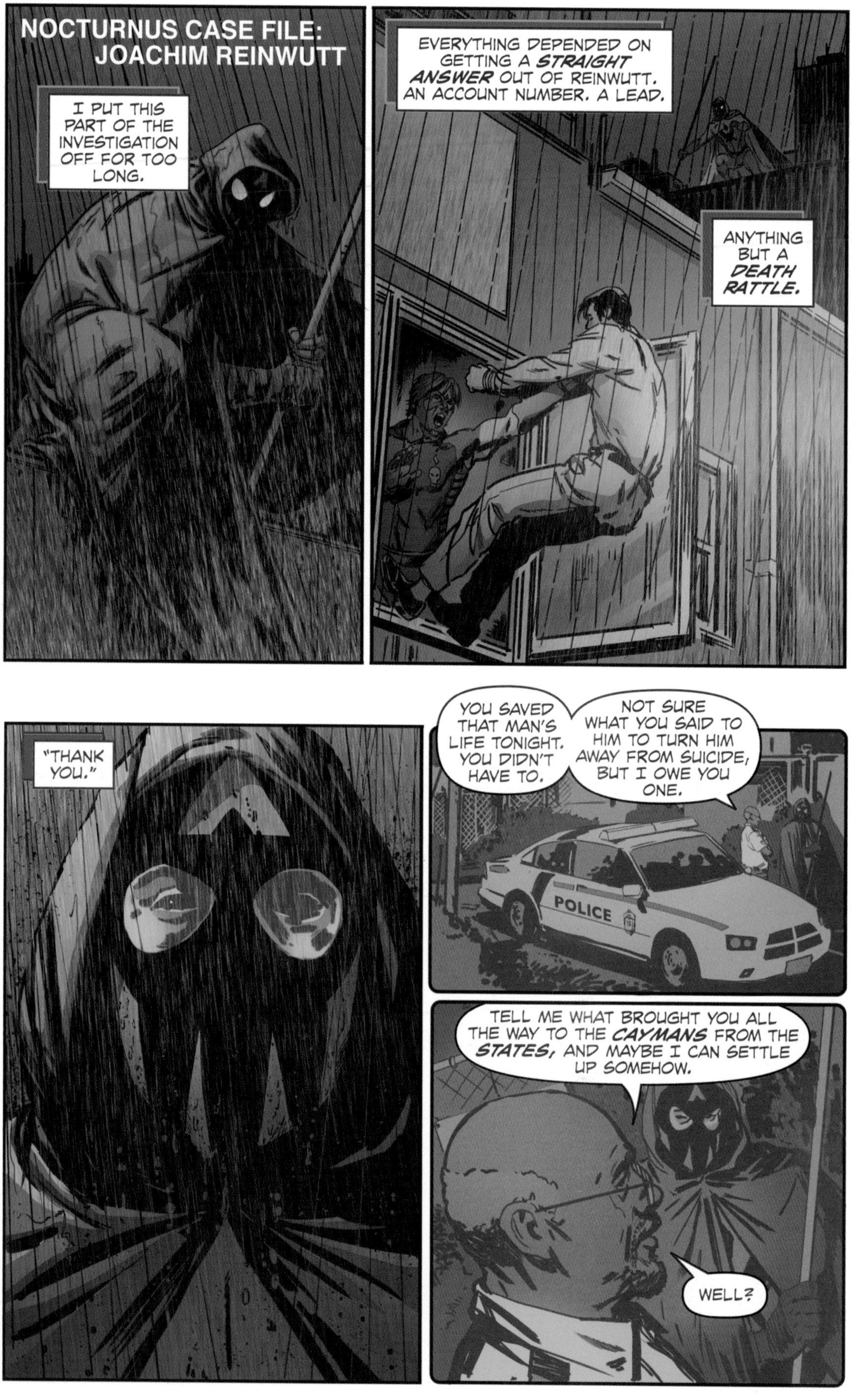
NOCTURNUS CASE FILE: JOACHIM REINWUTT
I PUT THIS PART OF THE INVESTIGATION OFF FOR TOO LONG.
EVERYTHING DEPENDED ON GETTING A STRAIGHT ANSWER OUT OF REINWUTT. AN ACCOUNT NUMBER. A LEAD.
ANYTHING BUT A DEATH RATTLE.
"THANK YOU."
YOU SAVED THAT MAN'S LIFE TONIGHT. YOU DIDN'T HAVE TO.
NOT SURE WHAT YOU SAID TO HIM TO TURN HIM AWAY FROM SUICIDE, BUT I OWE YOU ONE.
POLICE
TELL ME WHAT BROUGHT YOU ALL THE WAY TO THE CAYMANS FROM THE STATES, AND MAYBE I CAN SETTLE UP SOMEHOW.
WELL?

MY SON.

EXCUSE ME?

MY *SON.*

WE'RE HERE TO TRACK HIS STOLEN FORTUNE, BUT I'VE BEEN AVOIDING HIM.

BECAUSE...?

BECAUSE I DON'T WANT TO TELL HIM I CAN'T FOLLOW THE *MONEY TRAIL.*

I WOULD HAVE, IN MY PRIME. THESE DAYS, THOUGH, IT'S ALL ELECTRONICS AND KEYSTROKES.

I'M LOST.

LET ME HELP. WHAT CAN YOU TELL ME ABOUT THE THIEVES?

THIEF. THE SON OF ONE OF MY OLD ENEMIES.

KID NAMED JOACHIM REINWUTT.

SET HIMSELF UP AS GALAHAD'S OPERATIONS MANAGER, THEN STOLE EVERY CENT, FLED ON THE 27TH, I THINK *HERE.*

OKAY. HERE'S THE IMMIGRATION DATABASE FROM THAT DAY.

SEE IF THERE'S A FAMILIAR FACE BEFORE THEY FIND OUT I'M *IN* HERE.

"JACOB WHITE." THAT'S HIM. LOCAL CONTACT ADDRESS AND EVERYTHING.

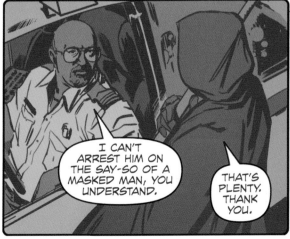

I CAN'T ARREST HIM ON THE SAY-SO OF A MASKED MAN, YOU UNDERSTAND.

THAT'S PLENTY. THANK YOU.

YOU *OR* YOUR SON GIVE ME ANYTHING *LEGIT* TO *BUST* HIM ON... *ANYTHING*...AND I'LL HAVE YOUR BACKS.

BUT LET YOUR KID KNOW, WITHOUT *RESERVATION*...

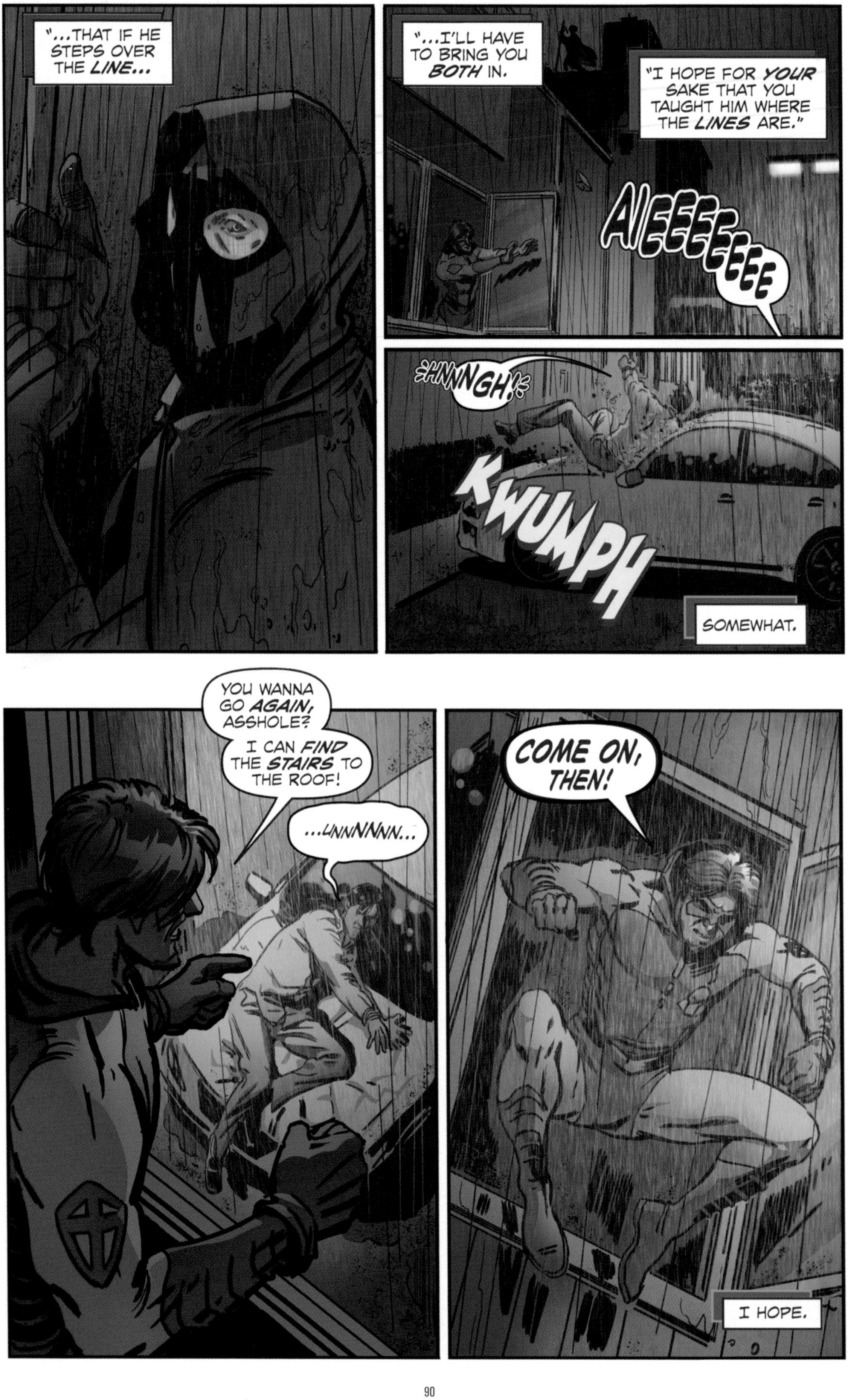
"...THAT IF HE STEPS OVER THE LINE...
"...I'LL HAVE TO BRING YOU BOTH IN.
"I HOPE FOR YOUR SAKE THAT YOU TAUGHT HIM WHERE THE LINES ARE."
AIEEEEEEEE
HNNNGH!!
KWUMPH
SOMEWHAT.
YOU WANNA GO AGAIN, ASSHOLE?
I CAN FIND THE STAIRS TO THE ROOF!
...UNNNNNN...
COME ON, THEN!
I HOPE.

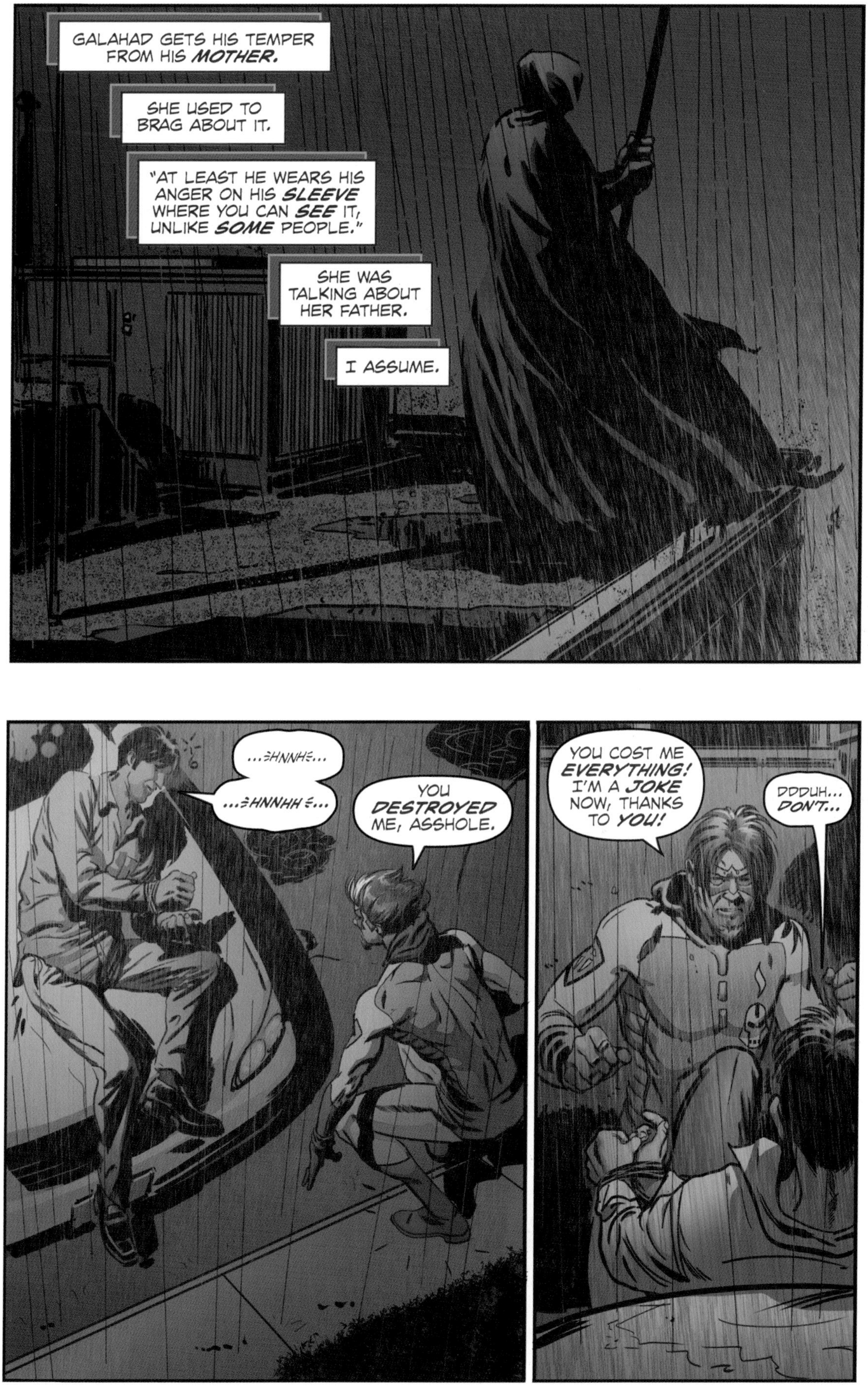
GALAHAD GETS HIS TEMPER FROM HIS *MOTHER.*
SHE USED TO BRAG ABOUT IT.
"AT LEAST HE WEARS HIS ANGER ON HIS *SLEEVE* WHERE YOU CAN *SEE* IT, UNLIKE *SOME* PEOPLE."
SHE WAS TALKING ABOUT HER FATHER.
I ASSUME.
...HNNH...
...HNNHH...
YOU *DESTROYED* ME, ASSHOLE.
YOU COST ME *EVERYTHING!* I'M A *JOKE* NOW, THANKS TO *YOU!*
DDDUH... *DON'T...*

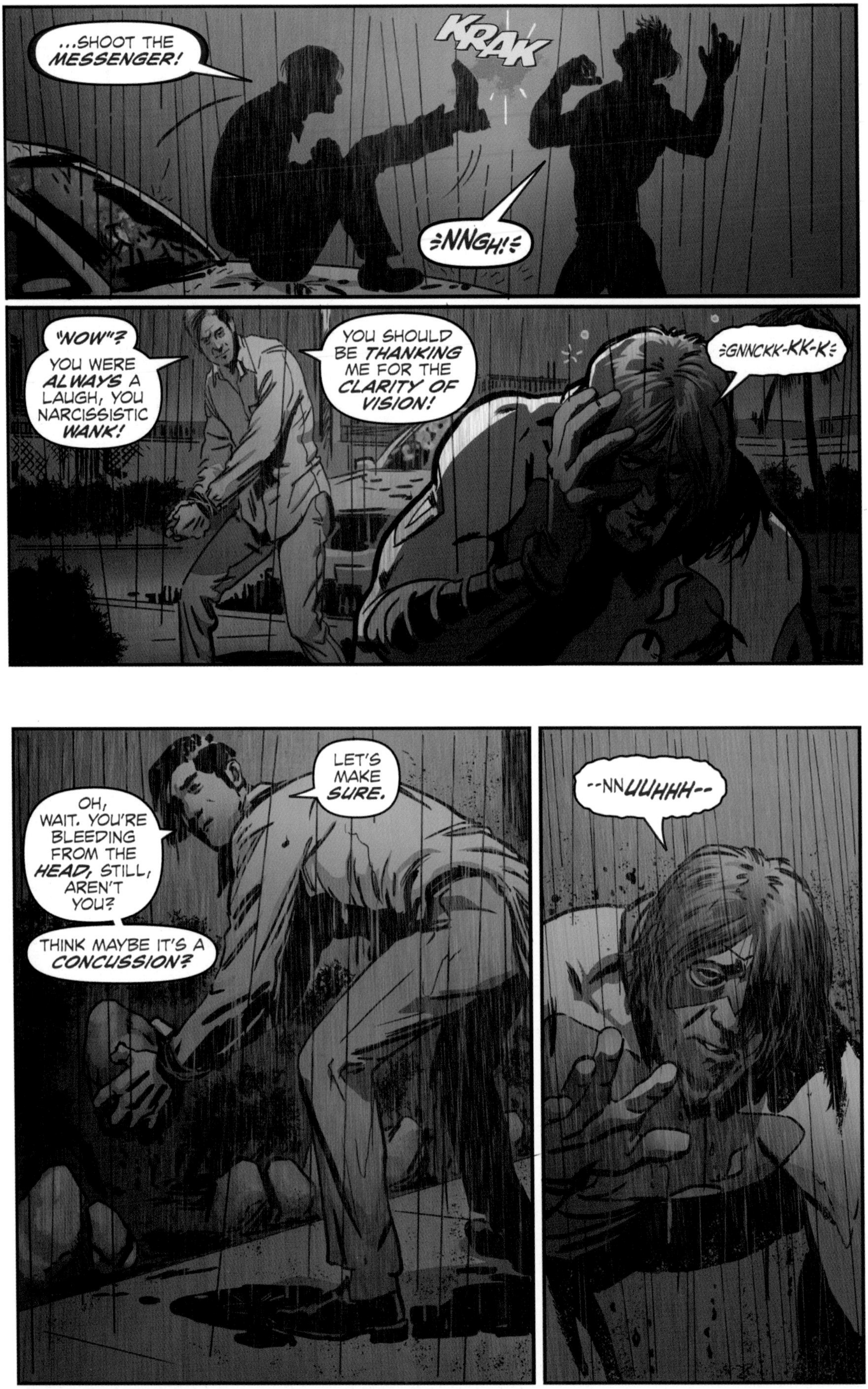
...SHOOT THE MESSENGER!
KRAK
NNGH!
"NOW"? YOU WERE ALWAYS A LAUGH, YOU NARCISSISTIC WANK!
YOU SHOULD BE THANKING ME FOR THE CLARITY OF VISION!
GNNCKK-KK-K
OH, WAIT. YOU'RE BLEEDING FROM THE HEAD, STILL, AREN'T YOU?
THINK MAYBE IT'S A CONCUSSION?
LET'S MAKE SURE.
--NNUUHHH--

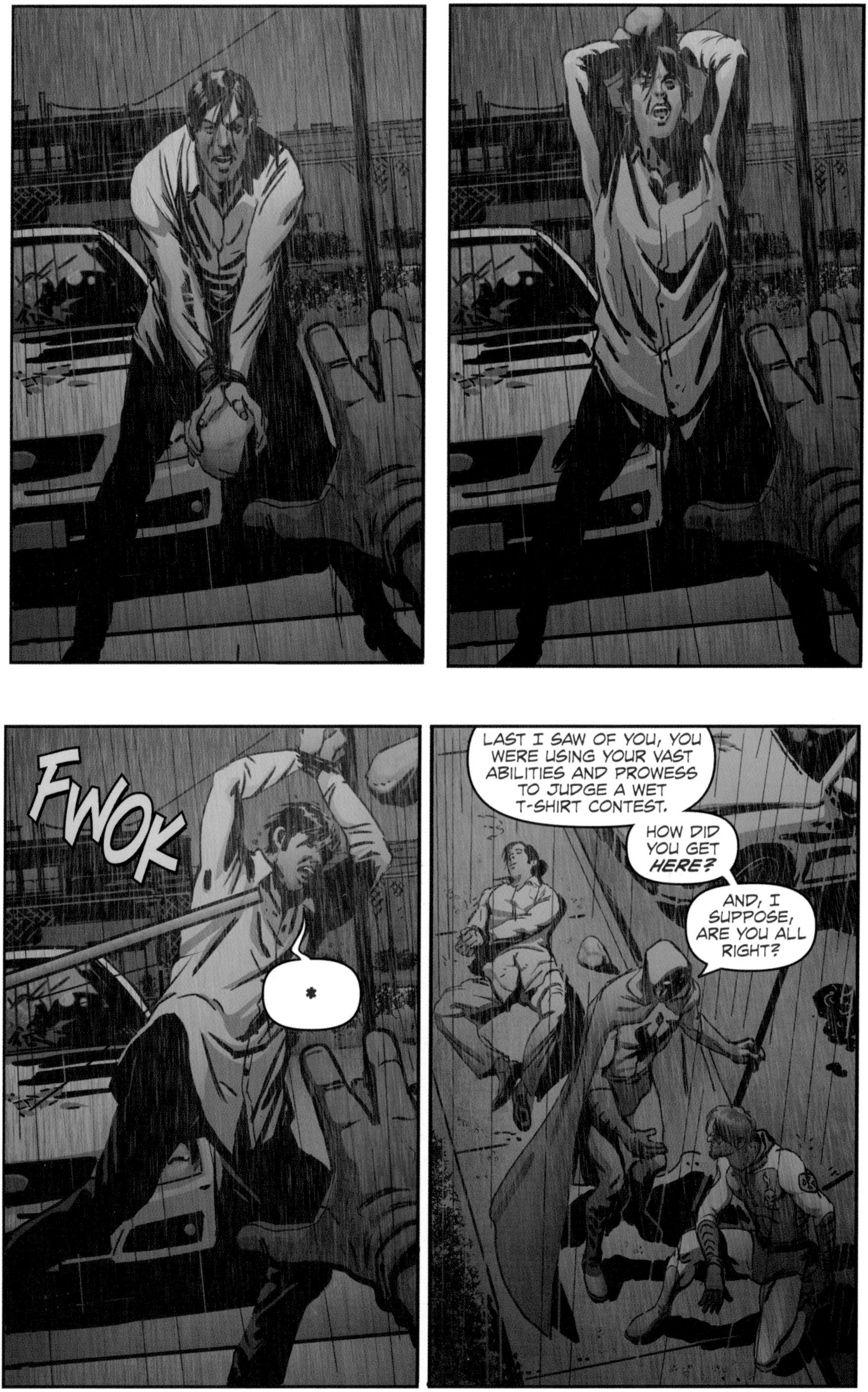
FWOK
*
LAST I SAW OF YOU, YOU WERE USING YOUR VAST ABILITIES AND PROWESS TO JUDGE A WET T-SHIRT CONTEST.
HOW DID YOU GET HERE?
AND, I SUPPOSE, ARE YOU ALL RIGHT?

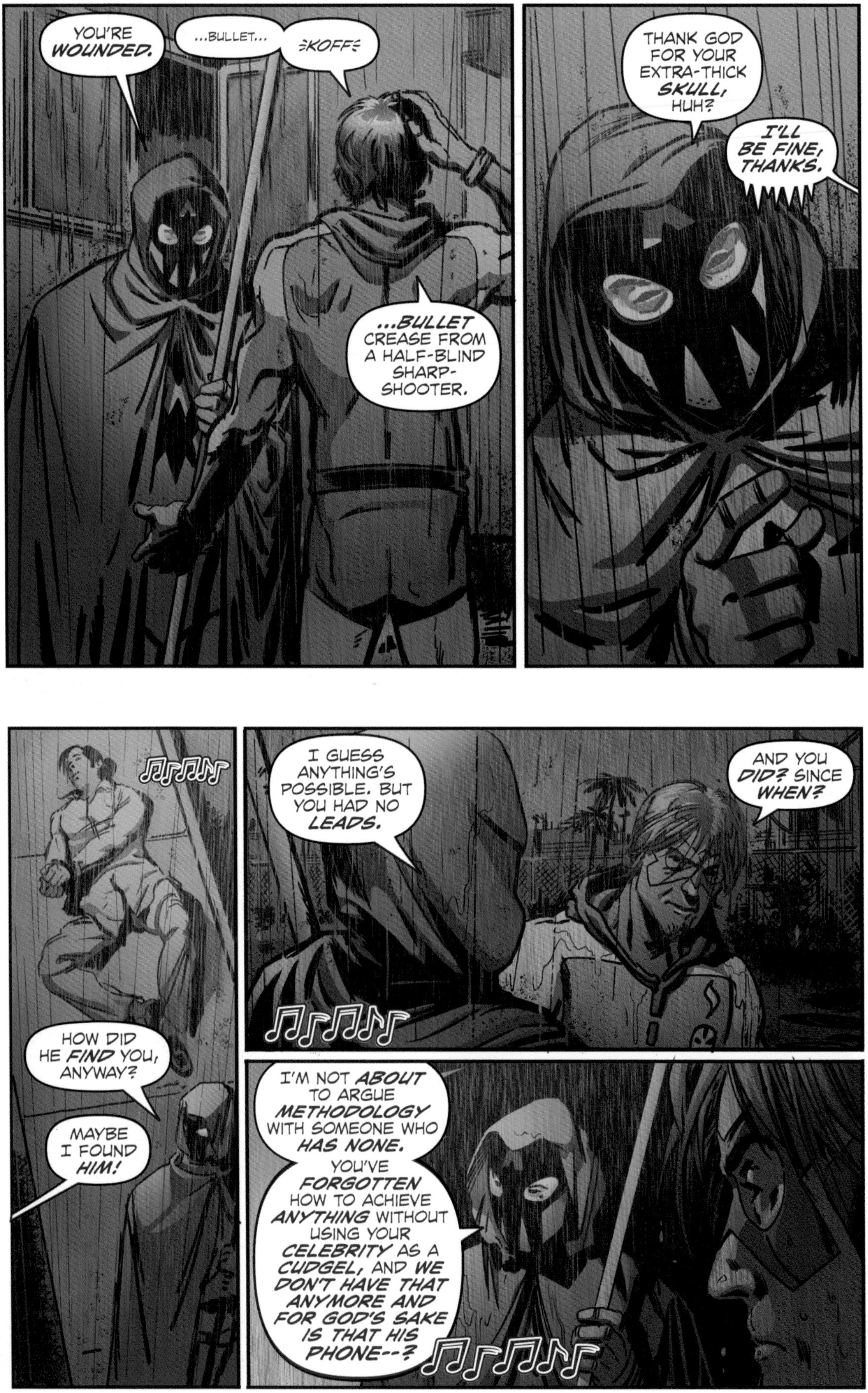
YOU'RE WOUNDED.
...BULLET...
≡KOFF≡
...BULLET CREASE FROM A HALF-BLIND SHARP-SHOOTER.
THANK GOD FOR YOUR EXTRA-THICK SKULL, HUH?
I'LL BE FINE, THANKS.
HOW DID HE FIND YOU, ANYWAY?
MAYBE I FOUND HIM!
I GUESS ANYTHING'S POSSIBLE. BUT YOU HAD NO LEADS.
AND YOU DID? SINCE WHEN?
I'M NOT ABOUT TO ARGUE METHODOLOGY WITH SOMEONE WHO HAS NONE.
YOU'VE FORGOTTEN HOW TO ACHIEVE ANYTHING WITHOUT USING YOUR CELEBRITY AS A CUDGEL, AND WE DON'T HAVE THAT ANYMORE AND FOR GOD'S SAKE IS THAT HIS PHONE--?

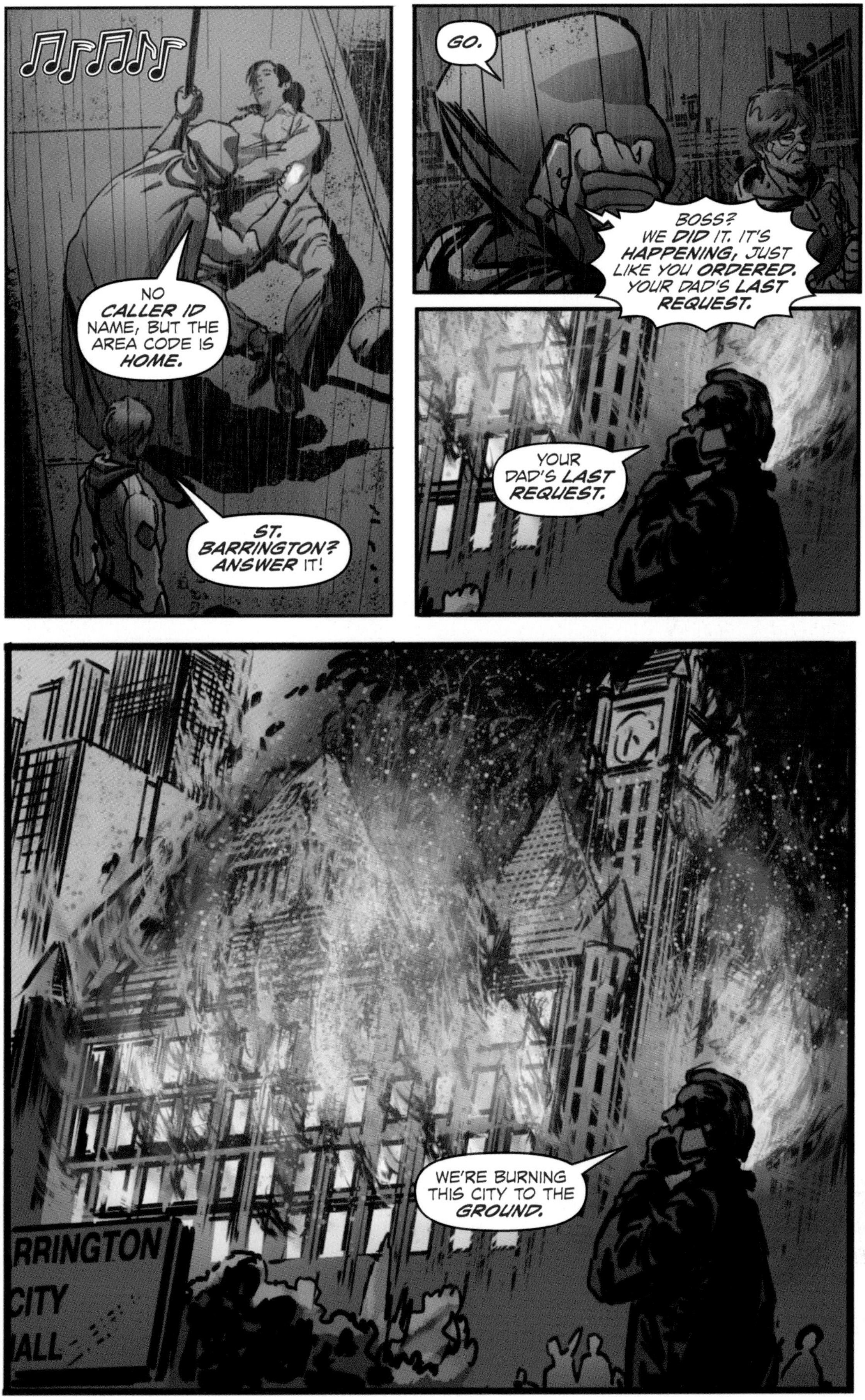
NO CALLER ID NAME, BUT THE AREA CODE IS HOME.
ST. BARRINGTON? ANSWER IT!
GO.
BOSS? WE DID IT. IT'S HAPPENING, JUST LIKE YOU ORDERED. YOUR DAD'S LAST REQUEST.
YOUR DAD'S LAST REQUEST.
RRINGTON
CITY
ALL
WE'RE BURNING THIS CITY TO THE GROUND.

CHAPTER 5

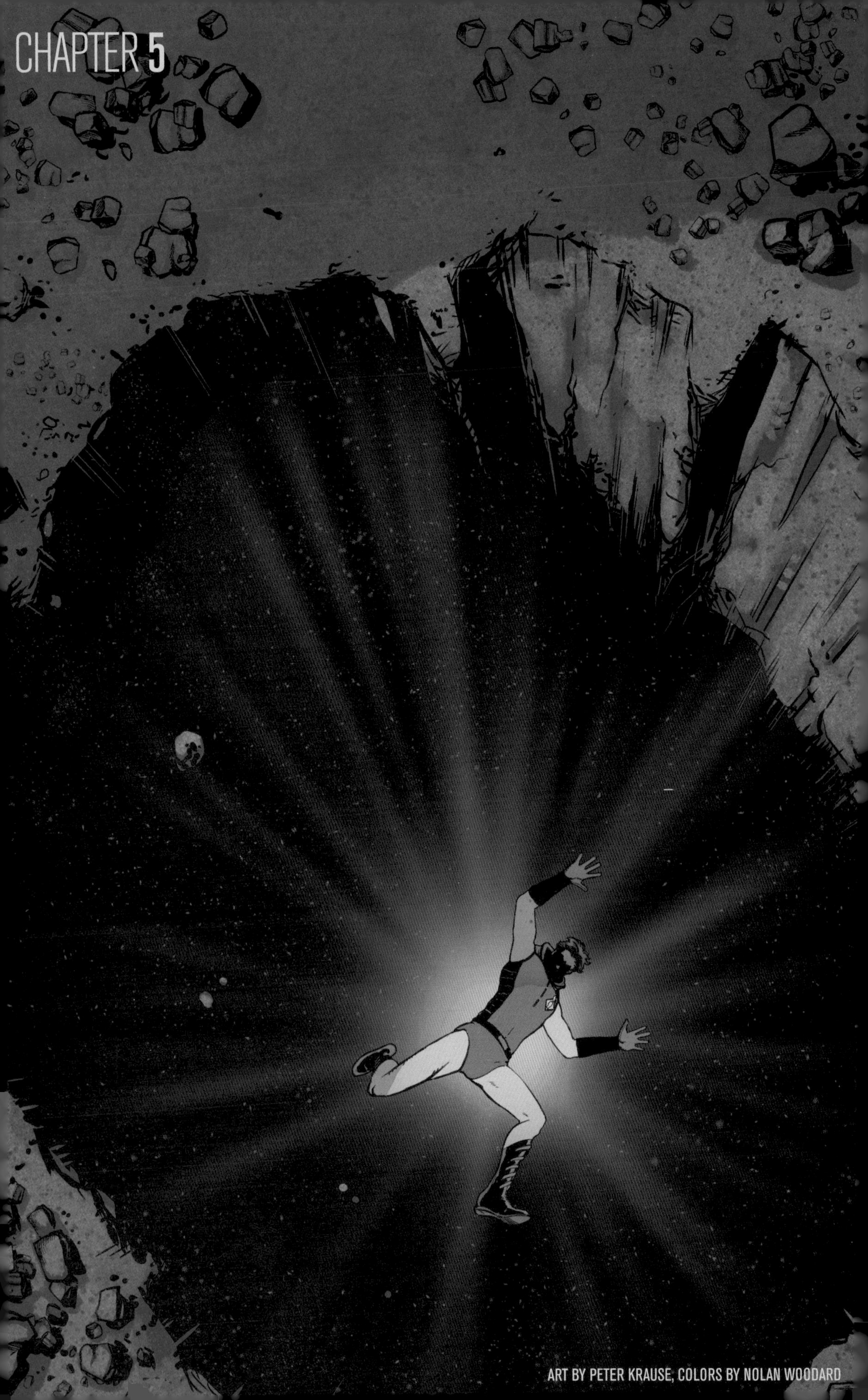

ART BY PETER KRAUSE, COLORS BY NOLAN WOODARD

I'M SORRY, DAD.

WE BOTH DIED FOR NOTHING, DIDN'T WE...? YOU TRIED TO TAKE THEIR LIVES AND I REALLY DID TAKE THEIR FORTUNE.

I'M GOING TO OPEN MY EYES IN HELL.

EXCEPT...

...EXCEPT WHAT I SMELL AROUND ME AS I WAKE ISN'T THE STINK OF BRIMSTONE.

WHAT I HEAR ISN'T THE SCREAMS OF THE DAMNED. NOT EXACTLY.

BUT KIND OF.

I KNOW THE VOICES.

NOCTURNUS IS SCREAMING AT GALAHAD.

GALAHAD IS SCREAMING AT NOCTURNUS

LIKE THEY COULD GO ON FOR HOURS.

OH, DAD...THIS ISN'T HELL.

IT'S HEAVEN.

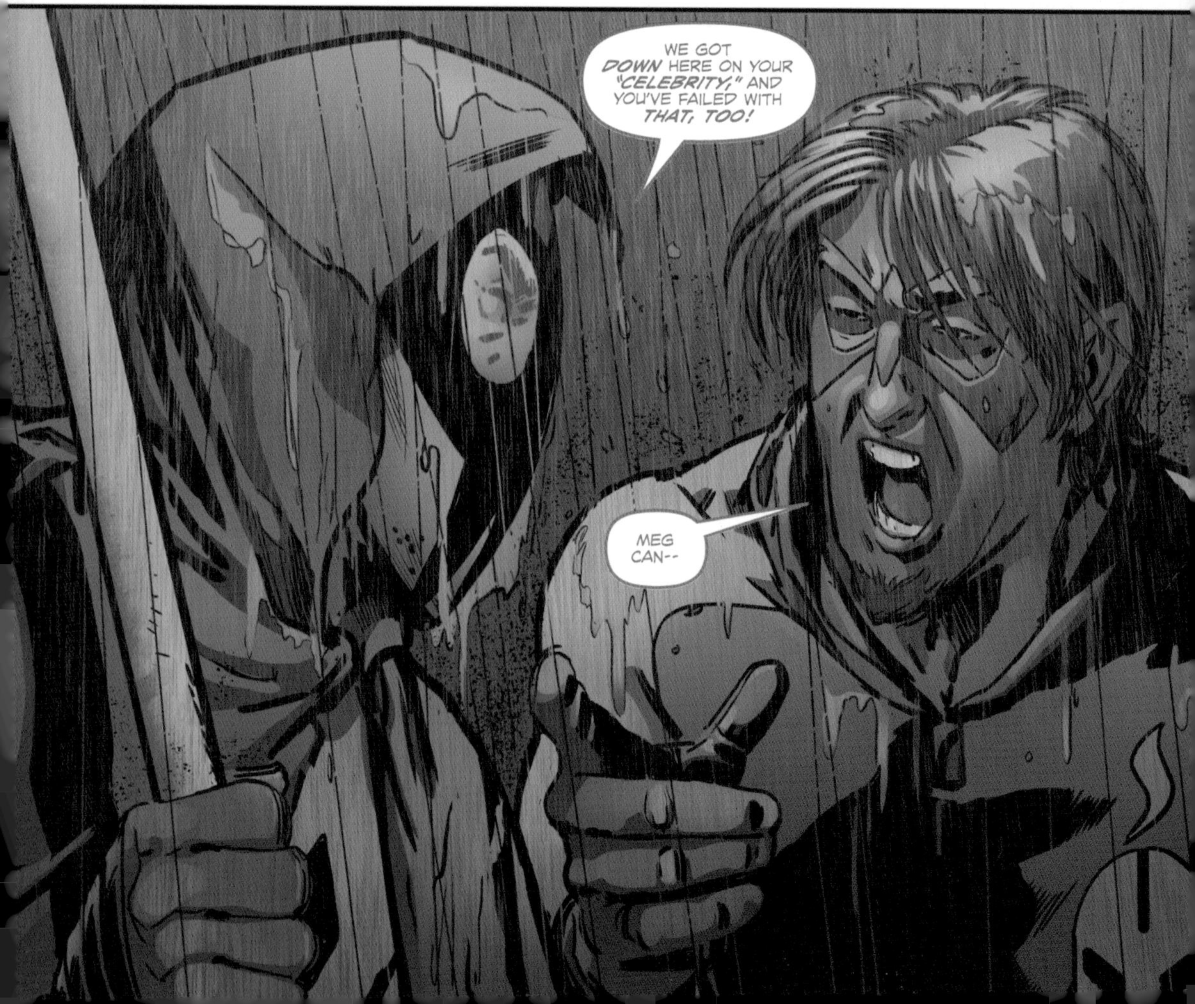
WE GOT *DOWN* HERE ON YOUR *"CELEBRITY,"* AND YOU'VE FAILED WITH *THAT, TOO!*
MEG CAN--

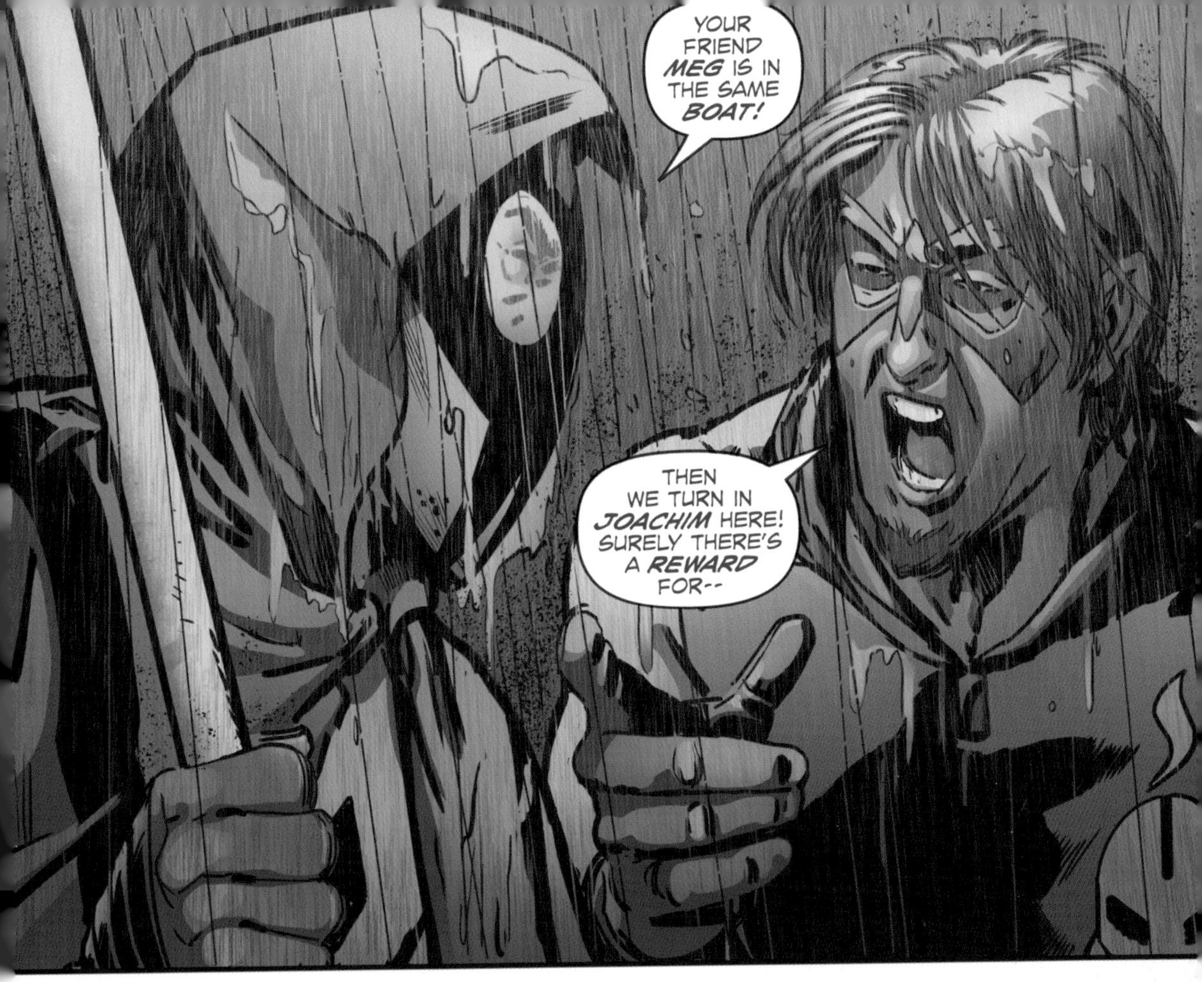
YOUR FRIEND MEG IS IN THE SAME BOAT!
THEN WE TURN IN JOACHIM HERE! SURELY THERE'S A REWARD FOR--

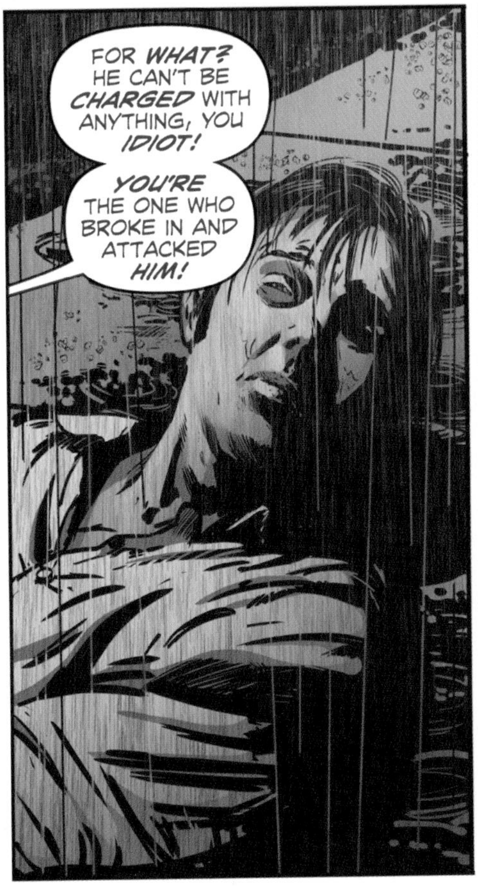
FOR WHAT? HE CAN'T BE CHARGED WITH ANYTHING, YOU IDIOT!
YOU'RE THE ONE WHO BROKE IN AND ATTACKED HIM!

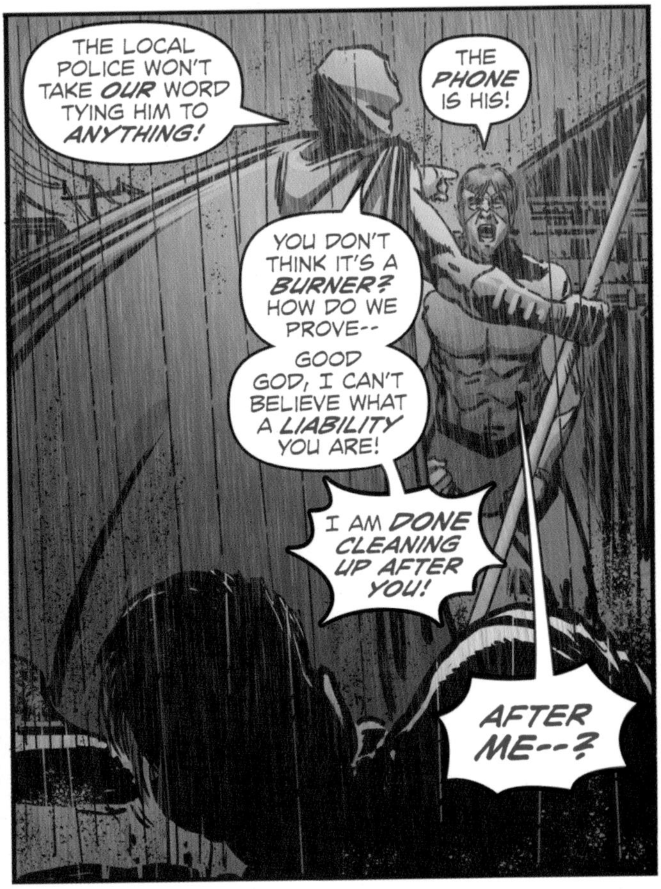
THE LOCAL POLICE WON'T TAKE OUR WORD TYING HIM TO ANYTHING!
THE PHONE IS HIS!
YOU DON'T THINK IT'S A BURNER? HOW DO WE PROVE--
GOOD GOD, I CAN'T BELIEVE WHAT A LIABILITY YOU ARE!
I AM DONE CLEANING UP AFTER YOU!
AFTER ME--?

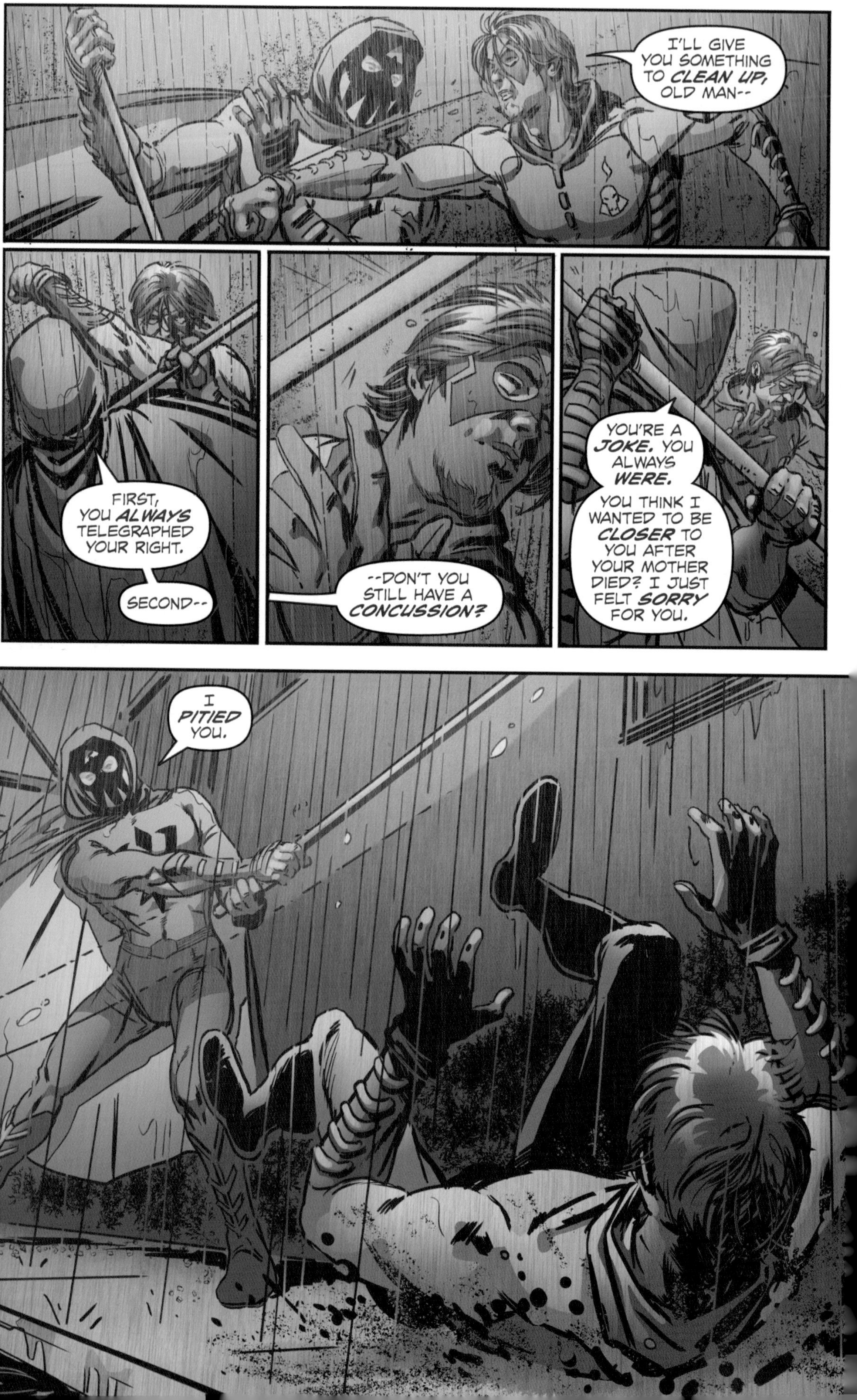
I'LL GIVE YOU SOMETHING TO CLEAN UP, OLD MAN--
FIRST, YOU ALWAYS TELEGRAPHED YOUR RIGHT.
SECOND--
--DON'T YOU STILL HAVE A CONCUSSION?
YOU'RE A JOKE. YOU ALWAYS WERE.
YOU THINK I WANTED TO BE CLOSER TO YOU AFTER YOUR MOTHER DIED? I JUST FELT SORRY FOR YOU.
I PITIED YOU.

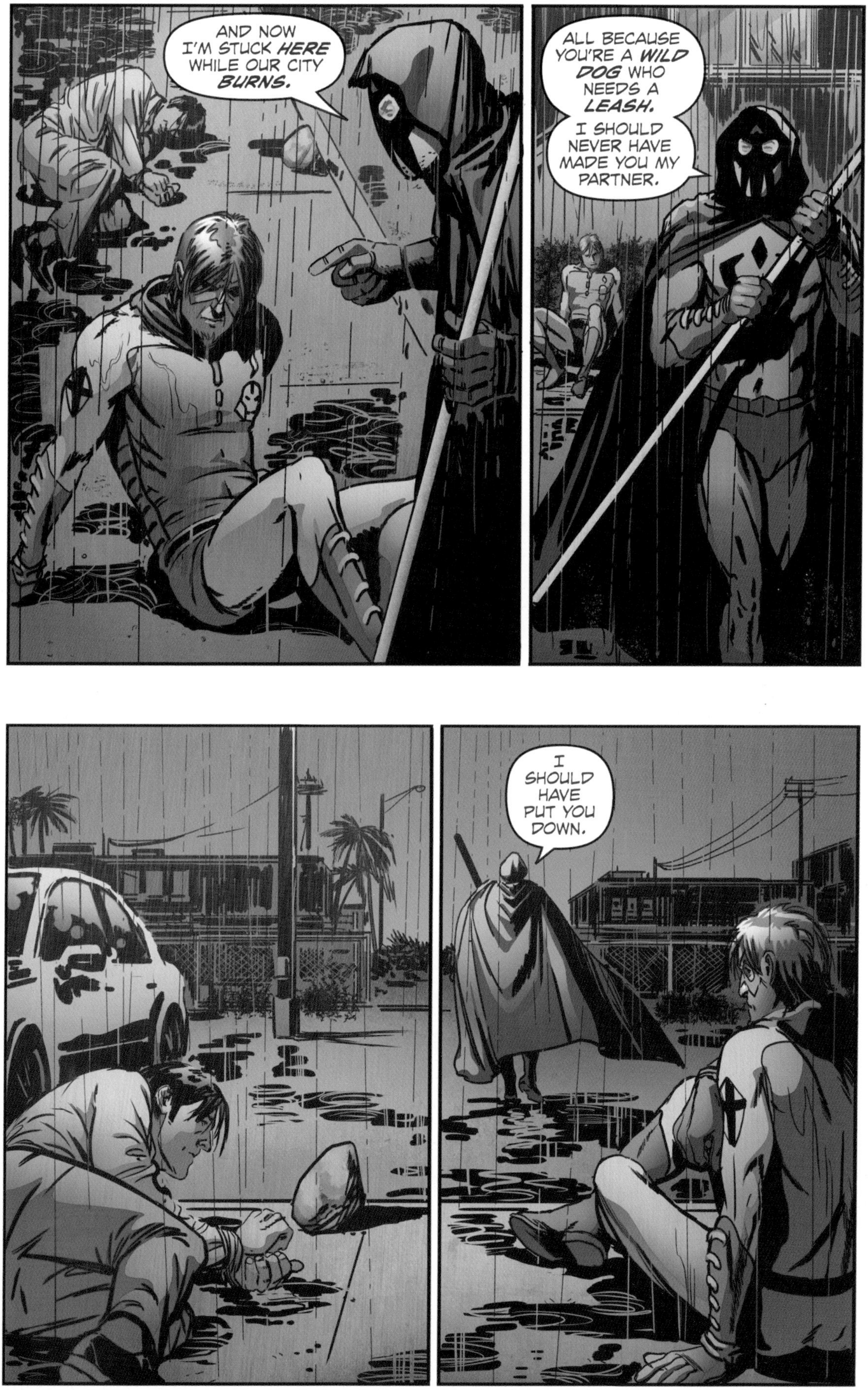
AND NOW I'M STUCK *HERE* WHILE OUR CITY *BURNS.*
ALL BECAUSE YOU'RE A *WILD DOG* WHO NEEDS A *LEASH.*
I SHOULD NEVER HAVE MADE YOU MY PARTNER.
I SHOULD HAVE PUT YOU DOWN.

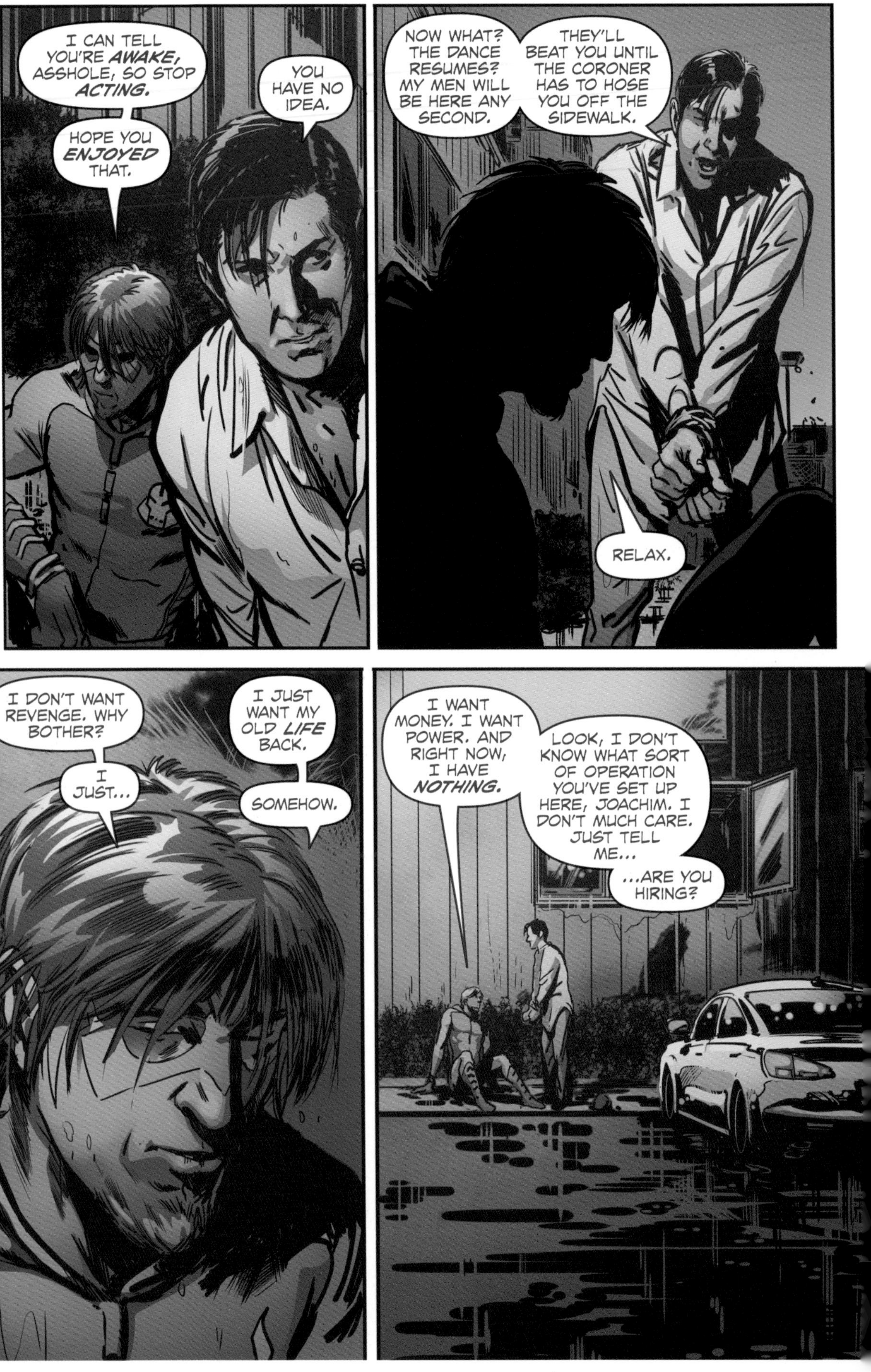
I CAN TELL YOU'RE AWAKE, ASSHOLE, SO STOP ACTING.
HOPE YOU ENJOYED THAT.
YOU HAVE NO IDEA.
NOW WHAT? THE DANCE RESUMES? MY MEN WILL BE HERE ANY SECOND.
THEY'LL BEAT YOU UNTIL THE CORONER HAS TO HOSE YOU OFF THE SIDEWALK.
RELAX.
I DON'T WANT REVENGE. WHY BOTHER?
I JUST...
I JUST WANT MY OLD LIFE BACK.
SOMEHOW.
I WANT MONEY. I WANT POWER. AND RIGHT NOW, I HAVE NOTHING.
LOOK, I DON'T KNOW WHAT SORT OF OPERATION YOU'VE SET UP HERE, JOACHIM. I DON'T MUCH CARE. JUST TELL ME...
...ARE YOU HIRING?

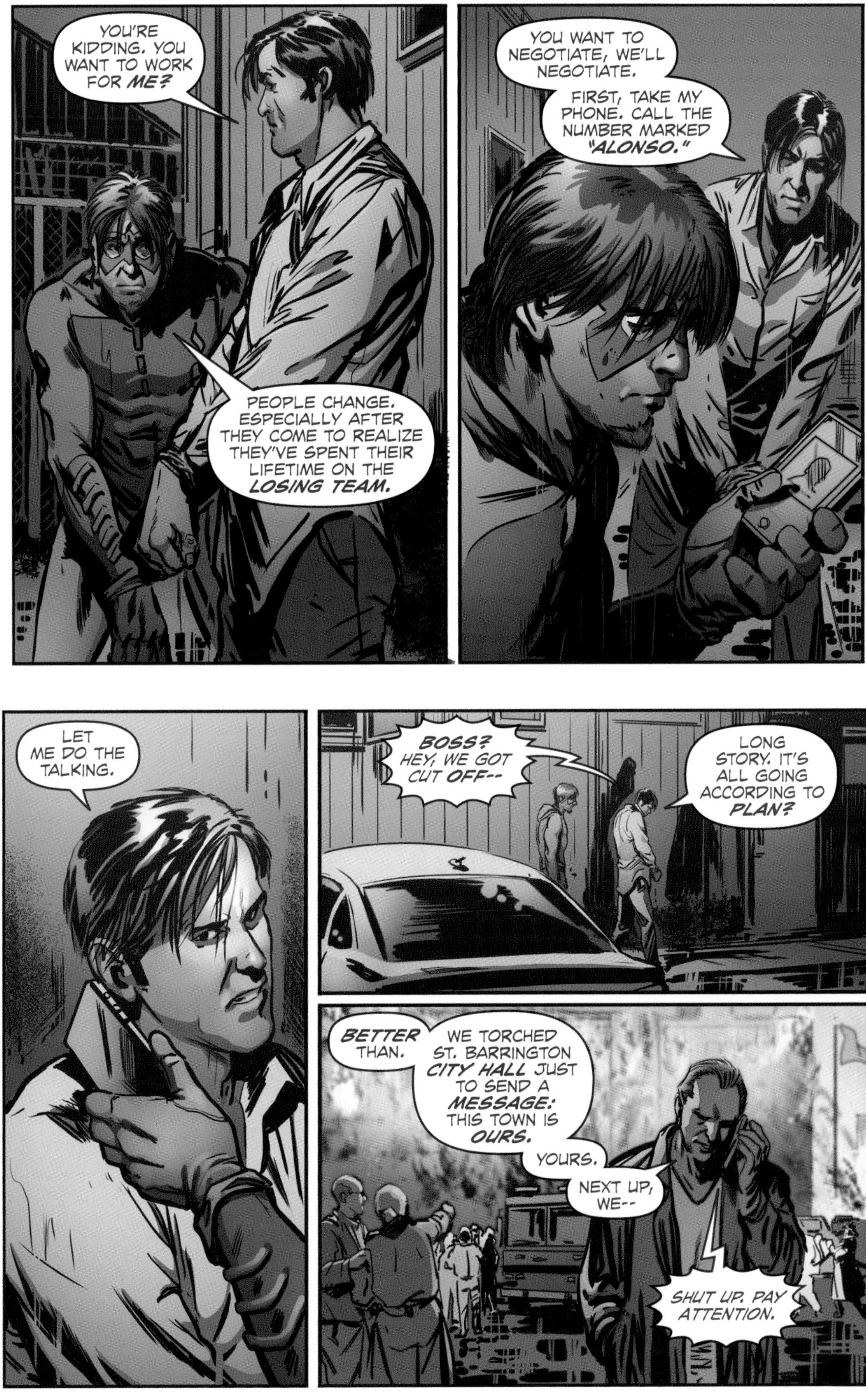
YOU'RE KIDDING. YOU WANT TO WORK FOR *ME?*
PEOPLE CHANGE. ESPECIALLY AFTER THEY COME TO REALIZE THEY'VE SPENT THEIR LIFETIME ON THE *LOSING TEAM.*
YOU WANT TO NEGOTIATE, WE'LL NEGOTIATE.
FIRST, TAKE MY PHONE. CALL THE NUMBER MARKED *"ALONSO."*
LET ME DO THE TALKING.
BOSS? HEY, WE GOT CUT OFF--
LONG STORY. IT'S ALL GOING ACCORDING TO *PLAN?*
BETTER THAN.
WE TORCHED ST. BARRINGTON *CITY HALL* JUST TO SEND A *MESSAGE:* THIS TOWN IS *OURS.*
YOURS.
NEXT UP, WE--
SHUT UP. PAY ATTENTION.

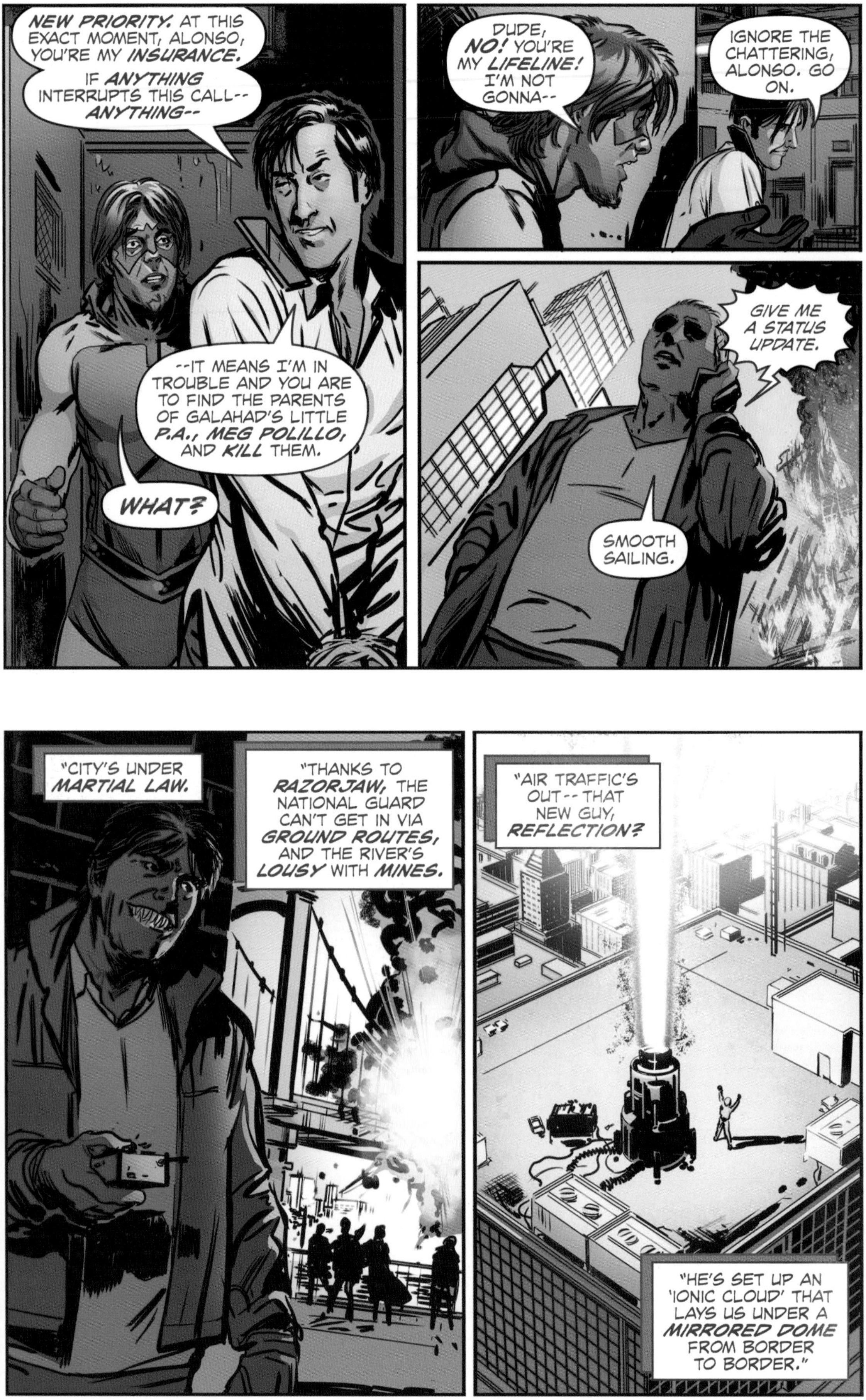

NEW PRIORITY. AT THIS EXACT MOMENT, ALONSO, YOU'RE MY INSURANCE.
IF ANYTHING INTERRUPTS THIS CALL-- ANYTHING--
--IT MEANS I'M IN TROUBLE AND YOU ARE TO FIND THE PARENTS OF GALAHAD'S LITTLE P.A., MEG POLILLO, AND KILL THEM.
WHAT?
DUDE, NO! YOU'RE MY LIFELINE! I'M NOT GONNA--
IGNORE THE CHATTERING, ALONSO. GO ON.
GIVE ME A STATUS UPDATE.
SMOOTH SAILING.
"CITY'S UNDER MARTIAL LAW.
"THANKS TO RAZORJAW, THE NATIONAL GUARD CAN'T GET IN VIA GROUND ROUTES, AND THE RIVER'S LOUSY WITH MINES.
"AIR TRAFFIC'S OUT-- THAT NEW GUY, REFLECTION?
"HE'S SET UP AN 'IONIC CLOUD' THAT LAYS US UNDER A MIRRORED DOME FROM BORDER TO BORDER."

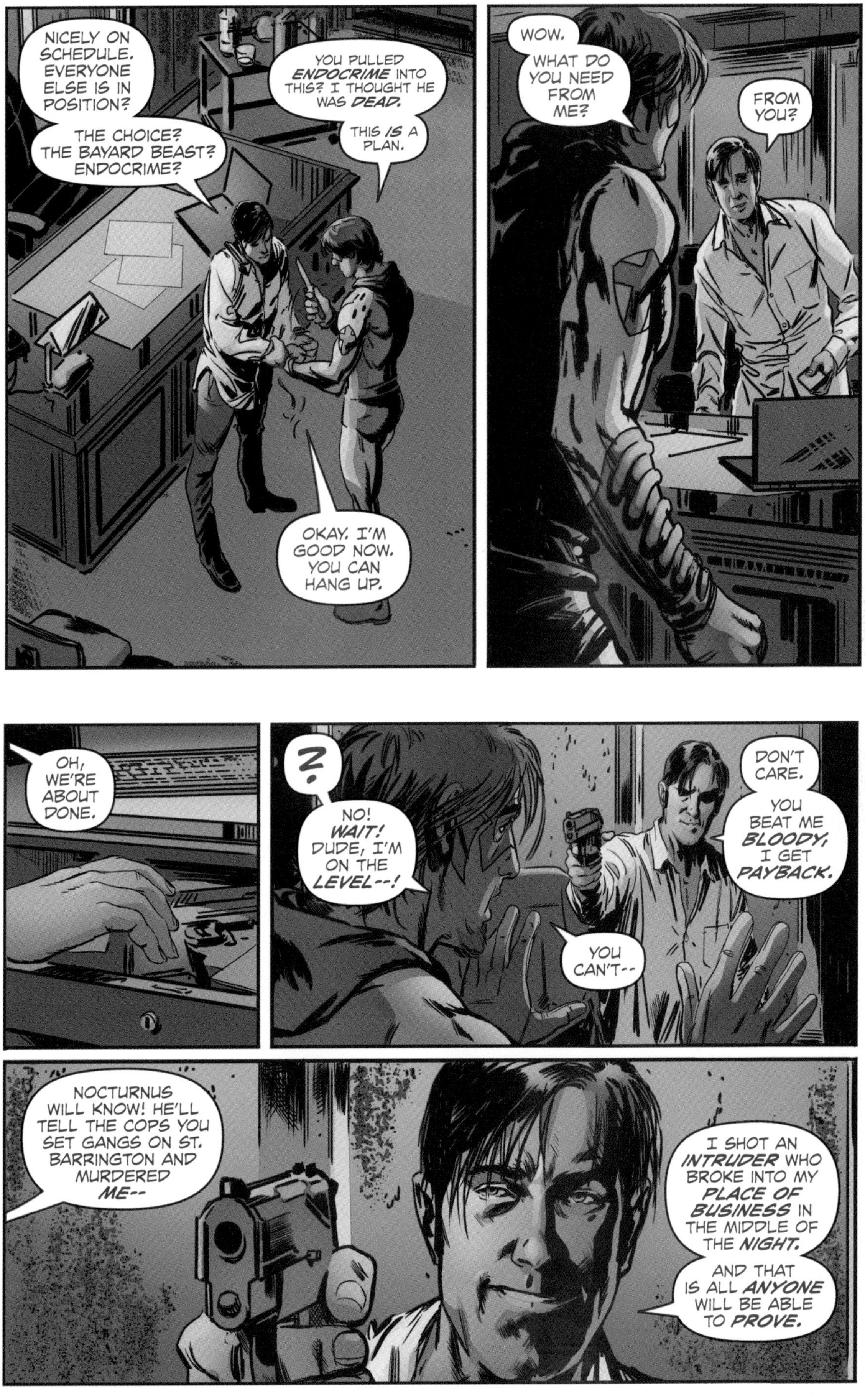
NICELY ON SCHEDULE. EVERYONE ELSE IS IN POSITION?
THE CHOICE? THE BAYARD BEAST? ENDOCRIME?
YOU PULLED ENDOCRIME INTO THIS? I THOUGHT HE WAS DEAD.
THIS IS A PLAN.
OKAY. I'M GOOD NOW. YOU CAN HANG UP.
WOW.
WHAT DO YOU NEED FROM ME?
FROM YOU?
OH, WE'RE ABOUT DONE.
?
NO! WAIT! DUDE, I'M ON THE LEVEL--!
DON'T CARE.
YOU BEAT ME BLOODY, I GET PAYBACK.
YOU CAN'T--
NOCTURNUS WILL KNOW! HE'LL TELL THE COPS YOU SET GANGS ON ST. BARRINGTON AND MURDERED ME--
I SHOT AN INTRUDER WHO BROKE INTO MY PLACE OF BUSINESS IN THE MIDDLE OF THE NIGHT.
AND THAT IS ALL ANYONE WILL BE ABLE TO PROVE.

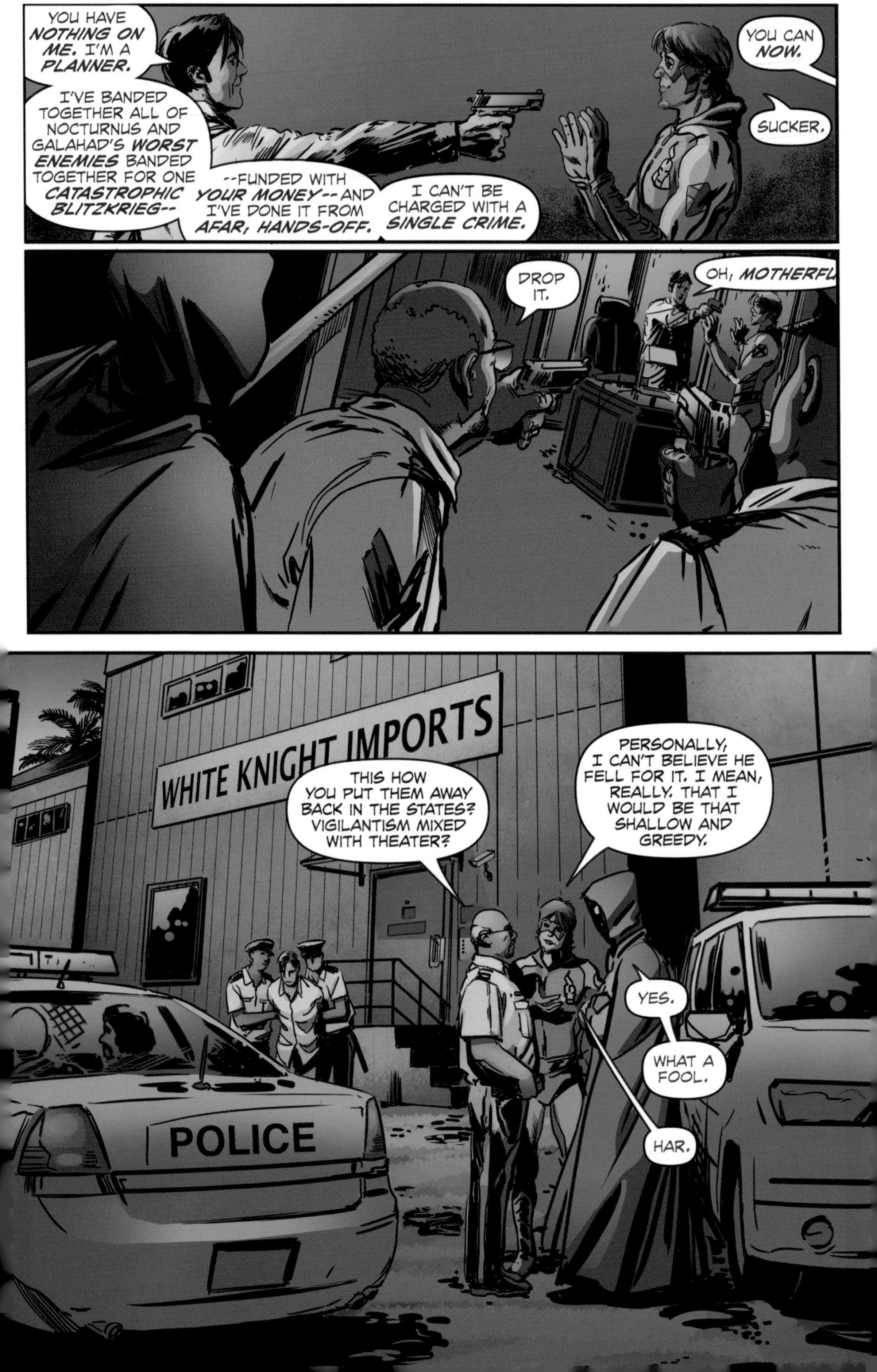

YOU HAVE NOTHING ON ME. I'M A PLANNER.
I'VE BANDED TOGETHER ALL OF NOCTURNUS AND GALAHAD'S WORST ENEMIES BANDED TOGETHER FOR ONE CATASTROPHIC BLITZKRIEG--
--FUNDED WITH YOUR MONEY--AND I'VE DONE IT FROM AFAR, HANDS-OFF.
I CAN'T BE CHARGED WITH A SINGLE CRIME.
YOU CAN NOW.
SUCKER.
DROP IT.
OH, MOTHERF
WHITE KNIGHT IMPORTS
THIS HOW YOU PUT THEM AWAY BACK IN THE STATES? VIGILANTISM MIXED WITH THEATER?
PERSONALLY, I CAN'T BELIEVE HE FELL FOR IT. I MEAN, REALLY. THAT I WOULD BE THAT SHALLOW AND GREEDY.
YES.
WHAT A FOOL.
HAR.
POLICE

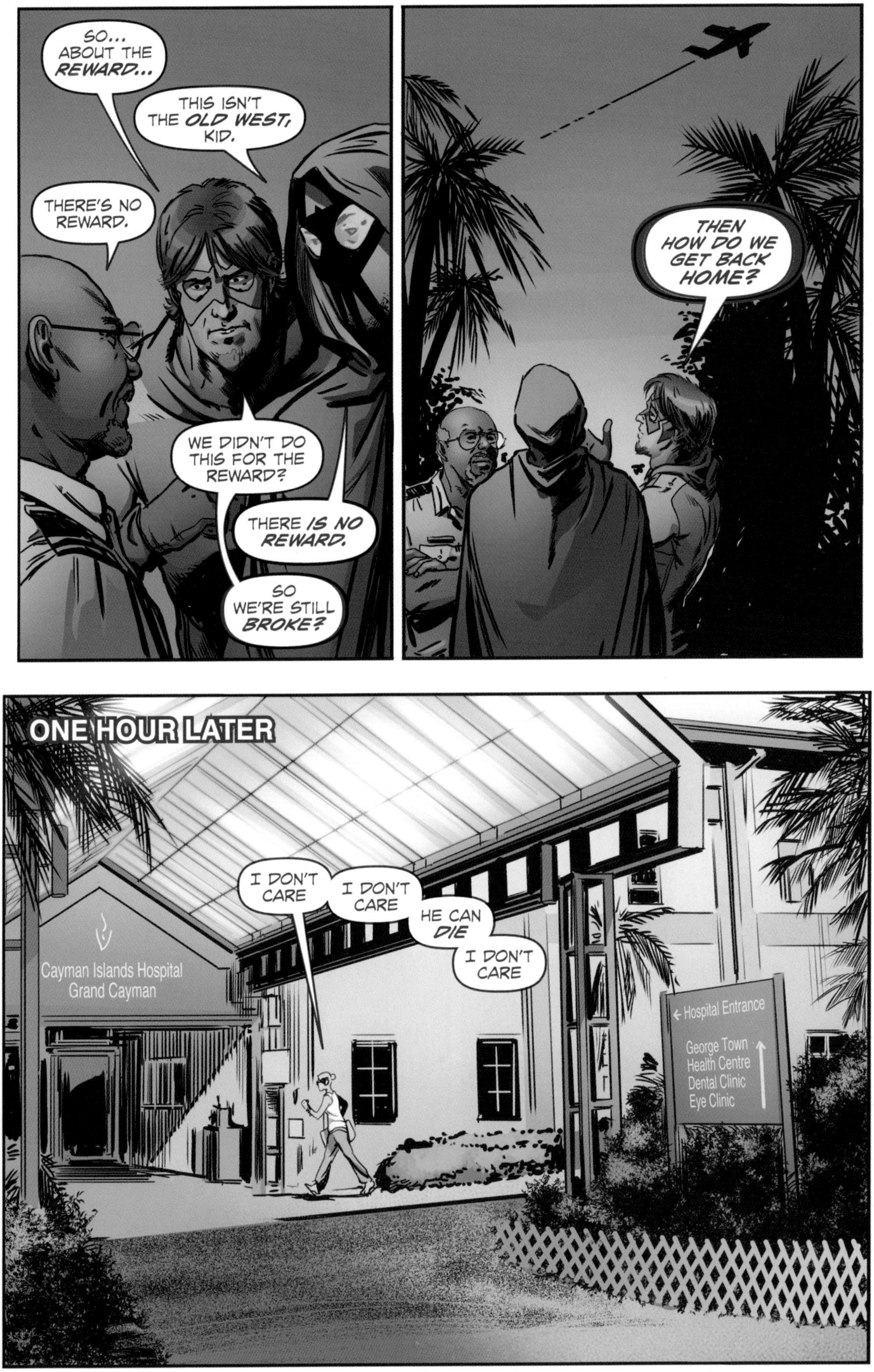
SO... ABOUT THE REWARD...
THIS ISN'T THE OLD WEST, KID.
THERE'S NO REWARD.
WE DIDN'T DO THIS FOR THE REWARD?
THERE IS NO REWARD.
SO WE'RE STILL BROKE?
THEN HOW DO WE GET BACK HOME?
ONE HOUR LATER
Cayman Islands Hospital
Grand Cayman
I DON'T CARE
I DON'T CARE
HE CAN DIE
I DON'T CARE
← Hospital Entrance
George Town
Health Centre
Dental Clinic
Eye Clinic

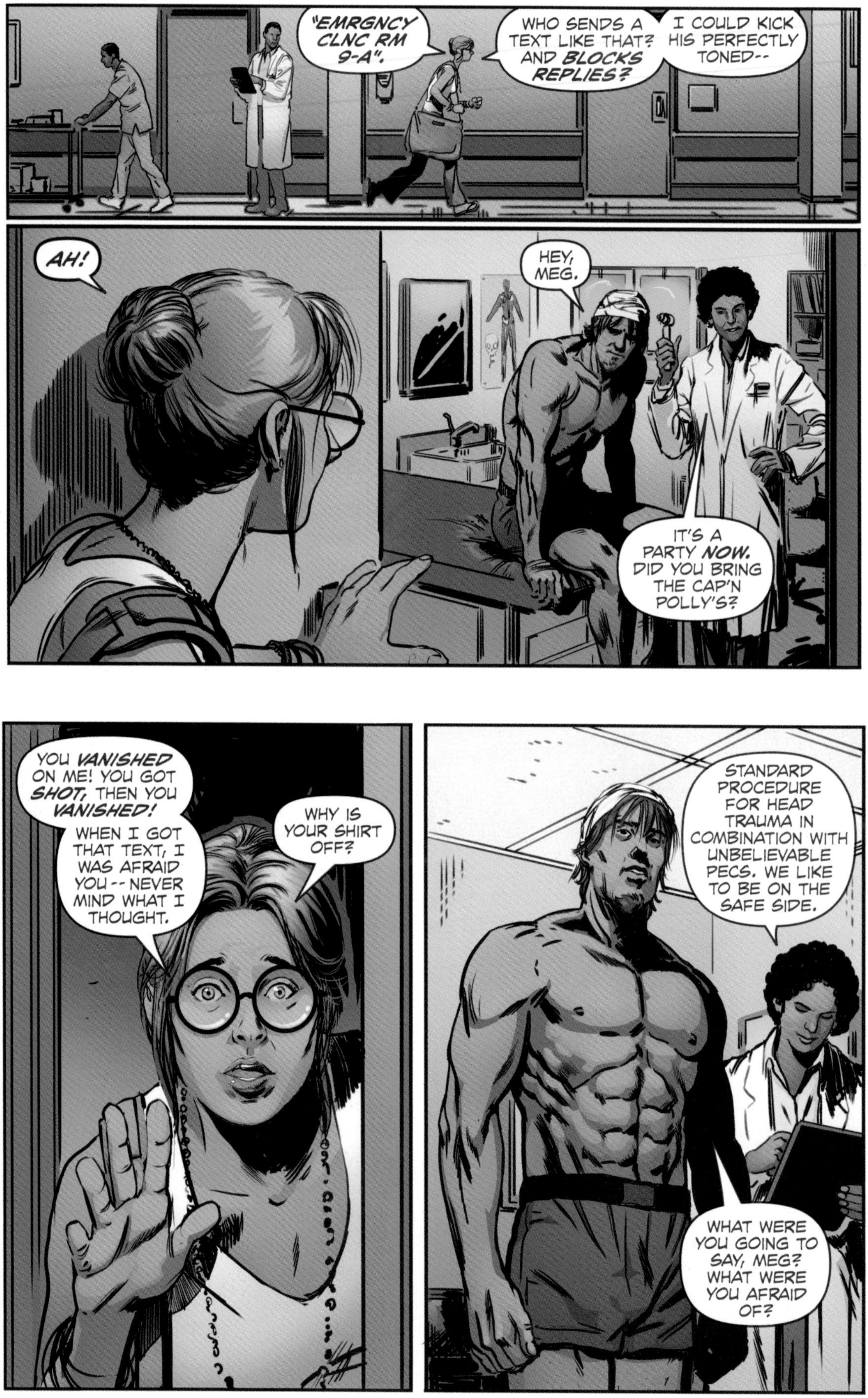
"EMRGNCY CLNC RM 9-A".
WHO SENDS A TEXT LIKE THAT? AND BLOCKS REPLIES?
I COULD KICK HIS PERFECTLY TONED--
AH!
HEY, MEG.
IT'S A PARTY NOW. DID YOU BRING THE CAP'N POLLY'S?
YOU VANISHED ON ME! YOU GOT SHOT, THEN YOU VANISHED!
WHEN I GOT THAT TEXT, I WAS AFRAID YOU -- NEVER MIND WHAT I THOUGHT.
WHY IS YOUR SHIRT OFF?
STANDARD PROCEDURE FOR HEAD TRAUMA IN COMBINATION WITH UNBELIEVABLE PECS. WE LIKE TO BE ON THE SAFE SIDE.
WHAT WERE YOU GOING TO SAY, MEG? WHAT WERE YOU AFRAID OF?

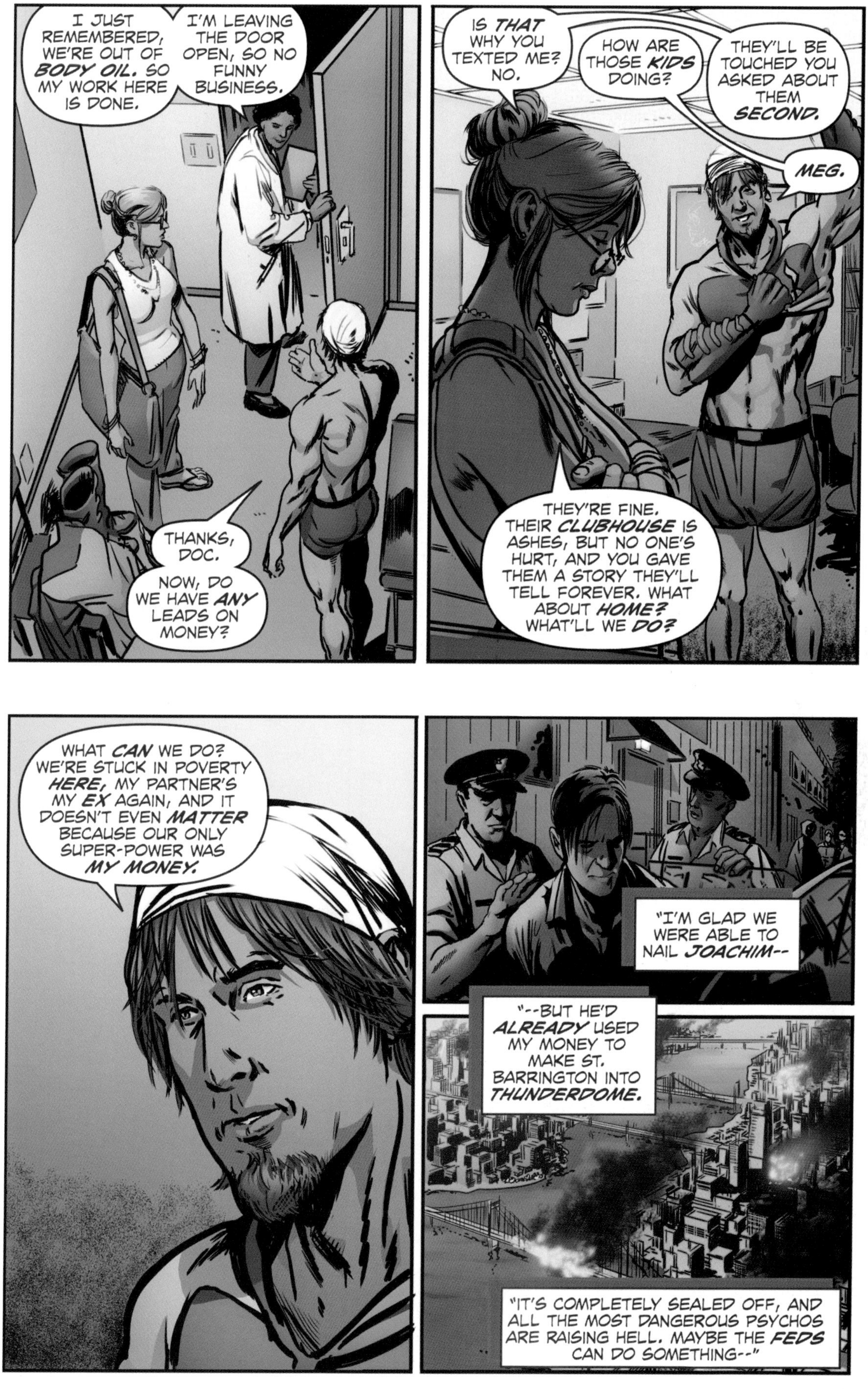
I JUST REMEMBERED, WE'RE OUT OF BODY OIL. SO MY WORK HERE IS DONE.
I'M LEAVING THE DOOR OPEN, SO NO FUNNY BUSINESS.
THANKS, DOC.
NOW, DO WE HAVE ANY LEADS ON MONEY?
IS THAT WHY YOU TEXTED ME? NO.
HOW ARE THOSE KIDS DOING?
THEY'LL BE TOUCHED YOU ASKED ABOUT THEM SECOND.
MEG.
THEY'RE FINE. THEIR CLUBHOUSE IS ASHES, BUT NO ONE'S HURT, AND YOU GAVE THEM A STORY THEY'LL TELL FOREVER. WHAT ABOUT HOME? WHAT'LL WE DO?
WHAT CAN WE DO? WE'RE STUCK IN POVERTY HERE, MY PARTNER'S MY EX AGAIN, AND IT DOESN'T EVEN MATTER BECAUSE OUR ONLY SUPER-POWER WAS MY MONEY.
"I'M GLAD WE WERE ABLE TO NAIL JOACHIM--
"--BUT HE'D ALREADY USED MY MONEY TO MAKE ST. BARRINGTON INTO THUNDERDOME.
"IT'S COMPLETELY SEALED OFF, AND ALL THE MOST DANGEROUS PSYCHOS ARE RAISING HELL. MAYBE THE FEDS CAN DO SOMETHING--"

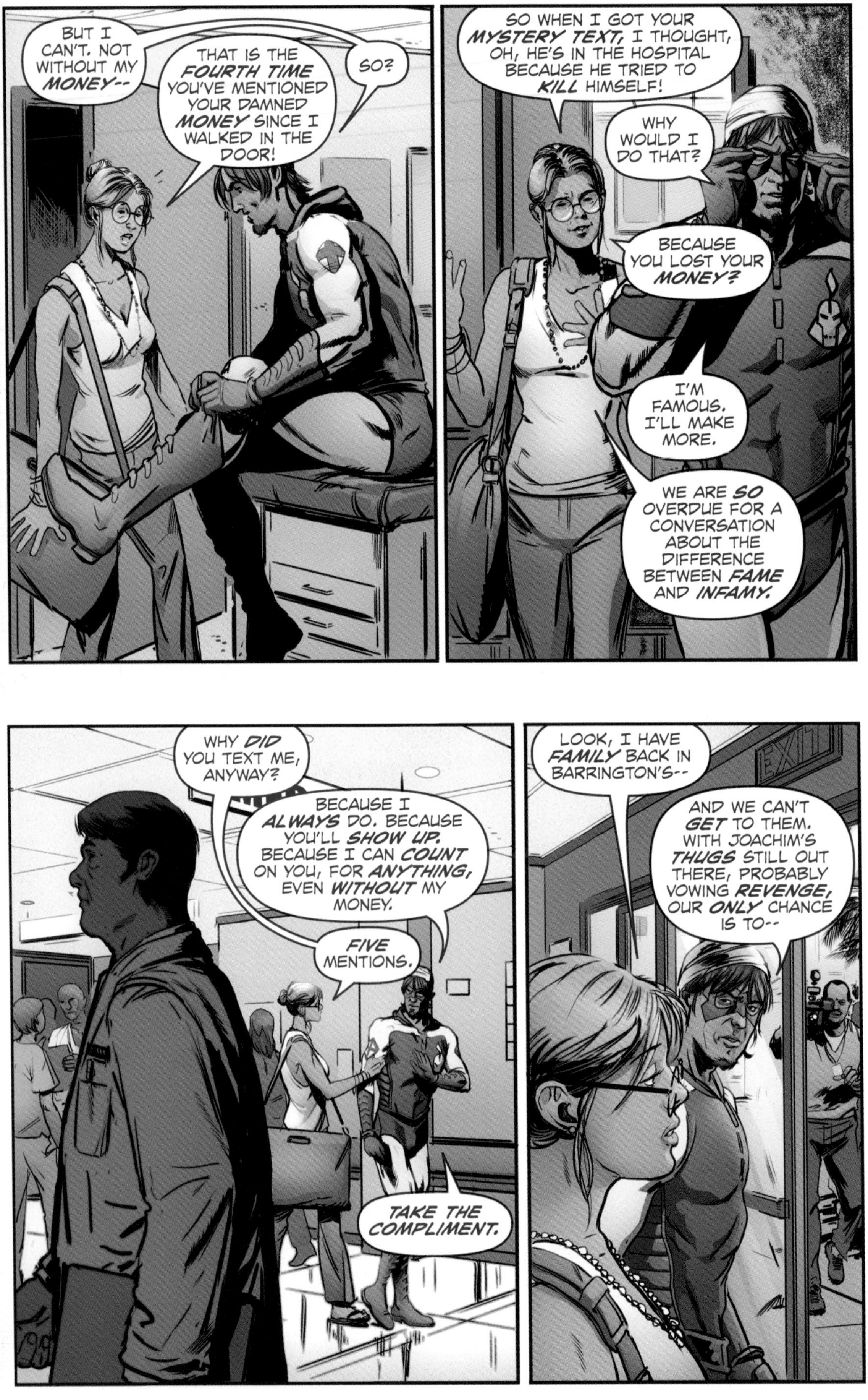

BUT I CAN'T. NOT WITHOUT MY MONEY--
THAT IS THE FOURTH TIME YOU'VE MENTIONED YOUR DAMNED MONEY SINCE I WALKED IN THE DOOR!
SO?
SO WHEN I GOT YOUR MYSTERY TEXT, I THOUGHT, OH, HE'S IN THE HOSPITAL BECAUSE HE TRIED TO KILL HIMSELF!
WHY WOULD I DO THAT?
BECAUSE YOU LOST YOUR MONEY?
I'M FAMOUS. I'LL MAKE MORE.
WE ARE SO OVERDUE FOR A CONVERSATION ABOUT THE DIFFERENCE BETWEEN FAME AND INFAMY.
WHY DID YOU TEXT ME, ANYWAY?
BECAUSE I ALWAYS DO. BECAUSE YOU'LL SHOW UP. BECAUSE I CAN COUNT ON YOU, FOR ANYTHING, EVEN WITHOUT MY MONEY.
FIVE MENTIONS.
TAKE THE COMPLIMENT.
LOOK, I HAVE FAMILY BACK IN BARRINGTON'S--
AND WE CAN'T GET TO THEM. WITH JOACHIM'S THUGS STILL OUT THERE, PROBABLY VOWING REVENGE, OUR ONLY CHANCE IS TO--
EXIT

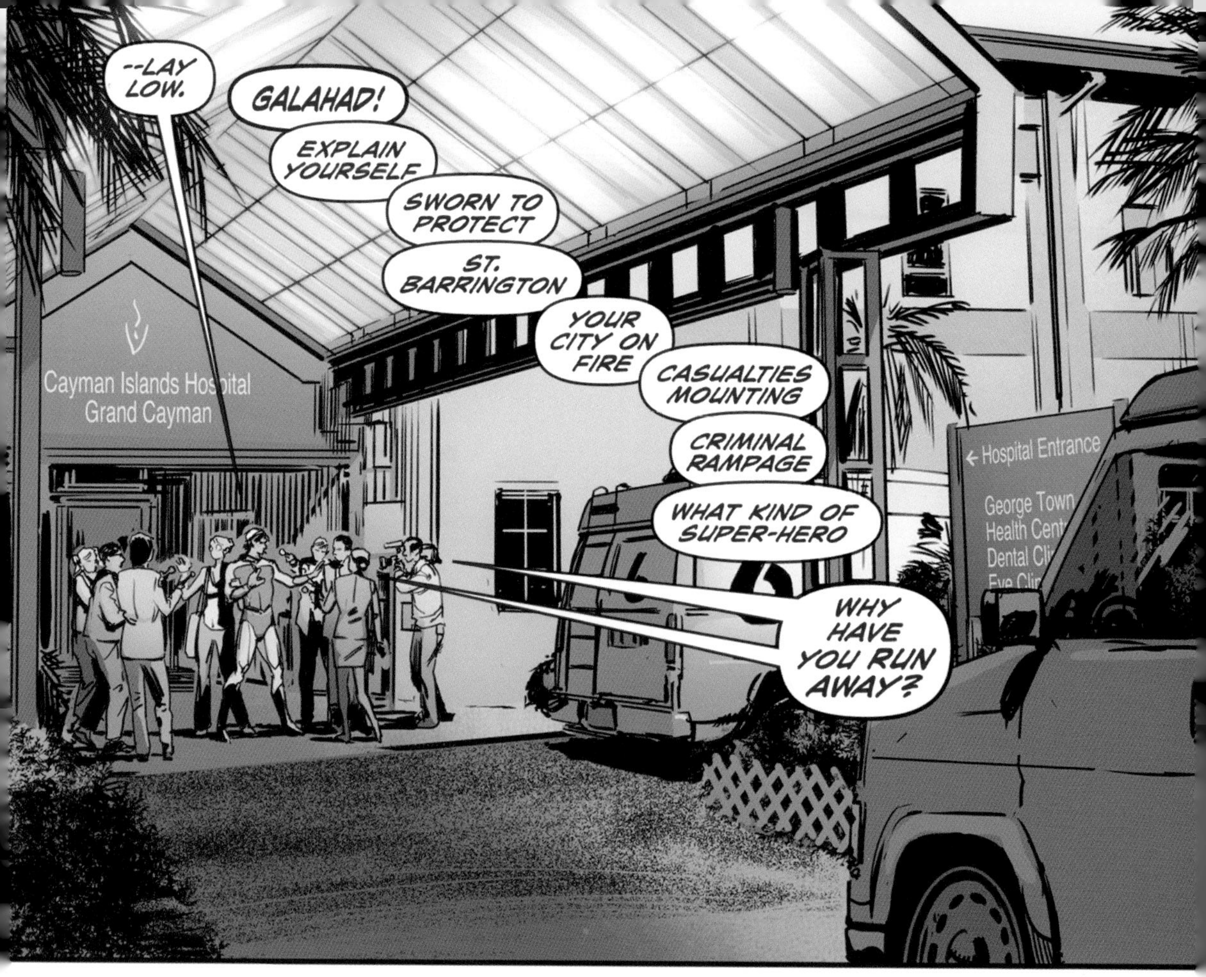
--LAY LOW.
GALAHAD!
EXPLAIN YOURSELF
SWORN TO PROTECT
ST. BARRINGTON
YOUR CITY ON FIRE
CASUALTIES MOUNTING
CRIMINAL RAMPAGE
WHAT KIND OF SUPER-HERO
WHY HAVE YOU RUN AWAY?
Cayman Islands Hospital
Grand Cayman
← Hospital Entrance
George Town
Health Cent
Dental Cli

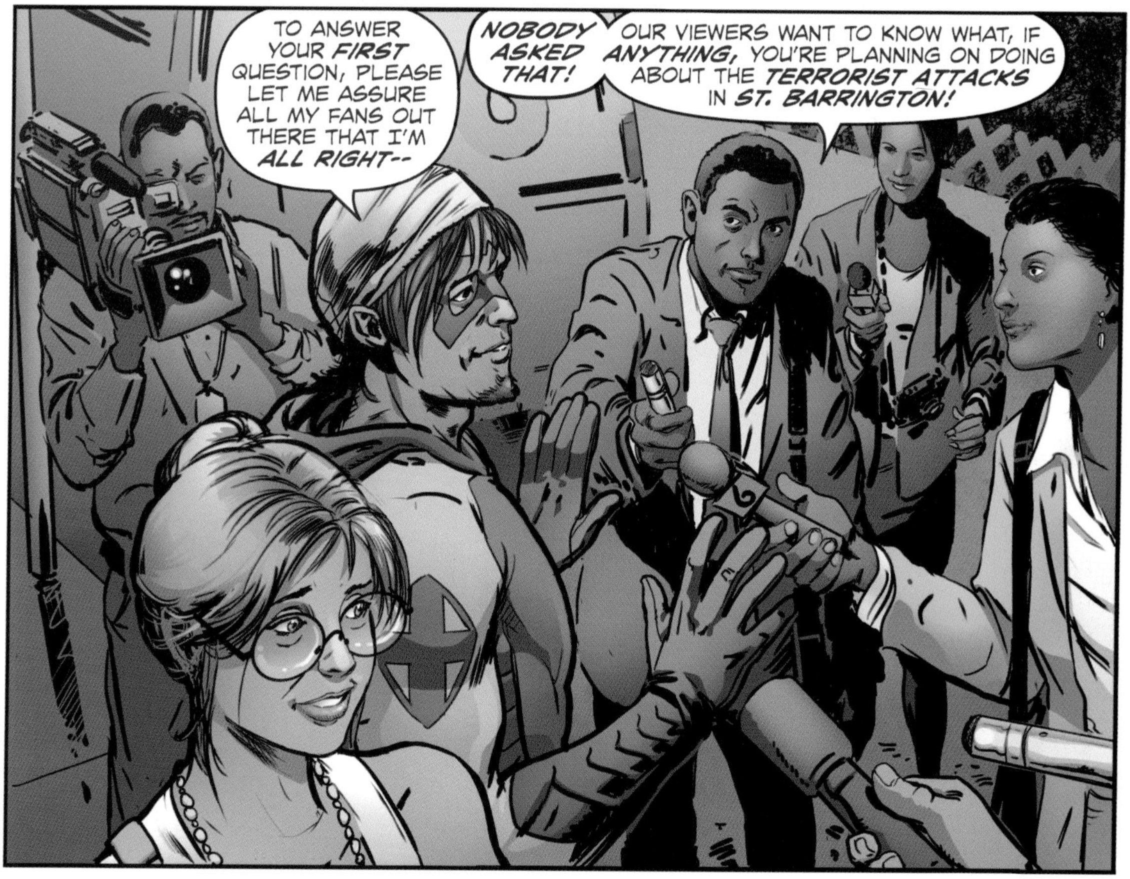
TO ANSWER YOUR FIRST QUESTION, PLEASE LET ME ASSURE ALL MY FANS OUT THERE THAT I'M ALL RIGHT--
NOBODY ASKED THAT!
OUR VIEWERS WANT TO KNOW WHAT, IF ANYTHING, YOU'RE PLANNING ON DOING ABOUT THE TERRORIST ATTACKS IN ST. BARRINGTON!

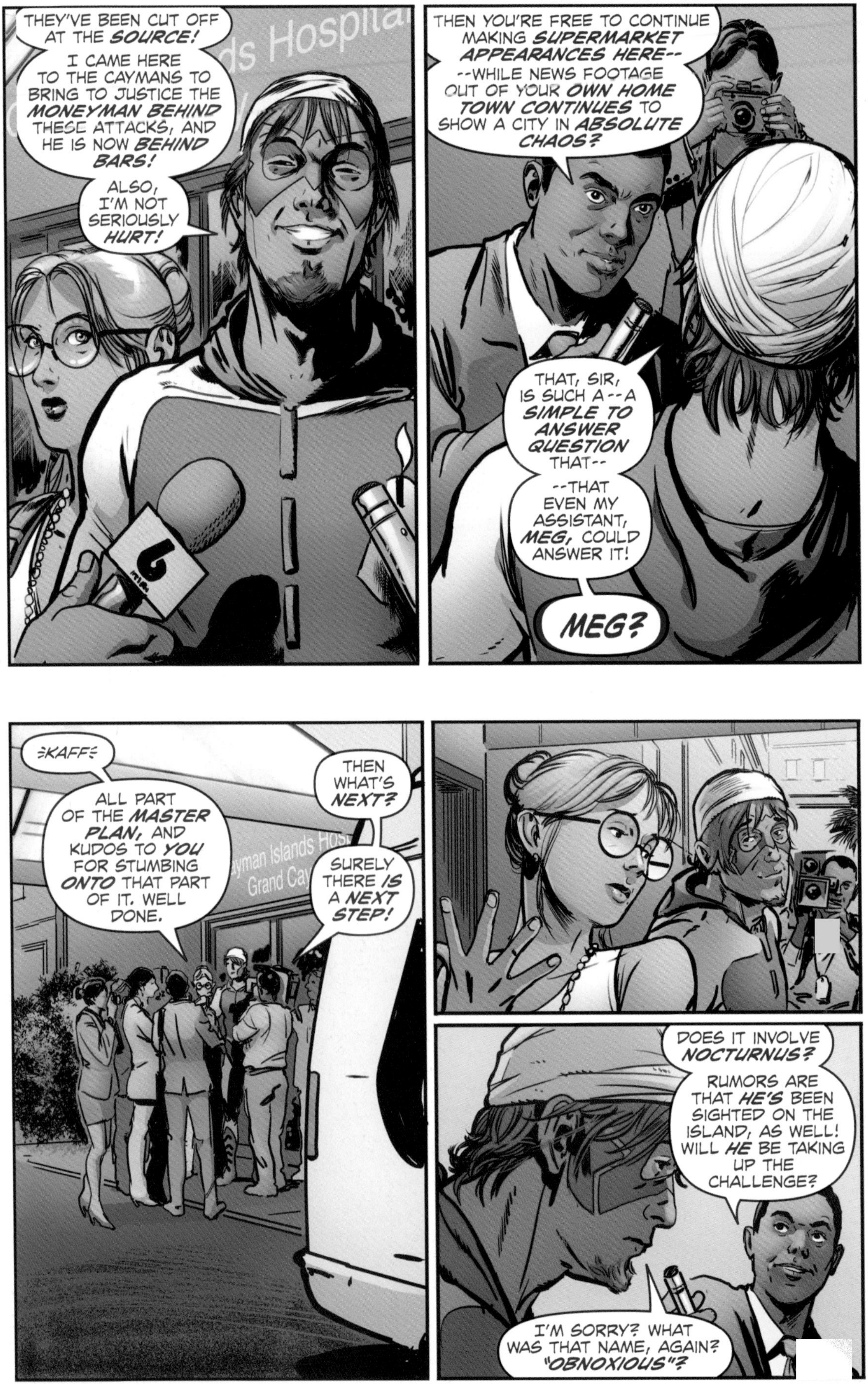

THEY'VE BEEN CUT OFF AT THE SOURCE!
I CAME HERE TO THE CAYMANS TO BRING TO JUSTICE THE MONEYMAN BEHIND THESE ATTACKS, AND HE IS NOW BEHIND BARS!
ALSO, I'M NOT SERIOUSLY HURT!
ds Hospital
THEN YOU'RE FREE TO CONTINUE MAKING SUPERMARKET APPEARANCES HERE--
--WHILE NEWS FOOTAGE OUT OF YOUR OWN HOME TOWN CONTINUES TO SHOW A CITY IN ABSOLUTE CHAOS?
THAT, SIR, IS SUCH A--A SIMPLE TO ANSWER QUESTION THAT--
--THAT EVEN MY ASSISTANT, MEG, COULD ANSWER IT!
MEG?
KAFF
ALL PART OF THE MASTER PLAN, AND KUDOS TO YOU FOR STUMBING ONTO THAT PART OF IT. WELL DONE.
THEN WHAT'S NEXT?
SURELY THERE IS A NEXT STEP!
ayman Islands Hos
Grand Cay
DOES IT INVOLVE NOCTURNUS?
RUMORS ARE THAT HE'S BEEN SIGHTED ON THE ISLAND, AS WELL! WILL HE BE TAKING UP THE CHALLENGE?
I'M SORRY? WHAT WAS THAT NAME, AGAIN? "OBNOXIOUS"?

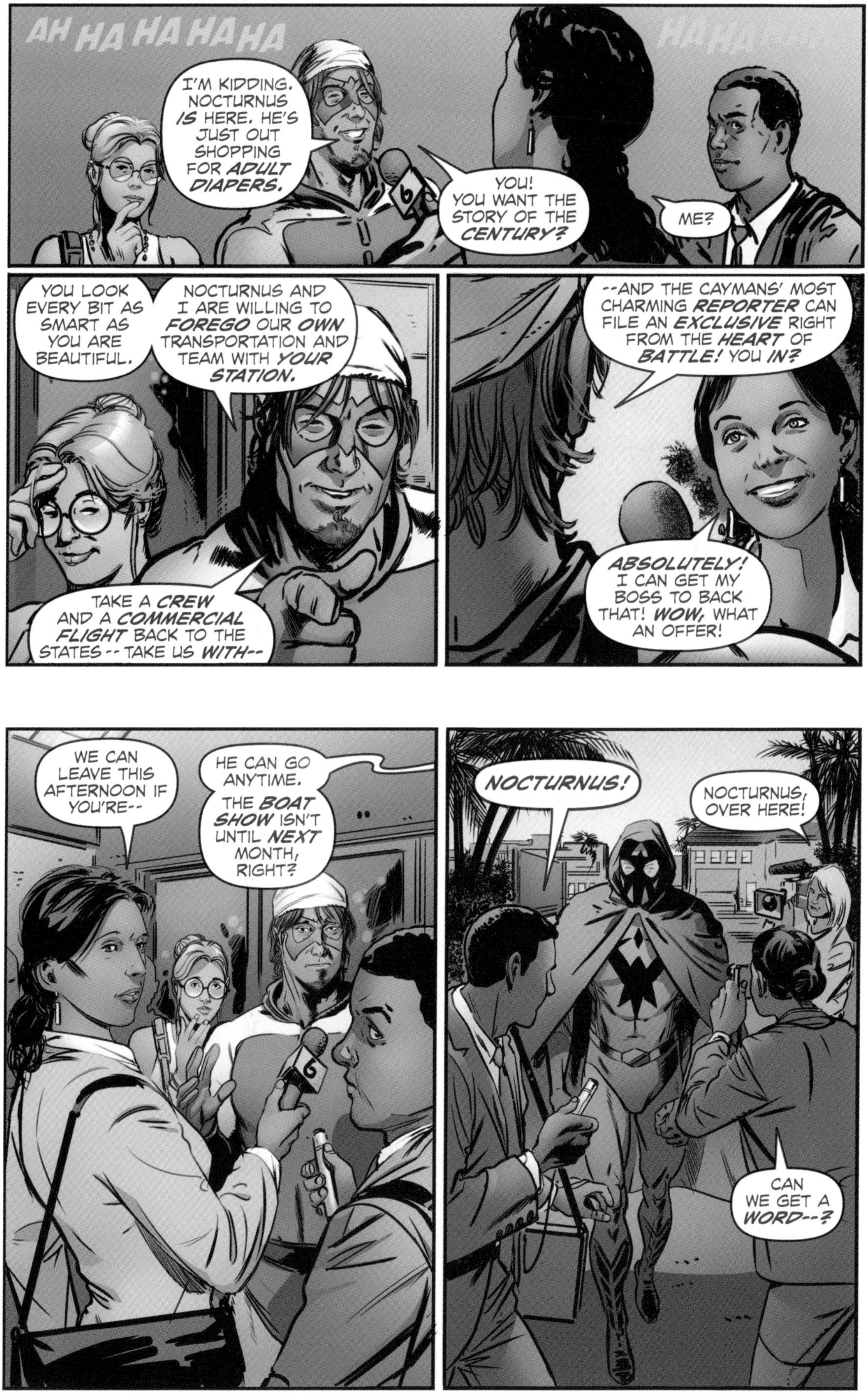
AH HA HA HA HA HA
I'M KIDDING. NOCTURNUS IS HERE. HE'S JUST OUT SHOPPING FOR ADULT DIAPERS.
HA HA HA
YOU! YOU WANT THE STORY OF THE CENTURY?
ME?
YOU LOOK EVERY BIT AS SMART AS YOU ARE BEAUTIFUL.
NOCTURNUS AND I ARE WILLING TO FOREGO OUR OWN TRANSPORTATION AND TEAM WITH YOUR STATION.
TAKE A CREW AND A COMMERCIAL FLIGHT BACK TO THE STATES -- TAKE US WITH--
--AND THE CAYMANS' MOST CHARMING REPORTER CAN FILE AN EXCLUSIVE RIGHT FROM THE HEART OF BATTLE! YOU IN?
ABSOLUTELY! I CAN GET MY BOSS TO BACK THAT! WOW, WHAT AN OFFER!
WE CAN LEAVE THIS AFTERNOON IF YOU'RE--
HE CAN GO ANYTIME.
THE BOAT SHOW ISN'T UNTIL NEXT MONTH, RIGHT?
NOCTURNUS!
NOCTURNUS, OVER HERE!
CAN WE GET A WORD--?

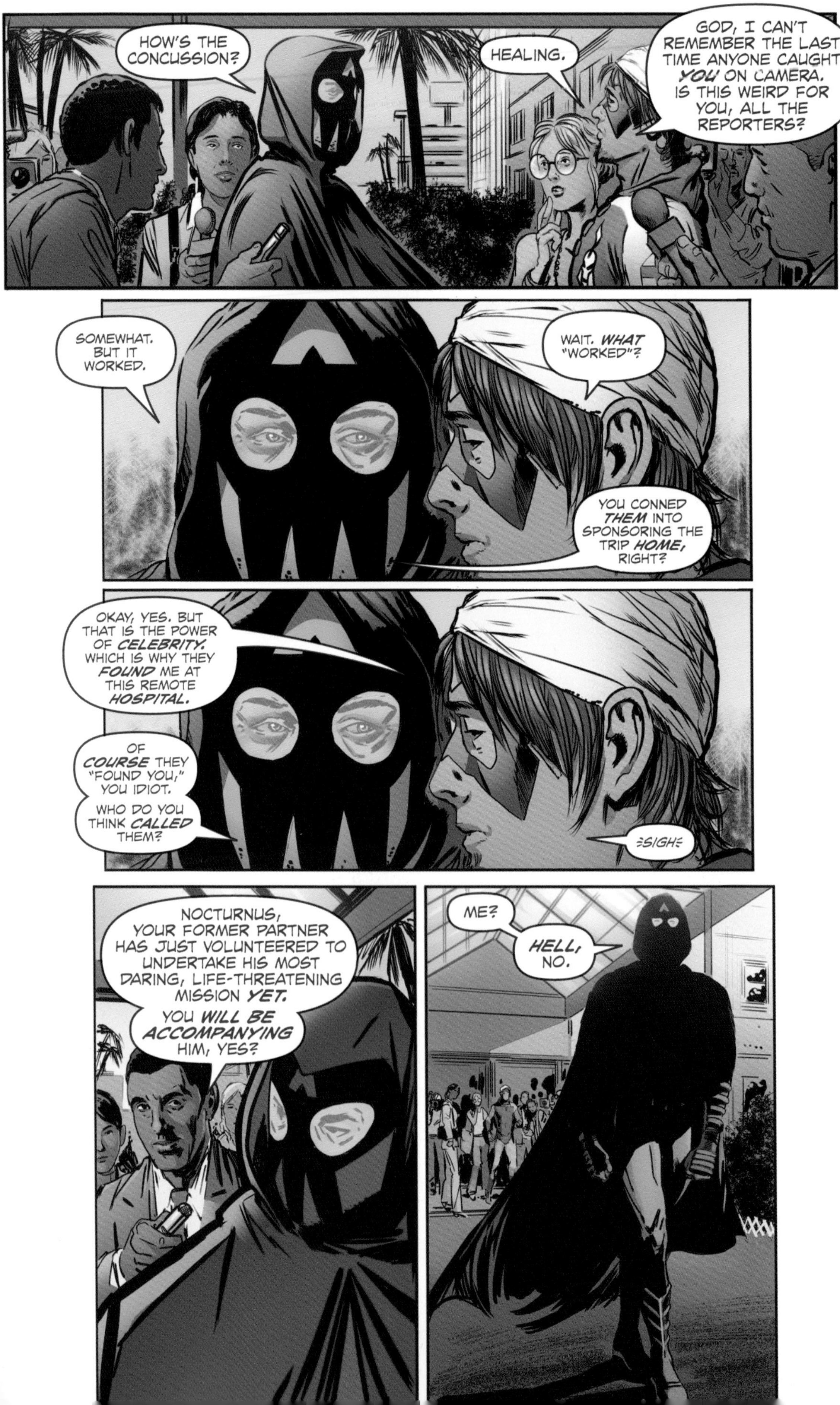

HOW'S THE CONCUSSION?
HEALING.
GOD, I CAN'T REMEMBER THE LAST TIME ANYONE CAUGHT YOU ON CAMERA. IS THIS WEIRD FOR YOU, ALL THE REPORTERS?
SOMEWHAT. BUT IT WORKED.
WAIT. WHAT "WORKED"?
YOU CONNED THEM INTO SPONSORING THE TRIP HOME, RIGHT?
OKAY, YES. BUT THAT IS THE POWER OF CELEBRITY. WHICH IS WHY THEY FOUND ME AT THIS REMOTE HOSPITAL.
OF COURSE THEY "FOUND YOU," YOU IDIOT.
WHO DO YOU THINK CALLED THEM?
SIGH
NOCTURNUS, YOUR FORMER PARTNER HAS JUST VOLUNTEERED TO UNDERTAKE HIS MOST DARING, LIFE-THREATENING MISSION YET.
YOU WILL BE ACCOMPANYING HIM, YES?
ME?
HELL, NO.

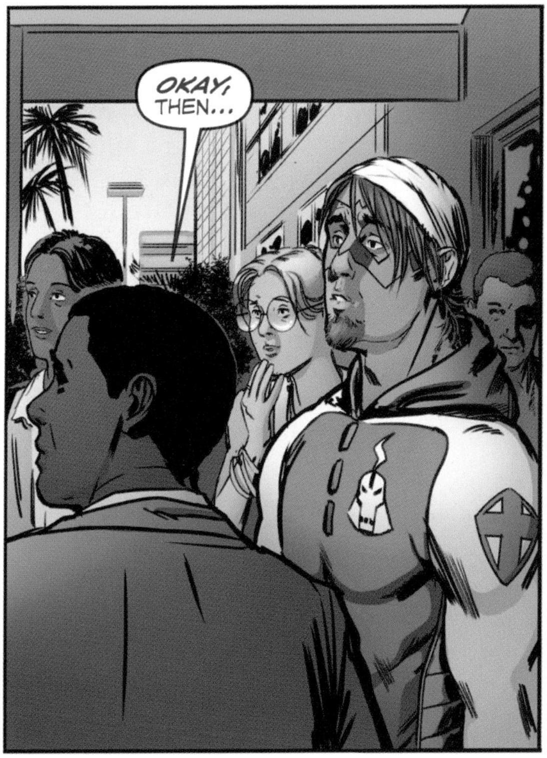
OKAY, THEN...

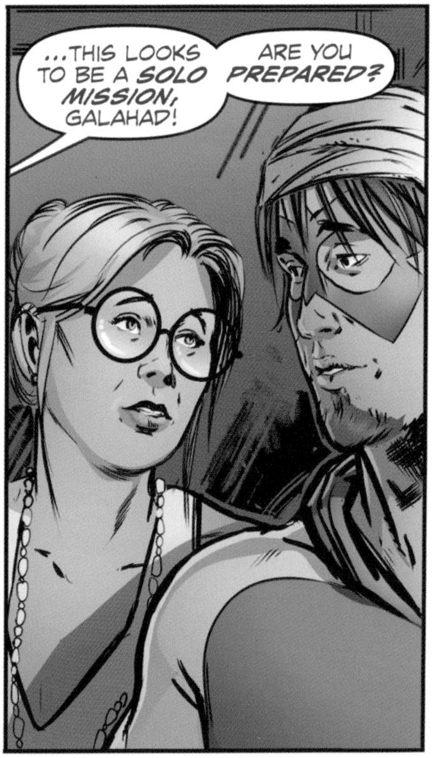
...THIS LOOKS TO BE A SOLO MISSION, GALAHAD!
ARE YOU PREPARED?

Hey,

By tonight I'll be home in St. Barrington. I hope. If Galahad can somehow get us through the tumult and the barricades. Even if he can't, it'll feel better not to be so far away. Just to breathe the familiar air again...

I'm so *done* with Cayman, living day-to-day, watching the cracks form in Galahad's façade as he hustles for money that never comes and for answers he doesn't like.

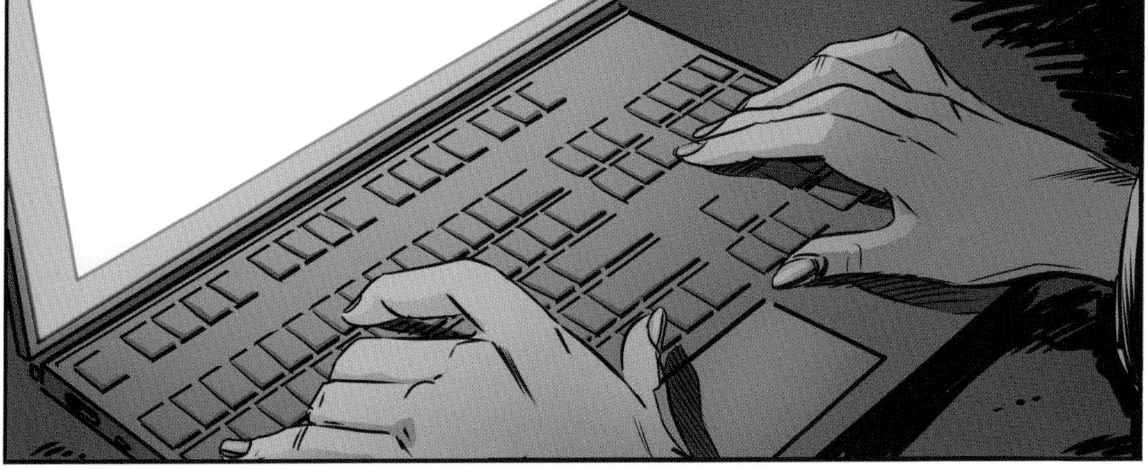

He's been the center of my life for three-plus years, ever since I went to work for Galahad, Inc. and even after the job evaporated. I've scheduled his Galahad time, covered up his Jarod mistakes, pulled him out of places he shouldn't be and into places he needed to be.

I've given him publicity and secrecy. I've wound him up and talked him down. He's depended on me, resisted me, frustrated me, ditched me, insulted me, and forgotten me.

I am seriously afraid of:
• His selfishness
• His impulsiveness
• His materialism
• His shallowness
• His disrespect
• His laziness
• His inattention
• The tantrums he throws when attention goes to anyone else but him
• The way he uses people like appliances
• How little most things interest him unless they immediately benefit him
• How boring he is
• How exciting he is
• How it makes me feel when he moves
• His eyes

Disappointing, isn't it? He gets my blood up, but that's not necessarily the same as passion, is it? If we were following the fiction-trope playbook, then naturally, predictably, inevitably, robotically, I'd start to fall for him. He is beautiful. He needs me.

Alternatively, it could be that, at a time of total uncertainty, I'm grasping at the nearest ripcord--
I mean, we're *all* free-falling, right? Maybe deep down I just see Jarod as my main chance at regaining my equilibrium.

Maybe I'm every bit as opportunistic as he. Maybe I'm no better.

Is what I'm feeling infatuation or desperation?

Budding love, or business-as-usual?

I wish you were here.

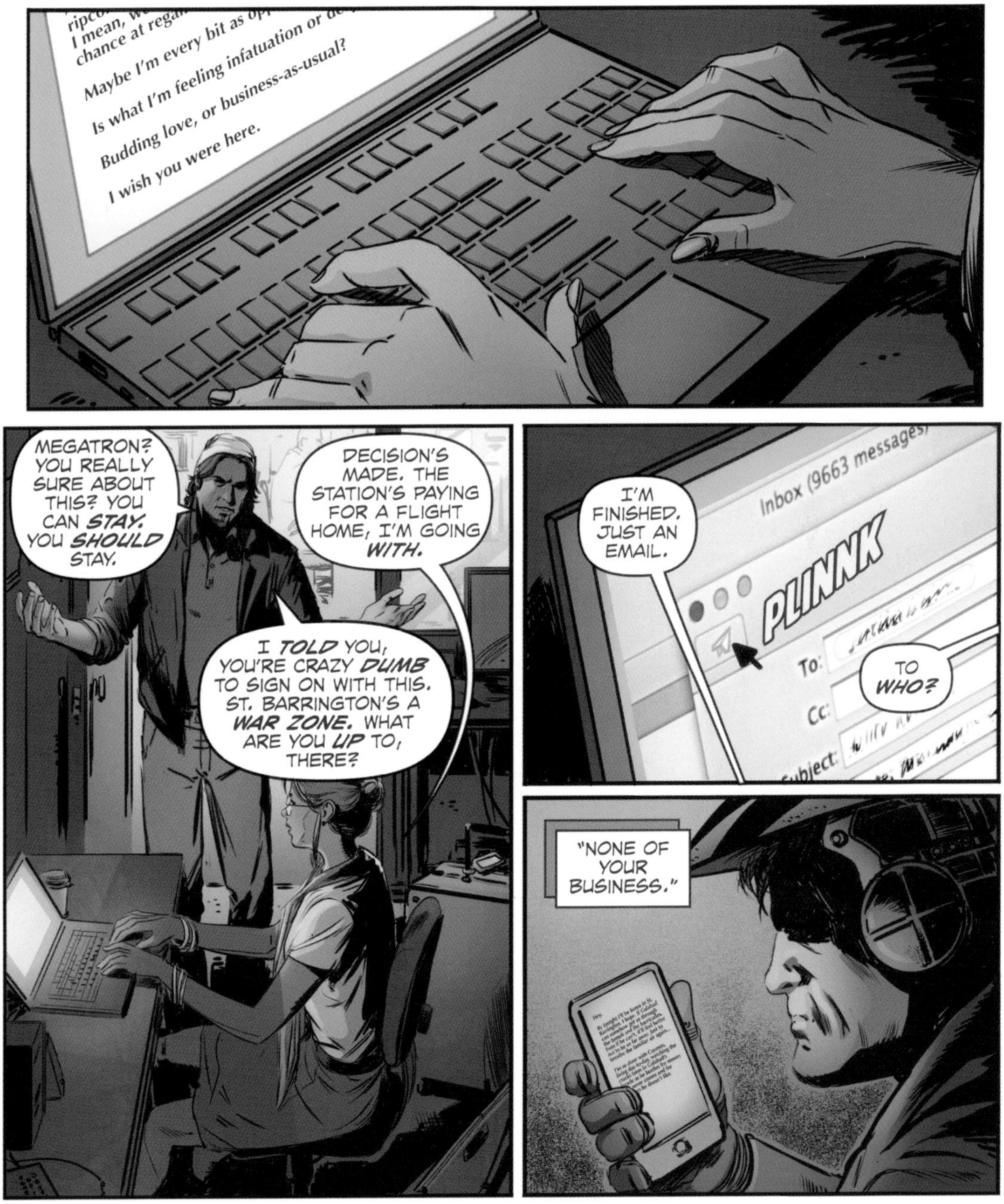
Is what I'm feeling infatuation or
Budding love, or business-as-usual?
I wish you were here.
MEGATRON? YOU REALLY SURE ABOUT THIS? YOU CAN *STAY.* YOU *SHOULD* STAY.
DECISION'S MADE. THE STATION'S PAYING FOR A FLIGHT HOME, I'M GOING *WITH.*
I *TOLD* YOU, YOU'RE CRAZY *DUMB* TO SIGN ON WITH THIS. ST. BARRINGTON'S A *WAR ZONE.* WHAT ARE YOU *UP* TO, THERE?
I'M FINISHED. JUST AN EMAIL.
Inbox (9663 messages
PLINNK
To:
Cc:
TO *WHO?*
"NONE OF YOUR BUSINESS."

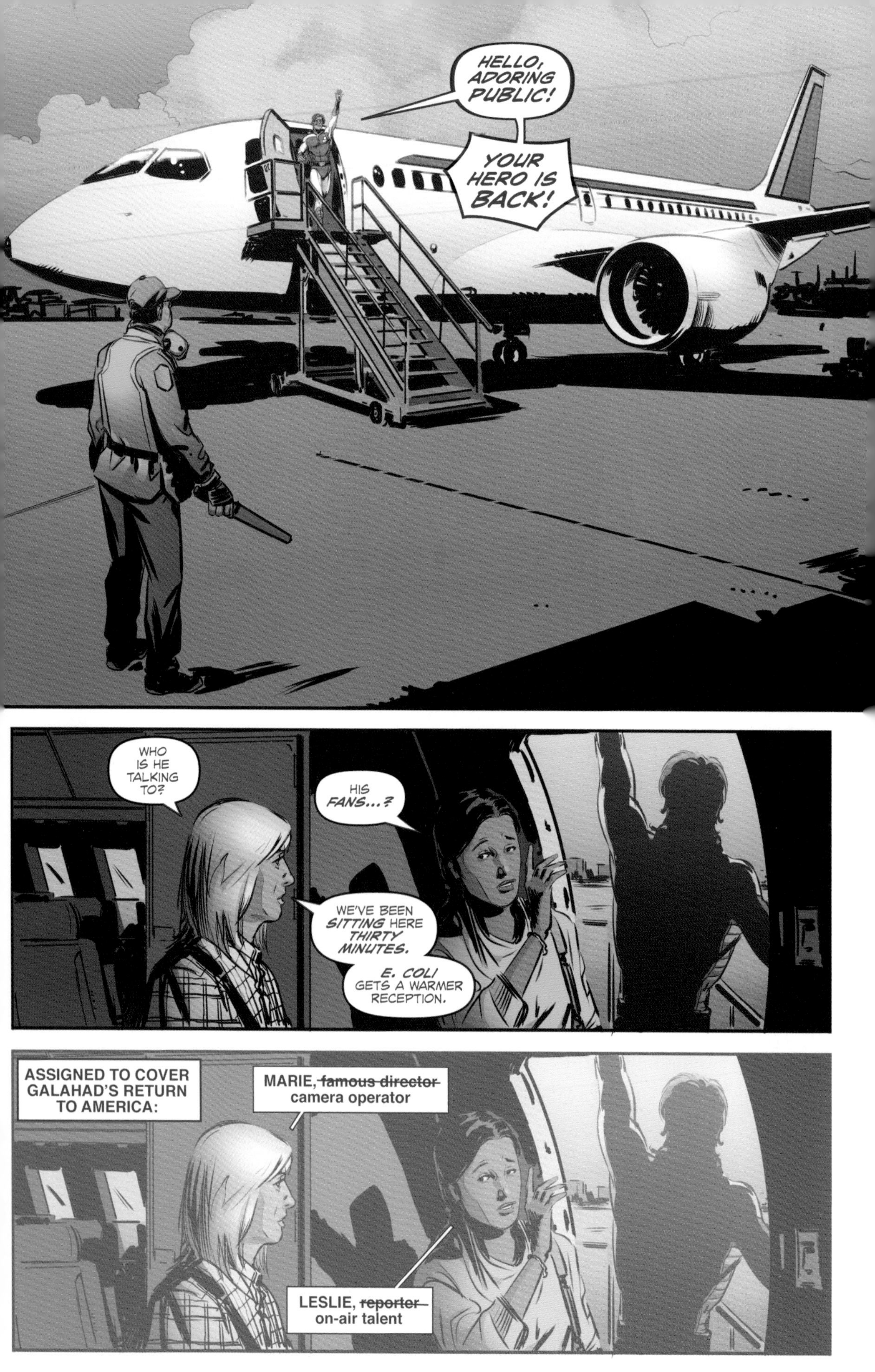
HELLO, ADORING PUBLIC!
YOUR HERO IS BACK!
WHO IS HE TALKING TO?
HIS FANS...?
WE'VE BEEN SITTING HERE THIRTY MINUTES.
E. COLI GETS A WARMER RECEPTION.
ASSIGNED TO COVER GALAHAD'S RETURN TO AMERICA:
MARIE, ~~famous director~~ camera operator
LESLIE, ~~reporter~~ on-air talent

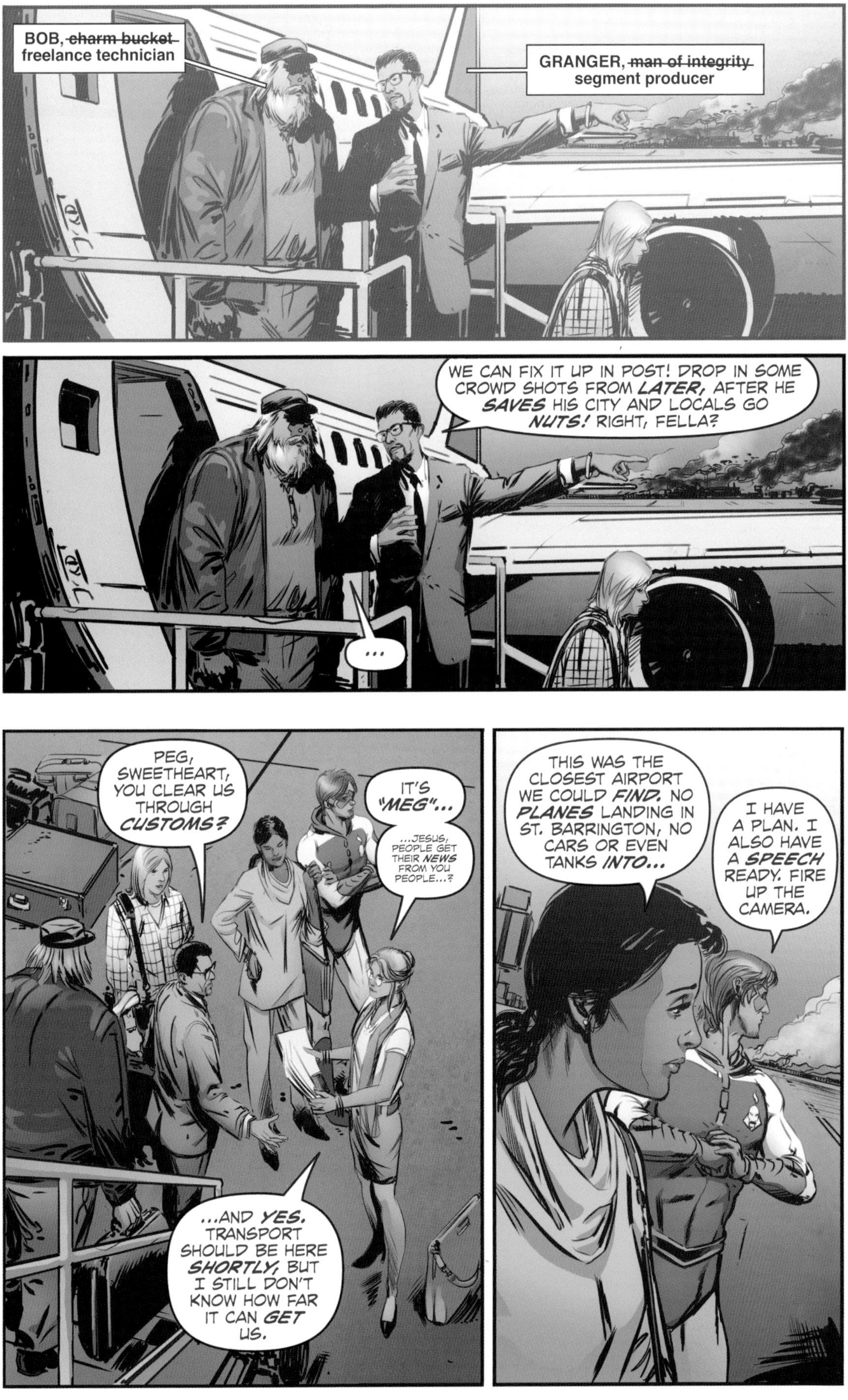

BOB, ~~charm bucket~~ freelance technician
GRANGER, ~~man of integrity~~ segment producer
WE CAN FIX IT UP IN POST! DROP IN SOME CROWD SHOTS FROM *LATER,* AFTER HE *SAVES* HIS CITY AND LOCALS GO *NUTS!* RIGHT, FELLA?
...
PEG, SWEETHEART, YOU CLEAR US THROUGH *CUSTOMS?*
IT'S *"MEG"...*
...JESUS, PEOPLE GET THEIR *NEWS* FROM YOU PEOPLE...?
...AND *YES.* TRANSPORT SHOULD BE HERE *SHORTLY,* BUT I STILL DON'T KNOW HOW FAR IT CAN *GET* US.
THIS WAS THE CLOSEST AIRPORT WE COULD *FIND.* NO *PLANES* LANDING IN ST. BARRINGTON, NO CARS OR EVEN TANKS *INTO...*
I HAVE A PLAN. I ALSO HAVE A *SPEECH* READY. FIRE UP THE CAMERA.

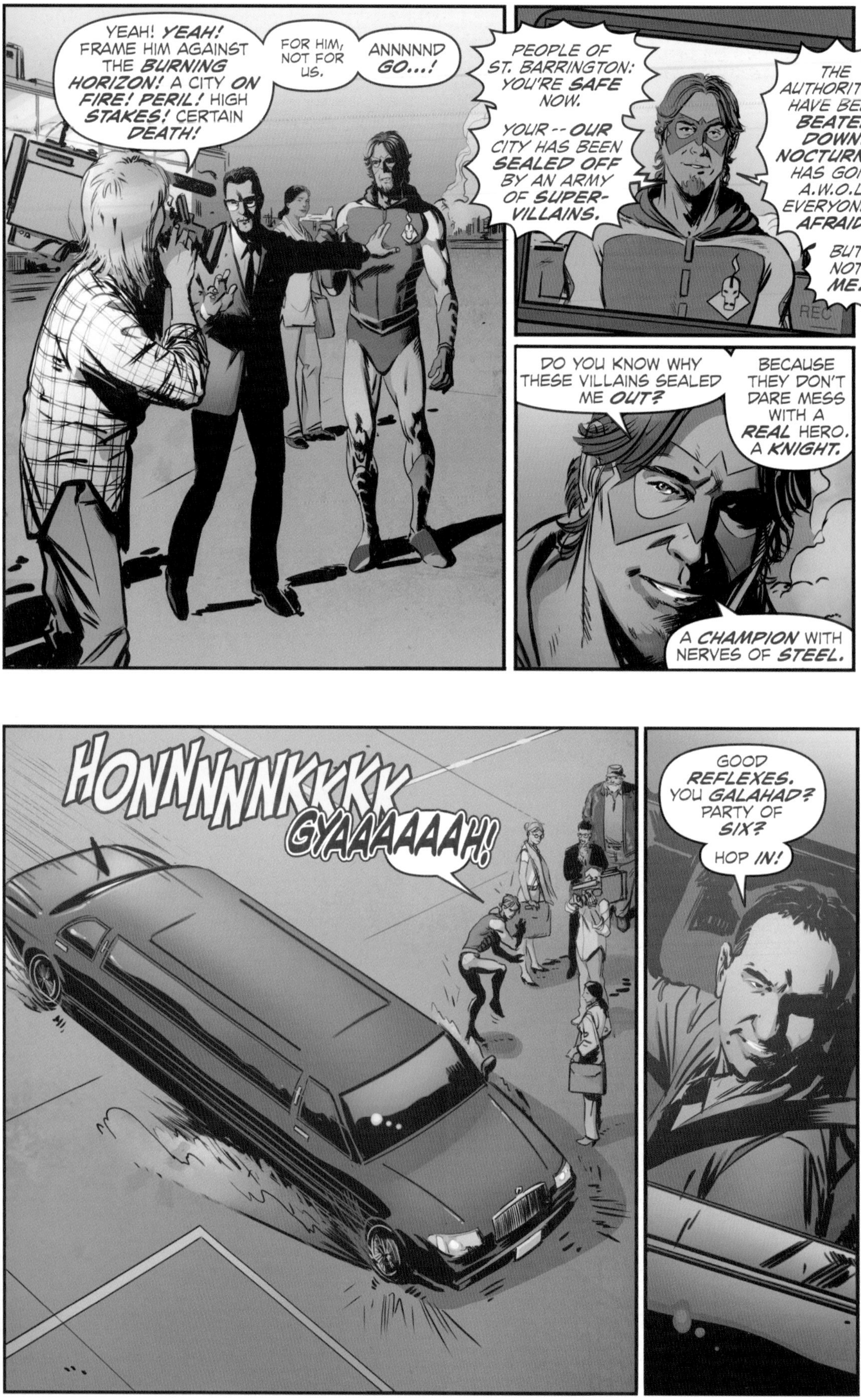
YEAH! YEAH! FRAME HIM AGAINST THE BURNING HORIZON! A CITY ON FIRE! PERIL! HIGH STAKES! CERTAIN DEATH!
FOR HIM, NOT FOR US.
ANNNNND GO...!
PEOPLE OF ST. BARRINGTON: YOU'RE SAFE NOW.
YOUR -- OUR CITY HAS BEEN SEALED OFF BY AN ARMY OF SUPER-VILLAINS.
THE AUTHORITIES HAVE BEEN BEATEN DOWN. NOCTURNUS HAS GONE A.W.O.L. EVERYONE'S AFRAID.
BUT NOT ME.
REC
DO YOU KNOW WHY THESE VILLAINS SEALED ME OUT?
BECAUSE THEY DON'T DARE MESS WITH A REAL HERO. A KNIGHT.
A CHAMPION WITH NERVES OF STEEL.
HONNNNNNKKKK
GYAAAAAAH!
GOOD REFLEXES. YOU GALAHAD? PARTY OF SIX?
HOP IN!

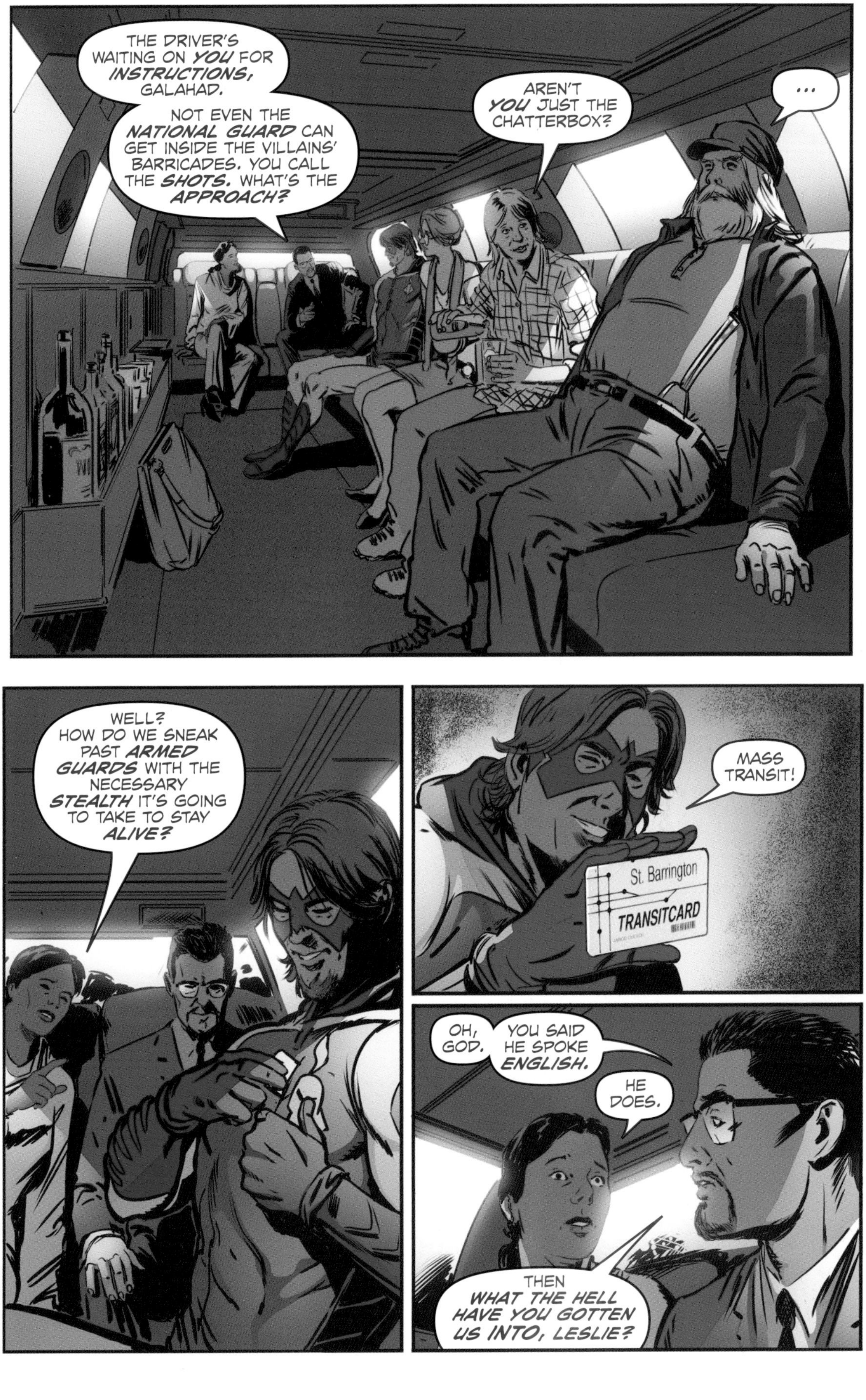
THE DRIVER'S WAITING ON YOU FOR INSTRUCTIONS, GALAHAD.
NOT EVEN THE NATIONAL GUARD CAN GET INSIDE THE VILLAINS' BARRICADES. YOU CALL THE SHOTS. WHAT'S THE APPROACH?
AREN'T YOU JUST THE CHATTERBOX?
...
WELL? HOW DO WE SNEAK PAST ARMED GUARDS WITH THE NECESSARY STEALTH IT'S GOING TO TAKE TO STAY ALIVE?
MASS TRANSIT!
St. Barrington
TRANSITCARD
OH, GOD.
YOU SAID HE SPOKE ENGLISH.
HE DOES.
THEN WHAT THE HELL HAVE YOU GOTTEN US INTO, LESLIE?

CHAPTER 6

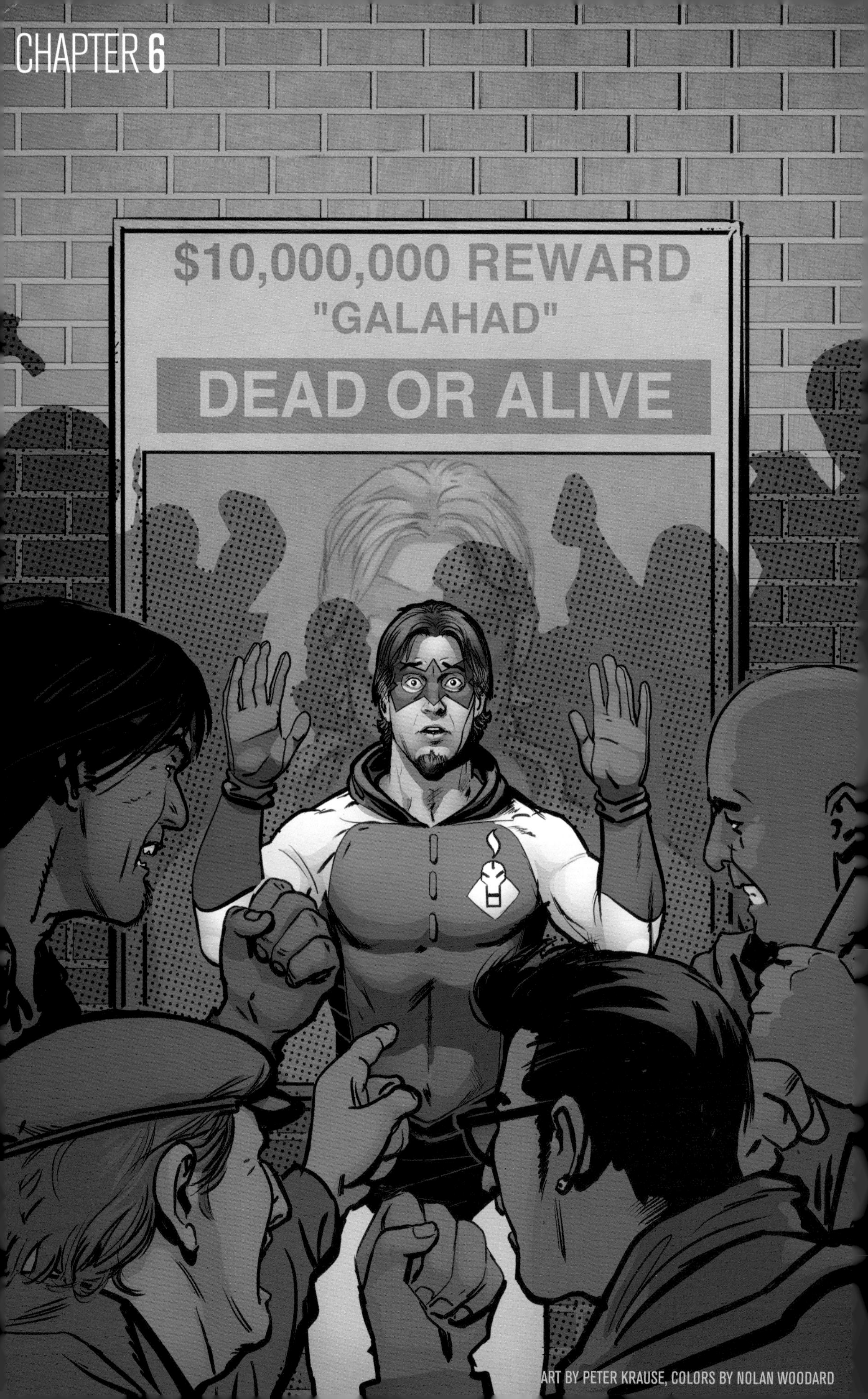

$10,000,000 REWARD
"GALAHAD"
DEAD OR ALIVE

ART BY PETER KRAUSE, COLORS BY NOLAN WOODARD

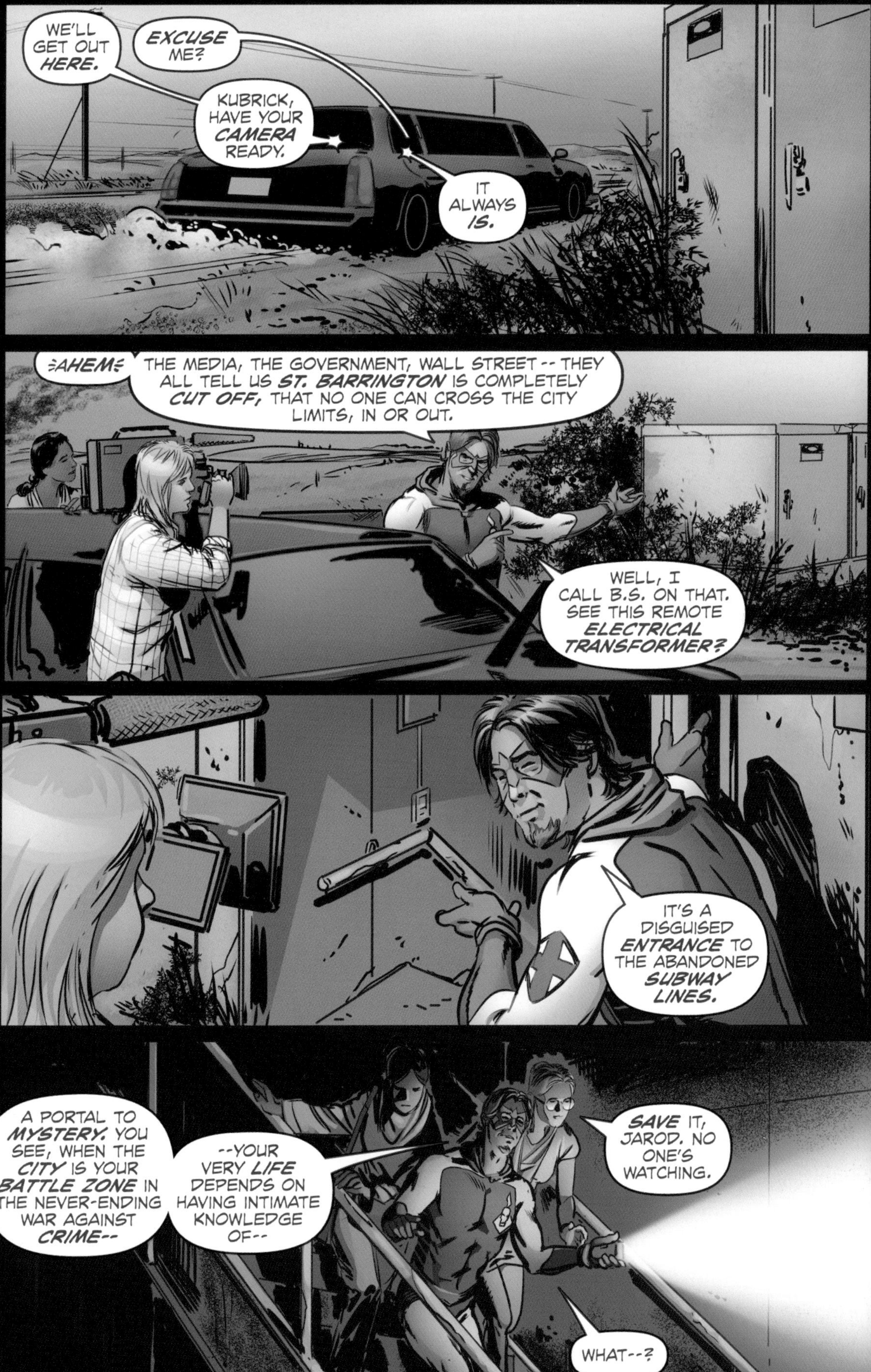
WE'LL GET OUT HERE.
EXCUSE ME?
KUBRICK, HAVE YOUR CAMERA READY.
IT ALWAYS IS.
AHEM
THE MEDIA, THE GOVERNMENT, WALL STREET -- THEY ALL TELL US ST. BARRINGTON IS COMPLETELY CUT OFF, THAT NO ONE CAN CROSS THE CITY LIMITS, IN OR OUT.
WELL, I CALL B.S. ON THAT. SEE THIS REMOTE ELECTRICAL TRANSFORMER?
IT'S A DISGUISED ENTRANCE TO THE ABANDONED SUBWAY LINES.
A PORTAL TO MYSTERY. YOU SEE, WHEN THE CITY IS YOUR BATTLE ZONE IN THE NEVER-ENDING WAR AGAINST CRIME--
--YOUR VERY LIFE DEPENDS ON HAVING INTIMATE KNOWLEDGE OF--
SAVE IT, JAROD. NO ONE'S WATCHING.
WHAT--?

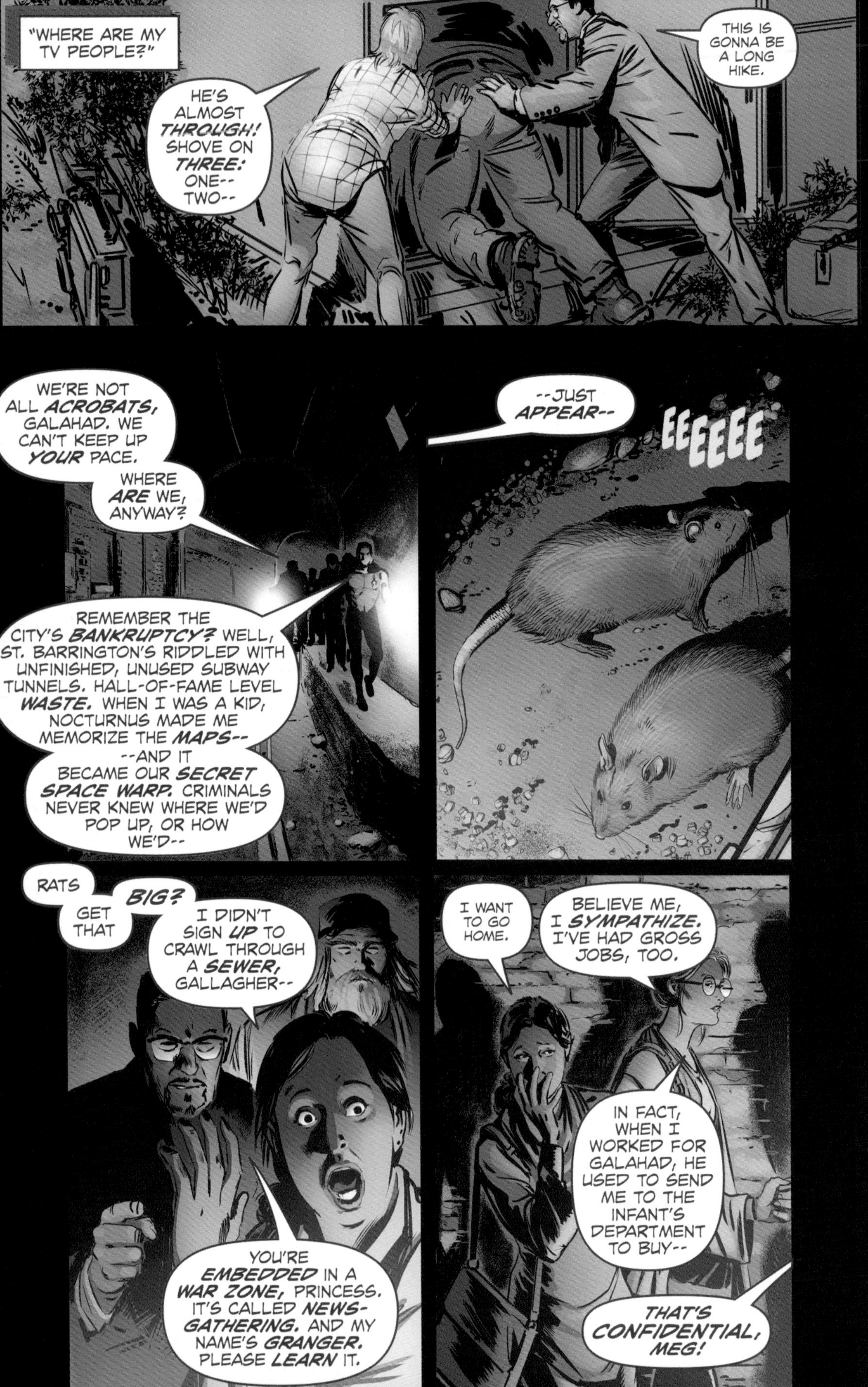
"WHERE ARE MY TV PEOPLE?"
HE'S ALMOST THROUGH! SHOVE ON THREE: ONE-- TWO--
THIS IS GONNA BE A LONG HIKE.
WE'RE NOT ALL ACROBATS, GALAHAD. WE CAN'T KEEP UP YOUR PACE.
WHERE ARE WE, ANYWAY?
REMEMBER THE CITY'S BANKRUPTCY? WELL, ST. BARRINGTON'S RIDDLED WITH UNFINISHED, UNUSED SUBWAY TUNNELS. HALL-OF-FAME LEVEL WASTE. WHEN I WAS A KID, NOCTURNUS MADE ME MEMORIZE THE MAPS--
--AND IT BECAME OUR SECRET SPACE WARP. CRIMINALS NEVER KNEW WHERE WE'D POP UP, OR HOW WE'D--
--JUST APPEAR--
EEEEEE
RATS GET THAT BIG?
I DIDN'T SIGN UP TO CRAWL THROUGH A SEWER, GALLAGHER--
YOU'RE EMBEDDED IN A WAR ZONE, PRINCESS. IT'S CALLED NEWS-GATHERING. AND MY NAME'S GRANGER. PLEASE LEARN IT.
I WANT TO GO HOME.
BELIEVE ME, I SYMPATHIZE. I'VE HAD GROSS JOBS, TOO.
IN FACT, WHEN I WORKED FOR GALAHAD, HE USED TO SEND ME TO THE INFANT'S DEPARTMENT TO BUY--
THAT'S CONFIDENTIAL, MEG!

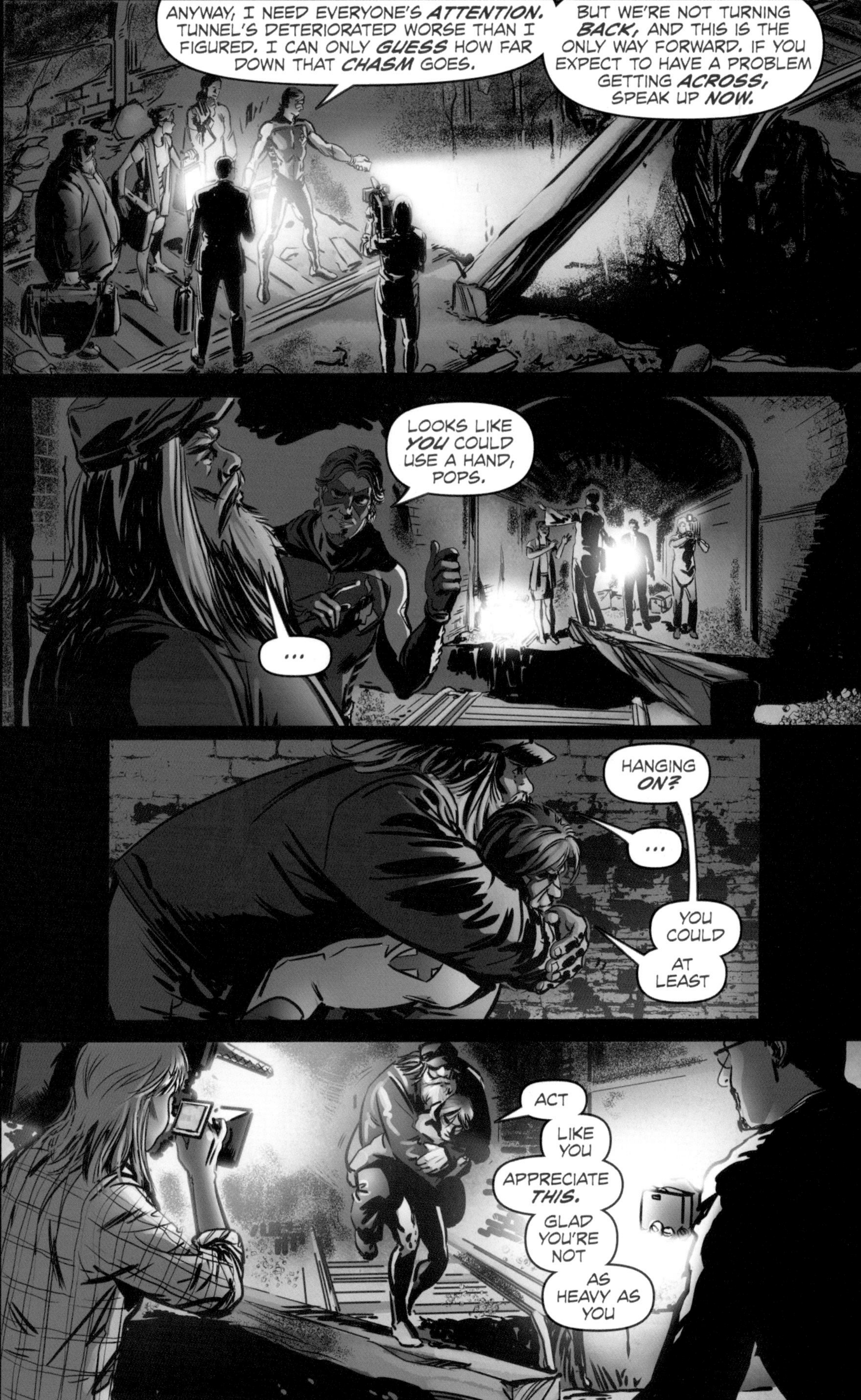
ANYWAY, I NEED EVERYONE'S ATTENTION. TUNNEL'S DETERIORATED WORSE THAN I FIGURED. I CAN ONLY GUESS HOW FAR DOWN THAT CHASM GOES.
BUT WE'RE NOT TURNING BACK, AND THIS IS THE ONLY WAY FORWARD. IF YOU EXPECT TO HAVE A PROBLEM GETTING ACROSS, SPEAK UP NOW.
LOOKS LIKE YOU COULD USE A HAND, POPS.
...
HANGING ON?
...
YOU COULD
AT LEAST
ACT
LIKE YOU
APPRECIATE THIS.
GLAD YOU'RE NOT
AS HEAVY AS YOU

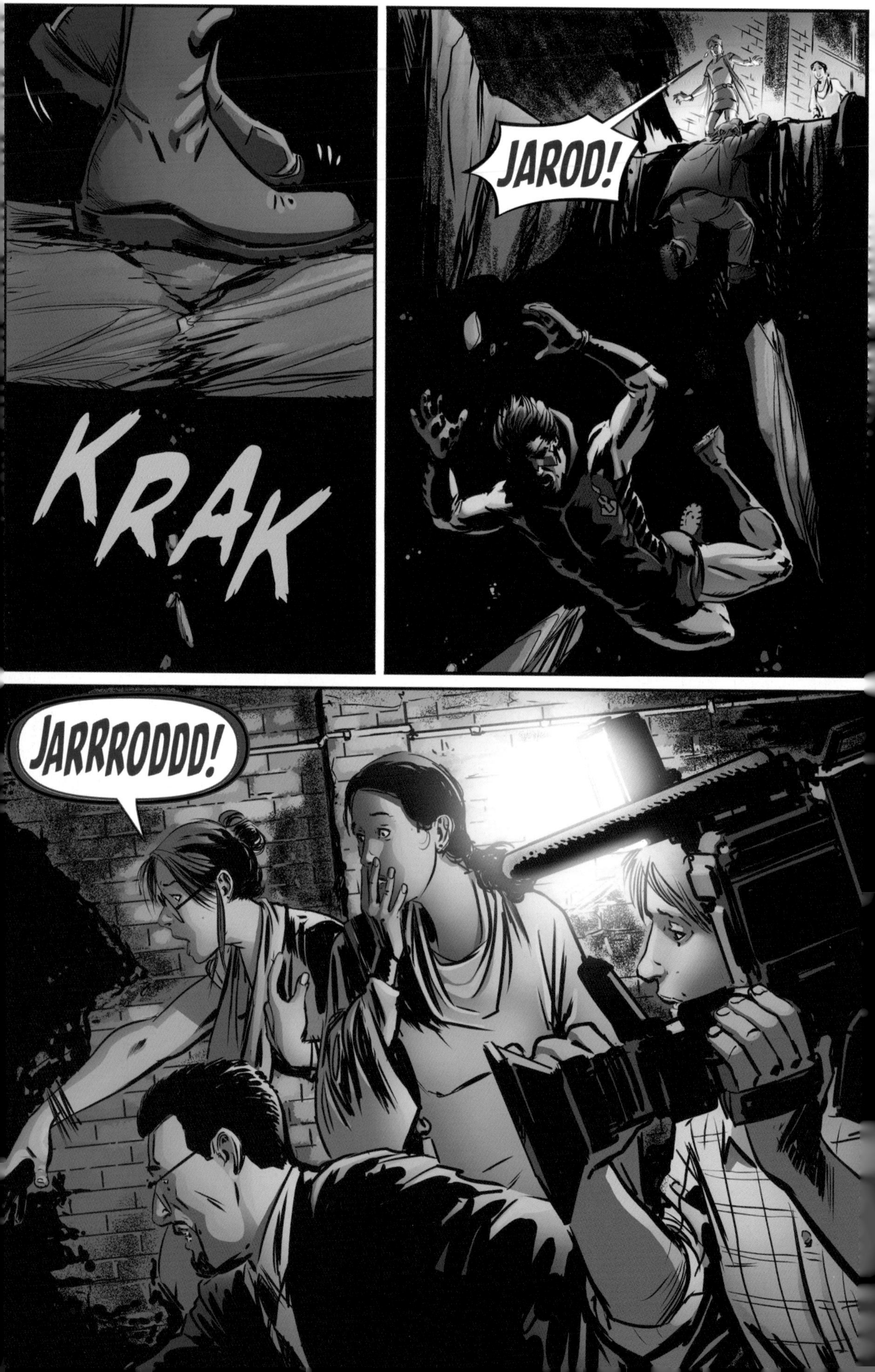
KRAK
JAROD!
JARRRODDD!

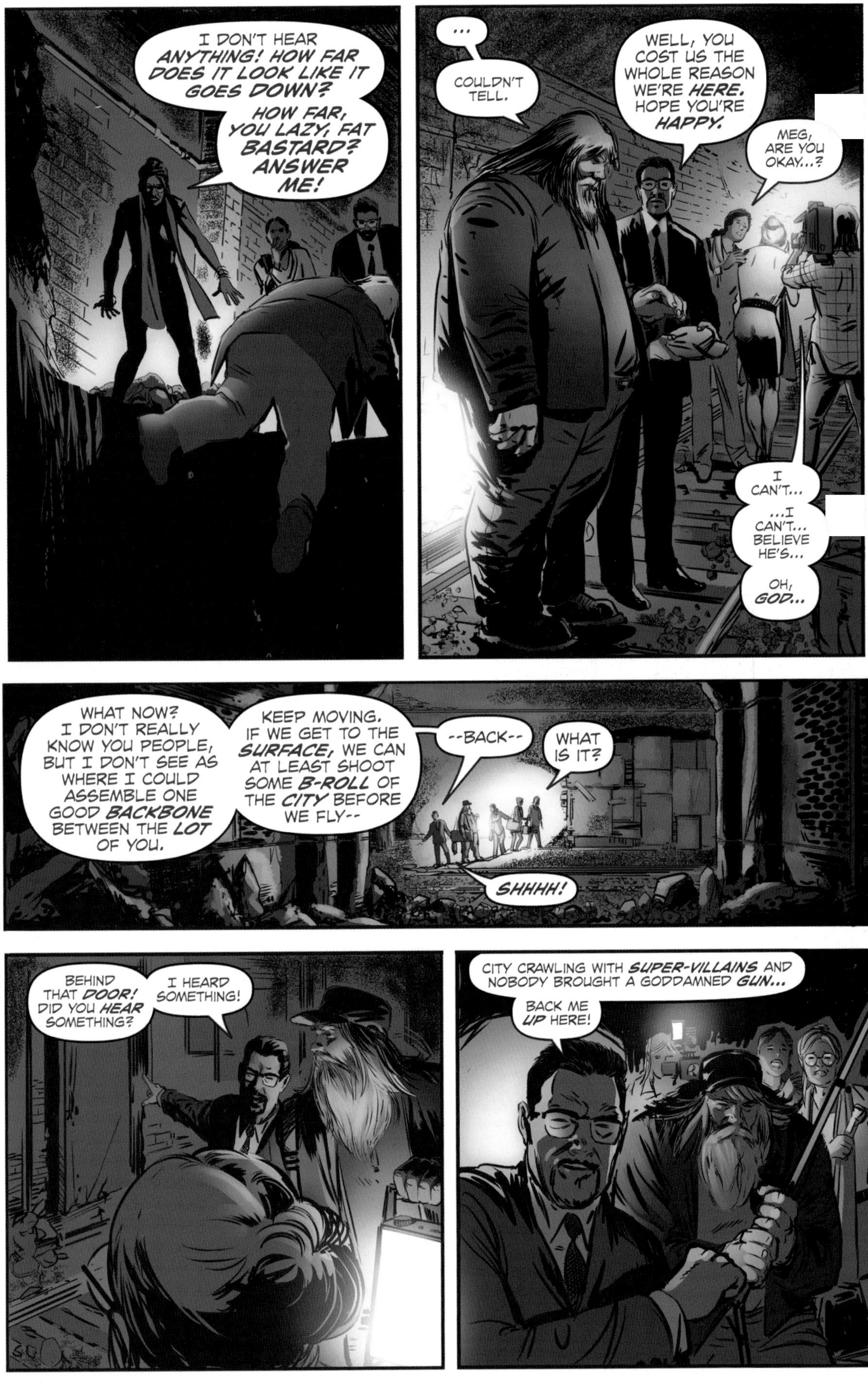
I DON'T HEAR ANYTHING! HOW FAR DOES IT LOOK LIKE IT GOES DOWN?
HOW FAR, YOU LAZY, FAT BASTARD? ANSWER ME!
...
COULDN'T TELL.
WELL, YOU COST US THE WHOLE REASON WE'RE HERE. HOPE YOU'RE HAPPY.
MEG, ARE YOU OKAY...?
I CAN'T...
...I CAN'T... BELIEVE HE'S...
OH, GOD...
WHAT NOW? I DON'T REALLY KNOW YOU PEOPLE, BUT I DON'T SEE AS WHERE I COULD ASSEMBLE ONE GOOD BACKBONE BETWEEN THE LOT OF YOU.
KEEP MOVING. IF WE GET TO THE SURFACE, WE CAN AT LEAST SHOOT SOME B-ROLL OF THE CITY BEFORE WE FLY--
--BACK--
WHAT IS IT?
SHHHH!
BEHIND THAT DOOR! DID YOU HEAR SOMETHING?
I HEARD SOMETHING!
CITY CRAWLING WITH SUPER-VILLAINS AND NOBODY BROUGHT A GODDAMNED GUN...
BACK ME UP HERE!

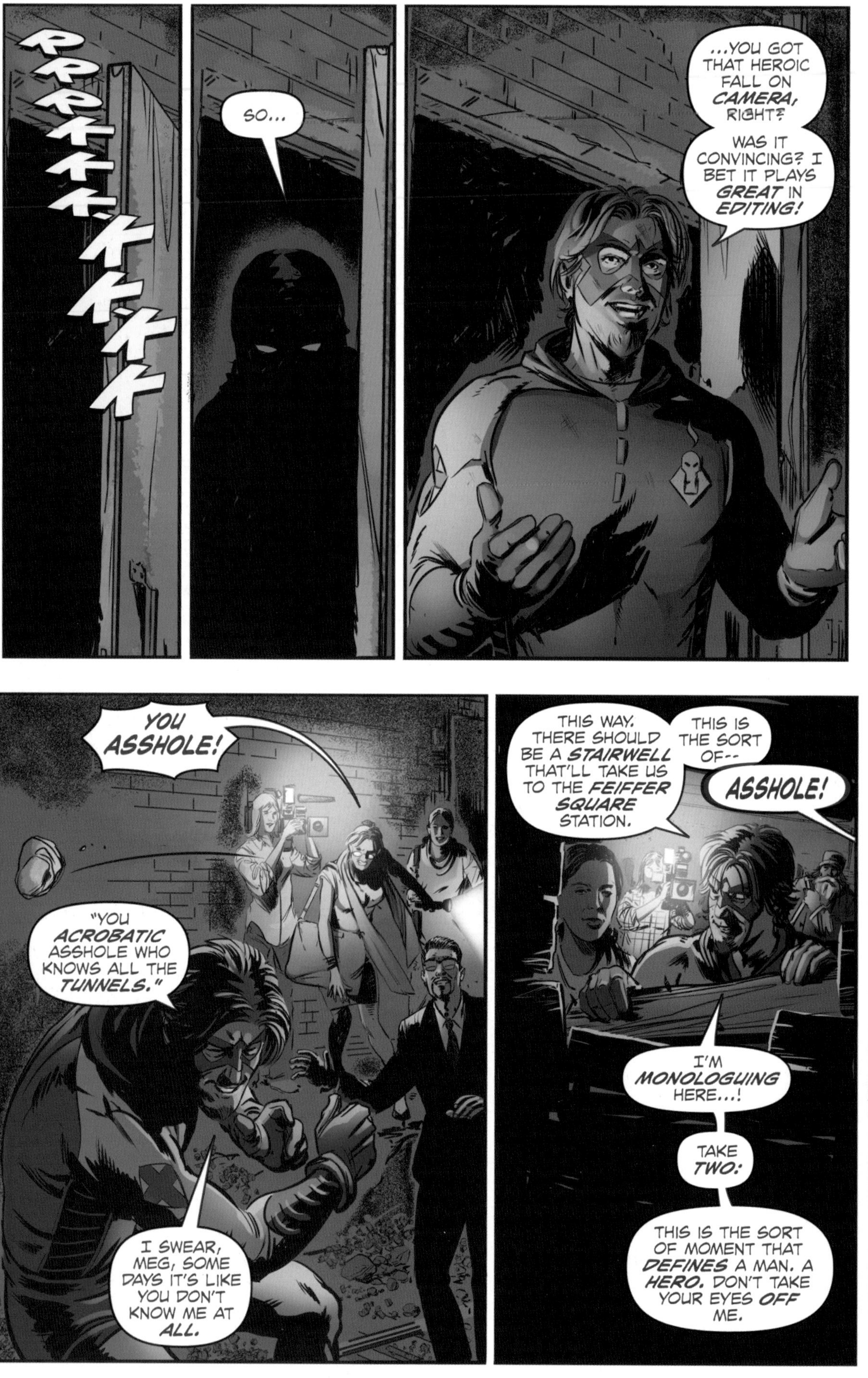
RRRKKK-KK-KK
SO...
...YOU GOT THAT HEROIC FALL ON CAMERA, RIGHT?
WAS IT CONVINCING? I BET IT PLAYS GREAT IN EDITING!
YOU ASSHOLE!
"YOU ACROBATIC ASSHOLE WHO KNOWS ALL THE TUNNELS."
I SWEAR, MEG, SOME DAYS IT'S LIKE YOU DON'T KNOW ME AT ALL.
THIS WAY. THERE SHOULD BE A STAIRWELL THAT'LL TAKE US TO THE FEIFFER SQUARE STATION.
THIS IS THE SORT OF--
ASSHOLE!
I'M MONOLOGUING HERE...!
TAKE TWO:
THIS IS THE SORT OF MOMENT THAT DEFINES A MAN. A HERO. DON'T TAKE YOUR EYES OFF ME.

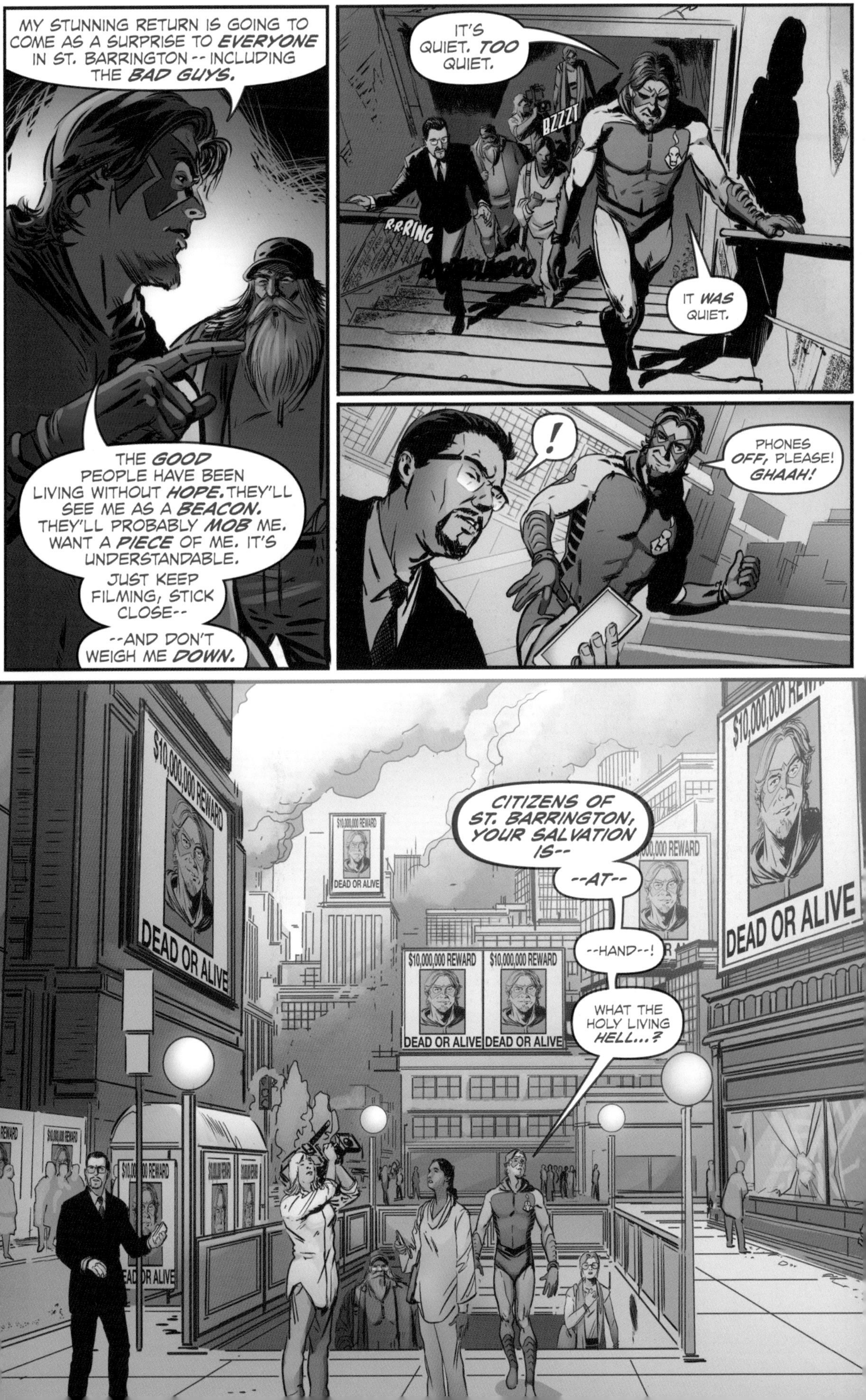
MY STUNNING RETURN IS GOING TO COME AS A SURPRISE TO *EVERYONE* IN ST. BARRINGTON -- INCLUDING THE *BAD GUYS.*
THE *GOOD* PEOPLE HAVE BEEN LIVING WITHOUT *HOPE.* THEY'LL SEE ME AS A *BEACON.* THEY'LL PROBABLY *MOB* ME. WANT A *PIECE* OF ME. IT'S UNDERSTANDABLE.
JUST KEEP FILMING, STICK CLOSE--
--AND DON'T WEIGH ME *DOWN.*
IT'S QUIET. *TOO* QUIET.
BZZZT
R-R-RING
IT *WAS* QUIET.
!
PHONES *OFF*, PLEASE! *GHAAH!*
$10,000,000 REWARD
DEAD OR ALIVE
CITIZENS OF ST. BARRINGTON, YOUR SALVATION IS--
--AT--
--HAND--!
WHAT THE HOLY LIVING *HELL...?*

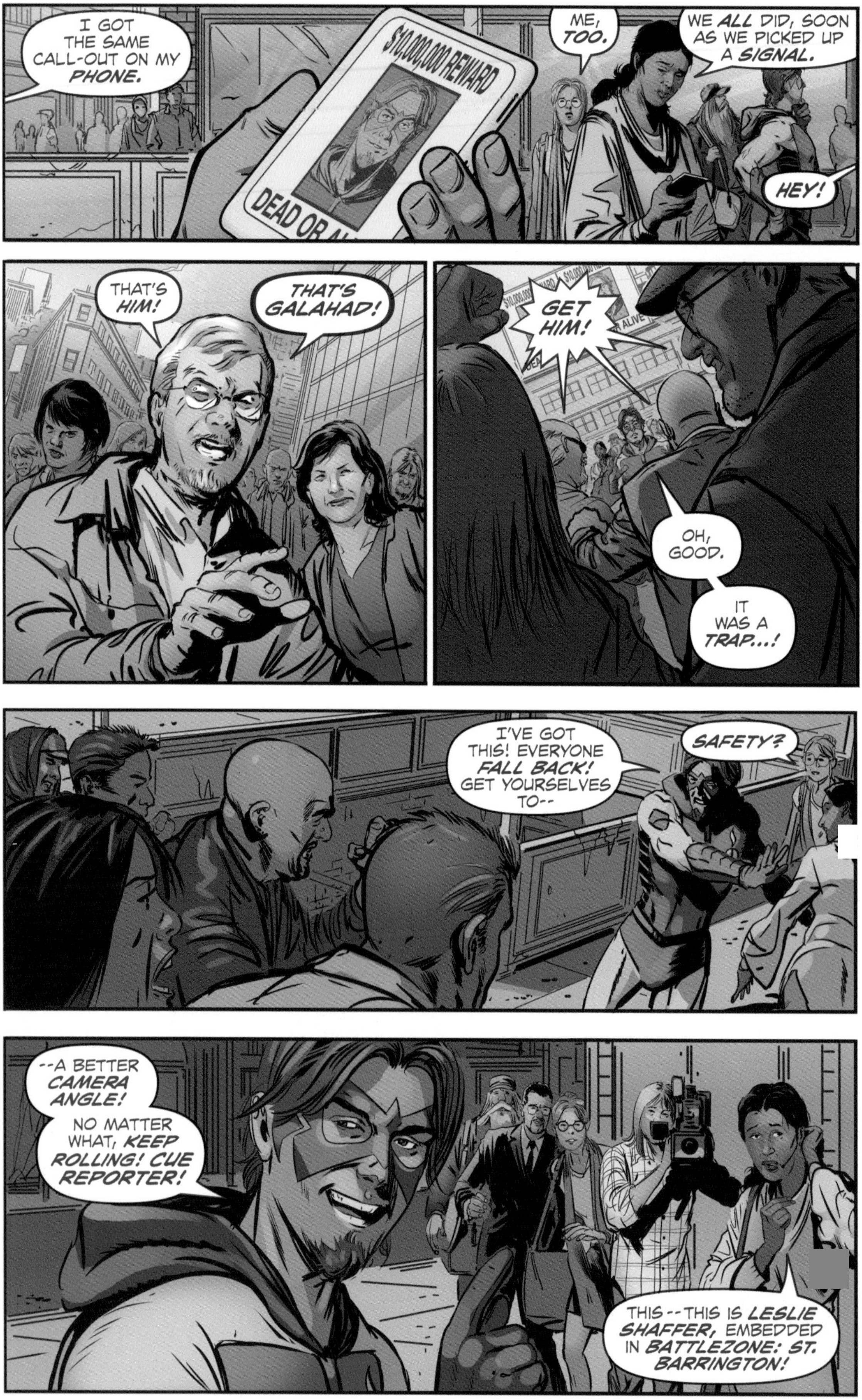
I GOT THE SAME CALL-OUT ON MY PHONE.
$10,000,000 REWARD
DEAD OR AL
ME, TOO.
WE ALL DID, SOON AS WE PICKED UP A SIGNAL.
HEY!
THAT'S HIM!
THAT'S GALAHAD!
GET HIM!
OH, GOOD.
IT WAS A TRAP...!
I'VE GOT THIS! EVERYONE FALL BACK! GET YOURSELVES TO--
SAFETY?
--A BETTER CAMERA ANGLE!
NO MATTER WHAT, KEEP ROLLING! CUE REPORTER!
THIS--THIS IS LESLIE SHAFFER, EMBEDDED IN BATTLEZONE: ST. BARRINGTON!

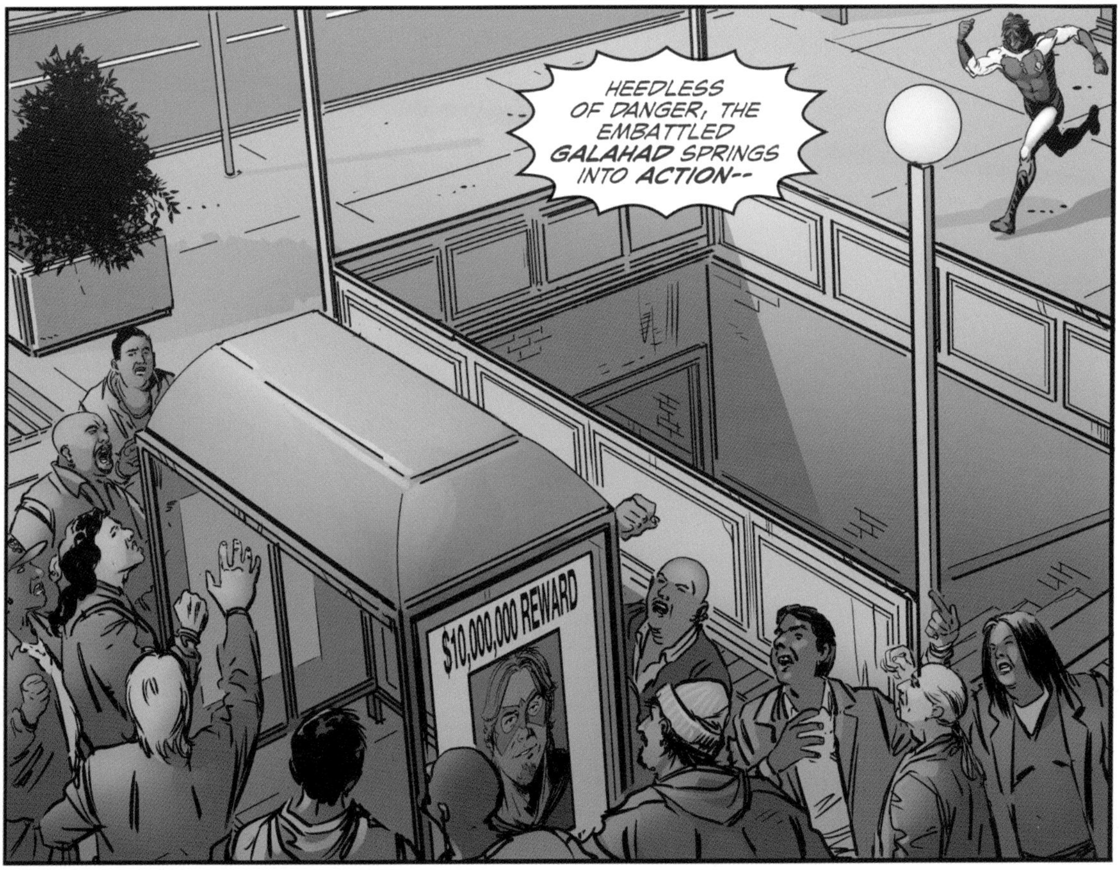
HEEDLESS OF DANGER, THE EMBATTLED GALAHAD SPRINGS INTO ACTION--
$10,000,000 REWARD

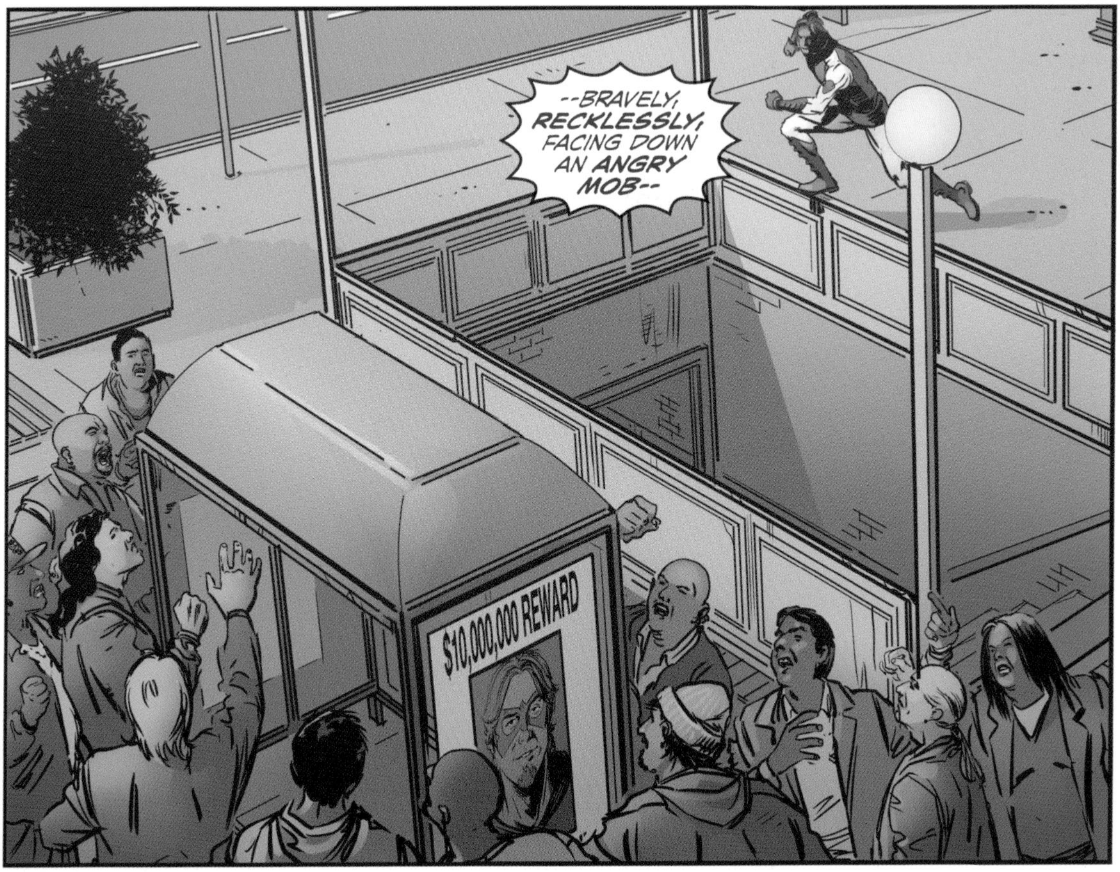
--BRAVELY, RECKLESSLY, FACING DOWN AN ANGRY MOB--
$10,000,000 REWARD

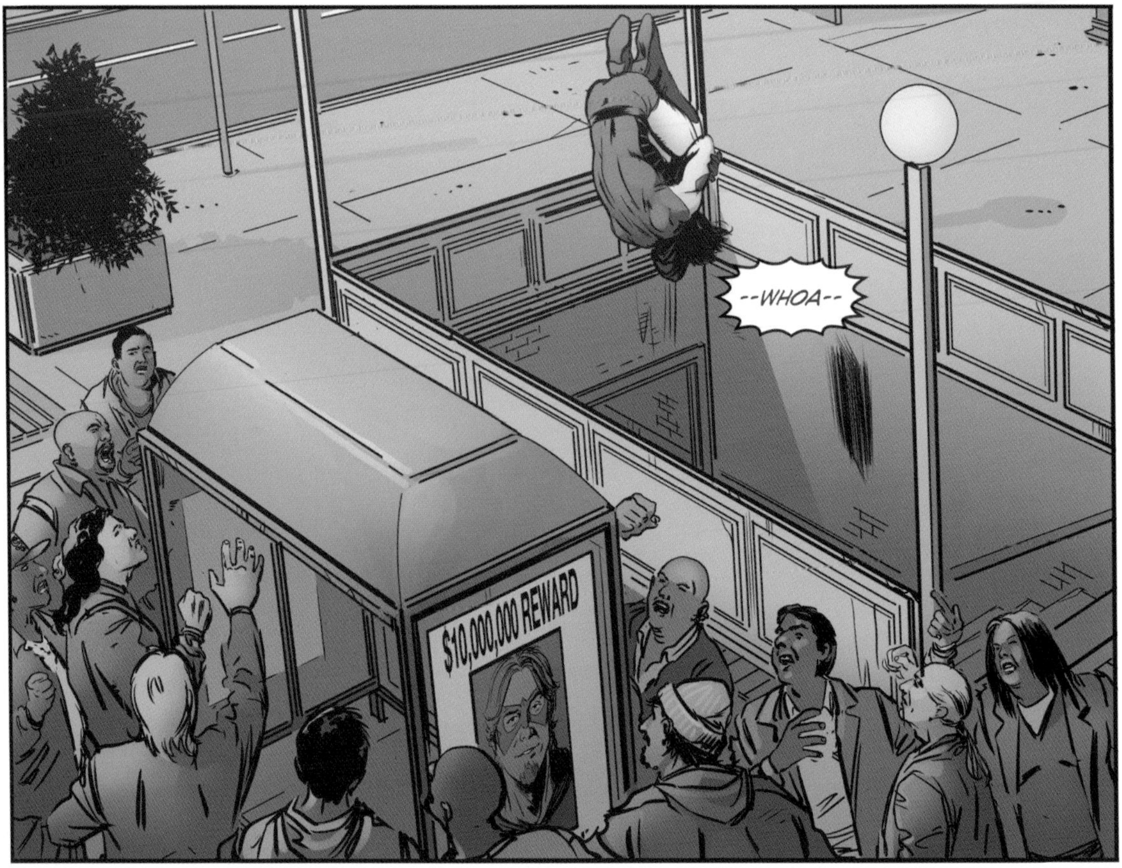
--WHOA--
$10,000,000 REWARD

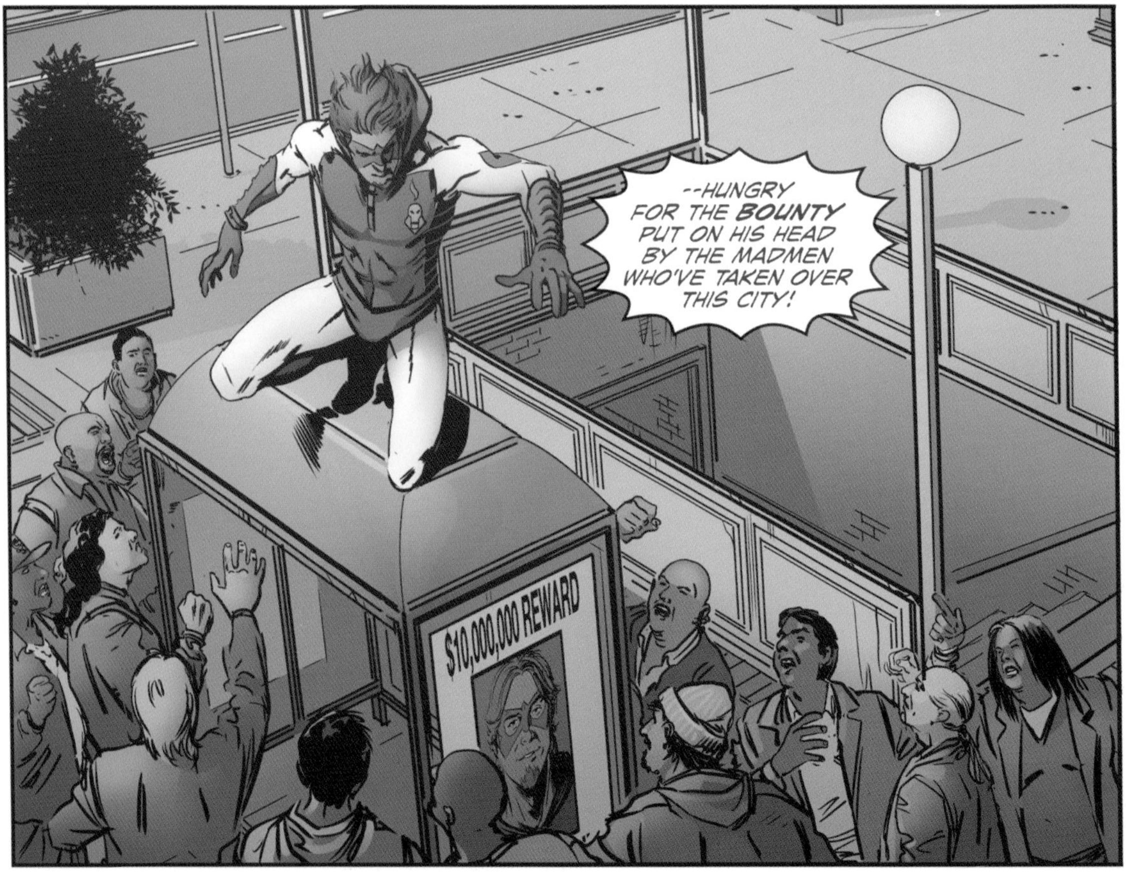
--HUNGRY FOR THE BOUNTY PUT ON HIS HEAD BY THE MADMEN WHO'VE TAKEN OVER THIS CITY!
$10,000,000 REWARD

EVERYONE *CHILL!* YOU'RE *SAFE* NOW! LET'S GET THIS CITY *RIGHTED!* WHO'S *WITH* ME!

YOU *ASSHOLE!*

NO! IT WASN'T *LIKE* THAT! I--

YOU WENT ON *VACATION* WHILE THIS CITY *BURNED!*

YOU LEFT US TO DIE!

$10,000,000 REWARD

DEAD OR ALIVE

THEY'RE RATIONING OUR *FOOD!*

IT'S EVERY MAN FOR *HIMSELF!*

AND OUR *WATER!*

GET HIM!

LADIES AND GENTLEMEN, YOU'RE WITNESSING THE FALL OF A--

--WELL-- SOME SAY *HERO,* OTHERS SAY *CELEBRITY*--

DEAD OR AL

--BUT, FROM WHERE I STAND, ULTIMATELY A SAD *MAN-CHILD* WHOSE *EGO* WAS HIS GREATEST DOWNFALL.

DEAD OR AL

AS HIS FORMER DEVOTEES TORE HIM *LIMB FROM LIMB,* THEY SHOWED *NO LOVE* FOR THE COSTUMED CHAMPION THEY'D *KILLED* WITH THEIR *BARE HANDS* -- CITIZENS TURNED *SAVAGES* BY THE HARSH --

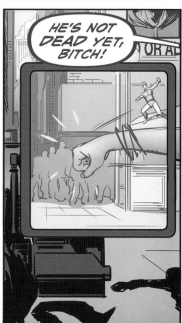

HE'S NOT DEAD YET, BITCH!

OR AL

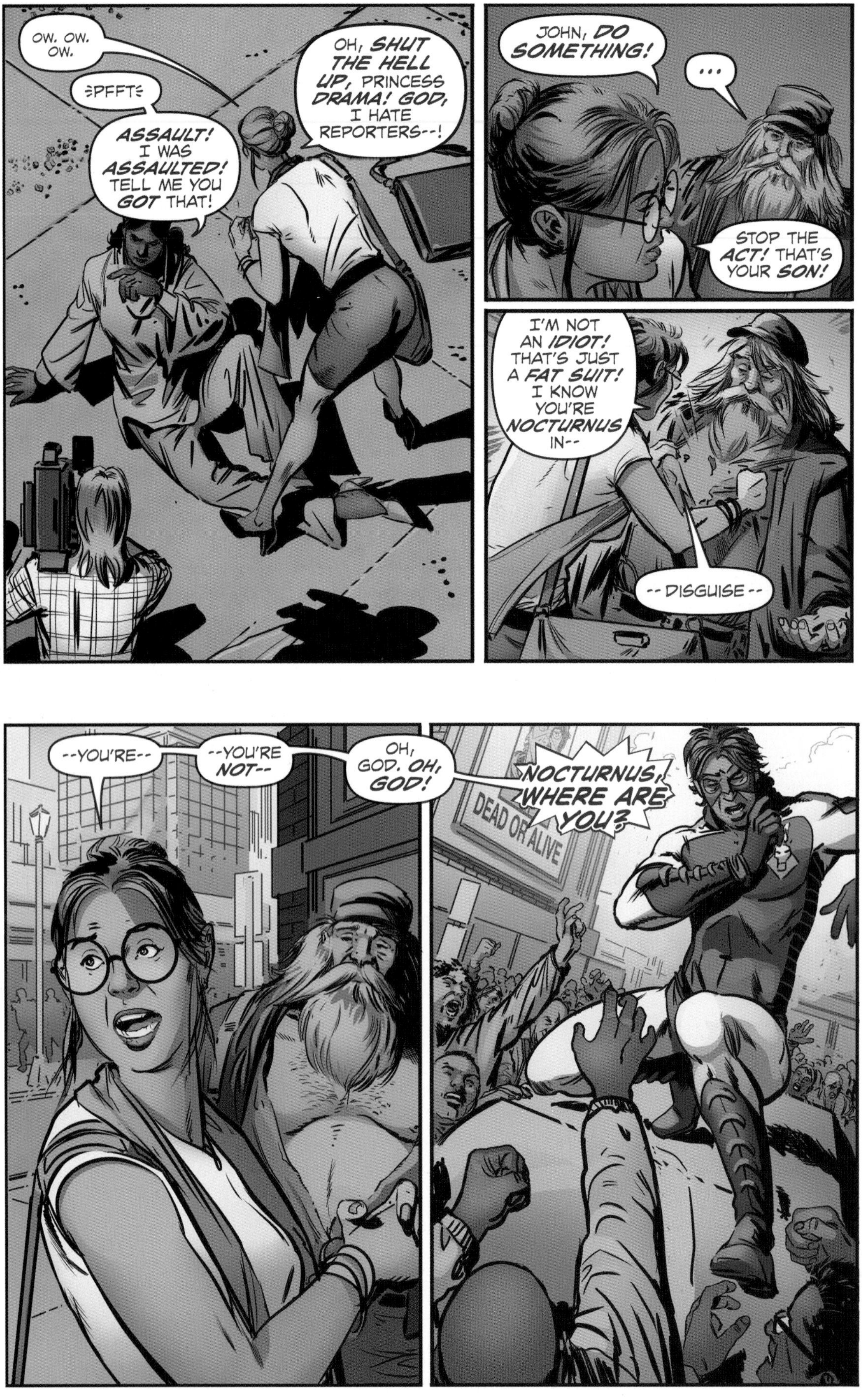
OW. OW. OW.
PFFT
ASSAULT! I WAS ASSAULTED! TELL ME YOU GOT THAT!
OH, SHUT THE HELL UP, PRINCESS DRAMA! GOD, I HATE REPORTERS--!
JOHN, DO SOMETHING!
...
STOP THE ACT! THAT'S YOUR SON!
I'M NOT AN IDIOT! THAT'S JUST A FAT SUIT! I KNOW YOU'RE NOCTURNUS IN--
--DISGUISE--
--YOU'RE--
--YOU'RE NOT--
OH, GOD. OH, GOD!
NOCTURNUS, WHERE ARE YOU?
DEAD OR ALIVE

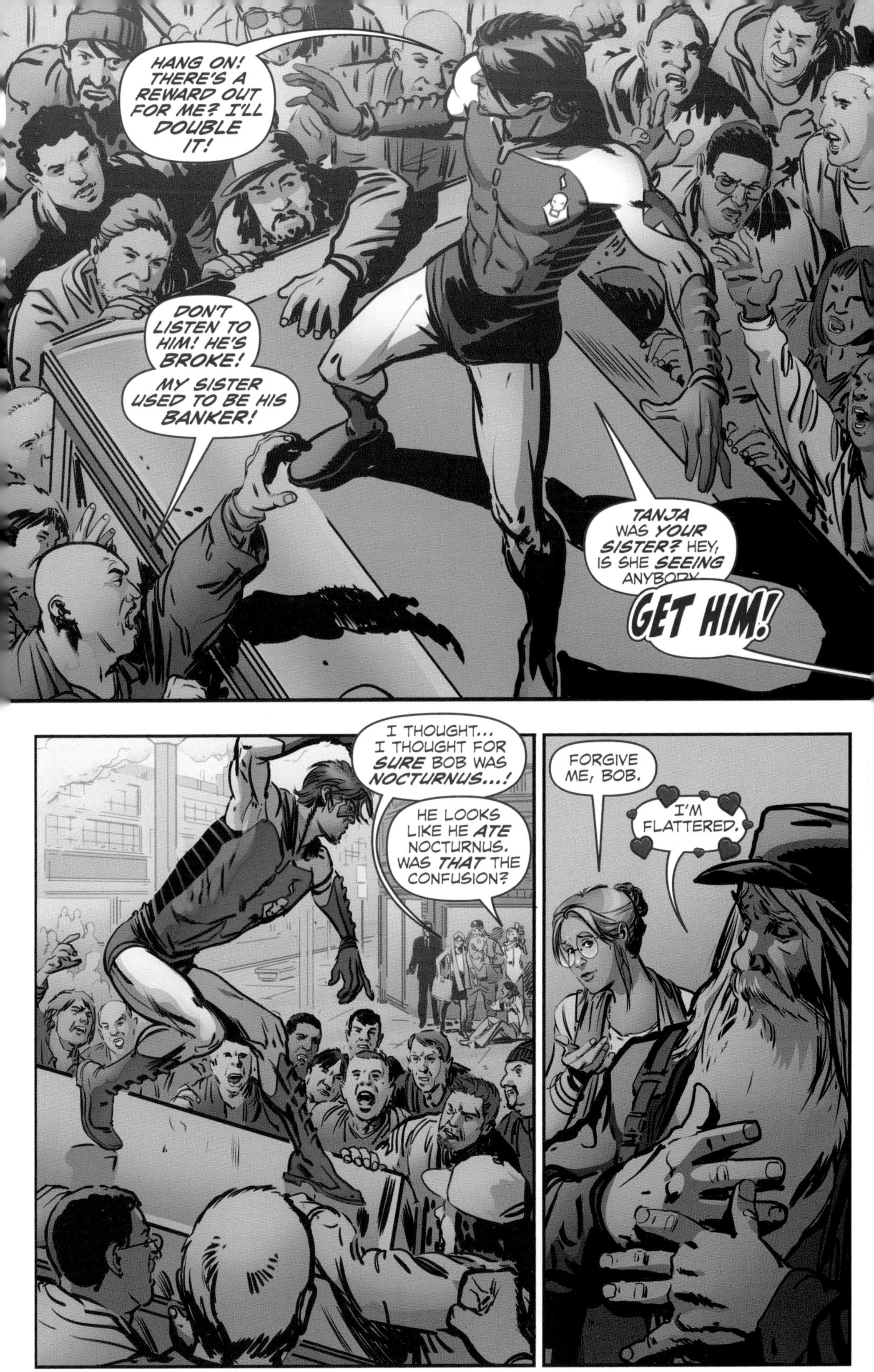
HANG ON! THERE'S A REWARD OUT FOR ME? I'LL DOUBLE IT!
DON'T LISTEN TO HIM! HE'S BROKE!
MY SISTER USED TO BE HIS BANKER!
TANJA WAS YOUR SISTER? HEY, IS SHE SEEING ANYBODY
GET HIM!
I THOUGHT... I THOUGHT FOR SURE BOB WAS NOCTURNUS...!
HE LOOKS LIKE HE ATE NOCTURNUS. WAS THAT THE CONFUSION?
FORGIVE ME, BOB.
I'M FLATTERED.

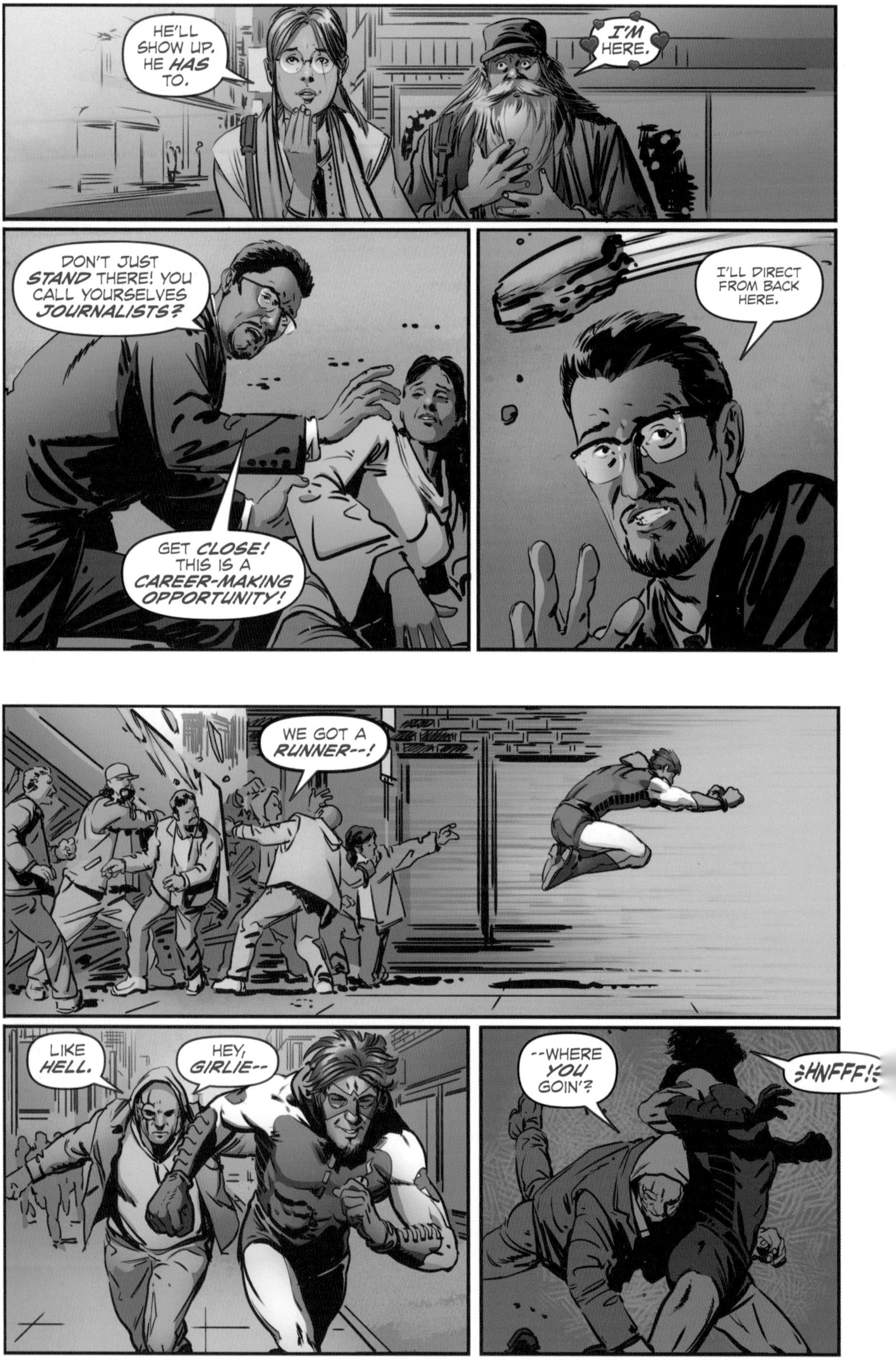
HE'LL SHOW UP. HE HAS TO.
I'M HERE.
DON'T JUST STAND THERE! YOU CALL YOURSELVES JOURNALISTS?
GET CLOSE! THIS IS A CAREER-MAKING OPPORTUNITY!
I'LL DIRECT FROM BACK HERE.
WE GOT A RUNNER--!
LIKE HELL.
HEY, GIRLIE--
--WHERE YOU GOIN'?
HNFFF!

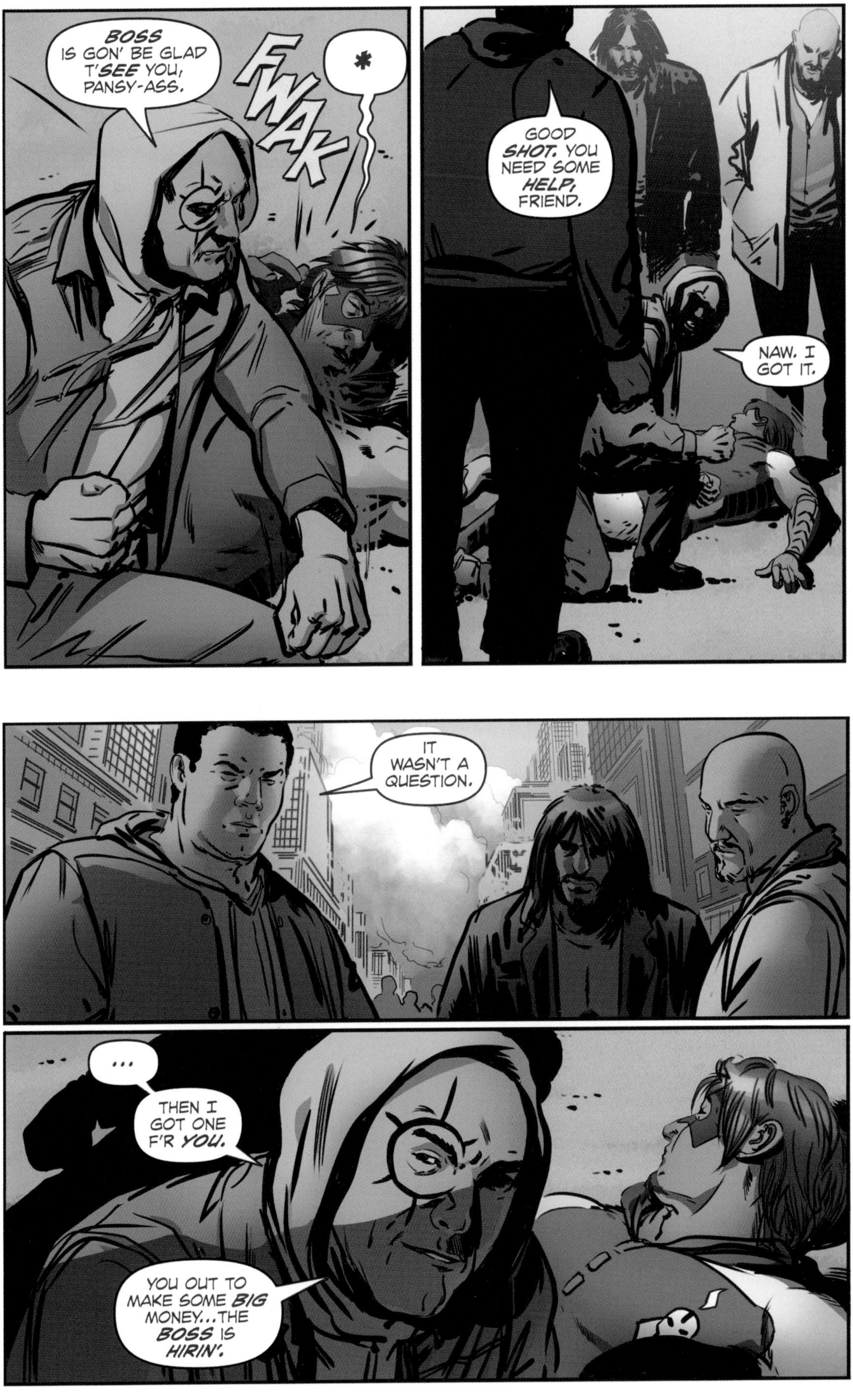
BOSS IS GON' BE GLAD T'SEE YOU, PANSY-ASS.
FWAK
*
GOOD SHOT. YOU NEED SOME HELP, FRIEND.
NAW. I GOT IT.
IT WASN'T A QUESTION.
...
THEN I GOT ONE F'R YOU.
YOU OUT TO MAKE SOME BIG MONEY...THE BOSS IS HIRIN'.

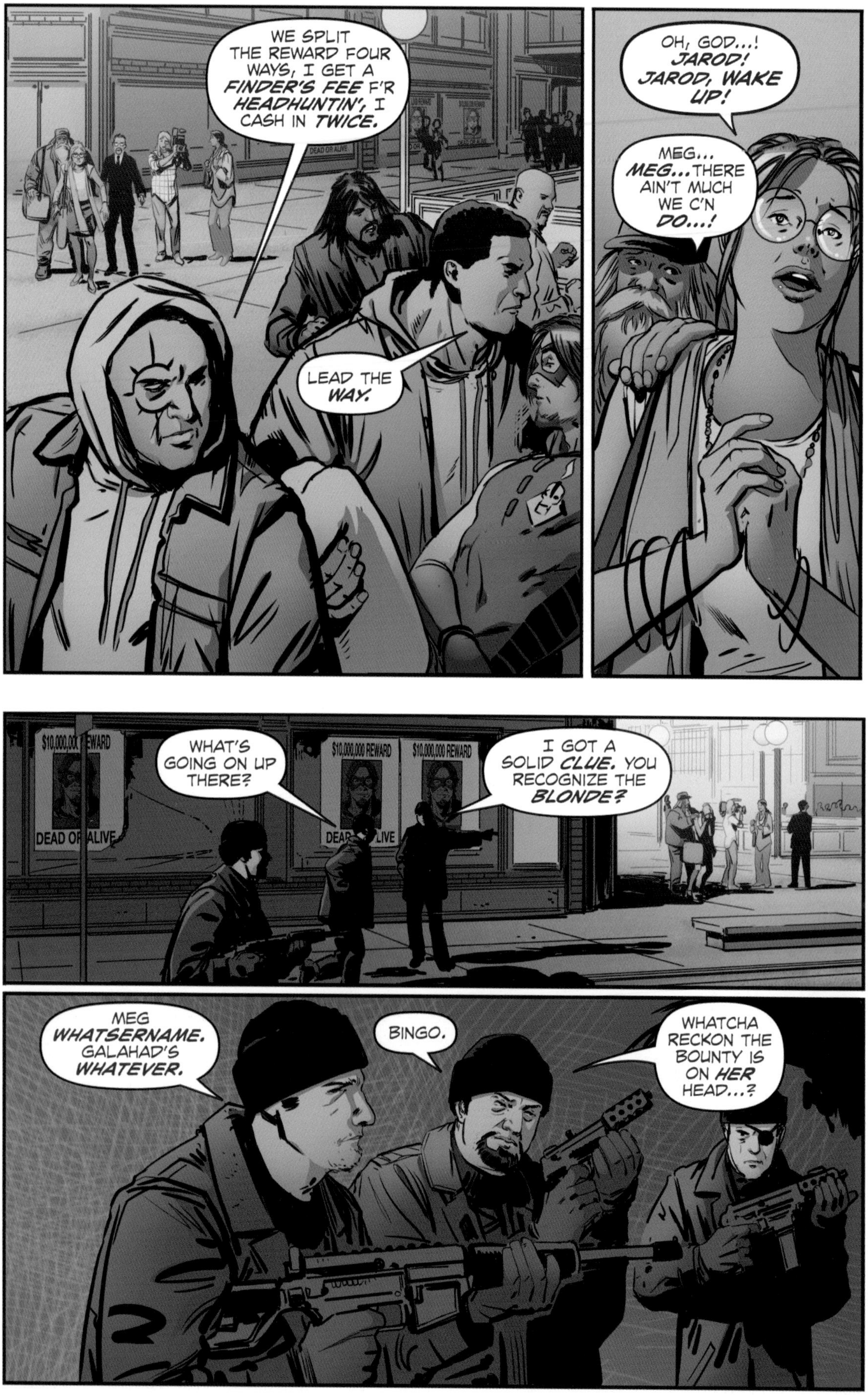
WE SPLIT THE REWARD FOUR WAYS, I GET A FINDER'S FEE F'R HEADHUNTIN', I CASH IN TWICE.
LEAD THE WAY.
OH, GOD...! JAROD! JAROD, WAKE UP!
MEG... MEG... THERE AIN'T MUCH WE C'N DO...!
$10,000,000 REWARD
$10,000,000 REWARD
WHAT'S GOING ON UP THERE?
I GOT A SOLID CLUE. YOU RECOGNIZE THE BLONDE?
MEG WHATSERNAME. GALAHAD'S WHATEVER.
BINGO.
WHATCHA RECKON THE BOUNTY IS ON HER HEAD...?

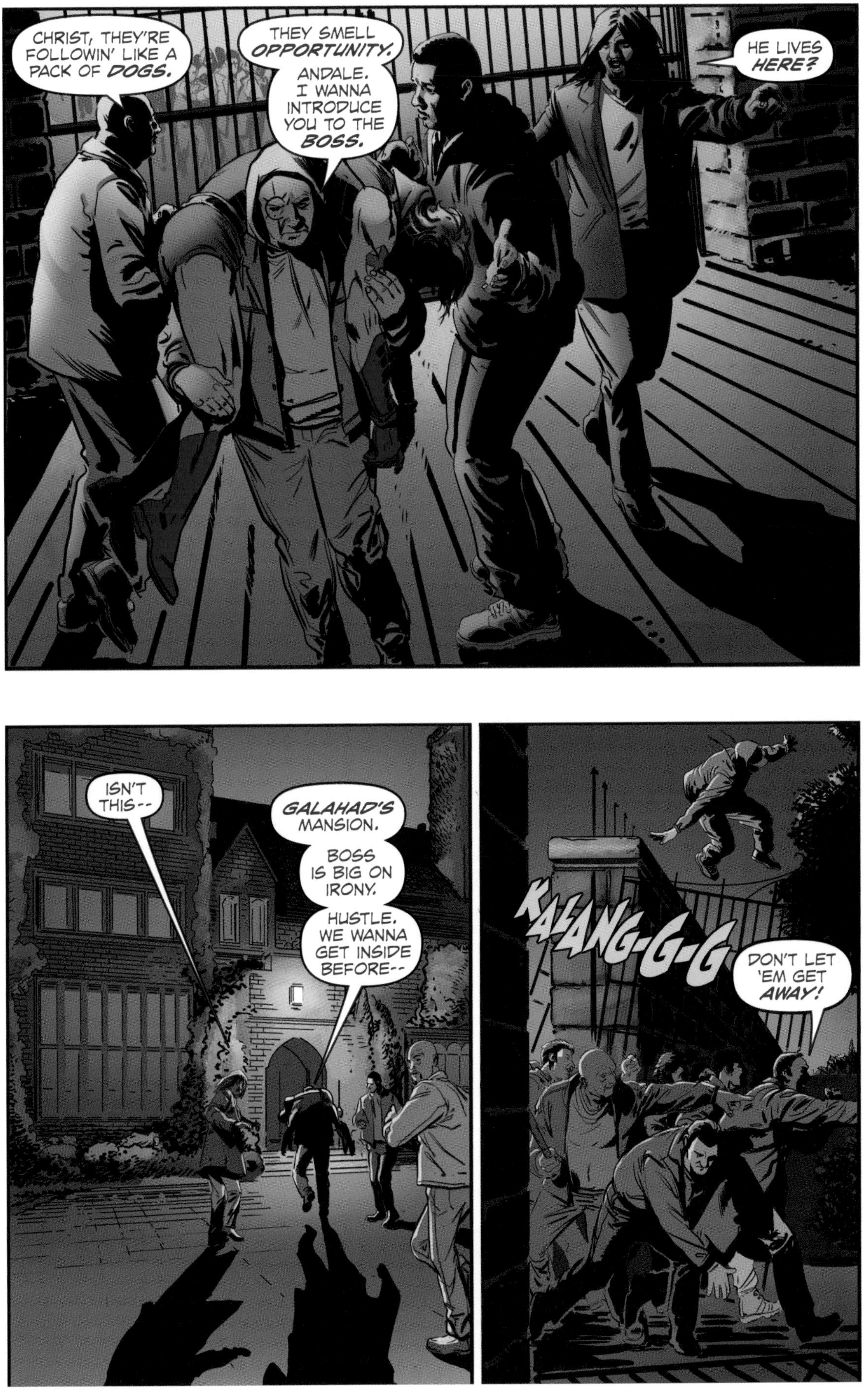
CHRIST, THEY'RE FOLLOWIN' LIKE A PACK OF DOGS.
THEY SMELL OPPORTUNITY.
ANDALE. I WANNA INTRODUCE YOU TO THE BOSS.
HE LIVES HERE?
ISN'T THIS--
GALAHAD'S MANSION.
BOSS IS BIG ON IRONY.
HUSTLE. WE WANNA GET INSIDE BEFORE--
KALANG-G-G
DON'T LET 'EM GET AWAY!

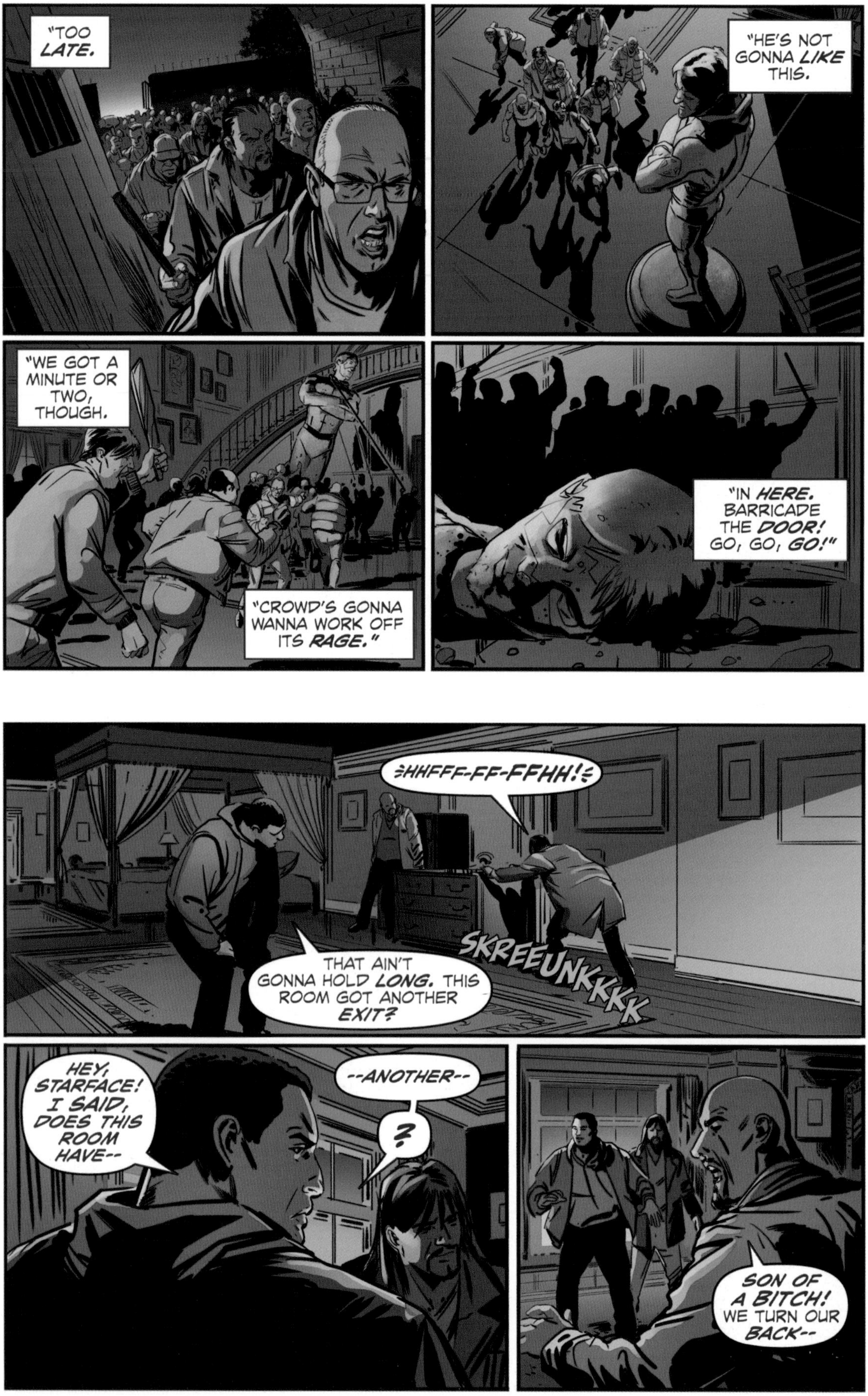
"TOO LATE.
"HE'S NOT GONNA LIKE THIS.
"WE GOT A MINUTE OR TWO, THOUGH.
"CROWD'S GONNA WANNA WORK OFF ITS RAGE."
"IN HERE. BARRICADE THE DOOR! GO, GO, GO!"
HHFFF-FF-FFHH!
SKREEUNKKKK
THAT AIN'T GONNA HOLD LONG. THIS ROOM GOT ANOTHER EXIT?
HEY, STARFACE! I SAID, DOES THIS ROOM HAVE--
--ANOTHER--
?
SON OF A BITCH! WE TURN OUR BACK--

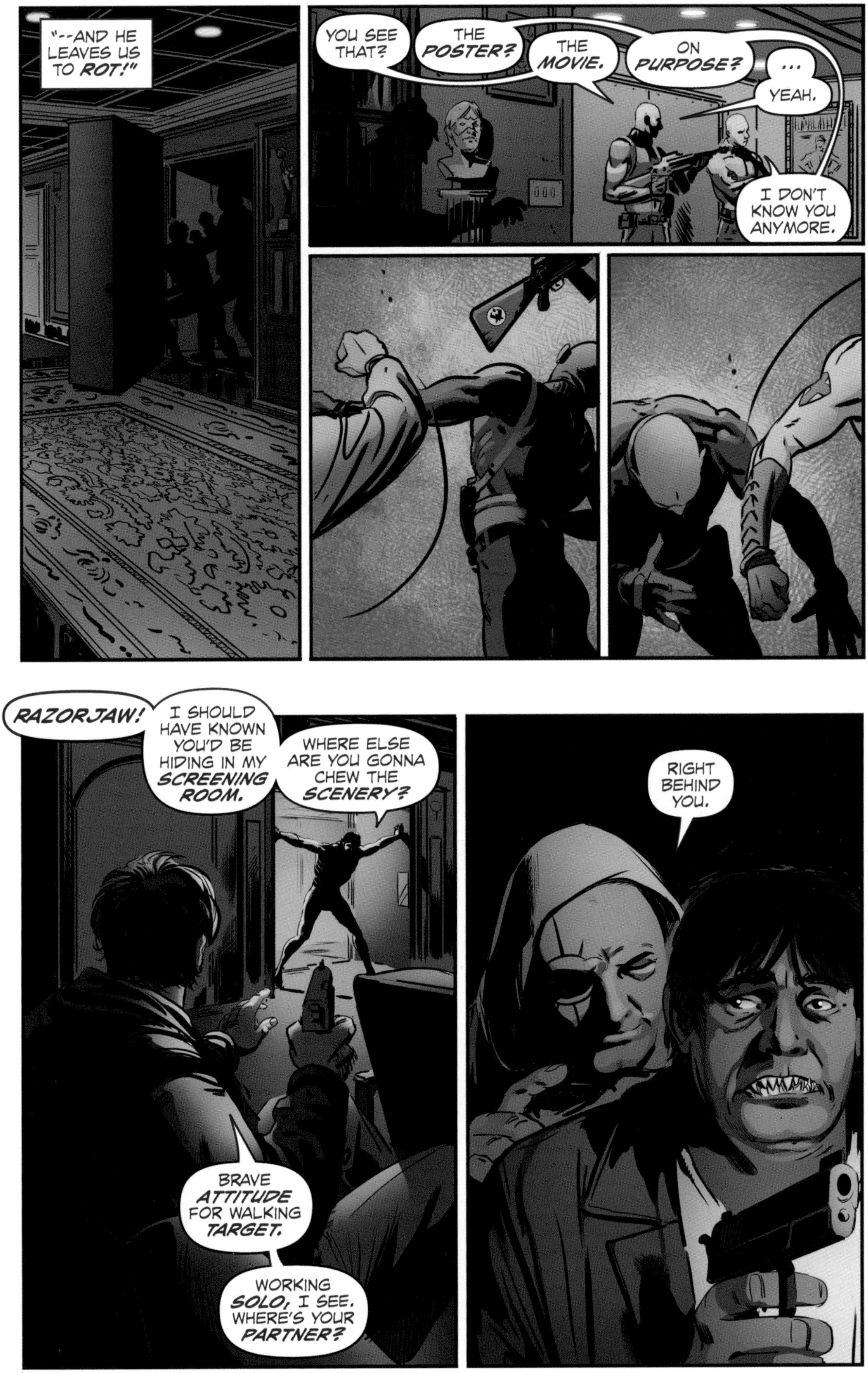
"--AND HE LEAVES US TO ROT!"
YOU SEE THAT?
THE POSTER?
THE MOVIE.
ON PURPOSE?
...
YEAH.
I DON'T KNOW YOU ANYMORE.
RAZORJAW!
I SHOULD HAVE KNOWN YOU'D BE HIDING IN MY SCREENING ROOM.
WHERE ELSE ARE YOU GONNA CHEW THE SCENERY?
BRAVE ATTITUDE FOR WALKING TARGET.
WORKING SOLO, I SEE. WHERE'S YOUR PARTNER?
RIGHT BEHIND YOU.

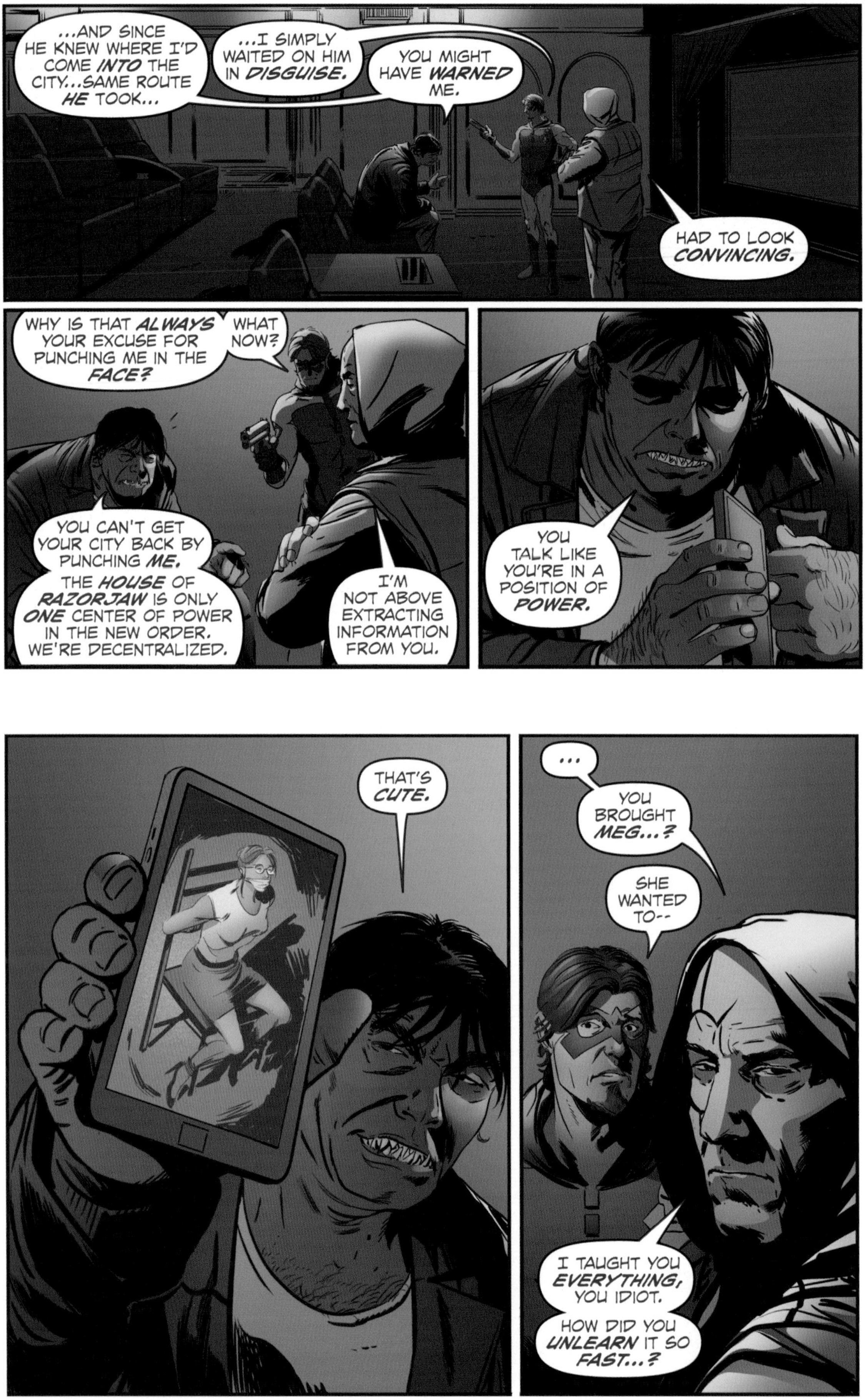
...AND SINCE HE KNEW WHERE I'D COME INTO THE CITY...SAME ROUTE HE TOOK...
...I SIMPLY WAITED ON HIM IN DISGUISE.
YOU MIGHT HAVE WARNED ME.
HAD TO LOOK CONVINCING.
WHY IS THAT ALWAYS YOUR EXCUSE FOR PUNCHING ME IN THE FACE?
WHAT NOW?
YOU CAN'T GET YOUR CITY BACK BY PUNCHING ME.
THE HOUSE OF RAZORJAW IS ONLY ONE CENTER OF POWER IN THE NEW ORDER. WE'RE DECENTRALIZED.
I'M NOT ABOVE EXTRACTING INFORMATION FROM YOU.
YOU TALK LIKE YOU'RE IN A POSITION OF POWER.
THAT'S CUTE.
...
YOU BROUGHT MEG...?
SHE WANTED TO--
I TAUGHT YOU EVERYTHING, YOU IDIOT.
HOW DID YOU UNLEARN IT SO FAST...?

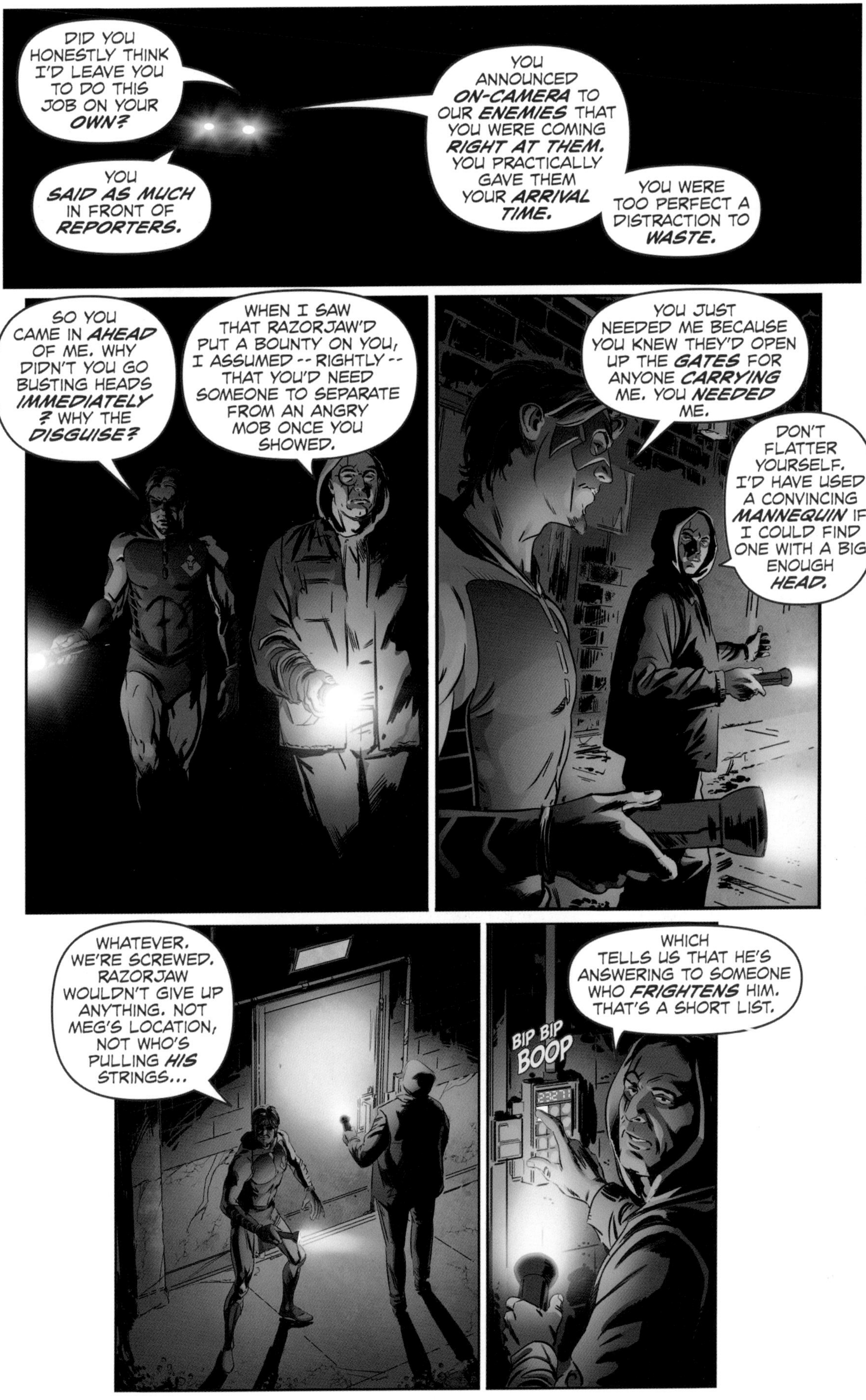
DID YOU HONESTLY THINK I'D LEAVE YOU TO DO THIS JOB ON YOUR OWN?
YOU SAID AS MUCH IN FRONT OF REPORTERS.
YOU ANNOUNCED ON-CAMERA TO OUR ENEMIES THAT YOU WERE COMING RIGHT AT THEM. YOU PRACTICALLY GAVE THEM YOUR ARRIVAL TIME.
YOU WERE TOO PERFECT A DISTRACTION TO WASTE.
SO YOU CAME IN AHEAD OF ME. WHY DIDN'T YOU GO BUSTING HEADS IMMEDIATELY? WHY THE DISGUISE?
WHEN I SAW THAT RAZORJAW'D PUT A BOUNTY ON YOU, I ASSUMED -- RIGHTLY -- THAT YOU'D NEED SOMEONE TO SEPARATE FROM AN ANGRY MOB ONCE YOU SHOWED.
YOU JUST NEEDED ME BECAUSE YOU KNEW THEY'D OPEN UP THE GATES FOR ANYONE CARRYING ME. YOU NEEDED ME.
DON'T FLATTER YOURSELF. I'D HAVE USED A CONVINCING MANNEQUIN IF I COULD FIND ONE WITH A BIG ENOUGH HEAD.
WHATEVER. WE'RE SCREWED. RAZORJAW WOULDN'T GIVE UP ANYTHING. NOT MEG'S LOCATION, NOT WHO'S PULLING HIS STRINGS...
BIP BIP BOOP
WHICH TELLS US THAT HE'S ANSWERING TO SOMEONE WHO FRIGHTENS HIM. THAT'S A SHORT LIST.

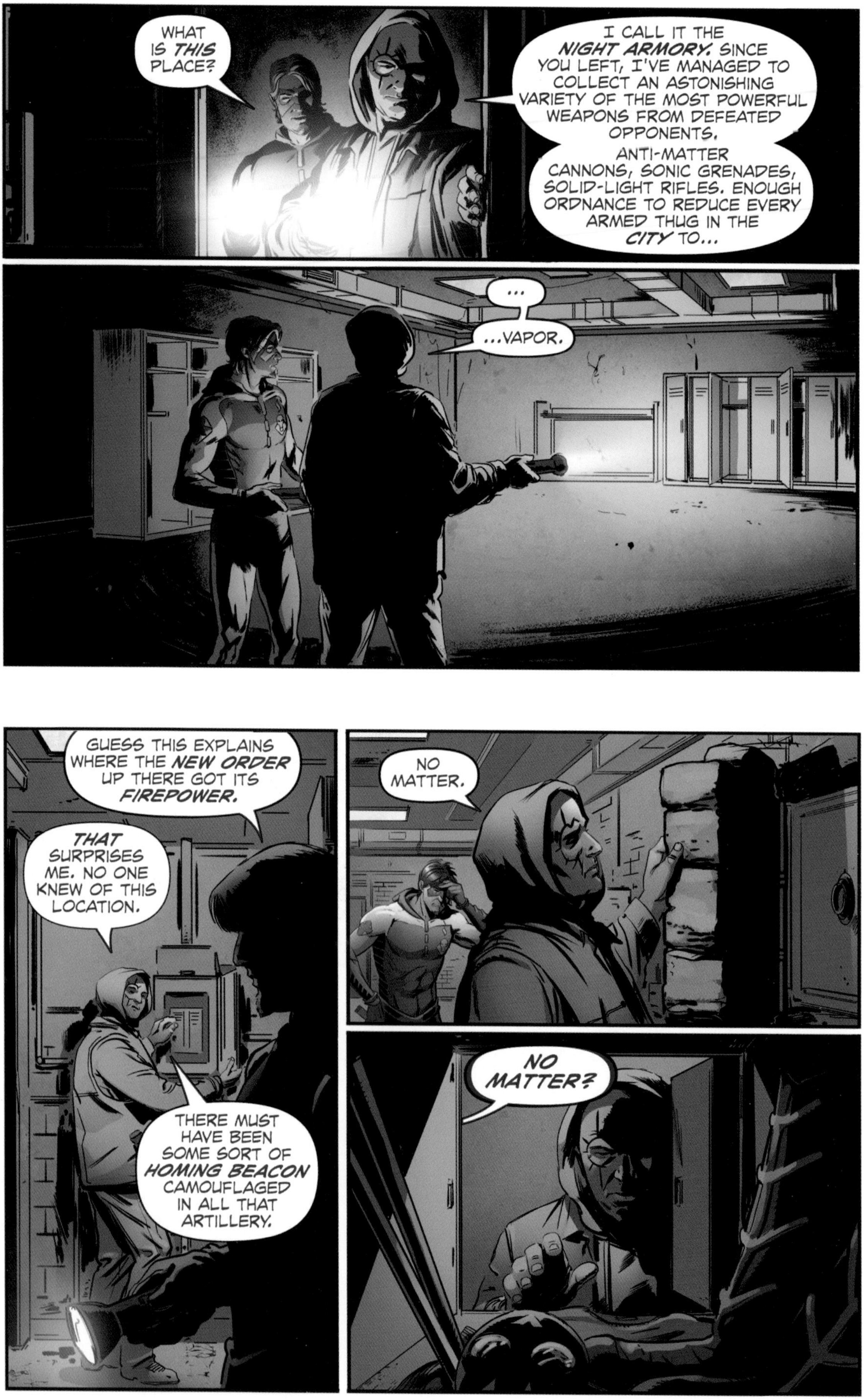
WHAT IS THIS PLACE?
I CALL IT THE NIGHT ARMORY. SINCE YOU LEFT, I'VE MANAGED TO COLLECT AN ASTONISHING VARIETY OF THE MOST POWERFUL WEAPONS FROM DEFEATED OPPONENTS.
ANTI-MATTER CANNONS, SONIC GRENADES, SOLID-LIGHT RIFLES. ENOUGH ORDNANCE TO REDUCE EVERY ARMED THUG IN THE CITY TO...
...
...VAPOR.
GUESS THIS EXPLAINS WHERE THE NEW ORDER UP THERE GOT ITS FIREPOWER.
THAT SURPRISES ME. NO ONE KNEW OF THIS LOCATION.
THERE MUST HAVE BEEN SOME SORT OF HOMING BEACON CAMOUFLAGED IN ALL THAT ARTILLERY.
NO MATTER.
NO MATTER?

WE WORK WITH THE RESOURCES WE HAVE.

UNTIL WE REGAIN CONTROL OF ST. BARRINGTON...

...UNTIL *MEG* AND ANY *OTHER* HOSTAGES ARE FREE AND SAFE...

...I WILL REMAIN IN THIS COSTUME. AS A FIGHTER.

AS A *SYMBOL.*

AS A SOLO ACT.

WHAT?

GET UP, JAROD. PEOPLE *NEED* YOU.

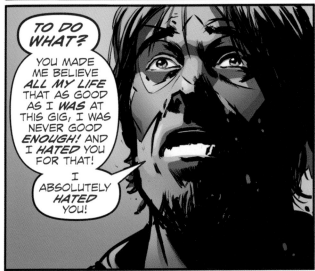

TO DO WHAT?

YOU MADE ME BELIEVE *ALL MY LIFE* THAT AS GOOD AS I *WAS* AT THIS GIG, I WAS NEVER GOOD *ENOUGH!* AND I *HATED* YOU FOR THAT!

I ABSOLUTELY *HATED* YOU!

WHY DID YOU HAVE TO BE RIGHT?

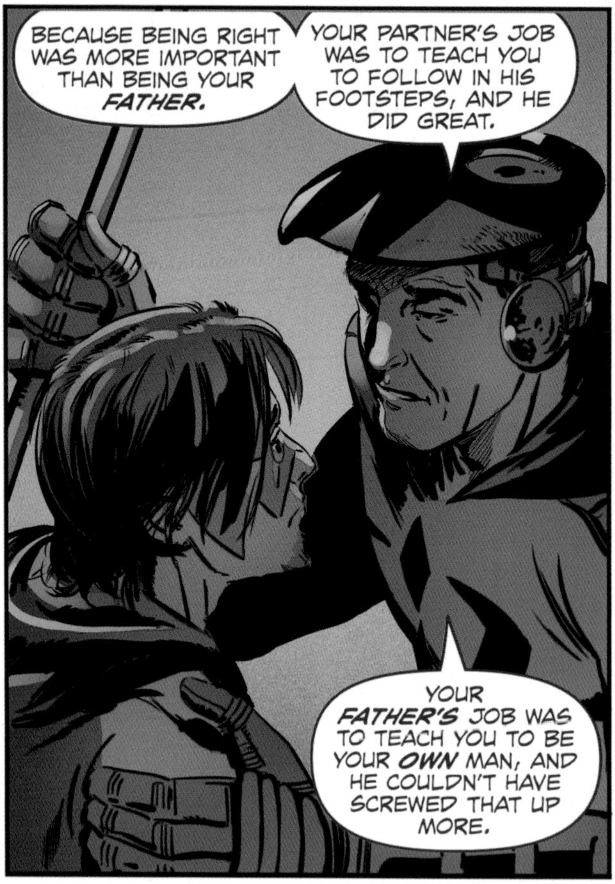
BECAUSE BEING RIGHT WAS MORE IMPORTANT THAN BEING YOUR FATHER.
YOUR PARTNER'S JOB WAS TO TEACH YOU TO FOLLOW IN HIS FOOTSTEPS, AND HE DID GREAT.
YOUR FATHER'S JOB WAS TO TEACH YOU TO BE YOUR OWN MAN, AND HE COULDN'T HAVE SCREWED THAT UP MORE.

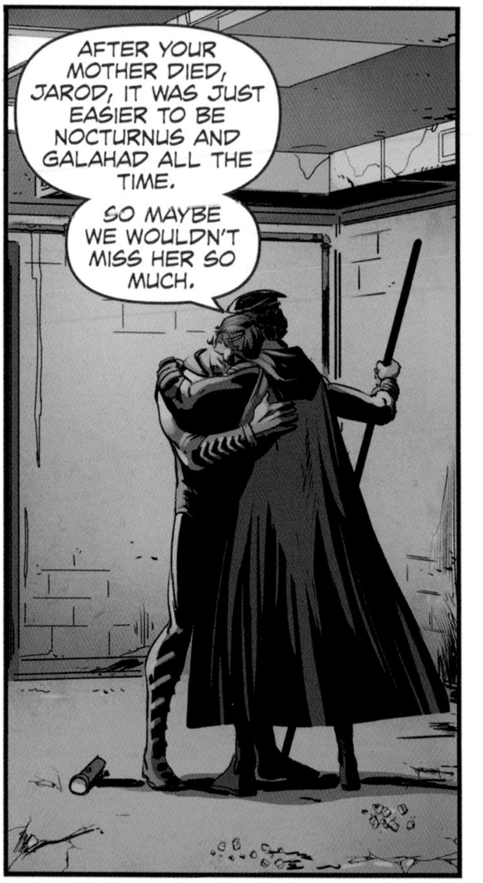
AFTER YOUR MOTHER DIED, JAROD, IT WAS JUST EASIER TO BE NOCTURNUS AND GALAHAD ALL THE TIME.
SO MAYBE WE WOULDN'T MISS HER SO MUCH.

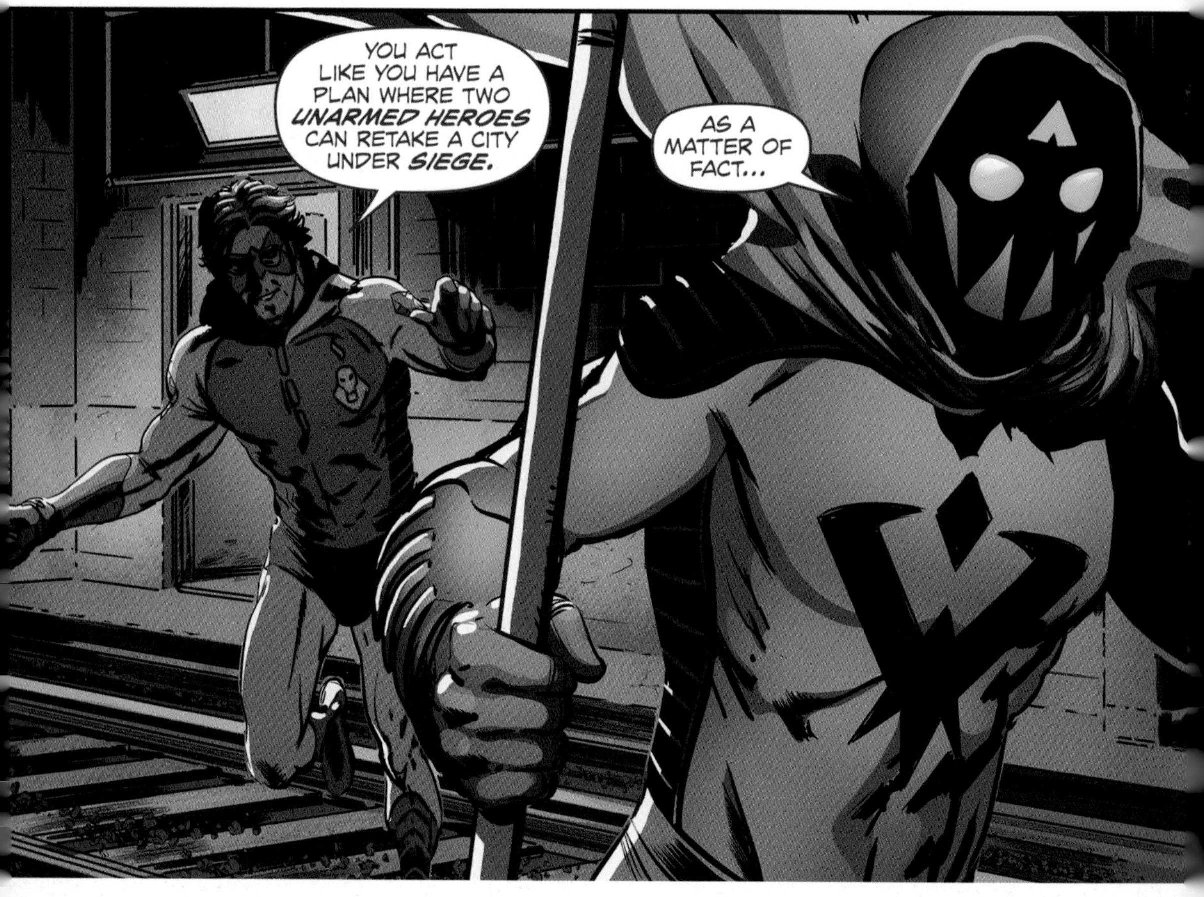
YOU ACT LIKE YOU HAVE A PLAN WHERE TWO UNARMED HEROES CAN RETAKE A CITY UNDER SIEGE.
AS A MATTER OF FACT...

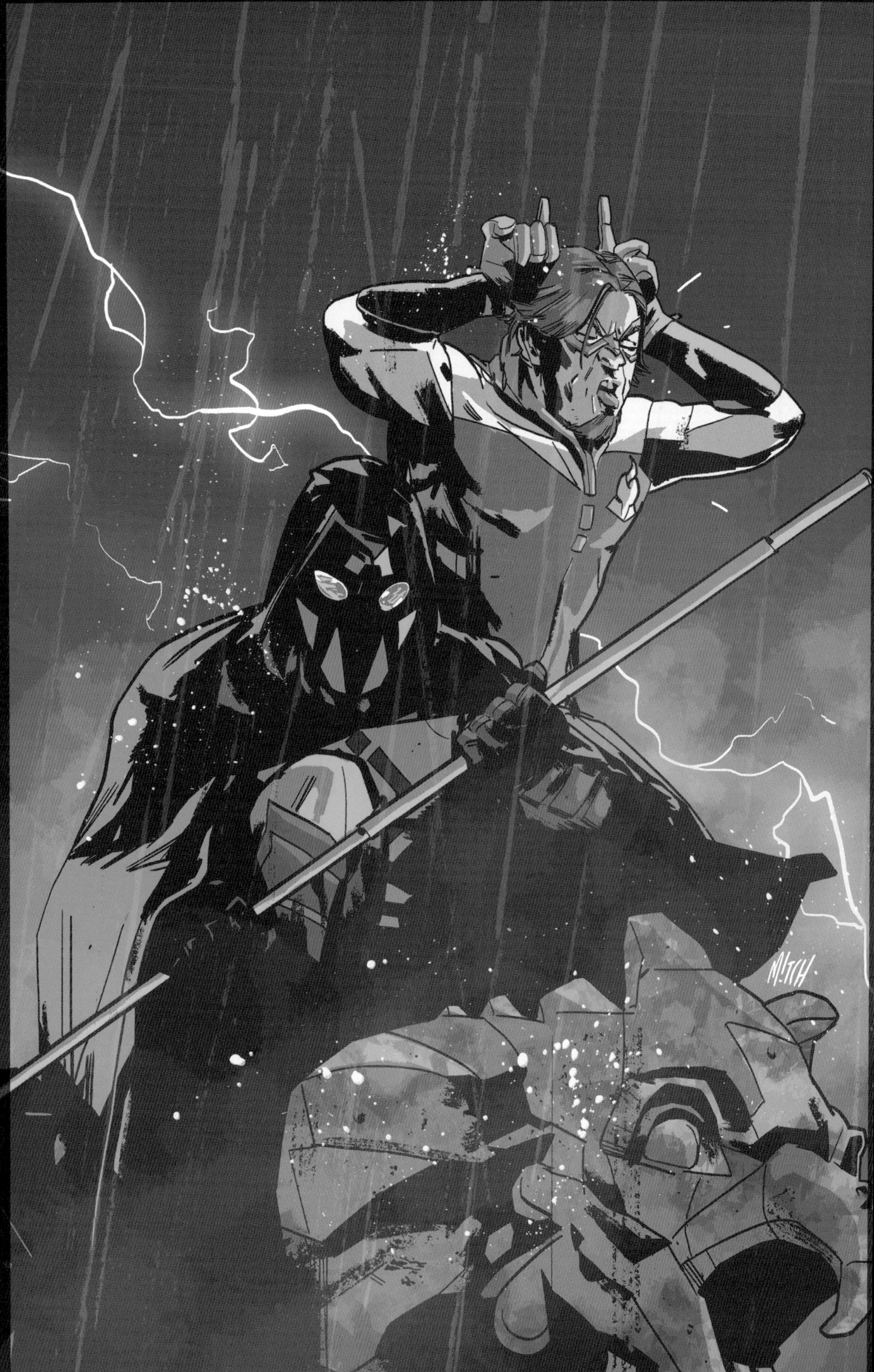

ART BY MITCH GERADS

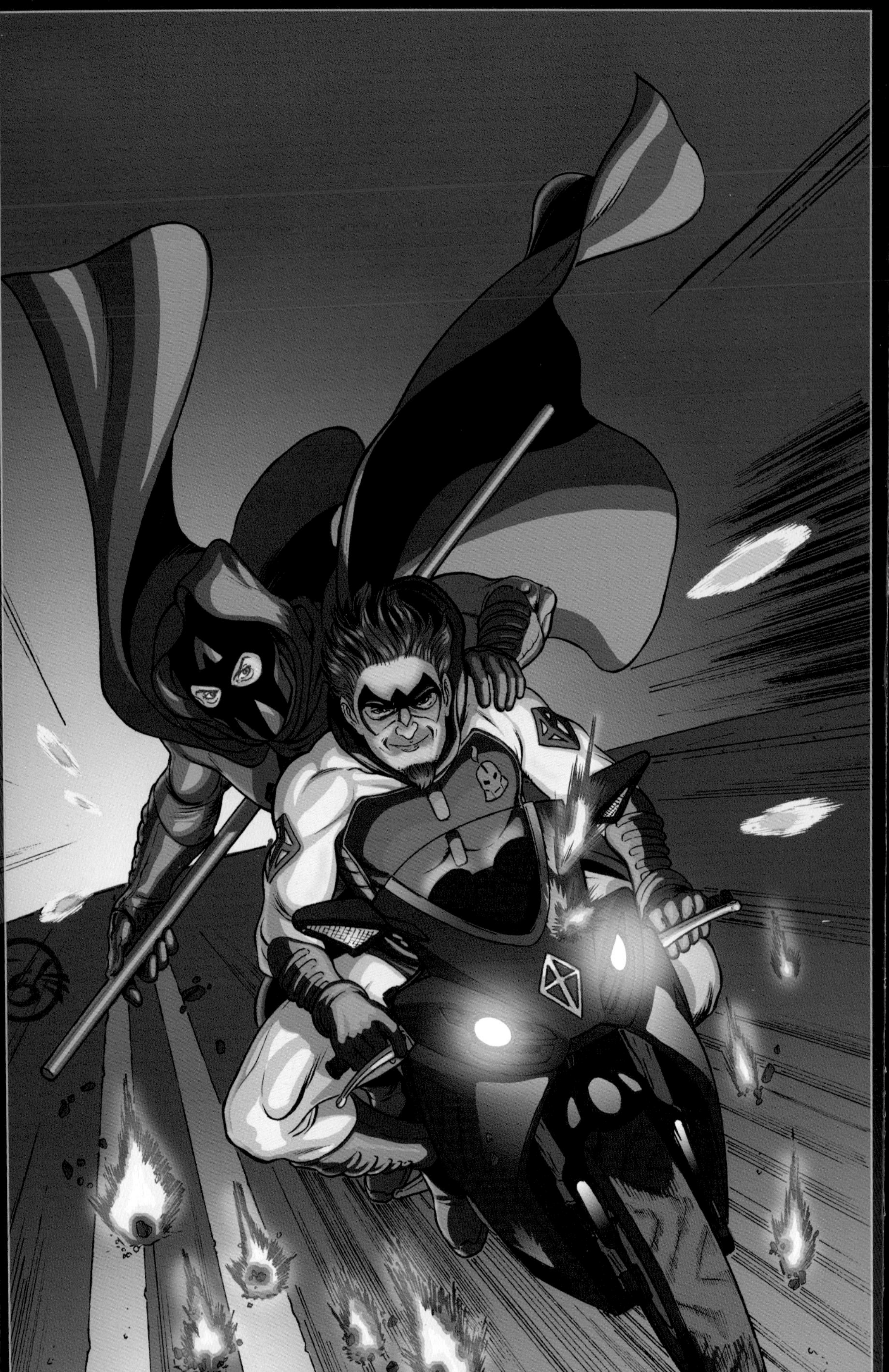

ART BY JAMAL IGLE

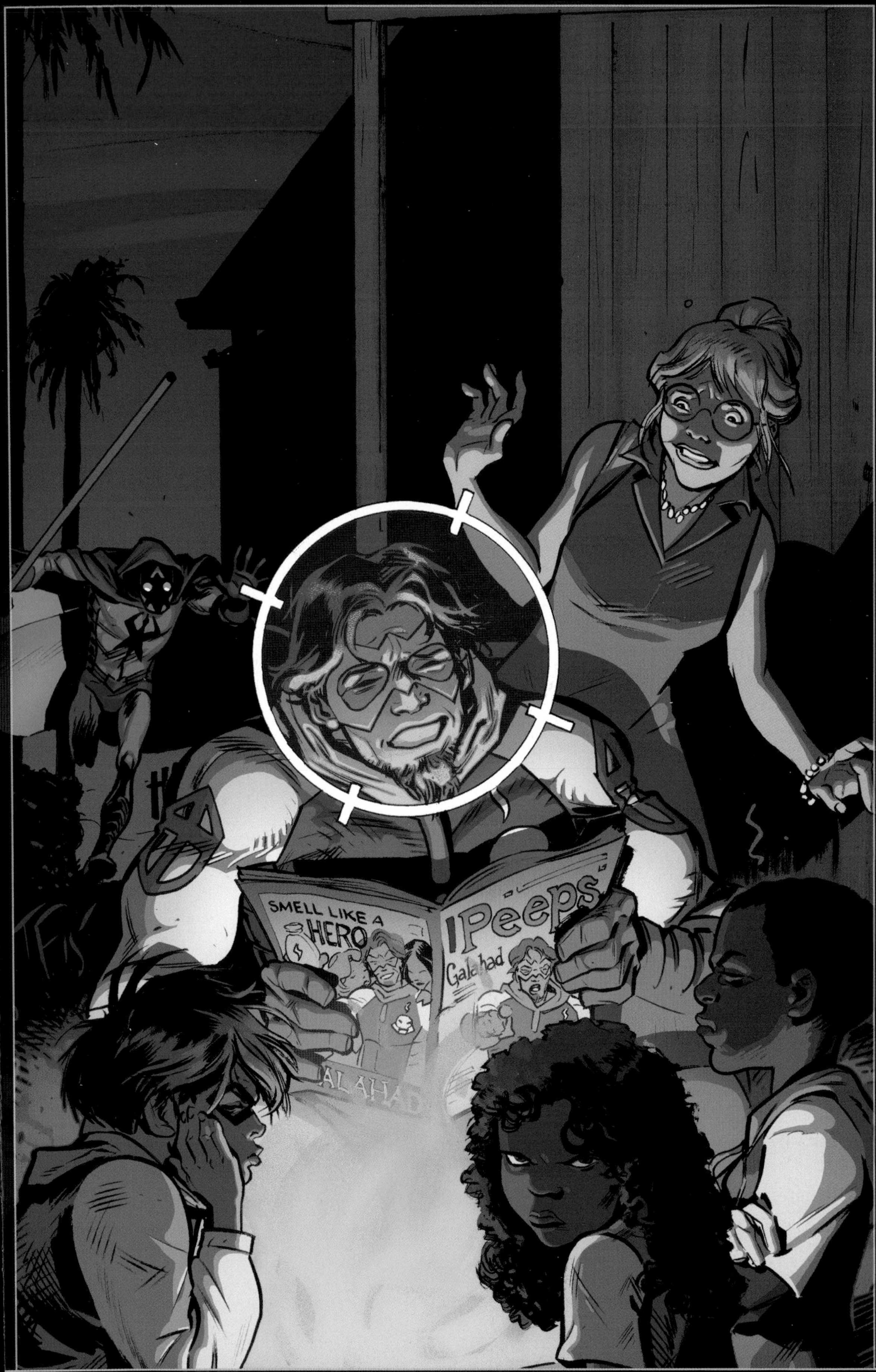
SMELL LIKE A HERO
Peeps
Galahad

ART BY TOM FOWLER, COLORS BY NOLAN WOODARD

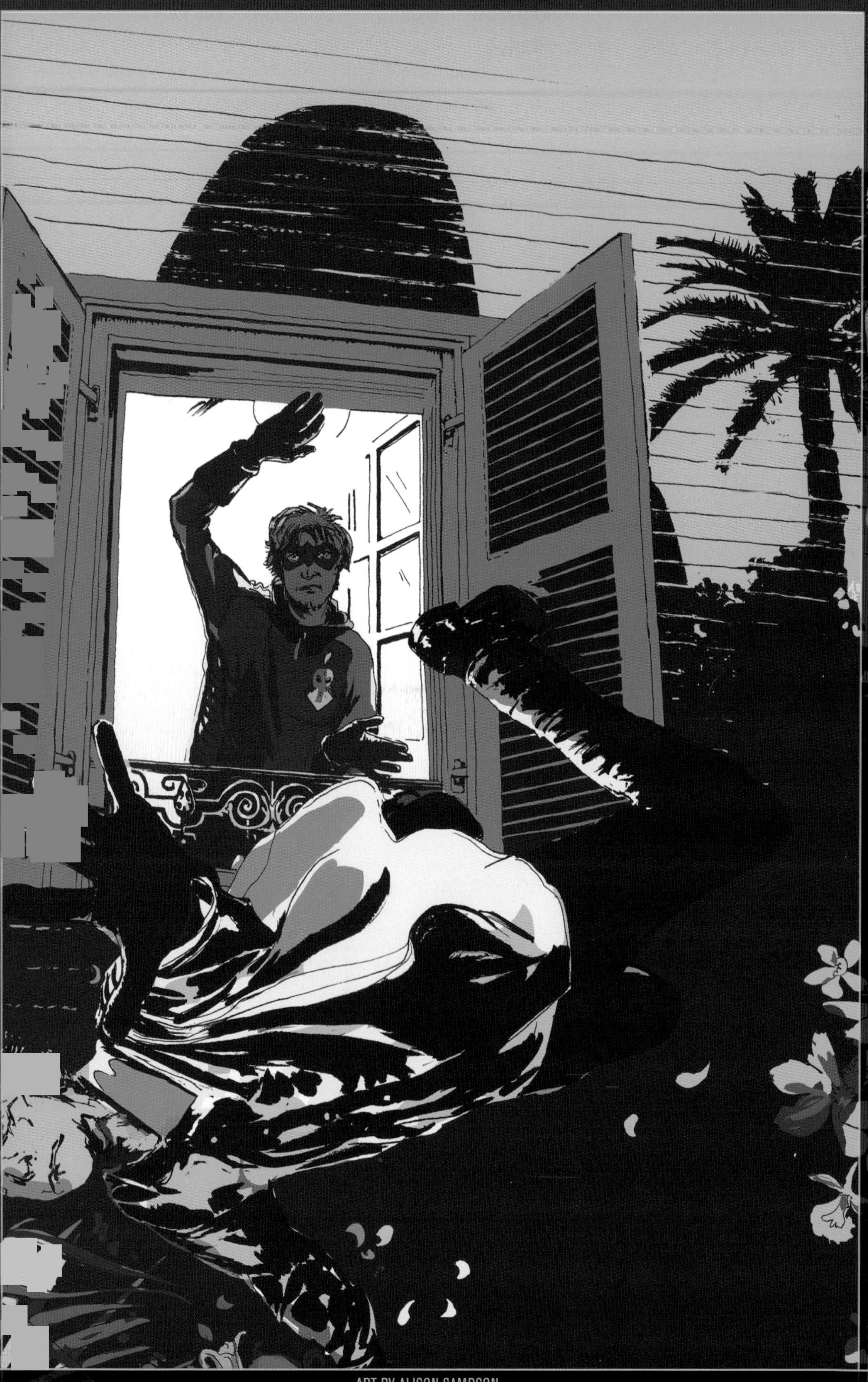

ART BY ALISON SAMPSON

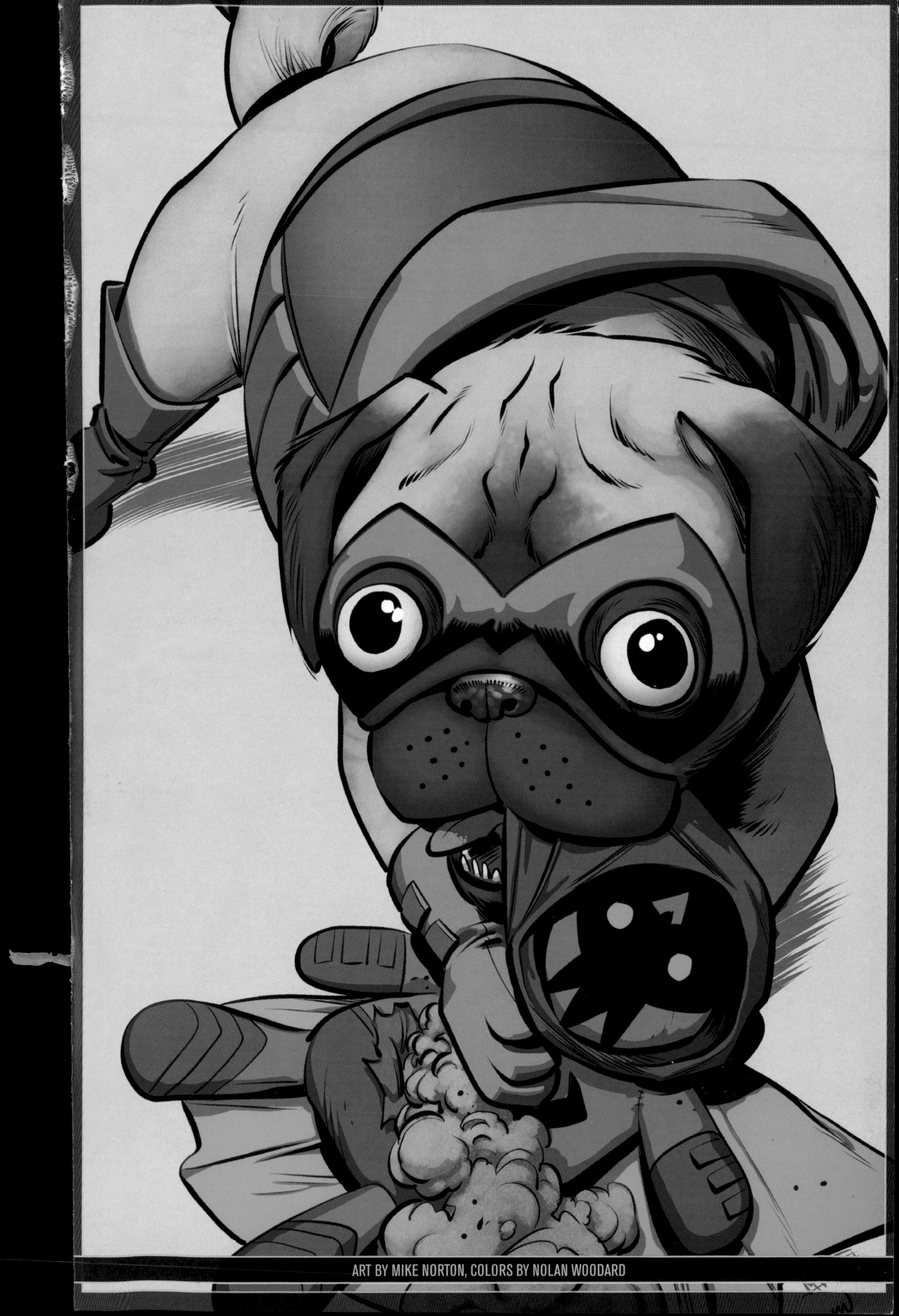

ART BY MIKE NORTON, COLORS BY NOLAN WOODARD

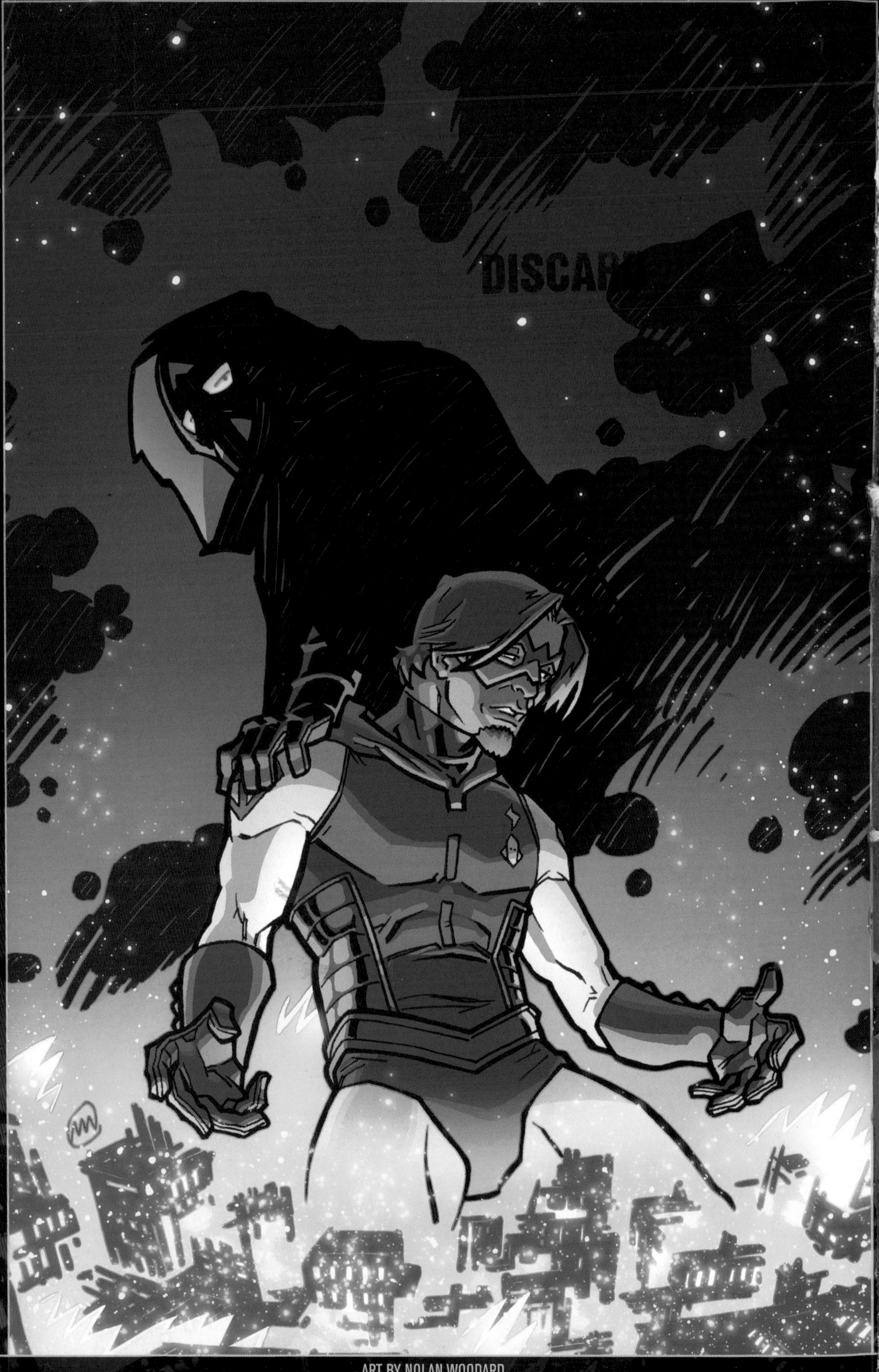

ART BY NOLAN WOODARD